哈尔滨工业大学外国语学院跨文化交际研究中心
中国跨文化交际学会

跨文化交际研究 第一辑

Intercultural
Communication Research

(Volume 1)

主　编　贾玉新
　　　　Guo-Ming Chen ［美］

副主编　孙有中
　　　　Ray Heisey ［美］

高等教育出版社
Higher Education Press

图书在版编目（CIP）数据

跨文化交际研究. 第1辑：汉、英/贾玉新主编. —北京：高等教育出版社，2009.6
ISBN 978-7-04-026757-0

Ⅰ. 跨… Ⅱ. 贾… Ⅲ. 文化交流－丛刊－汉、英 Ⅳ. G115-55

中国版本图书馆CIP数据核字（2009）第085037号

策划编辑	贾 巍	责任编辑	贾 巍 刘丽燕	封面设计	周 末
版式设计	刘 艳	责任校对	刘丽燕 贾 巍	责任印制	尤 静

出版发行	高等教育出版社	购书热线	010—58581118
社　　址	北京市西城区德外大街4号	免费咨询	800—810—0598
邮政编码	100120	网　　址	http://www.hep.edu.cn
总　　机	010—58581000		http://www.hep.com.cn
		网上订购	http://www.landraco.com
经　　销	蓝色畅想图书发行有限公司		http://www.landraco.com.cn
印　　刷	北京四季青印刷厂	畅想教育	http://www.widedu.com
开　　本	787×1092　1/16	版　　次	2009年6月第1版
印　　张	24.25	印　　次	2009年11月第2次印刷
字　　数	524 000	定　　价	45.00元

本书如有缺页、倒页、脱页等质量问题，请到所购图书销售部门联系调换。
版权所有　侵权必究
物料号　26757－00

Intercultural Communication Research (ICR)
跨文化交际研究

主办单位
哈尔滨工业大学外国语学院跨文化交际研究中心 (CICR-HIT)
中国跨文化交际学会 (CAFIC)

协办单位
国际跨文化交际研究学会 (IAICS)
高等教育出版社 (HEP)

主　编
贾玉新　哈尔滨工业大学
Guo-Ming Chen (美国) 罗得岛大学

副主编
孙有中　北京外国语大学
Ray Heisey (美国) 肯特州立大学

顾问委员会
主　任　　胡文仲　北京外国语大学
　　　　　Nobuyki Honna (日本) 青山学院大学

委　员　　（以姓氏字母排序）
　　　　　Hui-Ching Chang (张惠晶) (美国) 伊利诺大学芝家哥分校
　　　　　Ling Chen (陈凌) 香港浸会大学
　　　　　Michael Byram (英国) 杜伦大学
　　　　　Margaret D'Silva (美国) 路易斯维尔大学
　　　　　Brooks Hill (美国) 三一大学
　　　　　Bates Hoffer (美国) 三一大学
　　　　　Wenshan Jia (贾文山) (美国) 查普曼大学

Andy Kirkpatrick 香港教育学院
Zoya Proshina 俄罗斯莫斯科国立大学, 俄罗斯远东国立大学
Michael Prosser 上海外国语大学
Huizhong Shen (沈惠忠) (澳大利亚) 悉尼大学
Robert. N. St. Clair (美国) 路易斯维尔大学
Svetalana Ter-Minasova 俄罗斯莫斯科国立大学

编　　委　（以姓氏字母排序）

杜学增　北京外国语大学
傅　利　哈尔滨工业大学
高一虹　北京大学
顾嘉祖　南京师范大学
顾力行　(Steve Kulich) 上海外国语大学
关世杰　北京大学
贾　巍　高等教育出版社
李晓石　(美国) 密歇根州立大学
林大津　福建师范大学
刘长远　哈尔滨工业大学
宋　莉　哈尔滨工业大学
许力生　浙江大学
庄恩平　上海大学

执行编辑委员会

主　任　宋　莉　哈尔滨工业大学
　　　　刘长远　哈尔滨工业大学

执行编辑　贾雪睿　哈尔滨工业大学
　　　　　孟　劢　哈尔滨工业大学
　　　　　翟　峥　北京外国语大学
　　　　　张毅达　高等教育出版社

Intercultural Communication Research (ICR)

Sponsors:
Center of Intercultural Communication Research, Harbin Institute of Technology, China (CICK-HIT)
China Association for Intercultural Communication (CAFIC)

Co-Sponsors:
International Association of Intercultural Communication Studies (IAICS)
Higher Education Press, China (HEP)

General Editors
Jia Yuxin   Harbin Institute of Technology, China
Guo-Ming Chen   University of Rhode Island, USA

Associate Editors
Sun Youzhong   Beijing Foreign Studies University, China
Ray Heisey   Kent State University, USA

Advisory Editorial Board
Directors
Hu Wenzhong   Beijing Foreign Studies University, China
Nobuyki Honna   Aoyama Gakuin University, Japan

Advisors (in alphabetic order)
Hui-Ching Chang   University of Illinois at Chicago, USA
Ling Chen   Hong Kong Baptist University, China
Michael Byram   Durham University, UK
Margaret D. Silva   Louisville University, USA
Brooks Hill   Trinity University, USA
Bates Hoffer   Trinity University, USA
Wenshan Jia   Champman University, USA
Andy Kirkpatrick   Hong Kong Institute of Education, China

Zoya Proshina   Lomonosov Moscow State University; Far-Eastern National
                 University, Russia
Michael Prosser   Shanghai International Studies University, China
Huizhong Shen   University of Sydney, Australia
Robert. N. St. Clair   Louisville University, USA
Svetalana Ter-Minasova   Lomonosov Moscow State University, Russia

Editorial Board
Du Xuezeng   Beijing Foreign Studies University, China
Fu Li   Harbin Institute of Technology, China
Gao Yihong   Beijing University, China
Gu Jiazu   Nanjing Normal University, China
Guan Shijie   Beijing University, China
Jia Wei   Higher Education Press, China
Xiaoshi Li   Michigan State University, USA
Lin Dajin   Fujian Normal University, China
Steve Kulich   Shanghai International Studies University, China
Xu Lisheng   Zhejiang University, China
Zhuang Enping   Shanghai University, China

Executive Editorial Board
Directors
Song Li   Harbin Institute of Technology, China
Liu Changyuan   Harbin Institute of Technology, China

Executive Editors
Jia Xuerui   Harbin Institute of Technology, China
Meng Meng   Harbin Institute of Technology, China
Zhai Zheng   Beijing Foreign Studies University, China
Zhang Yida   Higher Education Press, China

Editorial

Globalization is in essence about changing perception of space and time. Globalization predisposes cultural globalization and cultural globalization thus refers to the process of changes of global cultures. This dynamic view of global cultures is becoming more and more important in the field of intercultural communication studies.

Cultural globalization is becoming a new context for intercultural communication and provides a new perspective for its study in the 21st century. This perspective is new and fresh in the sense that the scholars' main concerns are not only the phenomenon of global village, which is the result of "medium is the message", due to the "effect of technology" but also the directions and models of changing cultures and their possible impact on intercultural communication and cultural identification.

Which directions is cultural globalization oriented toward? Is it oriented toward unilaterality and homogeneity? Or heterogeneity and diversity? Stated differently, is it oriented toward localization or globalization? Or unity within diversity in which globalization and localization, "us" and "others" are complementally co-present, interact and reciprocate? In terms of changing models, is the "present" being separated and isolated from the past and modernity from tradition? Or is the "present" embedded in the past and modernity in tradition so that the past and tradition provide the network of meanings that gives meaning to the "present" and modernity? And following the model of the co-presence, we have the claim that the past and tradition give meaning to the present and modernity, and at the same time they are being reinterpreted, modified, and transformed to fit the context shaped by the present and modernity. These global questions under the discussion of this article have been the main concerns of the study of intercultural communication in recent years.

Culture has been a very important concept in the field of intercultural communication. It has been given new meanings in the 21st century. It is important not only because it is the major context that influences communication but also because it has become an important subject for many disciplines. It is regarded not only as "context" but also a "text" -a text that everyone must read and interpret. Facing the challenges of the ever increasing globalizing world, it is extremely important and necessary to read critically and interpret correctly the text of cultural globalization and to fully understand the complexities of intercultural interaction in today's global society.

Fortunately, in the first Volume of ICR, our distinguished scholars have addressed the core concepts of the intercultural communication issues, which are major global concerns and interest. Their original thought and insightful ideas will get the readers involved in thinking about today's intercultural learning and research. We, editors of ICR would like to say "Thank you, dear scholars and friends, for your help, support and love. You have paved the way for the forthcoming issues in ICR."

           Yuxin Jia President, CAFIC
           Guo-Ming Chen Executive President, IAICS
              April 7th, 2009

卷首语

  全球化是人类对时空感知的变化，在很大程度上，全球化是文化变化。全球化预设着文化全球化，文化全球化则顺理成章地意味着全球文化的变化。这种文化动态观在当前跨文化交际研究中的重要性变得越来越突出。

  文化全球化是21世纪跨文化交际的新语境、是跨文化交际研究的新视野。文化全球化的视野之所以"新"，是因为学者们关心的已不仅是电子时代所带来"媒体即信息"的"技术效应"——地球村现象；而是全球文化发展变化的趋势或走向、变化的形式、以及文化全球化对跨文化交际、跨文化认同所可能造成的影响。文化全球化走向何方？是西方文化的单向化、同质化、一体化，还是多样性、异质化、多元化？换句话说，文化全球化是走向全球化、地方化、还是二者共生共存、我者与他者 (Us and Others) 互动互惠 (Us-Others Reciprocity) 的"和而不同"？在变化形式方面，是过去与现在、传统与现代相互切割、相互独立，还是现在与过去、现代与传统共生共存 (co-presence)？这些全球性的问题近年来一直被普遍关注，是跨文化交际研究必须面对的问题。

  文化是跨文化交际中的重要概念，这一概念在21世纪又被赋予新的意义。它已不单纯被当作影响 (跨文化) 交际的环境因素，它本身已成为很多学科的研究对象。人们不仅把文化当作context (环境)，文化已是人们必须解读的text (课本)。面临全球化的挑战，深入解读全球文化这一"课本"，认清文化全球化的深刻含义，并懂得它与跨文化交际和跨文化认同的关系等，对跨文化交际研究至关重要。

  可喜的是，在我们的园地"《跨文化交际研究》(ICR)"刚刚问世的第一辑中，学者们就文化全球化这一21世纪跨文化交际的重大问题以及相关的问题各抒己见，这是对"ICR"的支持和厚爱，我们在此致以诚挚的谢意。

贾玉新 中国跨文化交际学会会长
陈国明 国际跨文化交际学会执行主席
2009年4月7日

序　言

跨文化交际研究在我国已经有了近三十年的历史。初期只是一些零散的文章问世，之后出现了论文集和国外跨文化交际著作的译本，再之后出版了专著。从上世纪80年代后期起，北京外国语大学、上海外国语大学、哈尔滨工业大学等高等院校率先开设了跨文化交际课程。至1995年，跨文化交际研究在我国已经有了相当的规模。也就是在这一年，哈尔滨工业大学主办了我国第一届跨文化交际国际研讨会，出席人数达到400余人。在会议期间成立了中国跨文化交际学会 (China Association for Intercultural Communication, CAFIC)。此后在学会的领导下，每两年召开一次全国性的研讨会，至今已经召开了七届。在此期间，跨文化交际研究在我国有了快速的发展，开设这一门课程的院校迅速增加。跨文化交际学已成为外语类硕士层次的规定课程。根据中国期刊全文数据库的统计，从1982年至2009年3月跨文化交际方面的论文和文章总数达到 11，312篇。国家图书馆馆藏图书中涉及跨文化交际的专著、论文集和硕士、博士论文共有 220种，其中专著和编著104部，硕士论文108篇，博士和博士后论文6篇，电子资源类2部。教师对于跨文化交际能力重要性的认识也越来越深化，在新制定的各个层次的外语教学大纲中都对于跨文化交际能力的培养作了规定。

尽管跨文化交际研究的发展势头很猛，但是，学者和教师的一个普遍反映是国内还没有专门发表跨文化交际研究成果的园地，教师通常都只能在外语类刊物或大学学报上发表自己的论文。学术研究和学术交流受到了一定的限制。虽然人们在会上会下多次呼吁，但由于现行的期刊制度多年来一直难以解决这一问题。

可喜的是，经过高等教育出版社和贾玉新教授的努力，在一段时间的筹备之后，终于出版了《跨文化交际研究》这一人们渴望已久的学术刊物。我相信，期刊的出版必将加强跨文化交际学者之间的交流，推动我国跨文化交际研究的发展，使我国的研究在现有的基础上更上一层楼。

中国跨文化交际学会名誉会长
胡文仲
2009年4月

Contents

INTERCULTURAL COMMUNICATION STUDIES IN THE CONTEXT OF GLOBALIZATION — 1

Jia Yuxin — 3
Cultural globalization and intercultural dialogues — Intercultural communication studies from the global perspective

Michael Byram — 16
Developing a concept of intercultural citizenship

Robert N. St. Clair — 30
The lamination of cultural space: A theoretical investigation of time in space

Steve J. Kulich   Chi Ruobing — 48
Developing intercultural communication as a discipline in China

Gao Yongchen — 75
Globalization: A new field for the development of intercultural communication

L. Brooks Hill — 83
The future of cross cultural communication: Perspectives from 20 years of the IAICS

Gu Jiazu — 109
Theorizing about intercultural communication: Dynamic semiotic and memetic approaches to intercultural communication

CULTURAL IDENTITY AND INTERCULTURAL COMMUNICATION — 117

William B. Gudykunst   Tsukasa Nishida — 119
The influence of culture and strength of cultural identity on individual values in Japan and the United States

Young Yun Kim — 136
Beyond cultural identity

Dai Xiaodong   **154**
Construction of intercultural identity—A two-directional extension model

DISCOURSE STUDIES IN CULTURAL CONTEXTS — 167

Guo-Ming Chen   **169**
On bian (change): A perpetual discourse of I ching

Ling Chen   **182**
Persuasion in Chinese culture: a glimpse of the ancient practice in contrast to the west

MULTICULTURALISM AND MULTILINGUALISM — 199

Nobuyuki Honna   **201**
English across cultures and intercultural awareness

Svetlana Ter-Minasova   **217**
Disadvantages of global English for English-speaking nations

Zoya Proshina   **227**
East-Asian cultures through a looking-glass of the English language thesaurus

INTERULTURAL MEDIA STUDIES — 245

Sun Youzhong   **247**
Intercultural mass communication: A new frontier for intercultural communication research

INTERCULTURAL COMPETENCE AND FOREIGN LANGUAGE EDUCATION — 259

Song Li   **261**
Teaching English as intercultural education: Challenges of intercultural communication

Zhang Hongling   **278**
Intercultural training for foreign language teachers

CROSS-CULTURAL TRANSLATION — 291

Xu Lisheng — 293
Intra-discourse translation and inter-discourse translation: A new approach to translation and culture

NON-VERBAL COMMUNICATION ACROSS CULTURES — 303

Richard L. Wiseman   Xiaohui Pan — 305
Smiling in the People's Republic of China and the United States: Status and situational influences on the social appropriateness of smiling

Bates L. Hoffer — 323
Aspects of intercultural nonverbal communicative competence

Contributors (in English) — 347

Contributors (in Chinese) — 357

Abstracts (in Chinese) — 364

目 录

全球化背景下的跨文化交际理论 —————————————————— 1

贾玉新 — 3
文化全球化与跨文化对话——全球化视野下的跨文化交际研究

Michael Byram — 16
培养跨文化公民的意识

Robert N. St. Clair — 30
文化空间的叠层：关于空间时间的探究

顾立行　迟若冰 — 48
国内跨文化交际／传播学学科发展现状综述

高永晨 — 75
全球本土化：跨文化交际学科发展应关注的新视域

L. Brooks Hill — 83
跨文化交际学的未来：二十年从事跨文化交际经验感悟

顾嘉祖 — 109
跨文化交际学的理论化：试论跨文化交际学的动态符号学、迷米学研究视角

文化身份与跨文化交际 —————————————————— 117

William B. Gudykunst　Tsukasa Nishida — 119
文化与文化身份对美日个人价值观的影响

Young Yun Kim — 136
超越文化身份

戴晓东 — 154
建构跨文化认同的路径——双向拓展模型

跨文化语篇 —————————————————— 167

陈国明 — 169
变："易经"永恒的论述

陈凌 — 182
论中国文化中的劝说：中西传统修辞对比研究

多语与文化多元化 — 199

Nobuyuki Honna — 201
跨文化英语与跨文化意识

Svetlana Ter-Minasova — 217
全球化英语对英语本族语国家的不利影响

Zoya Proshina — 227
透过英语辞典看东亚文化

跨文化大众传播 — 245

孙有中 — 247
跨文化大众传播研究:一个方兴未艾的领域

跨文化教育与外语教学 — 259

宋莉 — 261
跨文化教育英语教学:来自跨文化交际的挑战

张红玲 — 278
外语教师跨文化能力培训研究

跨文化翻译 — 291

许力生 — 293
话语内翻译与跨话语翻译:翻译与文化的新视角

非言语交际 — 303

Richard L. Wiseman　潘晓慧 — 305
中国人和美国人的微笑:社会地位和情景因素对微笑行为社会得体性的影响

Bates L. Hoffer — 323
非言语跨文化交际能力面面观

作者简介(英文) — 347

作者简介(中文) — 357

摘要(中文) — 364

INTERCULTURAL COMMUNICATION STUDIES IN THE CONTEXT OF GLOBALIZATION

Cultural globalization and intercultural dialogues — Intercultural communication studies from the global perspective

文化全球化与跨文化对话[1]：全球视野下的跨文化交际研究[2]

贾玉新

哈尔滨工业大学外国语学院

Abstract

This paper aims to present a framework for intercultural communication study in the perspective and context of globalization.

The study of intercultural communication falls in step with the progress of time. When the world enters into the 21st century which is characterized by the buzzword "globalization", it inevitably faces new challenges. Globalization predisposes cultural globalizations and globalization, localization, or glocalization potentially are a process of changing cultures today. Sharing the idea that "unity within diversity" (和而不同) is, potentially, the term that accurately describes the defining features of globalization, the author of this paper proposes that intercultural communication should be studied in the perspective of "unity within diversity". "Unity within diversity" is the Chinese cultural heritage and it inherently predisposes equality and diversity. It proposes equal dialogues between / among diverse cultures. Equal cultural dialogues between / among diverse cultures serve as the departure point for solving global problems and leading to global harmony. Cultural dialogues thus provide an ideal framework for the development of intercultural communication study in the 21st century. This paper, on the basis of an insightful study of the Confucian concept "unity within diversity" and rethinking of the Western "rhetoric of dialogue", develops the concept of the "rhetoric of dialogues" in the discourse of "unity within diversity" and uses it as a

---

1 此文中的"对话"及"对话"始于"倾听"的概念，是作者根据对儒家"仁道"、"恕道"、"恕道为敬"以及相关的思想的理解、并在全球化的语境重新解释的基础上提出来的。
2 本文阐述的思想和观点，在很大程度上受益于受杜维明、刘述先、汤一介等学者的新儒家思想以及国际学者关于全球化和"全球本土化"研究，没有他们的启迪，就不会有这篇文章。

guiding principle for the development of intercultural communication study in the context of globalization. This paper gives a clear explanation and analysis of the intercultural dialogues on the levels of cultural values and verbal / speech communications which are directly and immediately related to the concept of "unity within diversity". This paper suggests that the intercultural communication study adopt the dialectical approach that best complements the concept "unity within diversity" as it can incorporate not only cultural values of diverse and opposing nature, such as those of the East and those of the West. In so doing, the article attempts to explore the intercultural spaces where diverse cultures meet. This dialectical approach also incorporates the diverse approaches to the study of intercultural communication that is currently prevalent. It incorporates and integrates rather than separates and isolates values of diverse nature. In this approach, for example, it is viewed that the present is embedded in the past and thus modernity is embedded in tradition, and what is more, tradition should be redefined, modified, and transformed to meet the requirement of modernity. As such, dialectical approach may prove to be most instrumental to the understanding of the meaning of globalization.

1 解读"文化全球化": 跨文化交际研究的新视野和新语境

文化是跨文化交际中极其重要的概念, 是影响(跨文化)交际的最重要的环境因素。在当今全球化的时代, 这一概念的重要性已变得尤为突出, 人们已不仅仅把文化当作context(环境), 文化已是人们必须解读的text(课本), 它已成为很多学科关注的对象。面临全球化的挑战, 对跨文化交际的学者来说, 深刻解读文化全球化这一"课本", 读懂文化全球化的含义, 认清它与跨文化交际和文化身份建构的关系等, 对跨文化交际研究至关重要。

全球化实质上是文化变化, 全球化的过程是文化变化的过程, 全球化预设着文化全球化, 文化全球化则顺理成章地意味着全球文化的变化。这种文化动态观在当前跨文化交际研究中的重要性变得尤为突出。

跨文化交际研究与时俱进。20世纪50年代, 跨文化交往日益频繁, 此学科应运而生; 到了60年代, 高度发展的电子技术带来了以信息为中心的"地球村"(global village)时代, 跨文化交际研究随之达到高潮。当人类进入地球村概念越来越真实的20世纪90年代, 发达的经济导引的全球化代替了以信息为中心的"地球村"。 实际上, 全球化不仅是经济上的相互依存, 共存共荣, 它还涉及很多方面, 其中一个重要方面, 就是文化的全球化(cultural globalization)。文化全球化为跨文化交际提供了一个新视野。之所以"新"是因为学者们关心的已不仅仅是电子时代所带来"媒体即信息"的"技术效应"——地球村现象; 而是全球文化发展变化的趋势或走向、变化的形式以及文化全球化对跨文化交际、文化身份建构所可能造成的影响。

文化全球化走向何方？是西方文化的单向化、同质化（homogeneity）、一体化，还是多向化、异质化（heterogeneity）、多元化？是全球化、本土化、还是二者共生共存、我者与他者（us and others）互动互惠（us-others Reciprocity）的"和而不同"？

在变化形式方面，是过去与现在、传统与现代相互切割、相互独立，还是现在与过去、现代与传统共存（co-presence）？这些全球性的问题近年来一直被普遍关注，是跨文化交际研究必须面对的问题。

直到20世纪末、21世纪初，全球化和本土化有机相连，相互交汇，一个与时代相匹配的互动互惠的"全球本土化"（glocalization）概念问世。从此，本土与全球、"我者"（us）与"他者"（others）文化之间共存共荣、互动互惠（"us-others" reciprocity）、相互认同的"全球-本土"化成为跨文化交际的新语境，成为跨文化交际研究的新视点。无独有偶，"全球—本土"化概念与我国学者提出的"世界—民族"化概念，即"只有民族的，才是世界的"，反过来，"只有世界的，才是民族的"概念有异曲同工之妙。显然，本土与全球、民族与世界、互动互惠的"和而不同"的方向，是当前文化全球化的正确选择，"全球本土化"化或"和而不同"是跨文化交际的新语境，也是跨文化交际研究的新视野。

跨文化交际研究兴起至今，无论在学科建设和理论探索、还是发展文化交流、文明对话以及在外语教育等方面都凸显其重要作用。近年来，该学科在国内外发展迅速，成绩斐然，尤其理论上的进步标志着此学科日益走向成熟。W.B. Gudykunst在其重要著作《跨文化交际之理论》（*Theorizing About Intercultural Communication*，2005）中把现有的有关理论概括为十七种之多，此领域研究的繁荣与昌盛可见一斑。从研究视角来看，此学科研究大致分成三个学派：社会心理学派、"诠释"学派和"批判"学派（Martin & Nakayama, 2008），研究路径大致上有"主位"（emic）和"客位"（etic）两种。尽管研究视角和路径不同，对文化和交际的界定个性各异，但学者们的研究各有千秋，仁者见仁，智者见智。无论在研究理论框架、内容以及研究方法等方面，异曲同工：他们都视文化、语言与交际为一体，把交际分为文化和个体两个层面，并把文化当作对交际进行描绘、解释和预测的理论变量。

尽管跨文化交际研究取得长足进展，但目前有关研究无论在内容和方法都不同程度上滞后于全球化时代的发展。

全球化语境下的跨文化交际研究面临很多新课题：文化全球化、"全球—本土"化语境的界定、文化全球化的发展趋势、新语境对跨文化交际、跨文化认同以及对其研究产生什么影响；如何把截然不同的文化变化趋势（同质与异质、本土化与全球化）有机组合成互动互惠的统一体、如何发掘二者之间的交汇之处，以达到扩大共识、超越异同、扩大跨文化认同；"全球本土化"语境对语言和非语言交际有哪些作用、如何把"全球本土化"语境当作理论变量对跨文化交际进行描绘、解释和预测；还有相关的跨文化认同、多元身份建构、研究方法以及类似"文化动态／变化观"等相关概念的重新认识等，都等待我们去探索、发现和诠释。

当前全球性金融危机和其他全球性问题使国内外学者意识到，以往的文化和交际研究有明显的局限性。对此学科文化价值观等核心问题的认识和阐述有缺失，西方的启蒙精神往往被夸大成人类的最高价值，民主、自由、理性、个人权力以及与其相关的交往原则等被普世化；对人是世界主宰的"人类中心主义"（anthropocentrism）、工具理性、适者生存的"社会／文化达尔文主义"等价值的问题在认识上存在偏颇。相当数量的学者仍然把社会和文化变化与西方结构主义线性或时间性价值取向挂钩，造成过去与现在、传统与现代的脱节（J.W. Berry, 1980; St. Clair, 2009；贾玉新，1997）。在"二元对立"、"非此即彼"思维的笼罩下，西方文化价值、文化概念以及交往原则等被强加于非西方文化，被当作评断是非和取舍的标准，使包括儒家文化在内的非西方文化被边缘化，甚至被否定和排斥，使此领域的研究滞后于时代的发展。在交际研究方面，对与多元文化时代密切相关的文化相对性、文化的多样性、社会语言相对性和语用多样性以及文化概念的相对性（conceptual relativity）缺乏深刻认识和诠释。

该学科引进中国的30多年来，我国学者们学习借鉴国外理论，结合国内实际，从开创到发展，进展神速。但是，我国学者的研究基本上承袭了西方的研究理论，以上提及的问题在不同程度上都有所反映。此外，缺乏对自身文化和交际资源的认识与反思，缺乏独创性。研究主要集中在语言和交际行为的对比方面。静态研究多，动态研究少，缺乏量化研究，对语用多样性的认识明显不足；对包括交际在内的自身文化所具有的普世价值元素缺乏认识，对其阐述不到位，甚至出现偏颇。在内容方面，视野不够宽泛，"收集采购之功多，提炼转化之功少"。在研究方法上，西方的研究方法被视为具有普遍意义，缺乏自身文化特点，缺乏与"多元一体"相得益彰的辩证统一的认识观，这些问题都影响我们对此领域研究的开拓和发展。

总之，在充分解读文化全球化的意义和总结经验的基础上，我们要在文化全球化时代的视野下建构21世纪跨文化交际研究框架，设计相关的研究内容和方法，发展适应文化全球化语境的跨文化交际研究。

2 "文化对话"是全球文化价值重建的出发点，是搭建跨文化交际研究的平台

全球化加强了跨文化认同化和普遍化，也导引了强烈的本土化和个性化，二者之间我们不能做非此即彼的选择，既此既彼的"和而不同"是必然的发展趋势。

经济一体化使当今世界一荣俱荣、一损俱损，当前的金融危机就是明证。全球化不仅使不同文化相互依存、互动互补、相互合作、相互认同，也带来了空前的不确定性：冲突、仇恨、纷争、灾难、战争，乃至金融危机等等。随全球化产生的文化冲突尤其引起人们的关注和焦虑。全球化走向文明冲突和终结

（Huntington,1993），还是平等互动、相互融合、共存共荣？世纪之交，世界文明面临严峻挑战。在关键时刻，联合国大会倡导文明对话，这是极富智慧的正确的选择。越有冲突和矛盾，文明对话就越为必要。

文明对话预设着文化对话，文化对话是解决全球问题和建构全球和平的出发点，为跨文化交际搭建了一个理想的平台。

在"多元一体"的21世纪，各民族对平等权力和利益的诉求日益激烈，非西方文化的价值进入我们的视野。时代要求我们不以二元对立的思维对待非西方文化、要改变非西方文化的边缘地位，把多元文化价值当作营造全球和平的宝贵资源。中国的和平崛起改变了西方权势为主导的话语语境，并使中国成为解决全球问题、价值重建和"对话"的主角之一。

历史和现实证明平等对话已是解决全球问题和实现全球和平不可或缺的重要路径。但是，"对话"首先呼唤我们对自身文化深刻反思、对习以为常的西方的普世价值重新审视和全面阐述。对文化的反思和重新审视是"对话"的前提。

3 "和而不同"及其理念下的"对话"修辞

全球化是一个不可逆转的过程，全球化肇始于西方的现代化，但是，如同上文所讨论的，全球化不应是西化价值的同质化，也不是本土化。国家无大小之分，文化没有高低优劣，文化全球化发展趋势是"我者"（"us"）与"他者"（"others"）、本土与全球、民族文化与世界文化的共生共存、互动互惠和相互认同，他们的关系既对立又统一。

全球化意味着"全球文化多元化"，它承袭和发展了儒家文化的"和谐"这一核心价值，"和谐"的本质是"和而不同"。在"和而不同"概念中，"不同"指民族/本土文化的个性和独特性、指文化的差异性和多样性，而"和"意味着全球化。二者是"部分"与"整体"的关系，"和"如同"整体"，而文化之个性如同"部分"。这一比喻如同"全球—本土"、"世界—民族"概念中全球/世界与本土/民族是整体与部分的关系一样。时间和空间的紧缩、全球化的效应（包括现代的网络等媒体效应）带来的相互连接并不能取代文化边界。"和而不同"的理念是："不同而和"意味着长盛不衰，"同而不和"意味着衰亡和毁灭。"和而不同"准确地描绘了当前文化的全球化的性质。全球化是人类对时空感知的变化，这种变化好比硬币的两面："一方面，所有的边界都变得越来越向外延伸和扩大；但另一方面，自我边界又越来越清晰可见。"（Rico Lie, 2003）实际上，这就是全球化传递给人类的信息：当今世界不同文化既连接又独立、既对立又统一。在全球化过程中，个人、性别、种族、民族、宗教、政治、语言、文化等都在超越和扩大自己原有的边界，但它们无论怎样变化，都永远扎根在自己文化的土壤上。中国传统文化中的"螺旋"思维取向影响下的"万变不离其宗"的变化规律，讲的就是这个道理。文化的进步和文化趋同及认同的变化都需要文化间互动互补、相互渗透、共存共荣、相互认同。一种文明或文化，只有融入才能得到发展，在更为多样的文化中，才能得以生存和再生。"只有民族的，才是世界的"，但是，"只有世界的，才是民族的"，二者相辅相成，你中有我，我中有你。

这种既连接又独立、既对立又统一的"和而不同"预设着多样性文化之间的对话，通过"对话"才能深入认识和反思自己、扩大共识、扩大认同、开拓文化意识、互动共惠，共建"和而不同"的全球社会。

现代全球化视野下的"和而不同"语境中的"对话"预设着平等和差异，并倡导文化间平等对话，平等是对话的基础，没有差异则没有"对话"的必要（杜维明，2006）。在伦理上，"对话"要求开放性的心态：对差异的容忍、理解、尊重、欣赏、肯定和接纳。"对话"是对差异、分歧、矛盾以及冲突的和平协商；平等"对话"不是放弃自我，而是立足自身文化、开阔视野、扩大共识、扩大自身文化边界、扩大跨文化认同；同时对自身文化吐故纳新、推陈出新、有所突破和创建，从而再生和发展。

修辞是话语广义上的对话。亚里士多德把修辞看作关于"说服"的学问，修辞是"说服"的手段。在西方文化中，在独立自我、"二元对立"、线性思维以及普世主义影响下，"对话"成了"说服"的开场白和表白自己信仰及立场的平台（杜维明，2006）。这样，"对话"就成了改变、影响、教导、甚至命令和强加于人、甚至文化霸权的同义词。西方文化的"对话"是"教导文化"的产物（杜维明，2006）。这种对话修辞与儒家"和而不同"所倡导的平等互动、相互融合、共存共荣、扩大共识的价值取向大相径庭。

现代"和而不同"语境下的对话修辞应始于儒家"恕道"与"关系自我"取向下的"倾听"，"倾听"是一种谦虚的学习态度，是对差异的容忍和理解，是"学习文化"的产物。具体讲，"倾听"意味着谦卑、恭敬（"恕之敬也"）、敏感、同情和情感换位（empathy）；"倾听"从心开始，是全身心的投入，是情感、认知和行为的通力付出和投入，"倾听"是平等对话、和平协商、扩大共识、延伸自我、扩大文化认同的平台，是构建和谐的开场白。

以上"倾听"所传递的文化信息完全可以由象形会意的中国汉字"听"的繁体字"聽"的构造中解读出来。"聽"从"耳"、从"王"、从"德"，从"心"。"王者"为"圣"／"聖"，因为"聖"者从耳，故"聖"者善听，善听不同意见；"王"者天地人合一，由于善听，王者天文地理人事无一不晓。听者从"心"，心之功能则思，思为思考；"情"者从心，"心"者为情，"听"是情感投入。"聽"从"耳"、从"德"，"德"者"仁"，"仁"者爱人，"仁"者"忍"，"仁"者"恕"，"恕"之敬，"恕"之（同／移）"情"，"恕"者利人。"德"者谦虚，"德"者得天下，"德"者"得"也。听／聽从耳、从口，耳朵要听别人口中说话；"听"音通聪，聪从耳、从心，意味着聪敏智慧，兼听则明，耳听之后要分析，天地人为一体综合分析。分析后还要做道德判断。"听"／"聽"从"心"，根据中国传统文化，"心"者人也，而"仁者人也"。人固有恻隐之心（仁也）、羞恶之心（义也）、恭敬之心（礼也）、是非之心（智也）的品质。而"心"音通"新"，"新"者"变化"，推陈出新，吐故纳新。汉字形、音、意为一体，是文化的全息符号，是概念化文字。中国汉字文化告诉我们，"听"从"心"开始，用"心"去听，意味着全身心的投入和付出，"倾听"是行为、情感、认知、道德的全部投入和付出，所以"耳聪目明，圣听德贤"。

以"倾听"导引的"对话"是在不失去自我、不失去自己群体文化取向基础上的个人、性别、地区、宗教、民族、国家、区域以及国际等不同文化层面上的互动互惠、超越异同、扩大共识、延伸自我、扩大文化认同。正如费孝通先生所说的，不同文化间要做到"各美其美"、"美人之美"、"美美与共、天下大同"（2007）。显然，实现这样崇高的目标，应以"和而不同"理念下的"对话"为出发点，而这样的"对话"始于"倾听"。

4 "和而不同"视野下的跨文化对话

本节讨论跨文化"对话"所涉及的两个重要层面：文化对话和语言对话。

4.1 文化对话

价值是全球化的核心问题，也是跨文化交际的核心问题，因此，"对话"首先是多样性文化价值之间的对话。从东西方的视角来看，"对话"要求我们在对自身传统价值深刻反思和重建、对以启蒙精神为核心的西方价值重新审视和全面阐述的基础上，开展儒家人文精神与西方人文精神对话。

近几百年来，西方的启蒙文化为人类社会现代化做出了卓越的贡献，也使其一直处于强势地位，导引着世界文明和现代化。20世纪末，文化研究兴起新的高潮，包括西方文化学者在内的后现代主义、后结构主义以及跨文化交际学者开始对"自我中心"的文化进行反思，在哲学、文化学以及跨文化交际领域，开始注意和接纳儒家文化和其他非西方文化。当我们步入全球化的21世纪，残酷的现实使越来越多的学者意识到启蒙主义的缺失。他们对缺乏道德意识和社会责任感的极端"个人中心"主义造成的不良后果有切身体会，他们对西方普世价值在其他文化土壤的水土不服现象开始反思，对人是世界主宰的"人类中心主义"（anthropocentrism）的局限性，对工具理性、适者生存的"社会／文化达尔文主义"（Berry，1980；杜维明，2006）等西方文化固有的问题开始觉醒和批判。在重新审视和批判的基础上，学者们对西方价值有了新的认识。

在国内，从"五四"运动到20世纪七八十年代的近百年间，在西方启蒙心态和一切二分的"二元论"思维笼罩下，儒家精神一直被边缘化。20世纪的20、30年代的进步知识分子为追求民族独立和富强，倡导"民主"和"科学救国"、并取得所谓反传统的胜利，但因主张全盘西化和提倡"打倒孔家店"，在文化上造成传统与现代的脱节，致使文化发展停滞不前。解放后的年代里，政治上的极左路线使儒家文明被歧视、怀疑、否定和批判,而所谓右派倾主义,认为儒家过于迂腐,封建和落后,儒家精神被完全否定,文化在中国的发展严重滞后。

在当今全球化的21世纪,由于中国的和平崛起,被西方启蒙精神长期笼罩下的儒家精神重新进入人们的视野,在反思自身文化的基础上,一批学者认识到中国文化的核心概念"和谐"和"仁义"以及"一体之仁"、"人与天地万物为一体"等价值是具有普世意义的中国元素,在建构和谐全球社会方面有其特殊意义。

21世纪学者们的重新"审视"和"反思",为开展平等"对话"奠定了基础,使构建"和而不同"的全球价值和实现全球社会和平成为可能。

实际上,目前全球社会的发展已充分证明、并将进一步证明,只有通过平等的文化对话,全球问题才能得到解决;只有通过东西方"对话"、西方与非西方"对话",全球金融危机才能得到圆满解决。只有在东西方相互对立的文化价值中寻找契合点,在西方和非西方截然不同的价值中寻找交汇点,寻找共同之处,做到扬长避短、择善而从、兼容并蓄,达到"昌明国粹,融汇新知",全球和平才能得以实现。

笔者在一篇论文(2008)中曾指出,北京2008奥运会取得的无与伦比的成功,就是东西方文化价值平等互动、相互融合、共存共荣、跨文化认同的结晶。我国优秀运动员的双重文化身份已经体现出东西方价值的有机融合,他们的文化身份是集体主义和个人主义、儒家"仁义"和西方"个人尊严"、儒家的"和谐"与西方的"自由意志"等对立的价值相互交汇的结果,是跨文化认同的结晶。但我们同时也必须认识到,在我国文化中,东西方价值的融合是在传统的儒家传统框架内得以实现的,这一民族文化的独特性也正说明未来全球价值建构的多元性,他者文化价值必须与本土文化土壤相适应。缺乏自身文化土壤或文化根基的跨文化认同、或丢失自我文化身份的跨文化认同,在多元文化的现实世界不可能实现。

4.2 语言对话

"和而不同"的视野为对话提供了全新的"全球-本土"或"世界-民族"语境,在这一语境中,三种因素影响我们的交际:被人们广泛称之为的全球化、本土化,及"全球本土化"(East, M., 2008)。全球化曾意味着个人和群体以及他者之间在行为、认知和情感方面与西方认同。在国际交往中使用美式、英式英语,这显然是排斥"他者";与美国文化和语言的同质化,是没有"他者"的全球化或美国化,这是典型的语言或文化帝国主义。而极端本土化,则完全突出文化和语言使用的个性和独特性,这是一种排斥"他者"的趋势,是较为极端的文化相对主义和语言社会相对主义表现,是极端的文化和语言多元主义表现。而"全球本土化"或"世界—民族"化的视角则是较为积极的,这种视角把全球化和本土化、世界化和民族化相互对立的现实看成既对立又统一的一个整体,二者互动互惠,你中有我,我中有你,成为一个"我者"与"他者"之间相互交融、共生共存("us-others")、互动互惠("us-others" reciprocity)的有机体。

在语言使用方面则形成一个英语使用的双向性，英语同时受本土化和国际化的影响，这是英语全球化的发展趋势。其结果是英语因文化和地域差异而产生多样性和变异性，英语就成了因文化和地域而异的国际语或世界语，这显然是一种文化多元化和语言多元化的趋势，实际上，这是当前全球社会的现实。

全球多元化概念与我国传统价值"和而不同"有很多共同之处，这样的语境为语言研究提出两个任务，一是把英语作为国际语或世界语，把英语当作多元文化的语言，二是突出英语本土化的研究，即突出文化相对性、社会语言相对性的研究，这意味着要凸显作为国际语的英语的多样性或文化变异的研究。二者显然是部分与整体的关系，其互动和互惠反映出"全球"与"本土"之间辩证和统一的关系。

在全球化的视野下，"对话"预设着语言研究的新概念，即文化相对性（包括概念相对性）、社会语言相对性和语用多样性概念（Jia, Y. X. 2007, Spencer-Oatey.H. 1999; Jia X. R. 2009; Gudykunst, W.B. 2007）。在全球化的21世纪，这些新概念开始凸显其在跨文化交际研究中的作用。这意味着，除语言在语义、句法等方面的文化差异之外，与"和谐"或"和而不同"理念密切相关的，语言在和谐与调适人际和社会关系方面的社会功能的研究变得尤为重要（Spencer-Oatey, H., 2000; Brown, P. & Levinson, S.C,1987）。不同文化，尤其我们自己民族的语言在实施这一社会功能方面有其独到之处，它们是构建和谐全球社会的宝贵资源，在全球化的语境中会发挥重要的作用（Chen, 2007）。

社会语言相对性和语用多样性表现在跨文化交往的诸多方面：不同语言对纷繁复杂的文化环境和变化万千情景的适应能力、对文化和社会身份的表达与协商能力（Gumperz, J.J. 1982; Jia, X.L., & Jia, Y.X., 2004；Byram, M. 2008）以及对民族文化权力和利益诉求能力等方面。其多样性或差异体现在言语行为、交际方略、语篇和话语结构、交际风格、语码转换以及制约语言使用的社会文化和语用规范等诸多方面。

在跨文化交往中，社会语言相对性和语用多样性在很大程度上是通过世界通用语英语体现出来的，这就是全球化所带来的英语变异现象，这些变异现象显然是英语"全球化-本土"化语境影响下的必然结果。英语已经是不同文化共享的国际语，美式或英式英语已不再是唯一的标准英语，由于害怕新巴比主义的出现，有的学者呼吁重归美式或英式标准英语，或改变英语的多元文化趋势，这在文化多元的时代已成为不可能（Honna, N., 2008）。作为国际语，英语具有文化的多元性已经是全球社会的现实。这意味着，我们对英语多样性或变异现象，应有高度的意识性和敏感性；对全球化的语境及其对英语使用的影响以及英语的变异现象应展开深入的研究。

在全球化的语境下，用国际语英语在不同文化中进行交际的能力，已是全球公民所应必备的社会资本（Bourdieu, 1973）。它是人类通过沟通、交往和协商去完成交际任务、解决矛盾和冲突、表达和协商文化及社会身份、实现全球共存共荣以及扩大跨文化认同的文化资源转化成的社会资本。

5 "和而不同"视野下的研究方法：辩证法

"和而不同"是东方文化、尤其是中国文化的思维传统，充分体现对事物既对立又统一的辩证思维。"辩证"法是"和而不同"理念下对跨文化交际研究的理想路径，它与"多元一体"的视野相得益彰。辩证法对文化不黑白相分，是对西方"二元对立"、"非此即彼"以及线性思维定势的批判和超越。辩证法把相互矛盾和对立的价值和其他文化因素看作是一个互动互补的统一体。我们可以把"辩证"法当作是观察文化和交际中各种相关变量和现象的透视镜，在辩证法的透视下，东方与西方、西方与非西方、全球化与本土化、世界与民族、历史与现在、传统与现代、人与环境、差异与相似、静态与动态、人与自然、心与身、公平/正义与个人自由、理性与同情/情感换位、伦理道德/责任与工具理性、个人主义与群体主义（Hofstede, 1980）、体验/经验与先验/理性、直觉体征与逻辑实证（Hall, D.L.& Ames, R.T.（1987）、相对主义与普世主义等相互对立和矛盾的方方面面，都被看成既对立又统一的有机体，把对立和矛盾重新整合，并寻找交汇点、扩大视野、扩大跨文化认同。这意味着，应把对立和矛盾看作相互关联、相互补充、互动共生的（mutually formative）。在这样的视角下，我者与他者（us and others）变成既对立又统一的整体。

在辩证法的视角下的文化（价值）的动态观与西方结构主义文化动态观截然不同。根据西方结构主义，文化和社会之变化是在空间中的线性运动，这种线性运动的文化动态观认为，文化变化是某一静态时点（frozen time）的文化静态（steady state）到另一个静态时点的文化静态的变化。这样一来，在文化、社会的变化中，"现在"与"过去"、"现代"与"传统"就成为相互独立、截然相分的实体，这一观点显然与后现代的文化动态观大相径庭，它无法解释全球化时代中的"现代"概念的复杂现象，无法解释静态文化之间是如何衔接和演变的（St. Clair, 2009）。"辩证"视野下的文化动态观认为时间存在于空间，时间与空间一起变化和进步，"现在"与"过去"是一个相互依托和辩证的统一体，"现在"存在于"过去"之中，但"过去"在"现在"环境中要经过重新定义、突破、更新和创造，这也就是Kuhn"科学革命"理论中"现在与过去并存"（co-present）的观点。由此我们可以引伸出"现代"镶嵌在"传统"之中、或现代与传统共存共生的观点。诚然，传统在全球化的环境中不仅要"温故知新"、对自身文化还要"吐故纳新"、"推陈出新"，这种突破能力就是Boulding（1985）称之为人类的能力资源人类对现代环境的"创造性的适应能力"。（St.Clair & Williams, A.C.T., 2009）。但不管怎样，在变化过程中，正是不同文化在所扎根的传统或文化土壤之间的差异造成当今全球的文化的多元性。

"辩证法"倡导综合各相关学科理论，统筹认知、情感和行为等交际要素；对目前流行的"社会心理"、"诠释"和"批判"三个理论学派的理念，对流行的"客位"（etic）和"主位"（emic）的路径，对主观与客观以及定性和定量化的研究方法等进行客观审视、梳理、分析、对比和批判，并以此为基础，扬长避短，博采众长，兼容并蓄，使彼此对立或不同的观点和理念相互交融。

多元文化共存共荣或"和而不同"是全球化发展的必然路径，是人类共同理想。其理念下的"对话"呼唤我们从"辩证"的视角，透视和对待多样性的文化价值。"辩证法"所倡导的"万物并行而不相害，道并行而不相悖"的哲学思想，是跨文化交际的理想研究方法。

6 结语

全球化的21世纪预设着文化间相互依存、互动互补、相互交融、共存共荣的人类文明，但也带来了全球性的危机和空前的不确定性。这一充满诱惑和矛盾的时代是对跨文化交际研究全新的挑战。

"和而不同"是全球和谐发展的必然路径，也是跨文化交际研究的主导理念。作者认为"和而不同"理念下的"对话"是解决全球问题、矛盾和冲突，扩大视野、吐故纳新、推陈出新，文化认同、建构全球和平的出发点，因此，应在"对话"的平台上发展跨文化交际研究。本文在对"和而不同"理念理解的基础上，提出了"和而不同"理念下的对话修辞概念，提倡"对话"应始于"倾听"，而不是西方所倡导的"说服"；并以此为指导，对与"和而不同"密切相关的文化价值和言语层面上的对话，进行了较详尽的阐述和分析。本文还指出，未来的研究应采用"辩证"的研究方法，因为"辩证"法不仅能对所流行的研究理论和研究方法兼容并蓄，而且与构建全球和平的"和而不同"价值取向和理念相得益彰。本文对当前文化全球化过程中出现的新问题，如对文化全球化发展变化的两种截然不同的模式，从辩证法的角度进行解读。

References

Adler, P.S. (1987). Beyond cultural identity: Reflections on cultural and multicultural man. In L. Samovar & R. Porter (Eds.), *Intercultural communication: A reader* (4th ed., pp. 362-380). Bemont, CA: Wadsworth.

Berry, J. W. (1980). Social and cultural change. In H. C. Triandis, & R. W. Brislin (Eds.), *Handbook of cross-cultural psychology: Social psychology* (Vol.5, 211-279). Boston: Allyn and Bacon.

Boulding, K. (1985). *The World as a Total System*. London: Sage Publication.

Brown, P. & Levinson, S.C, (1987) Universals in language usage: Politeness phenomenon. In E.N. Goody (Ed.), *Questions and politeness: Strategies in social interaction*. (pp. 56-289.) Cambridge: Cambridge University Press.

Byram, M. (2008). *From foreign language education to education for intercultural citizenship*. Clevedon: Multilingual Matters.

Chen, G.M. (2007). A review of the concept of intercultural effectiveness. In Hinner, M.B. (Eds.), *The influence of culture in the world of business* (pp. 97-116). Frankfurt am Main, Germany: Peter Lang GmbH.

East, M. (2008). Moving towards Us-others reciprocity: Implications of globalization for language learning and intercultural communication. *Language and Intercultural Communication. Vol. 8*: 3. 156-157.

Giddens, A. (1990). *The consequence of modernity*. Cambridge: Polity Press.

Gudykunst, W.B. (2003). *Cross-cultural & Intercultural Communication*. Thousand Oaks: Sage Publications.

Gudykunst, W.B. (2005). *Theorizing about intercultural communication*. Sage Publications.

Gumperz, J.J. (1982). (Ed.) *Language and social identity*. Cambridge: Cambridge University Press.

Hall, D.L. & Ames, R.T. (1987). *Thinking through Confucius*. Albany, N.Y.: University State of New York Press.

Jia, Y.X. & Jia, X.L. (2008). *The Transition of cultural identity in China from 1950s to the 21st century*. Paper presented at International Conference at Shanghai Teachers University.

Jia, X. L. & Jia, Y. X. (2004). The construction and negotiation of individualistic identity with the traditional discourse in China *In Intercultural Communication Studies*. USA.

Jia,X.R. (2009). *A comparative study of Chinese and American communication styles*. Harbin: Harbin Institute Press.

Jia,Y.X. (2007). Pragmatic diversity, pragmatic transfer, and cultural identity. In Hinner, M.B. (Ed.). The Influence of Culture in the World of Business (pp. 431-434). Frankfurt am Main, Germany: Peter Lang GmbH.

Jia,Y.X. (2008). *China's cultural identity in transition* (1950-21st century), Paper Presentation at IAICS International Conference at Louisville, USA.

Jia,Y.X, & Jia, X. R.(2007). The study of Chinese language behavior cross-culturally: A sociolinguistic approach to intercultural communication. In Steve J.Kulich & Prosser, M., (Eds.) *Intercultural research on Chinese communication*（pp.129-174）. Shanghai: Shanghai Foreign Language Education Press.

Kuhn.T.S. (1962). *The Structure of scientific revolution*. Chicago: University of Chicago Press.

Spencer-Oatey.H. (1999). *Culturally speaking: Managing rapport through talk across cultures*. London: Assell Academic.

Hofstede, G.. (1980). *Cultures consequence: International differences in work related values*. Beverely Hills: Sage.

Honna, N. (2008). *English as a multicultural language in Asian contexts*. Tokyo: Kurosio Publishers.

Martin, J. & Nakayama, T. (2008). *Experiencing intercultural communication*. Boston, MA: McGraw Hill.

Rico, L. (2003). *Space of intercultural communication*. Greeskill, NewJersey: Hampton Press.

Spencer-Oatey, H. (2000). *Culturally speaking: Managing rapport through talk across cultures*. London: Continuum.

St. Clair, R.N.. & William A.C.T. (2009). The framework of culture space. in *intercultural commumication studies*. *Vol XVII*: 2. 1-13.

Ting-Toomey. S., & Oetzel, J. (2001). *Managing intercultural conflicts effectively*. Thousand Oaks, CA: Sage.

Ting-Toomey. S. (1999). *Communication across cultures*. New York, NY: The Gilford Press.

杜维明, (2006), 《儒家传统与文明对话》, 石家庄: 河北人民出版社, 第70-84页。

[Tu, W. M. (2006). *Dialogues between Confucianism and civilization*. Shijiazhuang: Hebei People's Press, 70-84.]

费孝通, (2007), 《论文化与文化自觉》, 北京: 群言出版社, 第315页。

[Fei, X. T. (2007). *Culture and cultural awareness*. Beijing: Qunyan Press, 315.]

郝大维、安乐哲, (2005), 《通过孔子而思》, 北京: 北京大学出版社, 第14-29页。

[Hall, D. L. & Ames, R. T. *Thinking through Confucius*. Beijing: Peking University Press, 14-29.]

贾玉新, (1997), 《跨文化交际学》, 上海: 上海外语教育出版社, 第55-88页。

[Jia, Y. X. (1997). *Intercultural communicatin*. Shanghai: shanghai Foreign Language and Education Press, 55-88.]

龙佳解, (2001), 《中国人文主义新论》, 长江: 湖南大学出版社。

[Long, J. J. (2001). *A new perspective on China's humanism*. Changsha: Hunan University Press.]

汤一介, (1988), 《中国传统文化中的儒道释》, 北京: 中国和平出版社。

[Tang, Y. J. (1988). *Interpretations of Confucianism in traditional Chinese culture*. Beijing: China He Ping Press.]

汤一介, (2007), 《新轴心时代与中国文化建构》。南昌: 江西人民出版社。

[Tang, Y. J. (2007). *A new axis and the construction of Chinese culture*. Nanchang: Jiangxi People's Press.]

哈佛大学、燕京大学, (2005), 《儒家传统与启蒙心态》, 南京: 江苏教育出版社。

[Harvard University / Yanching University (2005). *Confucianism and the enlightenment mentality*. Nanjing: Jiangsu Education Press.]

Developing a concept of intercultural citizenship

Michael Byram   University of Durham, UK

Abstract

"Education for citizenship" is a new concept but is related to old established functions of schools, i.e. to create identification with the nation-state. The new element in "education for citizenship" is that it includes teaching and learning objectives to take learners out of their schools to become active in their communities. However the largest community they engage with is the nation-state, and this is not enough in a globalised world where people need to interact in communities across state frontiers.

This article argues that foreign language teaching has a particular role to play in extending the concept of citizenship and activity to transnational civil society and transnational communities – small or large, permanent or temporary. It does so by showing that some of the objectives of foreign language teaching with intercultural competence as an aim overlap with some of the objectives of citizenship education, and simultaneously extend them and give learners the potential for interacting in transnational society. The overlap is in the notion that both citizenship education and foreign language education have "engagement" as one of their objectives. Citizenship education has practical applications in engagement in the community. Foreign language education promotes practical application in an international community.

Introduction

One purpose of this article[1] is to consider if and how the aims and objectives of teaching for intercultural communicative competence in a foreign language may be complementary to those of education for democratic citizenship in schools. The theoretical base for this lies in the concepts of intercultural competence and citizenship and in their

---

1   This article is based on a more detailed presentation in Byram, 2008, *From Foreign Language Education to Education for Intercultural Citizenship*, Clevedon: Multilingual Matters.

potential complementarity. I will discuss this potential relationship in terms of objectives for teaching and learning.

A second, more ambitious purpose is to consider if and how citizenship in a nation-state is compatible with international citizenship, and to suggest that "intercultural citizenship" is a useful concept for relating national and international citizenship, realisable in the practice of "education for citizenship" in schools.

National Identity, Language and Citizenship Education

Much of the thinking about education for citizenship is focused upon the nation-state. For example in a recent book edited by Lee et al. (2004), the authors of articles usually assume that citizenship education is an aspect of education in the nation-state and for the nation-state. For example, Kennedy (2004: 17) suggests that one significant role for citizenship education is in buttressing "the nation-state against fundamentalist extremism". This kind of thinking corresponds to Anderson's (1991) well-known notion of the nation as an imagined community. Anderson points to the significance of language and argues that the close relationship between language and nation was promoted from a European perspective, and was part of the "model" of the nation-state which was borrowed - or as he says, "pirated" — in many parts of the world. By referring not simply to language but to "print-language" and the power of newspapers and books to create a sense of community, Anderson also emphasises the significance of literacy. A nation-state is thus inter alia a community of communication which needs a shared language, and usually this shared language is what is designated as the national language[2]. Thus linguistic identity and national identity are closely connected through a formal, institutionalized "community of communication", which might however be better designated as a "society of communication" when communication takes place within state institutions and structures.

On the other hand, there are also other levels within a nation-state which are not necessarily formalised within and by the institutions of the nation-state, and therefore tend to have the characteristics of a community (Gemeinschaft). The organisations and institutions of "civil society" have differing degrees of formality, and where there is freedom of speech, these communities of communication can challenge the official discourses of the state (Kennedy and Fairbrother, 2004: 296). Nonetheless, such discourses are likely to be

---

2   There are of course many exceptions to this ideal-typical model, not least in Europe where the model originated. Where such exceptions exist, for example in Belgium or Switzerland, the ways in which a single-language state exists, are re-produced in the various sub-national sectors of the state, but there are exceptions to this too, notably in India, and my analysis can not deal with every case in detail.

conducted through the same national, officially recognized language(s), or in a variety of it/them, and again we see the significance of the national language(s) and the reinforcement of the relationship between the national language and national identity.

The question then arises as to what level of competence is expected of people who wish to be part of a national society. The usual assumption is that the competence norm is set by the "native speaker"[3]. This is made explicit whenever there are in-comers to the society, because they are expected to meet minimum requirements and attempt to develop competence which can be compared with the native speaker. Native speaker competence is developed above all in and through schooling, and is seen as a signifier of adherence to the nation-state and to the norms it demands of its citizens. The right of the nation-state to expect linguistic competence and linguistic identity goes largely unchallenged.

Only in the case of the European Union can we see nation-states gradually giving up some of their power and adopting a more trans-national, or more accurately European perspective. In such circumstances, there is encouragement for other languages to be given a status as part of the creation of identification with a society/community. This is made very clear in the EU's White Paper of 1995:

Languages are also the key to knowing other people. Proficiency in languages helps to build up the feeling of being European with all its cultural wealth and diversity and of understanding between the citizens of Europe.

(…) Multilingualism is part and parcel of both European identity/citizenship and the learning society.

(European Commission, 1995: 67 – my emphasis)

This is a statement where the word "European" could be substituted by the name of almost any nationality, and the parallels with the role of language in a national "imagined community" are clear; Europe is to become an international imagined community. It is also clear that, as in the nation-state, the types of communication involved are not only those which are formal and institutional, but also include those of civil society.

What makes the European example different is that it is not expected that people should be native speakers of all the languages they might acquire as part of becoming European citizens. All the work currently being carried out in Brussels by the European Union on the development of a "Europass" for languages" or in Strasbourg by the Council of Europe on a "European Language Portfolio" is a sign of the recognition by European authorities, and the national authorities which support them, that "plurilingual competence" of some kind is crucial. Thus, the assumption that native speaker competence is part of

---

[3] The concept of the native speaker is much debated but will have to be used here without entering into that debate (e.g. Davies, 2003).

identification with a polity is questioned, and replaced by plurilingual competence, as defined in the Common European Framework of Reference:

The ability to use languages for the purposes of communication and to take part in intercultural interaction, where a person, viewed as a social agent, has proficiency of varying degrees, in several languages, and experience of several cultures. (Council of Europe, 2001: 168)

The future success of a European imagined community of communication presupposes plurilingual competence so that discourses at formal level and in civil society can be extended beyond the national frontiers to European level.

The alternative to plurilingualism is to create a shared lingua franca – which at this point in history could only be English – but this is not politically acceptable since there would be accusations of linguistic imperialism. Nor would it be desirable. Trans-national discourses can not rely on a single, taken for granted, shared language and its meanings. For the discourse which is necessary is not simply a matter of establishing an agreement on and/or an exchange of information such as might be achieved through a lingua franca. The issues which arise in social discourse are shot through with contemporary and historical nuances and values, and the relationship between language and thought, between language and world-view, is crucial. An analysis of linguistic and conceptual relativism will show that a lingua franca will simply not cope with the nuances of communication necessary in social life.

Linguistic and Conceptual Relativism

It is not difficult to demonstrate that a public discussion in which people of different languages are participating, raises linguistic and conceptual complexities which cannot be overlooked. Let me do this in a brief way by considering the word "citizen" itself as it appears in writing about education for citizenship. One author is Norwegian and clearly has an excellent grasp of English:

At the conceptual level, the English words "citizen" and "civic" lack good synonyms in the Norwegian language. The most common translation borger, denotes meanings like "city dweller", bourgeois (as opposed to "peasant" or "worker') and "politically conservative". To overcome these problems the word medborger (co-citizen) seems to be gaining ground. To the extent that medborger colours the understanding of the concept, it probably gives more attention to the relational or collective elements. (Skeie, 2003: 55)

The author goes on to say that "to an international readership it may seem somewhat narrow-minded to go into linguistic details", but it is nonetheless revealing of historical developments and cultural values. On the contrary, far from being narrow-minded, this analysis reveals potential problems in public debate. Even if, as seems to be the case here, a speaker of Norwegian does not expect their interlocutors to understand the Norwegian connotations and collocations – a typical position, unfortunately, for speakers of less widely taught and spoken languages – his apparent assumption that if everyone speaks English as a lingua franca, mutual comprehension will ensue, is extremely unlikely to be true because the knowledge of English required would be too demanding for most people. Scholars such as Skeie know the anglophone literature and the British collocations and connotations of "citizen", are not representative of other Norwegians and other users of English as a lingua franca. Ordinary speakers of English as a lingua franca will not be able to adopt those connotations and collocations when speaking English – however good their grammatical and phonetic proficiency. Some would not even wish to do so, because of the hegemonic implications of adopting the language of the powerful, and in fact what seems to happen in lingua franca communication is that interlocutors introduce their own understandings, their own collocations and connotations, from their own language into the lingua franca (Meierkord, 2002).

Communication in a Transnational Civil Society

The significance of (plurilingual) language competence in citizenship becomes clear in a concept of society presented by Habermas. For Habermas, the model which should replace out-dated concepts of "the classic republican idea of the self-conscious political integration of a community of free and equal persons", is a model dependent on communication flows:

> a model of deliberative democracy, that no longer hinges on the
> assumption of macro-subjects like the "people" or "the community"
> but on anonymously interlinked discourses or flows of information
> (Habermas, 1994: 32)

This implicit critique of the concept of "the imagined community" as a description of a nation-state suggests that the nation-state is evolving and that communication competence has to become more complex if everyone is to participate in democratic life. It is all the more relevant as a description of democratic processes in a trans-national context, because there are certain assumptions in this analysis.

Communication flows and the "informal networks of public communication" presuppose favourable conditions for mutual understanding. At a national level, it can be assumed that the shared national language provides the necessary conditions but at a trans-national level, it can not be assumed that the conditions are favourable, unless there is plurilingualism among the social actors involved. With the potential for mutual understanding through plurilingualism, as argued in the previous section, there is a possibility of creating a community of communication which is trans-national. The parallel with the nation-state would then suggest that a community of communication can become a community of practice in a trans-national civil society, a community of citizenship and political practice. The question then arises as to whether a common set of values can be established, or is needed, as the basis for such political practice.

The most striking and demanding test of this possibility is currently found in the contrast between Western (i.e. European and American) and Asian (especially East Asian) philosophers of education for citizenship with their respective concepts of democracy and the relationship of the individual to the groups to which they belong, in particular the national group. One approach to the contrast and difference is to attempt to establish a common core of citizenship education as Kennedy proposes (2004). In this argument, citizenship education is still modelled on that of the nation-state and the purpose of a common basis is to ensure that different nation-states can support each other in maintaining their existing positions in the world. Even if it were possible, the starting point is still the unchallenged integrity of the nation-state.

An alternative view would be to facilitate co-operation at the level of civil society across state boundaries where a trans-national comity might evolve which would counterbalance what Dewey (1916: 87) called the anti-democratic tendencies of any closed group, including the nation-state. Furthermore the assumption that international co-operation and comity in civil society has to be based on common values – on a common core for citizenship education – is not a necessary conclusion. Indeed if this were the case, then the possibility of a trans-national civil society would be in doubt.

The issue is not whether successful communication and co-operation can be based only on the shared meanings in a shared language as is the case of discourse in the nation-state, but whether an alternative is available. In other words, rather than seeking common meanings, a common core in civil society communication – for example through a uniform concept of the citizen – we should be looking for a means of making communication across national boundaries possible whilst acknowledging linguistic and conceptual relativity.

The theory of intercultural competence proposes such an alternative and can be a complement to education for citizenship, and education for political action.

A Model for Intercultural Competence

I have proposed a model for intercultural (communicative) competence on a number of occasions, and it has been used for planning teaching, notably in some of the work collected in Byram, Nichols and Stevens (2001). The model is a prescriptive, ideal model from which objectives for foreign language teaching and learning can be derived, and it proposes an integration of linguistic/communicative objectives with intercultural competence objectives.

It is hence a model of intercultural communicative competence, and not just a model of intercultural competence. Of particular significance here is the fact that it includes the concept of "critical cultural awareness':

An ability to evaluate critically, and on the basis of explicit criteria, perspectives, practices and products in one's own and other cultures and countries.(Byram, 1997: 53)

What is at stake here is the ability to decentre from one's own culture and its practices and products and to gain insight into another. With the help of a comparative juxtaposition, one is able to apprehend what might otherwise be too familiar in one's own culture or too strange in another. One can then make judgements but such judgements must be on the basis of clearly articulated and justified criteria, and the judgements will be both negative and positive about both one's own and other cultures.

It is important to stress that criteria must be articulated and justified. Justification may be on rational grounds or as an act of faith, but without justification and explicitness, judgement descends into prejudice and relativism.

"Critical cultural awareness" is not a sine qua non of intercultural communication, but is an educational objective, i.e. an objective which is to be pursued where the language and culture teacher takes responsibility for the education of learners and not only the development of their communication skills. It is this aspect of the model[4] which I want to compare with political education and education for citizenship.

Critical Cultural Awareness and Political / Citizenship Education

The phrase "political education" probably needs "scare" quotation marks for many readers. It has negative connotations of indoctrination but more neutral phrases such as "civic education" are too narrow; they refer only what is called in current curricula in Britain "political literacy". In England, the phrase "education for citizenship" has been invented recently and defined as having three elements:

● Social and moral responsibility:

Pupils learning – from the very beginning – self-confidence and socially and morally responsible behaviour both in and beyond the classroom, towards those in authority and towards each other.

● Community involvement:

Pupils learning about becoming helpfully involved in the life and concerns of their neighbourhood and communities, including learning through community involvement and

---

4 For a representation of the model see Appendix 1

service to the community.
- ● Political literacy:

Pupils learning about the institutions, problems and practices of our democracy and how to make themselves effective in the life of the nation, locally, regionally and nationally through skills and values as well as knowledge – a concept wider than political knowledge alone.

http://www.dfes.gov.uk/citizenship/section.cfm?sectionId=3&hierachy=1.3

On the other hand, attention to political education (politische Bildung) has been evident in Germany for several decades, since the end of the Second World War and I shall draw on two writers from that tradition in particular as a starting point.

Gagel (2000) identifies three aims for political education in this sense:

Learning to consider personal involvement in political action as desirable;

Learning to recognize democratic forms of action as values (and only democratic forms); these can be called democratic "virtues";

Acquiring interest in public affairs, being prepared to be interested in political resolutions of social problems.

He summarises this by drawing attention to the combined emphasis on cognitive, evaluative and behavioural dimensions: "political education helps the individual towards an evaluative orientation in their environment and makes them capable of democratic behaviour" (2000: 24 – my translation).

Himmelmann (2003) prefers to refer to Demokratie lernen (learning democracy) instead of politische Bildung, and prioritises "affective / moral attitudes" because without a will or disposition to achieve common purposes, there can be no acquisition of knowledge or active engagement in democratic processes.

Himmelmann is concerned in his paper to define "standards" or agreed outcomes for political education, and derives from Audigier's (1998) paper for the Council of Europe the following list of affective / moral attitudes:

1. recognition of the principles of universality, interdependence and indivisibility of basic rights and freedoms
2. respect for the value, the dignity and the freedom of every individual person
3. acceptance of the rule of law, search for justice, recognition of equality and equal treatment in a world full of differences
4. recognition of the importance of peace, absence of violence, and the participatory and constructive resolution of social conflicts and problems
5. trust in democratic principles, institutions and modes of action and valorization of participatory citizenship
6. recognition of pluralism in life and in society, respect for foreign cultures and their contribution to human development

7. valorization of mutuality, co-operation, trust and solidarity and the struggle against racism, prejudices and discrimination
8. taking action in favour of the principles of sustainable development as a balance between societal and economic growth and the protection of the environment.

It is evident from this list that attitudes or commitments, as he also calls them, have to have an object towards which they are directed. The list reveals the principles and values which Himmelmann, and others, consider to be fundamental.

These same principles and values are also present in his second list of the elements of general cognitive capacity to:

1. recognize (repeating and describing) facts, a statement, a problem, a situation, a conflict
2. differentiate (and compare) statements, assertions, or facts according to different interests, needs or perspectives
3. discuss (and explain) different statements in a context, and develop further points of view
4. investigate (and explain) origins, background or history
5. critique (judge and evaluate) a position or perspective with respect to its consequences, its significance for the future, and its capacity for resolving problems
6. argue (and take a viewpoint) for or against a position; according to one's own explicit criteria
7. justify one's own position from a legal and moral perspective and evaluate possibilities of action
8. reflect on (and discuss) normative issues according to criteria of human rights, democracy, a state ruled by law, or moral beliefs; judge conflicts in decision and values

In this case Himmelmann derives the list from the National Standards for Civics and Government, published in the USA. He labels this list "knowledge" and he also has a separate list of the suggested contents of political education curricula of which learners would be expected to have knowledge. The first list is thus a definition of procedural knowledge ("knowing how") and the list of contents is knowledge about ("knowing that").

The third, behavioural, element of political education is again derived from Council of Europe work and there is some overlap with the cognitive capacities in the second list. This final list is labelled practical-instrumental capacities or skills and strategies:

1. grasp and take seriously the opinions and arguments of others, recognize those who have other opinions as people, be able to put oneself in the position of others, accept criticism and listen
2. make one's own opinions (needs, interests, feelings, values) clear, speak coherently, explain clearly

3. abandon every kind of violence, humiliation, insult (expressions of power) etc
4. take account of those who are weaker, reduce discrimination, integrate outsiders
5. organize group work, cooperate in the distribution of work, take on tasks, trustworthiness, perseverance, care and conscientiousness
6. tolerate plurality, divergences, differences, recognize conflicts, as far as possible crate balance, and resolve in socially acceptable ways, accept mistakes and differences
7. find compromises, seek consensus, accept majority decisions, tolerate minorities, promote encouragement, balance right and responsibilities, and show trust and courage
8. emphasize group responsibility, develop fair norms and common interests and needs, pursue common approaches to tasks

Put together, these three lists describe the desirable outcomes from political education/ democracy learning in terms of attitudes and capacities/skills. As Himmelmann points out, politische Bildung takes place, in Germany, in many parts of the curriculum and under many labels and guises. He lists 23 such labels.

Not surprisingly, there is no mention of language education, neither national nor foreign language education, but the definition of critical cultural awareness introduced earlier is comparable to items 5, 6, and 7 in the second list of elements of a general cognitive capacity listed above. In the further elaboration of critical cultural awareness in Byram (1997) the following objectives are specified for "the intercultural speaker" i.e. someone who is not attempting to imitate a native speaker of a foreign language but acquiring an ability to occupy the "space between" cultures of different groups and establish and mediate relationships between them:

Objectives (ability to):

(a) identify and interpret explicit or implicit values in documents and events in one's own and other cultures

The intercultural speaker:

* can use a range of analytical approaches to place a document or event in context (of origins/sources, time, place, other documents or events) and to demonstrate the ideology involved

(b) make an evaluative analysis of the documents and events which refers to an explicit perspective and criteria

> * is aware of their own ideological perspectives and values ("human rights"; socialist; liberal; Moslem; Christian etc.) and evaluates documents or events with explicit reference to them
>
> (c) interact and mediate in intercultural exchanges in accordance with explicit criteria, negotiating where necessary a degree of acceptance of those exchanges by drawing upon one's knowledge, skills and attitudes
>
> * is aware of potential conflict between their own and other ideologies and is able to establish common criteria of evaluation of documents or events, and where this is not possible because of incompatibilities in belief and value systems, is able to negotiate agreement on places of conflict and acceptance of difference

When critical cultural awareness is presented as part of foreign language teaching, it is focused on "otherness" incorporated in another language, and the access to other beliefs, values and behaviours is through another language as argued above with respect to linguistic and conceptual relativism. However, with some with minor changes – above all by substituting "social group" for "country" – the description of the elements of intercultural competence could provide the objectives for an education system which had an explicit purpose of ensuring social cohesion among disparate groups within one nation-state, where everyone can communicate through the national language. These could therefore be posited as some of the objectives for national language teachers and/or other teachers in a state/ public school, including teachers of political education/ politische Bildung in any of its guises. "Critical cultural awareness" can be a way of looking at other ways of life within one country; it is not necessary to cross nation-state borders to find "otherness".

The emphasis on the centrality of critical cultural awareness is similar to Gagel's suggestion that the central, unifying purpose of politische Bildung is the concept of politisches Bewusstsein (political awareness) defined as critical awareness, independent judgement and political engagement. The pre-condition for political engagement is that the citizen becomes aware of the relationship between the life of the individual and social processes and structures. Political awareness is formed through the recognition of one's own interests and through the experience of social conflicts and relationships of governance. The politically aware and informed person should not be a passive object of politics, but as a social actor should participate in politics (Gagel, 2000: 27). Gagel draws attention to the concept of engagement (a loan-word from French) and this corresponds to my use of the French phrase "savoir s'engager" for the concept of critical cultural awareness.

It would be possible but laborious to make a close comparative analysis of the nature of political education and of education for intercultural competence. There are strong parallels above all in the central idea of an awareness which leads to engagement, but there is also the significant difference that the model of intercultural competence becomes a model of intercultural communicative competence when it is part of foreign language teaching and learning and when the objectives include the acquisition of linguistic, sociolinguistic and discourse competence. It is through linguistic ability that people can be intercultural speakers mediating between cultures of different countries (nation-states) embodied in the (national) languages of those countries. In contrast, political/democratic education as presented by Gagel and Himmelmann seems to assume a common language among all those learning democracy. They do not address the practical linguistic skills necessary in international political engagement, even though Himmelmann's list of contents refers to globalization and foreign cultures:

A foreign language education perspective can complement and enrich this element of "democracy learning", not only by providing the linguistic competence necessary to engage with people of other countries in democratic processes but also, in the concept of critical cultural awareness, by introducing a process of comparison, mediation and negotiation which does not pre-suppose democracy as the only source of values and governance. For it is important to note that the definition of critical cultural awareness promotes the importance of individuals being aware of their own ideology – political and/or religious – and the need to be explicit about and justify one's criteria for evaluating other people's actions, or the documents and events of other cultures, as well as one's own. This would be crucial if education for citizenship were to engage learners with people of countries outside Europe where democracy is not assumed to be the only possible way of living together. Critical cultural awareness thus promotes the engagement of the individual with people of other ideologies: to look for common ground where possible, but also to accept difference. This includes, therefore, the acceptance of other systems of governance than democracy, and other types of democracy than that which is dominant in the European and North American thought[5].

Conclusion – towards a Concept of Intercultural Citizenship

Citizenship is often linked only to the nation-state, being a citizen of a particular state and sharing the values, beliefs and behaviours promoted by that state, through its education

---

5   It suggests therefore that, even within a framework of education for democracy, it is more important to be able to discuss different concepts of democracy Asian and Western for example as suggested in the work of W.O.Lee and colleagues — rather than to seek for a "common core of citizenship education" as Kennedy (2004) suggests.

system and other modes of socialization. Citizenship can also involve challenging what the state promotes through engagement in the life of civil society. Being and acting as a citizen of a particular state, depends on a shared language. Education for citizenship, or "learning democracy" to use Himmelmann's phrase, prepares young people for this.

However, in a world where states are economically and politically interdependent, education for citizenship has to take a wider perspective, involving engagement with people of other cultures, and acquiring some knowledge and skills in their language(s). Language teaching has a part to play in this but must go beyond the assumption that linguistic competence is sufficient, and must take intercultural competence as one of its aims. Intercultural competence includes the ability to compare and make judgements and in this respect language teachers and those who teach citizenship education are pursuing the same goals.

Education for citizenship goes further than language teaching, however, and leads to engagement and action. This suggests that education for intercultural citizenship should equally involve learners in engagement and action, at a trans-national level as well as at a local, regional or national level. Learners can engage in political and civil society at all these levels, provided they have the ability to engage in the language and culture at all levels.

Education for intercultural citizenship thus needs to bring together the hitherto separate concerns of citizenship teachers and language teachers, and future work needs to explore the practice of both to find common ground and new approaches.

References

Anderson, B. (1991). *Imagined Communities*. (2nd ed.) London: Verso.

Audigier, F. (1998). *Basic concepts and core competences of education for democratic citizenship*. Strasbourg: Council of Europe. (Ref: DECS / CIT (98) 35).

Byram, M. (1997). *Teaching and assessing intercultural communicative competence*. Clevedon: Multilingual Matters.

Byram, M., Nichols, A. & Stevens, D. 2001, Developing intercultural competence in practice. Clevedon: Multilingual Matters.

Council of Europe. (2001). *Common European Framework of Reference for Languages*. Cambridge: Cambridge University Press.

Davies, A. (2003). *The native speaker*. Clevedon: Multilingual Matters.

Dewey, J. (1916 / 1985). *Democracy and education*. Carbondale: Southern Illinois University Press.

European Commission, (1995). *Teaching and learning: Towards the learning society*. Brussels: European Commission.

Gagel, W. (2000). *Einführung in die Didaktik des politischen unterrichts*. Opladen: Leske and Budrich.

Habermas, J. (1994). Citizenship and national identity In B. van Steebergen, (Ed.), *The Condition of Citizenship*. London: Sage.

Himmelmann, G. (2003). — unpublished paper.

Kennedy, K.J. (2004). Searching for citizenship values in an uncertain global environment. In W.O. Lee et al.

Kennedy and Fairbrother (2004). Asian perspectives on citizenship education: postcolonial constructions or precolonial values. In W.O. Lee et al.

Lee, W.O. et al. (2004). *Citizenship education in Asia and the Pacific. Concepts and issues*. Hong Kong: Comparative Education Research Centre and Kluwer Academic.

Meierkord, C. (2002). Language stripped bare or linguistic masala? Culture in lingua franca communication. In K. Knapp & C. Meierkord, (Eds.), *Lingua Franca Communication*. Frankfurt a.M.: Peter Lang.

Skeie, G. (2003). Nationalism, religiosity and citizenship in Norwegian majority and minority discourses. In R. Jackson, (Ed.), *International perspectives on citizenship, education and religious diversity*. London: RoutledgeFalmer.

The lamination of cultural space: A theoretical investigation of time in space

Robert N. St. Clair   University of Louisville, USA

Abstract

Cultures change and the best way of comprehending this process is by investigating the layers of knowledge, social practice, and material artifacts that it deposits over time and space. Hence, the relationship of time and space to culture is not a linear one but an accumulation of layers of archeological space, sedimentations of culture over time. This archeological approach to culture is important because it allows historiographers of culture to better understand cultural change. The framework of cultural space is a model that brings the past and the present into a transformational space known as the co-present. It is in this space that the past is placed in a new configuration of the milieu of the present. In that process, the past never dies; it is either redefined, modified, revised, or even reinvented. What is important about this model is that it argues that the present is embedded in the past. One understands the present only because one knows the past. Similarly, in order to understand the future, one must turn to the present. Time, it is argued, is embedded in cultural space.

Introduction

Time and Space are always theoretically linked because space grows and develops in time. In the model of linear time, this linkage is based on the linear movement of time over space (St. Clair, 2006). What is missing from this temporal linear model is how cultural space changes over time. A resolution to this problem can be found in the insightful theories in the work of Foucault. In the Archeology of Knowledge (Foucault, 1969), he presents cultural space as the sedimentation of layers of historical space over time. A modification of this metaphor can be found in the sedimentation theory of time in space which envisions time as the accumulation of social practices layered in cultural space. In other words, it differs from the linear model of time in that it argues that time is embedded in space: the present is embedded in the cultural past and the future is embedded in the cultural present.

What is important about this framework of the sedimentation of time is that it accounts for many contemporary cultural constructs such as globalization and modernization. This investigation explains how cultural functions within several of the contexts space: colonialism, cultural habitus (Bourdeiu, 1977; 1984), global expansions, modernization, social scripts (St. Clair, Thomé-Williams, and Su, 2005), social structuration (Giddens, 1984) and mass media culture as the new-social-reality (Mehan and Wood, 1975). In essence, it claims that cultural change involves the retaining of some cultural practices along with the modification, revision, and re-invention of events in the co-present. Just as the present is embedded in the past, the future is embedded in the present.

Linear Time	**Sedimentary Time**
Time is based on movement over space	Time is embedded into strata of previous time. The present is embedded in the past; the future is embedded in the present
Space does not change; only time changes. The present is separated from the past and the future.	Both space and time change and are evidenced as vertical strata. The present emerges from the reconstruction of the past.
There are four possible models of linear time. In two of them, time moves in space (the future approaches the present); in the others people move in space and time remains immobile (one approaches the future). The direction of time is horizontal and linear	Space is the container of time. The present is embedded in the past; the future is embedded in the present. The direction of time is vertical.

The Sedimentation of Cultural Space

Defining culture is a difficult task because it brings into play so many different perspectives and one of the greatest dynamics has to do with change, a parameter that is the motivating force behind the Stratificational theory of time and space. There are many models of change, but one of the most influential models of change can be found in the work of Thomas Kuhn (1964; 1971). In this work, he argues that theoretical models of physics undergo structural changes from normal science to revolutionary science. Although this model of change accounts for the motivation of change in the natural sciences, viz., problem solving, it does not meet provide much insight into other aspects of the phenomena of change, especially cultural change.

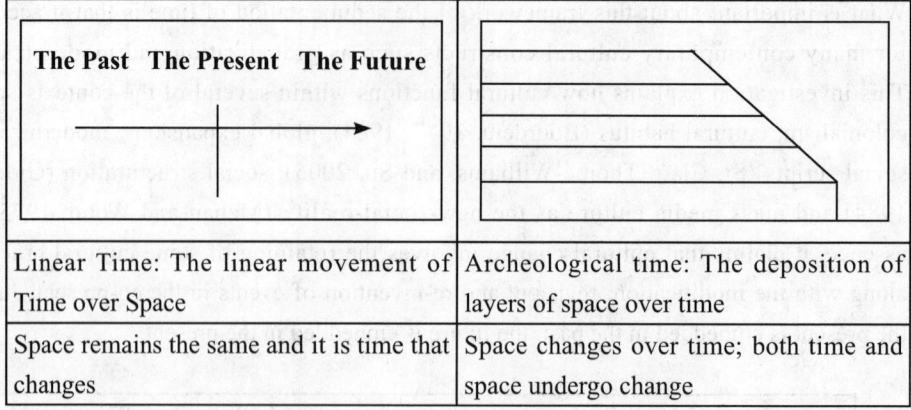

It is in the context of this model, that the concept of cultural emergence is investigated and discussed. It is argued that the present is constantly being socially constructed to make sense of a plethora of daily routines that constitutive the sociology of everyday life. These routines are integrated into the sociology of everyday life by individuals and this integration results in a sense of being centered and connected to the world. Many daily routines, however, are not integrated and left unresolved.

It is argued that in the context of the emerging-present (co-present), new levels of consciousness are raised and this leads to the creation of new perspectives and new forms of knowledge. This information is integrated into the emerging-present of those who share in these new experiences. When they are integrated into the daily experiences of individuals, they are also socially enforced by maintenance rituals and centered through meaning social interactions involving symbolic maintenance.

The Co-Present

When the present is emerging into a new level of consciousness, the co-present, it may come into conflict with many of the more established patterns of the past. These conflicts must be resolved. They are usually accommodated by redefining the past in order for it to make sense in the cultural present. The redefinition of the past is part of Kuhn's theory of scientific revolutions. After the new revolutionary science develops as the new reigning paradigm for a scientific community, the old patterns of thought are redefined in the context of this new framework. The past is re-presented into a new model of the present. It is taken out of its old context and placed into a new one. The result is a structured form of historical anachronism, a historical discontinuity.

Why is the study of cultural emergence important? It is important because cultural change is a constantly occurring phenomenon. The study of culture is not an established pronouncement of what happened in the past. It is not a body of knowledge that has been defined by cultural experts as a super-organic entity. Culture is dynamic. It has to do with sets of practices that change and redefine itself from one generation to the next. It creates a new-present and the new-future while redefining its past (old-present). This new future is a directional marker. It merely identifies the new forces that are taking place in the present and that assumed to continue to take place in the future. In order to make a transition into this new-future, the old past has to be redefined. It must be broken down and reorganized so that it can be understood in the cultural present. It must be made to fit into the new configuration of the present.

In order to explain the nature of the cultural dynamics outlined above, there are several concepts that need to be introduced and developed within the context of cultural emergence. These concepts include the archeology of knowledge, the concept of re-presentation, the structure of scientific revolutions, zones of proximal development, structuration, and the process of re-writing the past in order to make sense of the present.

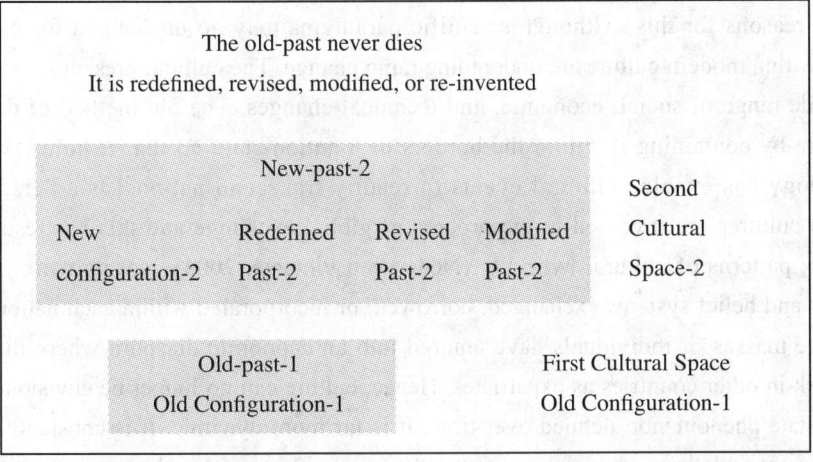

Explaining the Dynamics of Cultural Change

The traditional way of explaining change can be found in linguistic structuralism. It is assumed within that framework that change occurs when one steady-state of knowledge is replaced by a new steady-state. Examples of this approach can be found in historical linguistics where a steady-state of the later past, Old English, developed into a steady-state of the more recent past, Middle English. This is followed by the steady-state of the present, Modern English (Lehman, 1962). How does the movement from one state to the other take place? The answer to this question is described ex post facto by describing the sound changes that took place within the transition from one steady-state to the other. These laws are presented as the reason for the changes that occurred. The problem with this account is that it omits a discussion of the many epistemic ruptures (Foucault, 1969) that motivated those changes.

As noted earlier, Kuhn (1974) developed a theory of scientific revolutions within the natural sciences. Once again, his model of change is based on paradigm shifts from one steady-state (normal science) to another (revolutionary science). Kuhn argues that problem solving is the rationale for scientific change. When certain anomalies occur within a scientific discipline, this prompts the scientific community to engage in a quest to resolve those problems. There is a period of open discussion and debate (a period of crises) followed by the discovery of a workable solution in which a new paradigm emerges (period of scientific revolution). Within the historiography of the discipline, these transitions are seen as scientific events and are treated as historical discontinuities. Foucault (1969) considered these periods of events to be distortions of the historical record.

Within the humanities, models of structural change are not met with favor. There are several reasons for this. Although scientific paradigms may go unchanged for decades, events within modern culture are undergoing rapid change. The cultural present is immersed in a wide range of social, economic, and technical changes. The old method of defining a culture by containing it within the borders of a nation-state no longer holds. Modern technology has enabled cultural events to readily transcend national boarders. Many modern cultures are involved in the process of global exchange and this has resulted in complex patterns of cultural hybridity (Nederveen Pieterse, 2004). Not only are cultural patterns and belief systems exchanged, borrowed, or incorporated within each nation-state, but large masses of individuals have entered into an economic diaspora where they live and work in other countries as expatriates. Hence, culture can no longer be envisioned as a steady-state phenomenon defined over time. It is far more dynamic. It is constantly being redefined by a plethora of social and cultural forces within a cultural space and this space is no longer clearly defined by the borders of a nation-state. The forces of modernization have transcended local borders (Wallterstein, 2005). All countries are either engaged in or influenced by a Capitalist World-economic system (Wallerstein, 1977; 1980; 1989).

Model of Change	Re-presentation of Change	The parameters of Space
Structural Concept of Change	A system of ideas change over time. The model is static. It accounts for changes from one period of homeostasis to another.	Concepts occur over time. Cultural space is not accounted for.

Archeological Concept of Change	Human practices are documented over time within the same geographical space.	Modern space is superimposed over older layers of space over time.
Sedimentation Concept of Change	The layers of the past are not separated from the layers of the present. They are connected within the collective consciousness of those living in the co-present.	Many layers of the past remain in the present. The past never dies. It is redefined, modified, or reinvented to fit the contexts of the co-present.

Newly Emergent-realities

How do newly emergent-realties emerge from within a steady-state model? For example, how did these emergent structures arise from normal science within a scientific discipline? These mechanisms of change occur within the period of crises. What is important about the transition from normal science to revolutionary science is the fact that new structures emerge from the process of one paradigm shift to another. These structures are either a recombination of old structures or a re-presentation of old structures. This means that the past never dies. It can and does undergo one of several changes; while undergoing these changes, the past embedded within a new context where it is restructured, re-presented, or reinvented. This means that after the new paradigm of revolutionary science is established, the older form of normal science was re-written from the perspective of the new paradigm. This is not a radical phenomenon. Scientific textbooks also revise history and present information from the perspective of the new paradigm (Kuhn, 1962). The old structures undergo a transformation. They are elements of an embedded past that are reconstructed into a new component within the newer paradigm. Once these redefined units are introduced into the realm of revolutionary science, they come to designate a different level of consciousness within the present. They become part of the new-present.

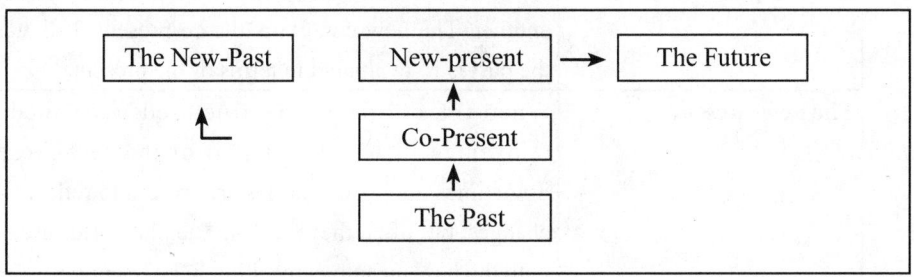

> The past and the present interact in the co-present. The past never dies. It is either accepted within the new structural configuration of the present (the new-past) or it is modified or redefined within the contexts of the present (the new-present). Ideas, concepts, beliefs, and practices may also be reinvented as newly emergent-realities. These provide the epistemological framework for the structuration of the future. The past remains as an active epistemological force that constitutes the present. The present is embedded in the past. It is redefined, modified in the co-present. Those aspects of the co-present that have been reinvented constitute the future, a newly emergent-reality. Hence, the present is embedded in the past; the future is embedded in the present.

The co-present contains the habitus of the past and the "newly emergent-realities" of the future. The co-present is where the phenomenon of change takes place. It is where the older structures are re-presented into new entities, the new-past and the new-present. Why does the past need to be restructured into different entities? It is because the contexts characteristically associated with the past have changed. When the present is embedded within the past, it brings into play new connotations and new associations that have to do with the co-present. The past has been re-contextualized. These re-presentations are important when they have been connected in a different way with the newly deposited layer of the co-present. In this case they are associated the context of a new level of consciousness. In the process of creating a co-present reality of structures within a paradigmatic shift, these re-presentations of the past may undergo further change. They are either brought into the co-present as an unmodified structure (the past) and remain within the habitus of the co-present realm or they are endowed with a heightened level of change that its presence demands that the past be redefined (the new-past).

The past	This is the past that belongs to an older paradigm. It is the past that is associated with what happened before it was brought into contact with the co-present. It is also the past associated with the unconsciousness.
The old-past	The past is taken out of one context and placed into another. The new context is the co-present. It is where the past is re-evaluated in terms of the present.
The new-present	When the old-past is restructured, redefined, or reinvented, it becomes a part of the new present. Sometimes new vocabularies are created to reflect these changes, but often they are not. The old worlds are used with the new meanings resulting in polysemy.

The co-present	This is where change takes place within the consciousness of the presence of everyday life. This is where the events of the past and the present collide. The retaining of old events in the present is the old-past. The revision of the past (restructuring, redefining, or reinventing) results in the new-present.
The newly emergent-reality	Within sedimentation theory, a new layer of practices may develop into a newer stratum of cultural space over the older strata. This new layer provides the basis for replacing older concepts, objects, and events with newer ones. They become the new-originals. The painting of Mona Lisa is the original; the replica or simulacrum of the painting in popular culture becomes the newly emergent-reality. It is called the emergent-reality because the newer generation within the co-present is not aware of the historiography of that object in the past and the new-past.

The fact that the past is always undergoing redefinition raises an important question for scientific research. What is the past? This is the question that Foucault (1969) sought to address. Why are such vagrant examples of historical anachronism allowed within a scientific enterprise? Why are historical discontinuities created in the historiography of a discipline? Can historical accounts of the past really be trusted? Do they have authenticity? Are primary sources just reconstructions of other allegedly primary sources? These are the kinds of questions being asked by postmodernists. With regard to culture, the co-present may contain a wide variety of cultural artifacts. Some of these exist within the realm of consciousness for experts and specialists as domains of knowledge, but how are they understood by others? Outside of the cultural sciences are non-specialists really aware of cultural theory? Can they articulate what constitutes culture? Is culture defined by what they do? Are nonverbal social scripts also a part of culture? If culture is to have permanence, is has to be a part of the past? The problem is whose version of the past? Whose version of the co-present defines the past? For many, the past is associated with new-originals. The co-present is where the past is ending and the future is beginning. It is a place of transition. It is a world in flux.

Constructing a Sedimentation Theory of Culture

There are several viable concepts that come together to constitute a model of cultural change. One of them is the concept of re-presentation that Foucault (1966) introduced in The Order of Things. He noted that the Middle Ages went through a time when the old idea of imitating nature was replaced by one in which the events of the present were re-presented and this meant that they were cast in a different code and possessed different social and cultural values. The way in which people think changed during this period of time. Instead of seeing are as copies of an original, the originals were re-presented and made into new entities. In this sedimentation theory, these new entities are called the new-originals. These developments occur within the co-present in the framework of a "contextualized emergence" in which some elements of the past are retained while others are modified or replaced with newer concepts. In terms of Foucault's sedimentation model of time, the layer of the present is placed onto the previous layer of the past. Hence, the present is embedded into the past. Those aspects of the past that undergo change come to represent the newest layer of sedimentation, the new-present or the makings of the future.

The implications of this investigation is that language is used to re-present the social construction of reality and in doing so, it redefines the past in terms of the relevancy of the present. As Kuhn (1964) noted in his model of the Structure of Scientific Revolutions, the past is rewritten to reflect the new paradigm. This phenomenon is not limited to the natural sciences but is endemic in daily social interaction involving language. The idea that scientific revolutions lead to new paradigms and new models of normal science is what Foucault (1969) sees as historical discontinuities. These models of the emergence of new knowledge frameworks is the by product of a process that begins with the anomies discovered in normal science, the attempts to correct them during the period of crisis, and the successful implementation of a new scientific paradigm during the period of scientific revolution. This is how natural and social scientists argue for a model of change. What they are revising and reconstructing is a system of thought, an old paradigm is replaced with a new one.

Towards a Theory of Cultural Change

Within the theory of the sedimentation of cultural time and space, it is agued that cultural consciousness plays an important role in the co-present, the place where the present is embedded in the past. It is in the co-present where the new-past is established and where traditions are redefined and given attributes that concur with its new contextual frame. It can be argued that the meaning of the present comes from the past. Old traditions provide road signs to the present. Old patterns of behavior provide social structures that legitimate the present. These patterns may not be obvious to the individuals functioning within the co-present. In such a case, the past becomes the new-past. However, where individuals are conscious of these transformations, the past becomes the new-present. They represent the newest layer of cultural space that is placed upon the co-present. This new layer will eventually form the old past for future generations of people inhabiting that cultural space.

Old-Past	New Past Redefined	New-Past Modified	New-Past Reinvented	Newly Emergent Realities
The Co-Present				
The Past				

It is also in the co-present where the new-present is created. This is because the future is embedded in the present. It is the place where human projections are created and where hopes and desires are developed and contextualized. Changes in the new-present are most obvious across generations within a social setting. A clear case of this can be found in the generation gap that has occurred among baby boomers from 1946-1964. Jones (1981), a demographer, studied this period in American culture and documented how the social construction of reality of the children of this generation differed substantially from those of their parents. There were several factors that led to this difference. It was during this time that people moved from the inner city to live in the suburbs. The automobile became a dominant means of transportation, and television the dominant means of entertainment. A plethora of new patterns of socialization led to the creation of a new mind set, a new cultural consciousness. The new-present of the children of this era differed significantly from the new-present of their parents. What the parents called the new-present, their children viewed the same phenomena as the new-originals.

Making the Present Coherent Through Habitus

Living in the co-present means that one inhabits a world that is in a state of flux. However, individuals who live in the co-present do not experience the sociology of everyday life as an unstructured and constantly changing world. Why is that? The answer can be found in the concept of Habitus (Bourdieu, 1977, 1984; Bourdieu and Wacquaint, 1992). The structures that underlie everyday life are the routines, habits, beliefs, and patterns of behavior that one acquires by living within a cultural complex known as one's social and cultural habitus. Life is embedded in this habitus. Without this habitus, life would undergo constant scrutiny. One would ask some very basic questions about the daily routines in life. What must one do when entering a restaurant? How does one go about ordering a meal? Life is full of these nonverbal social scripts. They are learned by living and participating in a cultural complex. Life makes sense because these routines provide daily activities and actions with a semblance of order. When others share the same social scripts, the result is a sense of social order. Primary and secondary socialization formed the training ground for the creation of this social order. Television programs also provide information on what is available for purchase in the common market. These programs also contain examples of social behavior in the form of soap operas, movies, and documentaries. Much of what constitutes culture exists in the forms of tacit knowledge. It can be found in the cultural habitus of daily living. Language, in particular, is full of grammatical and lexical devices that link the old-past with the new-past.

Re-Inventing the Cultural Past

There are many ways of knowing. Language as a medium of reality construction plays a large role in the Western tradition (Berger and Luckman, 1996). It is through language that the citizenry of a nation-state learns how to define the past, understand the present, and dwell on the future. Language is, after all, the medium of the public sphere (Habermas, 1989). As noted earlier, it is through language that the old-past is linked to the new-past. More will be said about language as a socializing medium and how it operates within a cultural space. At this point, it is important to note that language is not the only form of knowing. In the context of modernity, many social and cultural changes have taken place. Many of these are related to the emergence of mass media as an instrument of socialization where new forms of social reality are promoted by means of visual images (Debord, 1995). Many of these new images are not referenced to the old-past but function in the form of the new-present (Baudrillard, 1973; 1995). Many of the images found in contemporary mass media are not referenced to the old-past. They are new digital images which introduces a new world of virtual reality. In this context, the new-present is accepted and used to establish the new-past. In a world of simulations and simulacra (Baudrfillard, 1995), images have lost their authenticity (Sturken and Cartwright, 2001). The first evidence of this reinventing of the cultural past came about with the advent of the generation gap (Jones, 1981). Since then, many advanced modern societies have moved from print cultures to visual cultures and from linear reasoning to visual thinking (Mirzoeff, 1998).

Globalization is the new label that has replaced the concept of cultural diversity. Within the context of the archeology of knowledge metaphor, globalization is similar to a great flood that deposits new sediment that is deposited by the flood waters all over the land. After the flood is over, some portions of the land will remain unchanged as the water recedes and the high marks of the flood zone leave tell-tale signs and marks on city buildings and residential areas. Not all evidence of such a flood is washed away. Many areas remain inundated and the muddy waters hide or destroy the old-past. Some areas have new deposits of silt that have been integrated into the new landscape creating a new-present out of the old past. These metaphors provide insight into how the past is remembered (Connerton, 1989). With regards to sedimentation theory, globalization becomes a new layer in the terra firma of a cultural space. It is overlaid with new earth. The mores of other cultures and ways of life invade the cultural spaces of the past. Hence, the co-present is a mixture of not only new and old cultures, but also disparate cultures. There is another reason why globalization has been a more significant concept in modern times and this has to do with large movements of human beings going across international boundaries to resettle in a new land. The old concept of culture was defined by nation-states. It is what is within the political entity of a nation-state constituted its cultural framework. Once an individual leaves his country or nation-state, he enters into a new culture. With globalization such a definition of multiculturalism no longer holds. People are transported en masse in new cultures where they become hybrid citizens. In the old country, the present was embedded in the past. In the new host country, however, the cultural past is different. This means that their cultural identity has been compromised. They want to be participants in the new culture and yet remain favorable to their cultural past. This problem is resolved by transporting components of the cultural past and relocating it in the new home land. Those who reside outside of this phenomenon have labeled such communities as a ghetto, a little Tokyo, a barrio, or China towns. The reality is that has more to do with the making of a hybrid culture. It constitutes a new cultural space. Within the Foucault model of the archeology of knowledge, earth from the old country is brought into the new country and mixed with its new cultural space.

For those who are being bombarded with modernization in the form of new forms of architecture, new products, new languages, and new ways of thinking, the opposite is true. Their culture past has been placed into a new matrix, a new configuration, in which new forms of earth is being placed on it terra firma. These processes also constitutes a hybrid culture but of a different kind.

Emergent-Realities and the Cultural Construction

As noted earlier, one aspect of socialization that has not been fully addressed so far comes from the uses of mass media. This use of media comes in many forms and is directed to cultural niches. What one sees on television becomes a part of the conscious co-present. Those who share the same media use it as a way of reaffirming their social construction of reality. The soap operas, movies, and situation comedies that they watch are comparable to other forms of socialization except that the participation is passive and the messages may are tacit. Years after a certain event took place on television, individuals may invoke them in conversations and role playing. These invents are part of their virtual memory and form a part of their virtual culture. They function, in part, as a collective memory that has been distributed individually to individuals and these persons invoke the same memory at the same time in a public setting. They have become the new-originals. One can ascertain after a short conversation, for example, if another person subscribes to cable and what programs he or she watches on television. These forms of virtual memory become social markers of group coherence with regard to one event. It is as if there are niche cultures that can be invoked and used to unite disparate individuals by means of one event.

Sociologists do not want to deal with the concept of collective memory. They find it too mystical. This concept, it should be noted, was introduced by Durkheim (1951), one of the founders of sociology. Durkheim (1964; 1970) argued that individuals are bound together in society in two ways. They share their lives with others in a communal setting or they are bound together by institutions, laws, and regulations. Those who see life as a community share the same religion, the same hope, fears, and aspirations. Those who are bound by rules and regulations belong to a group but they do not feel bonded to the group. With the advent of television and the creation of the consumer culture, the kinds of bonding that occur in mass society have many of the elements associated with the primal communities that Durkheim discussed. Virtual cultures share virtual memories. They are bonded by virtual events. They have the same kind of deep emotional connection over events that earlier societal types encounter. If there ever was a time when a case could be made for the existence of fragments of a virtual memory distributed over a wide range of niche cultures, it is in the co-present world of television, the internet, blogospheres, and other forms of mediated communication.

Concluding Remarks

The concept of culture as a unit of knowledge shared by all individuals within a nation-state can no longer be maintained. Just as economic groups transcend national borders in order to do business, mass media transcends these same borders in order to market goods. What was once a simple matter of defining the mores of a tribal unit or a nation-state has emerged into a calculus of cultural artifacts that play a role in the co-present worlds of numerous consumer societies. How does one begin to explain this new form of cultural diffusion? How does one begin to define the forces behind these infusions of cultural symbols (1995)? How does one deal with the spectacle of life (Debord, 1995; Baudrillard, 1973)?

It was argued earlier in this investigation that Kuhn's theory of scientific revolutions provides a basis for the discussion of change within the cultural fabric of a society. Emphasis was placed on the period of crises where the social construction of reality is questioned and new potential paradigms emerge. It was argued that this locale is not the present but the co-present, the place where the past and the present encounter each other. It is where the present is embedded in the habitus of the past. It is also where the future is being created by means of new levels of consciousness raising and new re-presentations of the artifacts of the past. It is here that the rationale for change takes place. It is from this context that cultural changes emerge. Some of these function as new-originals. Others just remain as the new-present.

What this new framework for the study of culture proposes is that culture is a steady-state phenomenon that represents linear moments of frozen time in a dynamic realm of change. If modernity had to do with steady-state phenomena of the past and postmodernism has to do with the state of flux between steady-states, the question that needs to be asked is what comes after postmodernism. It will be another stable system surrounded by a flux of forces that contain the seeds of cultural change in the future. What is needed is a complexity theory of culture. It is under these circumstances that the nature of cultural change can be better examined, articulated, and defined.

References

Baudrillard, J. (1995). *Simulacra and simulation*. Ann Arbor: University of Michigan.

Baudrillard, J. (1973). *The mirror of production*. St. Louis: Telos Press.

Becker, H. (1973). *The outsiders: A study in the sociology of deviance*. NY: The Free Press.

Berger, P. L. and Luckmann, T. (1966). *The social construction of reality: A treatise in the sociology of knowledge*. Garden City: Doubleday.

Bourdieu, P. (1977). *Outline of a theory of practice*. Cambridge: Cambridge University Press.

Bourdieu, P. (1984). *The logic of practice*. Stanford, CA: Stanford University Press.

Bourdieu, P. (1986). The Forms of Capital. In J. G. Richardson, (Ed.), *Handbook for theory and research for the sociology of education*. NY: Greenwood Press.

Bourdieu, P. (1991). *Language and symbolic power*. Cambridge: Cambridge University Press.

Bourdieu, P. and Wacquant, L. J. D. (1992). *An invitation to reflexive sociology*. Chicago, Illinois: University of Chicago Press.

Brown, R. H. (1987). *Society as text: Essays on rhetoric, reason, and reality*. Chicago, Illinois: The University of Chicago Press.

Brown, R. H. (1977). *A poetics for sociology: Towards a logic of discovery for the* human sciences. Cambridge, England: Cambridge University Press.

Boas, F. (1928). *Race, language and culture*. NY: Macmillan.

Chomsky, N. A. (1957). *Syntactic structures*. The Hague, The Netherlands: Mouton and Co.

Chomsky, N. (1966). *Cartesian linguistics*. NY: Harper and Row.

Cooke, H. P. (Ed.). (1967). *The categories*. Cambridge, Mass.: Harvard University Press.

Cornford, F. M. (1957). *Plato's theory of knowledge*. Indianapolis, Indiana: The Library of Liberal Arts, The Bobbs-Merrill Company

Cornford, F. M. (1945). *The Republic of Plato*. Oxford, England: Oxford University Press.

Cornford, F. M. (1952). *Principium sapientiae: The origins of greek philosophical thought*. Cambridge, England: Cambridge University Press.

Cornford, F. M. (1937). *Plato's cosmology*. Indianapolis, Indiana: The Library of Liberal Arts, The Bobbs-Merrill Company.

Cornford, F. M. (1940). *Plato and Parmenides*. Indianapolis, Indiana: Bobbs-Merril Company Inc., The Library of Liberal Arts.

Coser, L. A. (2002). *The functions of social conflict*. NY: Basic Books.

Debord, G. (1995). *The society of the spectacle*. Cambridge, MA: Zone Books.

Derrida, J. (1976). *Of grammatology*. Baltimore: John Hopkins University Press.

Douglas, J. et al. (1985). *Introduction to the sociologies of everyday life*. NY: Academic Press.

Durkheim, E. (1951). *The elementary forms of religious life*. NY: The Free Press.

Durkheim, E. (1964). *The division of labor in society*. NY: The Free Press.

Durkheim, E. (1970). *The rules of sociological method*. London: Routledge and Kegan Paul.

Fish, S. E. (1972). *Self-Consuming artifacts: The experience of seventeenth-century literature*. Berkeley, California: University of California Press.

Forster, E. S. (1960). *Topica*. London, England: William Heinemann Ltd.

Foucault, M. (1966). *Les mots et les choses*. [English translation: *The Order of Things*]. Paris, France: Editions Gallimard.

Foucault, M. (1969). *L'Archéologie du Savoir Paris*. France: Editions Gallimard.

Foucault, M. (1971). *L'Ordre du Discours*. Paris, France: Editions Gallimard.

Foucault, M. (1982). *Ceci n'est pas une pipe*. Parid, France: Editions Gallimard.

Giddens, A. (1979). *Central problems in social theory: Action, structure and contradiction in social analysis*. London : Macmillan.

Giddens, A. (1984). *The constitution of society: Outline of the theory of structuration*. Cambridge: Polity Press.

Giddens, A. (1991). *Modernity and self-Identity: Self and society in the late modern Age*. Cambridge: Polity Press.

Goffman, E. (1959). *The Presentation of self in everyday life*. NY: Anchor, Doubleday and Company.

Goffman, E. (1959). *Asylum: Essays on the social situations of mental patients and other inmates*. Garden City, New York: Doubleday.

Goffman, E. (1961). *Encounters*. Indianapolis: Bobbs-Merril.

Goffman, E. (1963). *Stigma*. Englewood Cliffs, New Jersey: Prentice-Hall.

Goffman, E. (1967). *Interaction ritual: Essays on face-to-face behavior*. New York: Anchor Doubleday.

Goffman, E. (1971a). *Strategic interaction*. Philadelphia, Pa.: University of Pennsylvania Press.

Goffman, E. (1971b). *Relations in public*. New York: Colophon.

Goffman, E. (1974). *Frame analysis*. New York: Harper Colophon Books.

Hagstrom, W. O. (1965). *The scientific community*. NY: Basic Books.

Hanson, N. R. (1958). *Patterns of discovery: An inquiry into the conceptual foundations of science*. Cambridge, England: Cambridge University Press.

Jones, L. Y. (1981). *Great expectations: America and the baby boom generation*. New York: Ballantine.

Jourard, S. M. (1971). *The transparent self*. New York: D. Van Nostrand Company.

Karier, C. J., Spring, J. H., & Violas P. C. (1973). *Roots of crisis: American education in the twentieth century*. NY: Rand McNally.

Kuhn, T. S. (1964). *The structure of scientific revolutions*. Chicago: University of Chicago Press.

Kuhn, T. S. (1971). *The copernican revolution: Planetary astronomy in the development of Western thought*. Cambridge: Harvard University Press.

Lee, H, D, P. (Translator and Commentator) (1953). *The republic*. Baltimore, Maryland: Penguin Books Inc.

Lehmann, W. P. (1962). *Historical linguistics: An introduction*. NY: Holt.

Lippman, A. & A. Pentland. (2004). Organic Networks. *BT Technological Journal*, 22. 4, 9-12.

Lippman, A. & Reed. D. P. (2003). *Viral communication*. http://dl.media.mit.edu/viral/

Lloyd, G. E. R. (1990). *Demystifying mentalities*. Cambridge, England: Cambridge University Press, Themes in Social Sciences Series.

Luft, J. & Ingham, H. (1955). The Johari window, a graphic model of interpersonal awareness. *Proceedings of the western training laboratory in group development*. Los Angeles: UCLA

Marx, K. (1979). *A contribution of the critique of political economy*. New York: International Publishers.

Marx, K. (1973). *Grundrisse: Foundation of the critique of political economy*. NY: Vintage.

Marx, K. & Engels, F. (1965). The German Ideology. In E. Hobsbawm, (Ed.), *Precapitalist economic formations: Karl Marx* (pp. 121-139). NY: International Publishers.

Mehan, H. & Wood, H. (1975). *The reality of ethno-methodology*. New York: John Wiley and Sons.

Miller, D. R. & Bruenger, D. C. (2006). Virality: A postmodern cultural pandemic. http://music.utsa.edu:16080/musmkt/Virality_Postmodern_Pandemic_Miller_Bruenger.pdf

Miller, D. R. & Bruenger, D. C. (2005). Beyond cultural globalization: A postmodern interpretation of decivilization. http://music.utsa.edu:16080/musmkt/Beyond_Cultural_Globalization_Miller_Bruenger.pdf

Miller, G. A., Galanter, E., & Pribam, K.H. (1960). *Plans and the structure of behavior*. New York: Holt, Rinehart & Winston.

Minsky, M. (1988). *The society of mind*. NY: Simon & Schuster.

Pieterse, J. N. (2004). *Globalization and culture: Global mélange*. NY: Roman & Littlefield.

Prigogine, I. (1983). *From being to becoming: Time and complexity in the physical sciences*. San Francisco: W. H. Freeman.

Prigogine, I. & Stengers, I. (1997). *The end of certainty, Time, chaos and the new laws of nature*. NY: The Free Press.

Prigogine, I. & Stengers, I. (1983). *Order out of chaos*. NY: Bantom Books.

Rorty, R. (1991). *Objectivity, relativism, and truth*. Cambridge: Cambridge University Press.

Saussure, F. de. (1916). *Cours de linguistique générale*. Paris: Payot.

St. Clair, R. N. (2006). *The sociology of knowledge as a model for language Theory: language as a social science*. NY: Edwin Mellen Press.

St. Clair, R. N. (2002). *The major metaphors of European thought — Growth, game, language, drama, machine, time and space*. NY: Edwin Mellen Press.

St. Clair, R. N., Thomé-Williams, & Su, L. C. (2005). The role of social script theory in cognitive blending. In M. F. Medina & L. Wagner, (Eds.), *Special Issue of Intercultural Communication Studies XIV*.

Szasz, T. S. (1966). *The myth of mental illness*. New York: Anchor Doubleday.

Toffler, A. (1970). *Future shock*. NY: Bantam Books.

Toffler, A. (1980). *The third wave*. NY: Bantam Books.

Tredennick, H. (1967). *Prior analytics*. London, England: William Heinemann Ltd..

Tredennick, H. (1960). *Posterior analytics*. London, England: William Heinemann Ltd.

Turner, V. (1969). *The ritual process: Structure and anti-structure*. Chicago: Aldine Publishing Company.

Turner, V. (1972). *Dramas, fields and metaphors: Symbolic action in human society*. Ithaca, NY: Cornel University Press.

Turner, V. (1968). *The anthropology of performance*. NY: PAJ Publications.

Turner, V. (1982). *From ritual to theater: The human seriousness of play*. New York: PAJ Publications.

Walllerstein, I. (1974). *The modern world-system I: Capitalist agriculture and the origins of the European world-economy in the sixteenth century*. NY: Academic Press.

Wallerstein, I. (1980). *The modern world-system II: Mercantilism and the consolidation of the European world-economy, 1600-1750*. NY: Academic Press.

Wallerstein, I. (1989). *The modern world-system III: The second era of great expansion of the capitalist world-economy, 1730-1849*. NY: Academic Press.

Wallerstein, I. (2005). *World-systems analysis: An introduction*. Durham, NC: Duke University Press.

Van Gennep, A. (1960). *The rites of passage*. Chicago: University of Chicago Press.

Vygotsky, L. S. (1962). *Thought and language*. Cambridge, MA: MIT Press.

Vygotsky, L. S. (1978). *Mind in society: The development of higher psychological processes*. Cambridge, MA: Harvard University Press.

Developing intercultural communication as a discipline in China

Steve J. Kulich   Shanghai International Studies University
Chi Ruobing   Shanghai International Studies University

Abstract

With over two decades of development in the Chinese field of intercultural communication (IC), it is proposed that a comprehensive process of review, analysis and evaluation be applied to the curriculum, research and publication efforts nationwide. This paper summarizes key proposals from the series of articles on this topic published since 2002 in Wu Youfu & Feng Qinghua's edited Foreign Language and Culture Studies volumes published in Shanghai (SFLEP) and other recent chapters on IC disciplinary developments.

In an effort to encourage new steps in IC at other universities, this paper outlines the more than 10 years of history of IC at SISU illustrating the development of courses, teaching and training materials, instructors, research programs, as well as benefits from cooperation nationally and internationally. From this experience, suggestions are made regarding how an intercultural course can be expanded first into a broader curriculum, and then further developed into an academic direction or field.

Lessons learned from institutionalizing IC in the departments of SISU, such as the Overseas Training Center, the English College, and the College of Journalism and Communication, are highlighted. The paper seeks to provide a potential roadmap for other university IC teachers and researchers toward winning greater influence on their campuses. The aim of the paper is to motivate IC practitioners and researchers forward in building a more well-grounded, extensive and relevant IC discipline to meet the challenges and applications of the next decade.

Introductory Personal Address
Celebrating Our Shared Anniversaries and Prospects

Dateline: May, 21, 2005, Nanjing Normal University, by Steve J. Kulich
"At this 6th biennial Chinese Symposium for Intercultural Communications (CSFIC),

I am privileged to be invited to offer some congratulatory words, engage in a reflective review and suggest some prospects for the development of our field. A late-comer to the Chinese intercultural scene, I only share about a decade of this cooperative history, but the opportunity and contexts for which this paper is written are worth celebrating! These ideas arise out of some significant anniversaries and achievements, as well as anticipation for what lies ahead."

"With this conference we celebrate over 20 years of Intercultural Communications in China since He Daokuan's[1] first introductory articles (1983a; 1983b). But we especially congratulate this as being the 10th anniversary of the founding of the CAFIC. In a spirit of international cooperation, the 1995 joint conference with the IAICS[2] that was hosted at Harbin Institute of Technology marked the official beginning of our association and national awareness of shaping a field. The opportunity to regularly meet together and present papers at these biennial symposiums has sparked a significant decade of new book and article publication[3], of developing new courses and content, and of initiating new research topics and approaches."

"Though I had not yet managed to connect with most of you yet (remember, those were the days before e-mail or even easy access to telephones!), 1995 also marks the year of my first official grant proposal for 'Advancing Intercultural Communications in Shanghai[4].' That began a decade of continuous funding projects that allowed me to then join you in Beijing in 1997 and regularly since, and of developing teaching and research projects that would help move this field forward at SISU."

"At a personal level, I am pleased to celebrate many milestones with you. This is the capstone of my silver anniversary year in Asia. I consider it a privilege to have been able to sojourn for 25 years among Chinese communities, starting my teaching career in September, 1979 in Taichung, Taiwan, and continuing with years in Singapore, Xiamen, and now

---

1   Note that all Chinese names follow the Chinese convention of Surname followed by Personal Names: e.g. references under W. Z. Hu will be listed as Hu Wenzhong in the text.
2   The close cooperation of Jia Yuxin, Hu Wenzhong, Gao Yihong and others with IAICS founders John Khoo, Bates Hoffer and Robert St. Claire (the International Association of Intercultural Communication Studies, formally instituted in 1991) led to the 5th International Conference on Cross-Cultural Communication coming to Harbin Institute of Technology in 1995. This ground-breaking, first truly "international" (with 230 Chinese and 40 overseas participants), interculturally focused conference in China brought a great opportunity for Chinese scholars, with discussions there leading to the forming of our Chinese Association for Intercultural Communication (CAFIC) and to hosting these biennial symposiums.
3   Hu (2006) notes that the number of publications in 2004 was twenty-five times that of 11 years before, and that of the roughly 2000 articles or manuscripts published since the beginning of this area in China, 1066 articles were published from 1999-2002 and 541 appeared in 2004 alone, showing exponential growth (in his "Empirical Research" article).
4   Documented in Kulich (2003)

Shanghai. And according to the Chinese zodiac, as one born in the 'Year of the Rooster,' I am just completing my 4th cycle of life, half of that in China. In my 2nd benmingnian (本命年, 1981) I visited the Chinese mainland for the first time, and in my 3rd (1993), my family and I moved to Shanghai. So I also celebrate these rich years of experience here in China, where I have been able to witness the incredible changes and developments that continue to take place since the Reform and Opening Policy began."

"In many ways, my career history may bear some similar patterns as your own. Though first trained in natural science, I discovered by my third year of university that it was somehow my design and calling to be a teacher. The college years gave me rich international experiences and a strong interest in going abroad. So I began my career in Asia teaching language. That led not only to a strong interest in Chinese culture, but later to a research, writing and training job with an interpersonal communications group in Singapore, then to more Chinese language study in Xiamen. It was there that a Beijing Language Institute (now Beijing Language and Culture University) graduate, Zhu Linong, drafted a course book (中西文化比较课程) and introduced me to the topics, field and potential of cross-cultural communications."

"With these experiences came the hope to develop as a cross-cultural bridge person who could help westerners to understand China and the Chinese to understand other cultures. Since the mid-80s, I started on the task that many of you have also been devoted to – to seek to clarify the relationship of the Chinese language and its cultural context in contrast to other cultures. And since 1990, my focus has been on how the content of Intercultural Communications can help us perceive and bridge cultural gaps. I believe that this field and this association provide the ideas, tools and stimulus to keep moving in this direction and to build a solid discipline."

"So I celebrate our common history, congratulate your distinguished accomplishments as a group of scholars and students, and commemorate this important marker as a symbol of our continued efforts. I join you in looking forward to a bright future of new developments in this field.[5]"

Progress toward Developing IC as a Field in China
Our Context of Challenge, Opportunity and Development

China is a changing context, and the realities our citizens deal with since the mid-1990s are quite different from the traditional China we grew up in. This last decade of rapid

---

[5] Quoted from "Developing the Intercultural Filed: Lessons Learned at SISU," Keynote address at the 6th biannual Chinese Symposium for Intercultural Communications (CSFIC) held in Nanjing Normal University, May 20-22, 2005.

modernization and globalization has made our intercultural communications field more relevant than ever. We live in what is most likely the fastest changing economy and society ever in history! While the first decade of the Open Door Policy brought about some basic shifts in policy and posture, the last decade has brought about the rapid reality of social transformation. Every topic of intercultural communications can now be applied with rigor to the changes about us: what specifically are the values, identity, perceptual, attitudinal and communicative style shifts that are taking place? How are intercultural dimensions being expressed in education, the media, international business, or global diplomacy? If we were not busy as scholars and practitioners before, we have no excuse but to be so now in this period of dynamic international interface.

The good news is that we as teachers, trainers and as an organization have grown with the times. The 1980s seem to have been characterized by our efforts as language educators to find new ways to teach and evaluate progress in foreign languages. In the 1990s, cultural content was included to enhance our student's effectiveness in using the language appropriately. As the famous maxim states, "to learn another's language without learning his culture is a good way to make a fluent fool of oneself." This idea has guided our work to develop solid Foreign Language Teaching (FLT) approaches to culture teaching (as examples, Zhang Hongling, 2001, 2004, 2007; Yang & Zhuang, 2007).

And now, in this new century, Xu Lisheng (2006a) Song Li (2004), Dou Weilin (2005; 2007), Hu Chao (2005a) and many others are urging us to move forward to intercultural competence in this global, e- generation. No longer content to teach our students language, or even cultural history or information, we must now equip them with intercultural communication competence (ICC) if they are to survive and succeed in our internationalizing world. And where our students may have gone abroad a decade ago during the study abroad fever (chuguo re, 出国热), now the direction has changed – the world is coming to us. No longer can we train our students in one or two languages or specific cultural contexts – they now need a much broader cultural-general development – truly a global intercultural perspective.

We like to use the saying that is attributed to classical Chinese wisdom: "If you give a man a fish, you feed him for a day. If you teach a man to fish, he can feed himself for a lifetime (授之以鱼，不如授之以渔)." That might be true in stable contexts. But today, people are mobile and the fishing pools are changing. Thus, it is imperative that we expand the saying – to train and develop people to be competent all-rounded fishermen. The dictionary calls such fishing specialists "anglers" – a term whose root suggests "sharp like a hook," but also means "having well-honed skills" – "to use artful means to attain an objective." Such broadly developed people can skillfully fish in any pool that they come across. And because they know the process well themselves, they can train others in how to do it (cf. Kulich, 2007; 2008).

We believe that intercultural communications as a discipline gives us the capability to move beyond our roles as teachers and trainers to truly become this type of "people developers." And if English teaching has any similarity to learning fishing, then we have moved into this exciting stage of developing multi-talented multicultural people (cf. Kulich, Zhang & Zhu, 2005/2006).

This fish talk highlights another achievement – growing appetite. At our university, and probably yours, interest in the field of intercultural communication is high because our students and faculty feel a great need for it. With the overall increase in student intake (in the last seven years the SISU English Graduate School enrollment has increased from an annual intake of about 50 post-graduates to over 200) our IC course sizes have increased correspondingly, as has the number of other departments requesting a course in Intercultural Communications. At SISU, the English MA program in IC that started in 2002 with 7 students will have graduated 120 by the time this is published (our most recent intake group of 38 IC majors have just written and defended their MA theses)! This means that MA supervisors are hard pressed to have a broad enough palate of useful course and research topics to guide these eager post-graduates forward. The similar growth at other universities and the increasing size of our biennial conferences testify of this trend. Such interest and current opportunity is pushing us to a new level of need to ground IC as a solid, multifaceted discipline. There is much to anticipate and achieve in the coming years!

The Beginnings of Disciplinary Foundations

As a group of teachers, scholars and students, many of us have published excellent books and monographs (e.g. the new texts by Hu Chao 2005b; Xu Lisheng 2008; Yang Shu, 2006), or developed sets of notes and handouts for IC courses to help launch this field at the undergraduate and graduate level. But now with these new opportunities and challenges, we need to ask if we have an adequate tool kit to systematically ground and expand the field as a comprehensive discipline. Especially as we now have students who want to major in intercultural communications at the MA and Ph.D. levels, can we give them the comprehensive grasp of the field's history, conceptualizations, theories and applications both at home and abroad that they are needing or requesting?

This need has been at the forefront of our thinking at SISU. Wu Youfu, Feng Qinghua and others have been editing a series entitled Foreign Language and Culture Studies, a set of volumes published by SFLEP and readily available across the country. These volumes have provided an opportunity for Zhang Hongling and Steve Kulich to attempt to write some foundational articles for grounding IC and guiding our students.

The arrangement of these volumes reflects the general structure of language studies across China – we traditionally divide our work into the disciplines of Literature,

Linguistics, Pedagogy and now Translation Studies. Everything else gets relegated into the rather ambiguous or eclectic section called "related disciplines" (Fuhe Xueke, 复合学科). But with the growing interest and output of cross-cultural studies, we welcome the day when such volumes and our language and teaching journals will also contain a section clearly titled, "Intercultural Communication." We have made significant first steps forward with the SFLEP new series entitled Intercultural Research (e.g. Vol. 1, Kulich & Prosser, 2007), which seeks to do thematic topical "state of the art" volumes to help meet this need, and this new Intercultural Communication Research volume answers the call of many years for such a journal and manuscript outlet for our field.

Moving toward such these development were the specific focus of several of articles in the Wu and Feng edited series. Kulich (2002) reviewed the process and implementation of the first intercultural courses at SISU using a measure of cross-cultural adaptability to analyze the competence needs of some typical students and adapt curriculum design accordingly. Kulich (2003) went beyond course design to provide an initial overview toward content and research area development that would move "Beyond Language to Culture's Interdisciplinary Dimensions." That call for a broader and more clearly defined focus in intercultural communications also analyzed the unique development of IC here in China as compared to how the field developed in the US, and proposed an extensive set of field categories and sub-topics for future study and course expansion.

Kulich (2005) built on that and issued a call for a more thorough, systematic review of how the Chinese IC field has developed and where it can go. Kulich (2006) echoed Hu's (2006) call for a more scientifically grounded, data-based, theory-related approach to research projects and publications. Then Kulich (2006-7) extended this inductive approach, providing a graduated topological model for both past research analysis and future research development. Kulich and Zhu (2005) applied many of these concepts to their summary of developing a program of research for one core aspect of IC research – values studies. Together, those articles sought to lay foundations for students and scholars to reflect, think and plan more clearly how to proceed to build this field with solid academic underpinnings. In the following pages, we will highlight a few points from those articles to specifically address how we construe our field and how we can position, expand and develop it in our current Chinese context.

Reviewing IC as a Field – What are the Historic and Developmental Domains?

Though most have positioned IC in the language teaching domain in China, we might do well to consider a quick review of the roots of this field abroad. Many points of this history are known to most, but an integrated review might provide some insights for moving the field forward in our current context. Below is a brief history and graphical overview.

After World War II and in response to the pioneering books by anthropologist Edward T. Hall, interest in comparative cultural studies grew rapidly during the 1950s and 1960s in the US. Several main streams of investigation were developing, such as cross-cultural psychology, speech communication (with its emphasis on rhetoric, discourse analysis, semiotics), interpersonal communication, and mass media communications.

By 1970, leading scholars, in part arising out of several meeting organized by Michael Prosser, set out to establish IC as an academic field, and by the 1980s, intercultural communications was developing as a mature discipline. Improved textbooks emerged, solid academic theories were postulated (now in their 3rd generation of being tested), sub-fields were established, and research work diversified to examine cross-cultural issues in interpersonal and inter-group communication, psychology and cultural adjustment, international education and exchange, international organizations and international relations.

As can be seen in Diagram 1 below, IC developed both as an interdisciplinary field and with its own strong core of content and applications (details discussed more thoroughly in Kulich's "Beyond Language," 2003). In general, IC grew out from the American humanities and social sciences (top of the diagram), with a strong emphasis on the individual in his or her social context, to both micro domains (interpersonal and inter-group on the right) and macro domains (public education and information on the left).

Figure 1. Interdisciplinary Dimensions of Intercultural Communications[6]
This figure can help provide us with a roadmap for our own discipline development.

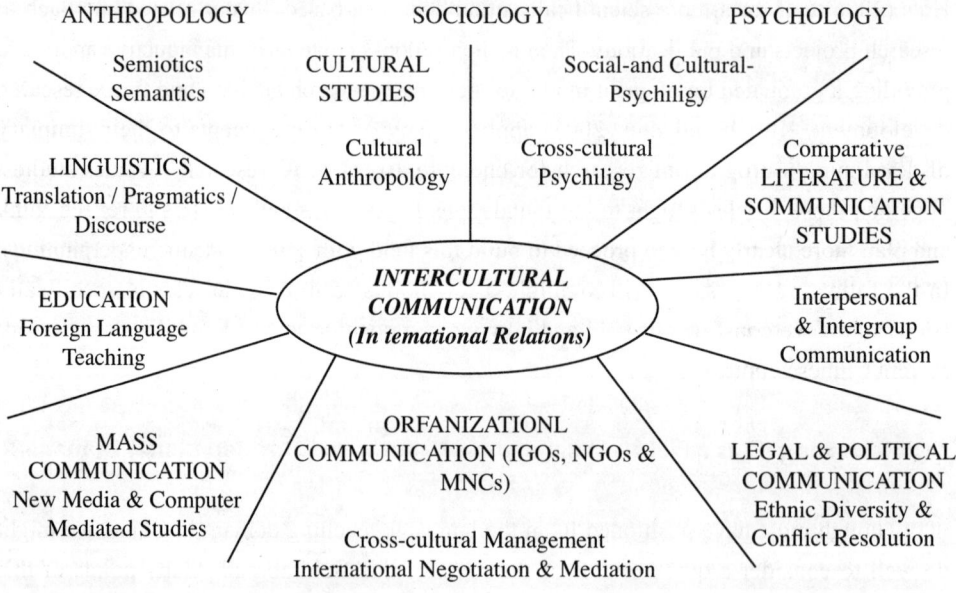

---

6 Taken from Kulich and Prosser (2007, p. 4).

Most would agree that our emphasis in China has been on the few segments on the left side of the figure (social linguistic, FLT, and communication areas). The question now is whether where the field started is where we want to remain long term. Though most IC instructors have started out as language teachers, now is an important time to develop ourselves into new competencies by starting to ask what areas of the global IC sphere are now needed or have perhaps been overlooked. What can we do to move our reading, coursework and research into the many other domains that we have largely left untouched, but which China in its rapid modernization and global integration may now urgently need?

In starting such an evaluation, it may help us to note the rather general nature of our course titles (e.g. Culture and Linguistics, Culture and Literature, Culture and Translation). These have been good starting points, but even in these familiar areas, we need to push toward more specific data-based and theoretical studies linking intercultural concepts with Social Linguistics (including Discourse Analysis, Pragmatics, and Semiotics, as Jia Yuxin and Gu Jiazu have both demonstrated in several conference keynotes, books and journals), Cognitive Psycho-Linguistics, Language and Culture Acquisition. For each of these domains, we need to re-examine the courses and texts we are using, design new studies and publish articles, chapters and books that move beyond the cultural generalities that some critics suggest we are reinforcing.

All of us probably need to start reading more in Social Psychology and Communication Studies and incorporate these concepts and theories into our work (highly recommended are Yan Wenhua's Intercultural Communication Psychology, 2008, and the translated version of Roger's A History of Communication Study, 2005, both in Chinese). It is important that both our courses and our research projects move on to examine the varieties of intercultural competence, the mechanisms of communication processes, and the personal psychology of communicators involved in these exchanges. How can these cross-disciplinary ideas be applied to cultural perceptions, attributions in stereotypes, culture shock analysis, new culture acquisition, cross-cultural adjustment or adaptation, conflict management and accommodation? How can each of these be pushed forward and applied into real-world spheres of media influence, audience response, organizational communication, cross-cultural management, international negotiation, global advertising, ethnic interaction, social conflicts, diplomatic processes and peace communication?

Further, as ground-laying scholars, we need to push ourselves to make new links with experts abroad, attend a wider variety of associations, read a broader palate of books. In this past year, many of the major academic presses in China have developed links with international publishers to issue complete series of original English textbooks at affordable prices for the Chinese mainland. Noteworthy is Beijing University's new series (in coordination with presses like Pearson, Thompson, McGraw-Hill) on basic communication studies, media studies, psychology, sociology and social theory. These should be on all of our shelves and reading tables. And our students should be urged to be reading them as well so that we can expand our foundations to make IC a truly connected, interdisciplinary, academically-grounded and practically-related field.

Such reading should lead to new curriculum that provides a deeper analysis of those fields most directly related to our endeavor, with course titles like: Cross-cultural Psychology, Social Ethnography, Cultural Anthropology, or Interpersonal Communication. Also urgently needed is the next challenging step to apply each of these areas to varied practical contexts such as classroom teaching and work settings (Interpersonal Social Networking, Organizational Communication, Educational Psychology, International Relations, and Public Relations). Such a multi-disciplinary approach benefits IC because it helps us face true social realities and consider how to apply our theories, observations and experiences to meet the real-world needs of our students, clients and citizens.

As we grow in this direction, IC should also become a key course for the benefit of the entire university (in a similar way that "Public English" now is). In keeping with the call to not only teach language, culture and their application to related disciplines, but also develop cultural competence, IC as a field can serve a primary role in internationalizing our students and equipping them for increasingly multi-cultural contexts (as Dai Weidong, 2004; and Wu Youfu, 2006, have called for on different occasions; cf., Kulich, 2008; 2009). All departments of any university can greatly benefit from a strong and well-developed intercultural communication program. At all levels of cultural analysis (national, regional, sub-cultural group or individual), understanding the basic perceptions, identity, values and psychological expectations of diverse participants, their varied communication styles and differing cultural norms can inform and enhance the development of more globally-minded students, more widely-contexted research and more relevantly-applied teaching across the entire university.

How Might IC Develop? – SISU as a Case Study for New Proposals

A recent survey of intercultural communications literature suggests that quite a number of universities have been producing CNKI-listed publications, with Shanghai International Studies University (SISU) among the top ten. ECNU (East China Normal University) and SISU have produced the most doctoral dissertations related to IC (Song Ying, 2009), with He Jiaoxiong and Hu Shuzhong leading the way as supervisors, each having directed several intercultural PhDs. A number of SISU professors or foreign experts touched on the relationships of culture and language in the 1980s and 1990s. Early courses on culture and translation have been offered by Professors Feng Qinghua and Fang Yongde for many years. The more international as well as indigenous approach to IC as described above was primarily developed at SISU by the first author in collaboration with Zhang Hongling. This history is described below:

"In 1993, I was invited by the Overseas Preparatory Department (not the Overseas Training Center) to teach English as a Foreign Expert. During those years of expanding enrollments and programs, many of our students were not only going abroad, but moving from state-run corporations to multinationals. Therefore I proposed that they needed cross-cultural adjustment training, and offered a new course dedicated to those qualifying for the Advanced Classes. This Intercultural Communications course was first taught in 1994 and continues until today (with other instructors teaching it since the fall of 2004).[7]"

"This course was annually upgraded and word got out to other departments, so I was invited to serve as a resource to various SISU teachers or post-graduates, working with Zhang Hongling for her Ph.D. dissertation in 1999, Fan Zheng for management applications in 1999, and Yu Zhaohui for her work in International Public Relations starting in 2003. In 1999, the College of Journalism and Communication invited me to open a similar course for 3rd year students in Communication Studies and Educational Technology and concurrently for their MA students and teaching staff. 3rd year Advertising majors also joined the course in 2000 and other Journalism direction students could choose it as an elective."

"That led to the Graduate School inviting me to offer the first upper level course (Intercultural Communication: Theory & Practice) to all 1st year English major postgraduate students in 2000 (with 59 students completing it). In May 2001, I began a new appointment as Professor in the Graduate School to develop and offer more IC courses to more students. Concurrently, Zhang Hongling was awarded an American Fulbright Scholarship to be a visiting scholar in Intercultural Communications and Education at the University of Minnesota (one of the most productive early homes of IC in the US) for the 2001-2002 academic year and we have worked closely on developing curricula for various departments since. She has taken on the teaching of the course for media majors since 2003 (Educational Technology, Advertising, Broadcast Media) and has taught the course each fall to International Relations majors since 2004."

"In locating IC in the Graduate School in 2002, our courses were placed under the Culture Direction of the College of English, joining Prof. Wang Enming's focus on American Culture, Society and Politics and Prof. Chen Hanshen's focus on British Culture, Society and Politics. Enrollment in the introductory course (Intercultural Communications Theory & Practice) continued to grow rapidly (77 completing it in 2001-2002 and 113 completing in 2002-2003). Therefore, the course was split into an English major's and Non-English major's sections since 2003, as well as offered to adult working students enrolled in our weekend tongdeng xueli (同等学历) program since 2001. To date, over 600 regular MA

---

7 Documented in Kulich (2002)

post-graduates and 400 weekend applicants have enrolled in this course."

"Of the 1000 post-graduates who have completed the course requirements in the past five years, over 500 were English majors. But we have had post-graduates from each of our other colleges (from International Trade, International Relations, Communications, Journalism, International Cultural Exchange, Comparative Literature, and Business Management), and from most of our other language majors (Russian, French, German, Italian, Spanish, Japanese, Arabic) as well as over 50 jinxiu (进修) students from other colleges and universities. Even though the course has increasingly rigorous assignments and is only an elective for most students, the academic and personal benefit of working through such an intercultural course has been continually expressed in participant feedback."

Developing a Post-Graduate IC Direction at SISU

In response to this growing interest and to further develop the foundations of IC as an academic field, we opened two other post-graduate courses in sequence:

International Values Studies (a deeper IC theory and concept course surveying most of the intercultural frameworks), started the fall of 2002, and IC Research and Training Methodologies (an application course toward research and thesis writing, and business training applications) since 2003.

Thus, SISU became perhaps the first program in China to offer a multiple-course intercultural-focus major at the post-graduate level[8]. This curriculum became an independent direction in 2005 and has expanded now into a comprehensive curriculum for IC majors at SISU including ten courses touching most of the applied areas. And the program continues to attract more enrolled students and new faculty members.

Teaching in China we are well aware that adequate literature resources have been a limitation, especially for an emerging field. The first author started seeking grants for research projects and literature purchases starting in 1995, but these efforts to collect important books and monographs became a high priority with the start of the post-graduate program (the scope and structure of this now over-2000-volume library is currently being documented).

From these expanding collections, that first group of students (2002, including the co-author) started compiling sets of resource literature for core courses. At present, we are updating and improving several representative draft volumes, including:

---

8   The syllabi and assignments for these and other courses are available upon request from the SII at SISU for those interested in developing similar coursework, student handbooks or research resources.

The Intercultural Communications Foundations Series:

Volume 1: The Intercultural Values Studies Reader 1: Concepts of Culture and Values, Kulich (Ed.), 2003,

Volume 2: The Intercultural Values Studies Reader 2: Comparative Values Study Frameworks, Kulich (Ed.), 2003, and The Chinese Values Readers Series:

Volume 2: Chinese Values in Comparison: The Way We Have Been, Kulich (Ed.), 2003.[9]

Other disciplinary development course supplement and research manuscripts have been developed by the SISU Intercultural Institute (SII) as working papers or course collections:

Toward Mapping the Chinese Intercultural Field, SII Working Paper 1, Kulich (Ed.), 2006,

Interpersonal Communication Reader, Wakefield (Ed.), 2006, 2007, 2008 editions,

Cultural Analysis of Film, Wakefield (Ed.), 2007, 2008, 2009 editions,

Investigations into Chinese Identity, SII Working Paper 3, Kulich (Ed.), 2008,

Intercultural Values & Core Culture Studies: A Student Sourcebook, Vol. 1 (International Studies) and Vol. 2 (Chinese Studies), Kulich (Ed.), 2008.

Cooper Wakefield has further documented the development of the two courses for which the collections by him are a part (Wakefield, 2007; 2008a). More updated course or resource books need to be developed on other foundational intercultural topics like perception, cultural awareness, IC competence or cross-cultural adjustment (cf., Zhou & Knapp's guidebook, 2007). Such a call is based on the fact that these extended IC topics consistently draw attention from not only our intercultural students, but also from Culture, Teaching Methodology, Linguistics, Translation and Literature majors. The interest and relevance of our field as well as its content and research methodologies are appealing to and seem to be needed by many areas, so it behooves us to strengthen it.

Most recognize that graduates of IC need both solid academic grounding and specific real-world practice. If any course or curriculum should be based on the principles of liberal education, inductive inquiry, critical thinking and "learning by doing," this field should be the example in order to apply theoretical conceptions to life and develop true intercultural competence (cf. Wakefield, 2008b). Thus, the first group of majors to graduate at SISU with this focus (the seven who started in 2002) worked hard at this "learning by doing approach" and sought to broaden their exposure by attending and presenting papers at national and international conferences, interacting with guest speakers, and seeking opportunities to

---

9 Volume 1 "The Way We Were," and Volume 3 "What We Are Becoming" have not yet been issued.

work with international companies or go abroad.

Each conference attended and each talk with an overseas scholar brought growth, confidence and clarified research development. The efforts of Zhuang Enping at Shanghai University to organize such conferences (e.g. the Shanghai International Symposium on Intercultural Communication in 2006 that introduced China to the international authors of the newly published SFLEP series[10], and his work with that press to organize IC teacher training seminars), of Yan Jinglan (ECUST) to initiate the first Shanghai MA symposium at SHNU (2007), where six universities in the city each sent their top two MA graduates that year to present papers as a stimulus to faculty and the next generation of students, and of Vice President Lu Jianfei and Dai Xiaodong, not only in hosting that MA symposium, but also the first national thematic IC conference on Identity (December 2008 at Shanghai Normal University)[11] are all to be applauded! City-wide and regional networking is important for building our fledgling field.

Another important consideration was that an intercultural major needs to become an internationalized person. Though such an agenda may have been difficult to fulfill in the 1990s, it is more realizable since 2000 with the signing of the WTO agreement, growing globalization and cultural exchange now in both directions. Our students now have new opportunities for cross-cultural interaction (like joining the AIESEC student volunteer program abroad, or applying for the Erasmus program in Europe). We as instructors need to motivate our students to seek out such avenues, provide more opportunities by inviting overseas scholars or representatives, and be willing to have our students go beyond our own limits. Since the SISU program began in 2002, we worked hard to make contact with overseas scholars by email and invite those who already had travel plans to China[12]. Each international encounter has had a positive impact, and upgraded the level of paper and thesis writing.

Regarding theses, the selection of topics is an area that may also need development. After conducting a broader review of the current state of our research (as has been proposed in Kulich 2005; 2006), IC professors may want to guide their students to foundational, building-block topics centered on key themes. On this, the Zhejiang University Department of Psychology is a good model. There Dr. Zhang Qiuhe (Hora Tjitra) has been guiding his students to work as research teams on key projects, one on IC competence, another on complex cross-cultural problem solving, and now one organizational culture and

---

10 See a conference report http://www.zjuc.org/content/view/78/27/ (Retrieved March 23, 2009)
11 See the conference webpage at http://202.121.63.16/icc/ (Retrieved March 23, 2009)
12 e.g., Professor Michael Prosser was our first guest lecturer in 2004 and he has significantly strengthened our IC program in his four years working at SISU, as well as help recruit many other international speakers.

performance. In cross-cultural psychology at ECNU, Yan Wenhua's national-funded key project involving her post-graduates on foreigners' cross-cultural perception of and adaptation in China is also a good example. Such teamwork allows each student to focus on one important step or topic in the overall research project process, instead of writing papers that attempt to be too broad and thus become general overviews.

At SISU we have been seeking to narrow down to similar foci. The first year theses focused on topics related to clarifying intercultural values, identity, and cross-cultural competence, and the second year doing more on these areas and also extending them to interpersonal communication and IC teaching. In the third year, some theses built these topics further, and others moved into intercultural conflict, IC and the Internet, and IC in business topics. The fourth year saw more extensions, and added culture shock, family communication and cultural adjustment, and year five's students took new angles on IC teaching/training, values/identity studies, and looked at IC related to the adjustment of migrants within China, to intercultural media (Internet, TV show, fashion magazine, film analysis), to new IC business topics.[13] We propose that each IC-related staff member of each university evaluate what their unique contribution to the field can be in helping students link their research efforts (along the lines of a graduated topology, proposed in Kulich, 2006) to strengthen and fill in the research gaps of our growing field.

Implementing steps like these, helping students write better thesis papers, and attracting over 30 students to study this area, the College of English felt that the time was ripe to expand the program to "direction" status starting the fall of 2005. This meant that the three-course program needed to be expanded to more than five, and that more professors needed to be recruited to supervise post-graduates. Concurrently as "Translation" split into two, creating a new "Oral Interpretation" direction, so the "Culture" direction split to create an "Intercultural Communications" direction. With such a demarcation now in place, it may first help to clarify the difference we see between "Cultural Studies" and "IC."

Clarifying the Foggy Overlap of Culture Terms and Related Disciplines

It is our understanding that "Cultural Studies" (whether in language or "Area Studies" programs) focuses on specific information about one distinct national culture (e.g. American, British), and the starting points are analyzing that nation's political, educational, social systems and their historical development. "Intercultural Studies" seeks to look across cultures (including sub-cultures or contexts) with the starting point being how differing

---

13 A comprehensive list of the 120 IC thesis topics now completed is available from the SISU Intercultural Institute by contacting the authors, and are also downloadable for reference from the SISU Library.

individuals or groups perceive and respond to different social or psychological cultural stimuli. Each of the closely-related "Cross-cultural" fields compares and contrasts these factors, dimensions or syndromes between cultures (usually taking national cultures as a variable of comparison). Thus understanding cultural values, identities, expectations and other aspects of a groups' or people's psychology are important for useful comparisons and adjustments to differences. "Intercultural Communication" (IC) then looks at how these dynamics function in interactive settings (often at the interpersonal level, but these can also be extended to the diplomatic or global media level). Academically, IC as a field seeks to develop both local and global theoretical frameworks for clarifying meaningful comparisons and contrasts toward enhancing communication between groups.

Though each has a unique perspective, Cultural Studies and IC serve each other. Students in culture courses can greatly benefit from the interpersonal and psychological analysis that IC develops, helping them to better understand national cultural systems at a personal level. And IC students greatly benefit from several electives on specific countries to deepen their knowledge about the history, power influences and social nature of specific contexts. "Own-culture awareness" is particularly useful and necessary as a starting point, like Fang Yongde's approach to teaching "Culture and Translation" which focuses on elucidating Chinese culture (e.g. one needs to know his own cultural system well before being able to translate to another cultural system effectively). But to further develop in this field, IC majors need a full palate of courses that teach them not just cultural knowledge, but cross-cultural analysis and comparative skills. Such a discipline can contribute to enhancing students' all-round competitiveness, including strong language competency, relevant interdisciplinary applications, and effective cross-cultural skills.

We further suggest that more attention be given to clarifying the use of the words "culture," "comparative culture," "cross-cultural," and "intercultural" (as we have sought to do briefly above). They all seem to be in vogue, attract attention, and make good-selling book titles, but as a growing discipline, it is our responsibility to bring clarity to our terminology and usage. To this end, at SISU we currently assign all incoming students an assignment to track "the concept of culture and IC in my field." We are seeking to map out who have been the introducers of key terms or culture-related foci to each academic area, and trying to discover the variety of ways in which each term is used, much as Kluckhohn & Kroeber did for the US in their seminal work.[14]

---

14 See Kluckhohn & Kroeber's classic monograph, "Culture: A Critical Review of Concepts and Definitions," available online at http://www.questia.com/PM.qst?a=o&d=100067373 and in the institute.

What Constitutes a Mature Discipline? Considering Developmental Stages

When we evaluate the state of our field, it is helpful to consider the disciplinary markers that are reflected in the growth and development of other fields. In conjunction with a 211 disciplinary develop project, the SISU Intercultural Institute team have been specifically reviewing the development of the communication studies discipline in the US. This has been documented extensively in Rogers (1994), Schramm (1997), Park & Pooley (2008), in the JOC special issue "Ferment in the Field" (1983) and the more recent double special issues on key topics in the field (Benoit & Pfau, 2004; 2005). Concurrently, discussions about the beginnings of the intercultural communication field in the US and China and how it moved toward disciplinary status have been instructive (cf., Guan, 2007; Prosser, 2007; Yin, 2006; Zhang, 2009).

Below we put forward a suggested progression of disciplinary development stages:

The Burgeoning (Interest) Stage

1. Imported ideas and new concepts have been introduced in academic journals and public forums
2. Definable content is being established (concepts, topics) and trial or topical courses are being offered
3. A list of pioneering and leading scholars is emerging from initial publications

The Building (Integration) Stage

4. More courses are being offered, syllabi clarified, curriculum developed
5. Teaching is taking place at multiple levels (from BA to MA)
6. Conferences are being held, from sub-topics in related disciplinary conferences, to holding independent conferences, to hosting specific research theme symposia
7. A recognizable list of focused and influential scholars has emerged, evident from their conference papers and published articles and monographs
8. Textbooks are being produced, and core-content topical manuscripts and volumes are being published

The Institutionalizing (Field) Stage

9. Research is developing through MA theses and PhD dissertation being produced so that the requirements are standardized and more topics are covered
10. Existing journals are increasingly welcoming field articles, creating dedicated columns, inviting special issues, such that new field journals are being established to publish the field's core content
11. Related-field associations have developed "interest groups" or "divisions" for this field, and new field associations are being established

12. Theoretical ideas are being developed, from the establishing of key constructs, factorial analysis of dimensions, hypotheses being put forward and systematically tested, theories being postulated, quantitatively tested, critically challenged, revised and fine-tuned theoretical frameworks are emerging

The Maturation (Disciplinary) Stage

13. A clear set of disciplinary theories, their leading scholars, and a wide range of extensions or applications are recognized and documented
14. Funding sources are being established, research projects are gaining prominence and producing locally and nationally viable results
15. Career options are emerging, creating a recognizable identity for field graduates and professionals who keep on training newcomers
16. Professional competencies have been standardized, certificate programs established
17. Disciplinary status is being recognized and approved by government and educational bodies
18. Awards and honors are being given to field leaders to promote excellence, social recognition is growing

We propose that the above list can serve as markers for measurement of our current status, potential areas for development, and future milestones for progress. The purpose of this article will not be to specifically measure our current levels of progress or success. All of the above areas can be worked on in the coming years. But from a general evaluation of where we are at, we will make some specific proposals deemed relevant for the next stage of our progress. From a brief retrospective overview, we find that the development of IC in China has taken a strikingly similar road as that of the field of Communication in the United States. A summary historical account of the latter may shed some light on our future efforts to build IC as a discipline.

Being the crossroad of many disciplines, the study of communications attracted many scholars in its early days. This brought in various theories and research methodologies from sociology, psychology and information science (which the forefathers of Communication Study represented). Only a few courses on communication were scattered in different departments and universities in the beginning. It did not become a discipline until Schramm founded the first doctoral program in the University of Iowa (where the first two graduates got their degrees in 1948). He then spent his whole life developing courses, writing comprehensive textbooks, establishing and running research centers at the University of Illinois, Stanford and Hawaii. The institutionalization of Communication as a discipline took about a decade. (cf., Rogers, 1994, pp. 1-32; Schramm, 1997, pp. 125-154).

A number of institutions in China have been a part of the collective script-writing toward IC field development. Scholars and the courses or research programs they have developed at Peking University, Beijing Foreign Studies University, Harbin Institute of Technology, Fuzhou Normal University and many other institutions have been both cradle and catalyst. At SISU we have sought to duly note these foundations and foster cooperation toward building a comprehensive IC program. Having gone through the course, curriculum and research center development periods, we hope summarizing this process can also serve as an incitement for further establishing the independent disciplinary base of IC in China.

Proposals for the Development of an IC Discipline
Expanding IC Relevance, Topics and Coursework

It is obvious that Chinese culture is developing and changing rapidly under the influence of the WTO, globalization, international information, media impact, and increased international exchanges. English speaking countries are also changing quickly, especially influenced by the emerging global youth culture facilitated by mass media and the Internet. Whatever we do in intercultural communication studies, we must consider and compare the changes in China with trends in other societies.

There is thus a need for future IC research topics to focus on the influences on cultural reception and perception, the meanings associated with images or icons, varied media usages and their influences, personal and cultural identity and in-group shifts, traditional and modern value transitions, interpersonal conflict and communication patterns, regional expressions and variations, diverse teaching and learning styles, varied work expectations and practices, and other related applications of IC concepts. All of these topics would fall under the rubric of studies on "China in transition" or "the influences of modernization, globalization and post-modernism."

Other topics might chronicle the historical development of IC overseas as a model for improving the research, coursework and teaching modules here. As IC is a relatively young field to China, it is important to develop in similar ways as other new "studies" have, focusing both on practical, paradigmatic and historical topics to lay a solid foundation for a discipline, both at the MA and Ph.D. level. And to become universities or colleges strong in "cross-cultural skills" or "intercultural communicative competence (ICC)," a wide range of studies need to be conducted to evaluate what aspects of ICC are relevant and useful for China's development.

As we consider these needs at SISU, we have determined to build on the courses already offered, extend them to deepen the theoretical foundation of our students, and broaden the practical applications of the field, making our graduates more marketable for a variety of university teaching, corporate work or human resource training roles. We are also glad to see that many former IC graduates have found positions in universities or colleges to open similar courses or integrate IC into their language teaching or training practices.

Any curriculum arises out of the opportunities, faculty, interests and context of the specific institution. Certainly, having qualified and committed faculty join us, such as Michael Prosser, Zhang Hongling, Cooper Wakefield, David Henry, and now the annual lectures of Myron Lustig, have made a large contribution. Here we list the recommended, required and elective course listing as it has now developed at SISU at the MA level (where most majors take eight to ten of the 12 courses offered):

First Semester (entry level – getting exposed to the IC major)

*Introduction to IC Concepts and Awareness (a personal orientation course, which for non-English majors is still entitled: IC Theory & Practice)

*IC Studies Foundations – History and Status of the Field

Chinese Culture Awareness (actually titled: Culture and Translation)

+ an application course elective, either

    Interpersonal Communications (personal level)

    Intercultural Business Communication (professional level)

    Global Media and Culture (mass media level)

Second Semester (deepening in the IC major)

*Comparative Culture Research Methodologies

Communication Theory and Applications

IC Values, Identity and Core-Culture Studies (theory applied)

+ another application course elective, either:

    IC Education and Cross-cultural Training (professional Level)

    The Cultural Analysis of Film (mass media level)

    Model United Nations Security Council (international diplomatic level)

Linking Interdisciplinary Approaches to IC

This curriculum is now in place for our IC majors in the College of English. But how are the needs of other departments with an interest in IC to be met? Working closely with the College of Journalism and Communication, a new IC MA direction was established in 2007. Those students currently take the starred subjects (*) as their core required courses. Now that a university-wide intercultural institute is established, we are working across interdisciplinary lines to build more IC competence in other established majors. Ideally, a range of IC electives should be offered in other colleges so that each post-graduate can pursue the course concentration that suits their interests best. Beyond those currently offered above, such courses could include:

    IC in Pragmatics and Translation (applied to Discourse and Textual Analysis)

    IC in Literature (in the paradigms of Culture, Literature and Critical Theory)

    IC in International Business Organizations (in Management, HR, Negotiation)

IC in Mass Media (in TV Broadcasting, Advertising, International Journalism)
IC in International Relations (in Diplomacy, Politics and Public Relations)
IC Case Analysis (applied to solving various types of cross-cultural problems)

Expanding IC Doctoral Programs

Eventually, dedicated Ph.D. programs will develop in China. Hu Wenzhong, Jia Yuxin, Dai Weidong, He Zhaoxiong and others have already pioneered the first coordinated social-linguistics doctoral program giving PhD students access to a number of universities and well-known language and culture scholars. Guan Shijie opened the first intercultural communication doctoral program in the College of Journalism and Communications at Peking University (since 2006). Wu Youfu and Guo Ke are directing doctoral students at SISU with a focus on International and Public Relations Communication.

To strengthen the field, doctoral content will need to move beyond our present courses to include other foundational intercultural areas and based more on indigenous approaches and studies. Since solid doctoral programs need to succeed in publishing and most overseas IC journals have a data-driven focus, our CAFIC association and our universities will need to be developing a core of IC faculty who can advise on quantitative studies, assist with data entry and statistical analysis and help in the writing and statistical reporting of research reports. As language educators, it is imperative that we expand our competence in data analysis. Higher levels of social and cultural analysis are also needed in our qualitative methodologies.

Lin Dajin and Xie Chaoyang's (2005) book certainly provides a new level of academic foundations for upper post-graduate work. And as the title reminds us, intercultural communication is a balance of theory and practice. The growing interest across Chinese universities to open intercultural courses and the growing needs of society must converge to make sure that our coursework makes a usable contribution. Our graduates will be presented with unparalleled business and government consulting opportunities. So how can our courses equip them to be well-read, well-communicating, effective practitioners?

Fostering City-wide or Regional Networking

Though several of our campuses nationwide are building a solid beginning, we acknowledge the limits of one institution to meet all the needs of post-graduate students. Hu Wenzhong alluded to this at Xiangtan (October, 2003) and suggested that Shanghai seemed uniquely positioned to start a model for the development of a city-wide network of intercultural scholars and teachers. Therefore, a CAFIC Shanghai Branch was established in 2003 and this network of interested scholars and students at several universities continues to develop. Through meeting several times a year to discuss shared interests, inviting distinguished IC experts as guest speakers, giving our graduate students opportunities for exchange (like the MA paper conference), and other interaction, cross-city cooperation is being strengthened.

Considering Coordination through Diversified IC Centers

With China's increasing role and reputation as a significant global player, we believe there must also be correspondingly new levels of intercultural training and international awareness. Each strategic region of China would benefit greatly from establishing some form of an intercultural center that would link the scholars of our various universities, colleges and institutes with the leaders of key government departments and those of both national and international corporations[15]. Such centers can play a stimulating role in developing research, teaching and training programs that enhance international understanding and cooperation at government, business and educational levels. These eventual centers or institutes could consider some of the possible "*Five I*" goals listed below, and adapt them to their own regional needs and opportunities:

Be *Interdisciplinary* and Cooperative. Center affiliation should link staff from many different disciplines to contribute to a core mission of promoting cross-cultural comparisons, intercultural competence, and coordinated national- and international-level research.

Be *Interactive* and Responsive. A center would seek to relate theory to practice, principles to people, and develop staff that investigate real-world needs, research relevant problems, publish academic works, and design practical training tools, materials and websites that expands the field. Hosting forums, seminars, public lectures and interacting with both corporations and the community should help keep each center engaged, relevant and on target.

Be *Innovative* and Groundbreaking. A center can provide a seedbed for research topics and projects where there are not yet majors, becoming a creative impulse for the development of new studies, curriculum, courses, theories and approaches that can be implemented to serve the broader university's, city's, region's and country's development.

---

15 To our knowledge, such centers have already been established at Shanghai International Studies University, Peking University, Beijing Foreign Language University, Zhejiang University, Shanghai University, Chinese University of Mining in Xuzhou, Huazhong University of Science and Technology, Wuhan, and China Jiliang University (Hang Zhou). Most likely this list needs to be updated, and readers are asked to contact the SISU IC Institute with updated information.

Be *Integrative* and Bridge Building. A center can link academic and corporate worlds, fostering cooperation between the university and industry and relating education to society, as well as strategic linkages between other centers in the country for the extension of the field.

Be *International* and Multicultural. A center can also dynamically link local and foreign experts, building relationships with other centers world-wide, participating in educational exchanges and cooperative programs, seeking to address today's multicultural and global issues.

Developing Influence through Dedicated IC Publications and Journals

Most of us agree that key need in our field is to develop a strong, integrated publishing program. The Beijing Foreign Language Teaching & Research Press (FLTRP) has wonderfully led the way in the last decade publishing many important resources. We applaud the many excellent text books, topical publications and articles coming out from other presses and in many journals. But for us as scholar-authors (or teacher-researchers), local pressures might be pushing us too much to try to produce our own definitive works instead of mapping out a broader perspective and plan of what is needed to develop the field nationally. We suggest a "publications" round-table symposium is needed to discuss and agree together what types of books, topics or studies are most urgent for us to address at this time.

In this line, we are grateful for the new efforts of the Shanghai Foreign Language Education Press (SFLEP) in publishing its new series of 10 highly regarded international IC works in their original English format with Chinese notes contributed by local scholars. Concurrently, their series of locally developed works (e.g. Xu, 2007b; Zhang, 2007; Zhuang, 2004) are moving the field forward in the Chinese context, as is the Intercultural Research series of topical volumes. These three series will continue and include more diversified works so that they will be an asset to all of our teaching and research programs.

Long term, our research and broader IC agenda need an article outlet, and though some of our seminal papers are getting published, Li, Li & Wang (2005) show in their citation study that the percentage of articles is still small and limited. IC in China needs its own publishing home, as the International Journal of Intercultural Relations (IJIR) and Intercultural Communication Studies (ICS) have similarly served the US-based field. Responding to the call we and others have issued before, the launching of this journal/ manuscript series is breakthrough step forward, joining the efforts that Chen Guo-ming and Zhao J.J. Edmondson have made in establishing China Media Research (which also is publishing intercultural papers). Such journal give hope toward a more comprehensive scope of publishing to make sure that they encourages and addresses the broader interdisciplinary areas of IC, both the theoretical and applied domains, as shown earlier in Diagram 1.

Conclusions

In these pages we have given a brief review of our field, its core content both at home and abroad, some applications in Shanghai, and some of the opportunities and challenges facing the field. As Hu Wenzhong noted in the closing comments of the Nanjing conference in 2005, even with 20 some years of history and over 2000 publications, IC is entering a new phase of development and in some ways a new beginning. Our hope is that this overview helps further this process of "coming of age" and motivates both scholars and practitioners to consider anew the current state of our field so that we can partner together to develop it into a vibrant discipline. Together, developing IC as a discipline in China can become a reality that makes a great contribution to our own development as scholars, to equipping our students, and to serving the needs of our nation at this important historical juncture.

References

Benoit, W. L., & Pfau, M. (2004). Introduction to the special issue: The state of the art in communication theory and research, Part 1. *Journal of Communication, 54*(4), 588.

Benoit, W. L., & Pfau, M. (Eds.). (2005). The state of the art in communication theory and research, Part 2. *Journal of Communication, 55*(3), Special Issue.

Gerbner, G. (1983). *Ferment in the field: Journal of Communication, 33*(3), Special Issue.

Guan, S. J. (2007). Foreword in S. J. Kulich & M. H. Prosser, (Eds.), *Intercultural Perspectives on Studying the Chinese, Intercultural Research*, Vol. 1 (pp. i-xiii in Chinese; ix-xvi in English). Shanghai: Shanghai Foreign Language Education Press.

Hu, W. Z. (2006, May). *On empirical research in intercultural communication*. Paper presented at the 6th Chinese Symposium for Intercultural Communication, CAFIC, Nanjing Normal University.

Kluckhohn, C. M. F., & Kroeber, A. L. (1952). *Culture: A critical review of concepts and definitions. With contributions from Alfred G. Meyer & Wayne Untereiner.* New York: Alfred A. Knopf/Random House. (Originally published as Vol. XLVII — No. 1 of the Papers of the Peabody Museum of American Archaeology and Ethnology, Harvard University)

Kulich, S. J. (2002). Using a Measure of Cross-cultural Adaptability to Develop Intercultural Communications in China – Introducing the CCAI. In Y. F. Wu & Q. H. Feng, (Eds.), *Foreign language and culture studies, Vol. 2* (pp. 934-961). Shanghai: Shanghai Foreign Language and Education Press.

Kulich, S. J. (2003). Beyond language to culture's interdisciplinary dimensions – Toward a broader focus in intercultural communications (Introducing the "Advancing Intercultural Studies" project). In Y. F. Wu & Q. H. Feng, (Eds.), *Foreign language and culture studies, Vol. 3* (pp. 848-869). Shanghai: Shanghai Foreign Language and Education Press.

Kulich, S. J. (2005). Back to the future – Proposing an inductive review of Chinese intercultural communications toward building the field. In Y. F. Wu & Q. H. Feng, (Eds.), *Foreign language and culture studies, Vol. 5* (pp. 831-848). Shanghai: Shanghai Foreign Language and Education Press.

Kulich, S. J. (2006-7). Toward a graduated research topology for field and publication analysis. In Y. F. Wu & Q. H. Feng, (Eds.), *Foreign language and culture studies, Vol. 6* (pp. 839-859). Shanghai: Shanghai Foreign Language and Education Press.

Kulich, S. J. (2008). An interdisciplinary framework for (inter) cultural studies. In Y. Z. Sun, (Ed.), English Education and Liberal Education (pp. 278-296). Beijing: Foreign Language Teaching and Research Press.

Kulich, S. J. (2009). Teaching toward psychological competence through an intercultural FLT pedagogy. In W. D. Dai, (Ed.), *New directions in foreign language teaching methodology, Vol. 3* (in press). Shanghai: Shanghai Foreign Language and Education Press.

Kulich, S. J., & Prosser, M. H. (2007). *Intercultural Perspectives on Studying the Chinese, Intercultural Research, Vol. 1.* Shanghai: Shanghai Foreign Language Education Press.

Kulich, S. J., Zhang S. T., & Zhu, M. (2006). Global Impacts on Chinese Education, Identity and Values – Implications for Intercultural Training. *International Management Review, 2*(1), 41-59.

Kulich, S. J. & Zhu, M. (2004). Getting to the Core of Culture – Introducing the

Shanghai Chinese Values Project (SCVP). In Y. F. Wu & Q. H. Feng, (Eds.), *Foreign language and culture studies*, *Vol. 4* (pp. 805-832). Shanghai: Shanghai Foreign Language and Education Press.

Li, A. C., Li, Y., & Wang, J. (2005, May). *Exploring a decade of development for IC in China – A review of three representative foreign language teaching journals (1995-2004)*. Paper presented at the 6th Chinese Symposium for Intercultural Communications, CAFIC, Nanjing Normal University.

Park, D. W., & Pooley, J. (2008). *The history of media and communication research*. New York: Peter Lang.

Prosser, M. H. (2007). One world, one dream: Harmonizing society through intercultural communication: A prelude to China intercultural communication studies. In S. J. Kulich & M. H. Prosser, (Eds.), *Intercultural perspectives on studying the Chinese, Intercultural research*, *Vol. 1* (pp. 22-91). Shanghai: Shanghai Foreign Language Education Press.

Rogers, E. M. (1994). *A history of communication study: A biographical approach*. New York: The Free Press.

Schramm, W. L. (1997). *The beginnings of communication study in America: A memoir*. Thousand Oaks, Sage Publications.

Song, Y. (2009). *Evaluating 10 years of doctoral dissertations on intercultural communication in Mainland China*. Unpublished master's thesis, Shanghai International Studies University.

Wakefield, C. S. (2007). Culture as personally active: Bridging intercultural with interpersonal communication courses. In Dai, W.D.(Ed.), *Opportunities and Challenges of Foreign Language Teaching: Symposium of the 2nd International Conference on Foreign Language Teaching Methodology in China* (pp. 467-478). Shanghai: Shanghai Foreign Language Education Press.

Wakefield, C. S. (2008a). Course proposal for "Culture in film." In Sun, Y.Z. (Ed.), *English education and liberal education* (pp. 297-310).Beijing: Foreign Lanugage Teching and Research Press.

Wakefield, C. S. (2008b, December). *A missing link to Intercultural Communication: A preliminary investigation into Shanghai student's critical thinking competence based on oral English speeches, interviews and discussions*. Paper presented at the Conference on Intercultural Communication and Identity, Shanghai Normal University.

Xu, L. S. (2006a, May). *Intercultural Communication Competence*. Paper presented at the 6th Chinese Symposium for Intercultural Communications, CAFIC, Nanjing

Normal University.

Yin, G. (2006). *A glimpse into intercultural communication study in America: Evaluating 35 years of Samovar & Porter's Intercultural Communications: A Reader.* Unpublished master's thesis, Shanghai: Shanghai International Studies University.

Zhang H. L. (2001). Language and culture teaching. In Y. F. Wu & Q. H. Feng, (Eds.), *Foreign language and culture studies, Vol. 1.* Shanghai: Shanghai Foreign Language and Education Press. (In Chinese)

Zhang H. L. (2004). The trend of English education teaching English as an international language in Y. F. Wu & Q. H. Feng, (Eds.), *Foreign Language and Culture Studies, Vol.4,* Shanghai: Shanghai Foreign Language and Education Press.

Zhang, L. (2009). *Investigations into the influence of an intercultural communication founder: Michael Prosser and the early scholars.* Unpublished master's thesis, Shanghai International Studies University.

Zhou.Z. (周真) & Knapp, D. R. (2007), *Experiencing another culture.* Kunming: Yunnan People's Publishing House.

戴炜栋, (2004), 大学发展的新趋势: 从适应市场走向国际化 (在"2004年亚洲大学校长论坛"上的演讲). http://www.sh.xinhuanet.com/zhuanti/xiaozhang/baogao/bao06.htm <2009年3月23日>

[Dai, W.D. (2004). New trend of university development: from market accomodation to internationalization (speech at Asian University Presidents Forum 2004. Retrieved March 23, 2009from http://www.sh.xinhuanet.com/zhuanti/xiaozhang/baogao/bao06.htm.]

窦卫霖, (2005),《跨文化商务交际》, 北京: 高等教育出版社。

[Dou, W.L. (2005). *Intercultural business communication.* Beijing: Higher Education Press.]

窦卫霖, (2007),《跨文化交际基础》, 北京: 对外经济贸易大学出版社。

[Dou, W.L. (2007). *Fundametals of intercultural communication.* Beijing: Higher Education Press.]

何道宽, (1983a), 介绍一门新兴学科——跨文化的交际,《外国语文》第2期。

[He, D.K. (1983a). Introduction of a new discipline—Communication across cultures. In *Foreign Language,* Vol.2]

何道宽, (1983b), 比较文化我见,《读书》第8期, 第104-111页。

[He, D.K. (1983b). My view of comparative cultural studies. *Dushu,* Vol.8, 104-111.]

胡超, (2005a),《跨文化交际: E-时代的范式与能力建构》, 北京: 中国社会科学出版社。

[Hu, C. (2005a). *Intercultural communicaiton.* Beijing: China Social Sciences Press.]

胡超, (2005b),《跨文化交际实用教程》, 北京: 外语教学与研究出版社。

[Hu, C.(2005b). Intercultural communication: *A practical coursebook*. Beijing: Foreign Lanugage Teaching and Research Press.]

林大津、谢朝阳,(2005),《跨文化交际学:理论与实践》,福州:福建人民出版社。

[Lin, D.J. & Xie, Z.Y. (2005). *Intercultural communication: Theory and practice*. Fuzhou: Fujian People's Publishing House.]

罗杰斯,(2005/1994),《传播学史——一种传记式的方法》,殷晓蓉(译),上海:上海译文出版社。

[Rogers, E. M.(2005/1994), *A history of communication study: A biographical approach*. Yin, X.R. (trans). Shanghai: Shanghai Translation Publishing House.]

宋莉,(2004),《跨文化交际导论》,哈尔滨:哈尔滨工业大学出版社。

[Song, L. (2004), *Gateway to intercultural communication*. Harbin: Harbin Institute of Technology Press.]

吴友富,(2006),《国际化视野中上外的创新和跨越》,<2009年3月23日> http://www.xizuo.com/yingyujiaoshibokejingxuan/yingyulunwen2/30072.html

[Wu, Y.F. (2006). *Innovation and transformation of SISU from an international perspective*. Retrieved March. 23, 2009 from http://www.xizuo.com/yingyujiaoshibokejingxuan/yingyulunwen2/30072.html <2009]

许力生,(2006b),《语言研究的跨文化视野》,上海:上海外语教育出版社。

[Xu, L.S. (2006b). *Studying language and its use: An intercultural approach*. Shanghai: Shanghai Foreign Language Education Press.]

许力生,(2008a),《跨文化交际(学生用书)》,上海:上海外语教育出版社。

[Xu, L.S. (2008a). *Intercultural communication (Student's book)*. Shanghai: Shanghai Foreign Language Education Press.]

许力生,(2008b),《跨文化交际(教师手册)》,上海:上海外语教育出版社。

[Xu, L.S. (Xu, L.S.2008b). *Intercultural communication (Teacher's guide)*. Shanghai: Shanghai Foreign Language Education Press.]

严文华,(2008),《跨文化沟通心理学》,上海:上海社会科学出版社。

[Yan, W.H. (2008). *Cross-cultural communication: A psychological persepective*. Shanghai: Shanghai Academy of Social Sciences Press.]

杨盈、庄恩平,(2007),构建外语教学跨文化交际能力框架,《外语界》第4期第13-21页。

[Yang, Y. & Zhuang, E.P. (2007). The Construction of Intercultural Communication Competence Framework for Foreign Language Teaching. *Foreign Langugae World* Vol.4, 13-21.]

张红玲,(2007),《跨文化外语教学》,上海:上海外语教育出版社。

[Zhang, H.L. (2007). *Intercultural Approach to Foreign Language Teaching*. Shanghai: Shanghai Foreign Language Education Press.]

庄恩平,(2004),《跨文化商务沟通案例教程》,上海:上海外语教育出版社。

Globalization: A new field for the development of intercultural communication

全球本土化：跨文化交际学科发展应关注的新视域

高永晨

苏州大学

Abstract

As a phenomenon and result of the contradiction in motion between global culture and national or local culture, glocalization has been the most striking characteristic of the era of cultural globalization, and thus has opened up a brand-new field for both the study of intercultural communication and the disciplinary development. Under the influence of globalization, various kinds of "intercultural" disciplines are increasing daily, transnational cooperative researches becoming extensive and profound, and a series of new things and problems turning out new topics for research. Hence the discipline of intercultural communication can be developed both in depth and in breadth.

1 引言

与经济全球化同时并存的文化全球化导致了"全球本土化"（globalization）的崭新景象。"全球本土化"的内涵和意义并不简单地体现在它是"全球化"（globalization）和"本土化"（localization）这两个词的合成上，而更多地表现在由全球文化与国家、民族和地区等本土文化的既冲突又融合的双向互动上，即促使跨文化交际研究领域的拓宽、研究内容的增多以及研究方式和研究格局的改变上。一方面，全球本土化导致了跨文化交际研究领域的拓宽，出现了如同戴维·哈维（David Harvey）所描绘的一种时空还原阶段（phase of reduction of time and space）的到来，随着跨文化交际研究时空的转换，跨文化交际研究领域会不断扩大。另一方面，全球本土化并不意味着全球文化与本土文化的二元对立，相反，全球本土化促使各民族本土文化以更加开放的态势与多样性的异域文化进行积极的对话，在相互交流中补益和发展自身，出现全球文化的统一性与多样性、普遍性与独特性并行不悖的生动格局。揭示全球本土化趋势如何成为推动跨文化交际学科发展的动力源泉的内在原因，预测在全球本土化态势下跨文化交际学学科发展的主要特点以及基本趋势，对于顺应全球本土化带来的新变化，促进跨文化交际学的学科建设以及指导跨文化交际的实践都具有很重要的理论意义和实践价值。

2 全球本土化推动着以"跨文化"命名的学科不断增加

全球本土化作为全球文化与本土文化矛盾运动的产物，以文化的全球本土化和本土全球化这两种迥异的形式表现出来，呈现出文化的统一性与多样性相互交融、相互促进、协调发展的生动景象。作为现代新兴文化交际工具的国际互联网络和现代交通技术的空前发达，跨国界大众传播和人际传播交往的空前频繁，显示了英国著名学者吉顿斯先生所说的"全球化使时间和空间压缩"这句话的真理性。[1]与此同时，吉顿斯先生又将时间和空间的压缩反证为时间和空间的延伸，说明在全球本土化时代，全球文化或本土文化创新的速度、多元文化交往的频度以及相互之间协调和沟通的程度都是历史上从来没有过的。在全球本土化时代，现代意义上，或者说是全世界真正意义上的跨文化交际的大格局才得以形成，换言之，全球本土化或本土全球化才以内在的张力促成了无论是深度还是广度都名实相符的跨文化交际。弗雷德里克·杰姆逊深刻地指出："全球化是一个传播性概念，交替地掩盖与传递文化或经济含义。"[1：55]他的话意味着全球化是从经济和文化两个层面同时展开的，在正视经济的全球化现象时，不能无视文化的全球化。而他所强调的全球化是一个传播性概念，就包括了文化的全球本土化和本土全球化的双向运动。全球本土化，无论是对其概念的解读，还是对其内容的学理阐述都成了真正的跨国研究，或者说是一种真正的跨国界现象和跨国界理论。全球本土化与本土全球化是文化全球化所表现出来的两种基本形式，它们既内在地蕴涵着跨文化交际的新情况，是跨文化交际在新时期的产物和必然结果，又强有力地推动着跨文化交际从深度和广度两个方向发展，为人们研究跨文化交际在新时期的嬗变和新的建构提供了又一个新的视角，为指导人们在新时期的跨文化交际实践提供了又一行之有效的方法论。

全球本土化时代也是文化的综合和分化的趋势日益增强的时代。无论是社会科学的研究，还是自然科学的研究都出现了既不断分化又高度综合的趋势。不断分化的趋势，就是各门学科由于研究的深入，分得越来越细。不断综合的趋势，就是分得越来越细的各门学科，它们之间的内在联系也越来越紧密，互补性和渗透性的趋势日益明显。越是将它们联系起来研究，就越能够发现其中蕴涵着的共同本质和规律。

---

① 参见詹姆斯·H. 米特尔曼著，刘得手译，全球化综合征. 北京：新华出版社。2002：5。

全球本土化，其概念的意蕴就体现在全球文化向本土文化的渗透和本土文化向全球文化的扩张上，推动着各门学科在综合中分化和在分化中综合。自从跨文化交际学作为一门学科产生以来，各种以"跨文化"命名的学科就如雨后春笋般地涌现，如跨文化教育学、跨文化管理学、跨文化心理学、跨文化市场营销学、跨文化经营学、跨文化谈判学、跨文化传播学、跨文化比较研究学、跨文化广告学、跨文化领导学、跨文化行为学、跨文化哲学、跨文化历史学、跨文化文献学、跨文化美学、跨文化社会学等。这些以"跨文化"命名的学科的不断产生，都源于传统学科无法适应新时期出现的新问题的需要，以及全球文化与民族本土分化之间既高度综合又日益分化的趋势。都可谓应时代之运、问题之运、研究对象需要应运而生。全球本土化趋势，为这些以"跨文化"命名的学科的发展增加了新的活力。

跨文化交际学与这些以"跨文化"命名的学科，因为各自的研究对象、研究领域、研究范围、研究方法、研究手段以及研究学科使用的原理原则以及方法论等方面的差异性，都存在着各自的适用范围，学科之间的性质具有明显的差别性。但是，跨文化交际学与这些以"跨文化"命名的学科从本质上说，在具有差异性的同时，又有着一致性。因为这些学科都要研究和揭示不同文化背景中的人们在各种文化活动中面临着的文化的特殊性和统一性之关系等问题，都要在各种文化活动中进行从个别到一般，再从一般到新的个别的逻辑分析和学理阐述。在研究使用的材料以及研究的结论等方面都存在着交融性和互补性。直言之，跨文化交际学的发展离不开以"跨文化"命名的各种学科的发展，以"跨文化"命名的各种学科越发展，跨文化交际学越能从中吸收对学科建设有用的理论成果，推动跨文化交际学科的丰富和完善。

各种以"跨文化"命名的学科，与跨文化交际学的学科发展有着非常紧密的关联性，对跨文化交际学科建设都起着直接或间接的影响和推动作用。例如，跨文化心理学和跨文化教育学，对跨文化交际学的发展有着直接的促进作用。因为跨文化交际的过程，实质上就是跨文化心理调适和互动的过程，同时也是跨文化学习和教育的过程。不同民族的文化都与不同民族的心理紧密联系在一起。而不同的民族心理都由不同民族的教育方式、教育内容、教育环境等决定。对于不同的民族心理和民族教育的深入研究，有助于为跨文化交际研究提供大量的实证经验材料，推动跨文化交际研究的深入进行。

跨文化交际学与跨文化心理学之间的内在关联性是很明显的。学界一般都认为，英国人类学家、心理学家米勒是跨文化心理学的奠基人，他在其著作《逻辑体系》一书中初步体现出跨文化心理学思想。米勒认为跨文化心理学家要研究适用于任何国家、任何民族的基本心理规律，强调研究人的心理时不应忽视文化环境。他开创性地提出了"习性学"（一门研究人的性格的学科）的概念，指出这一学科在探讨个体性格的形成与发展时，必须注重个体与环境的交互作用，按照一定的规律去研究文化对人的性格的影响。20世纪上中叶的一批人类学家和心理学家，如摩尔根、巴蒂斯安、马林诺夫斯基、博阿兹、本尼迪克特和米德、卡尔纳等人对跨文化心理学进行了深入的描述与实证研究，这些研究成果对于跨文化交际研究都有着重要的借鉴作用。在当今的文化全球化时代，不同文化背景下的人们的交往过程，就是跨文化心理的顺应和调适过程。实践证明，越是深入地了解和研究跨文化心理学，越能有效地推进跨文化交际学。

跨文化交际学与跨文化教育学之间的关系也是十分紧密的。其互为动力的作用表现为，一方面，跨文化教育学的发展强有力地推动着跨文化交际学的发展；另一方面，跨文化交际学的发展也是推动跨文化教育学发展的强大动力。跨文化教育学，一般是指在两种或多种文化之间进行的一种教育。从教育人类学的角度看，人类的一切教育活动都是建立在某种特定文化基础之上的，教育是传承文化的载体。每一个人都具有一定的民族属性，而每一种教育也都与特定的民族文化密不可分。具有不同文化的民族，都会选择和确立具有自己民族特色、有助于本民族文化传承和发展的教育模式。教育具有"单一文化教育"和"跨文化教育"两种基本类型。前者是指受教育者所受教育基本上仅局限于一个民族的文化，具有单一的民族属性。而后者，则是在两种不同文化之间进行的。进行跨文化教育，如移民教育、殖民地教育、留学生教育、多民族国家中的少数民族教育和多元文化教育等，有助于推进跨文化交际的深入进行。文化全球化也意味着教育全球化。跨文化教育不仅在学校教育中越来越成为非常普遍的现象，而且也越来越成为社会中非常普遍的现象。跨文化教育的理论和实践直接推动跨文化理论的发展和学科建设。

各种以"跨文化"命名的学科不断增多，或者说是"跨文化学科丛林"的出现，既反映了全球本土化时代文化繁荣和学科繁荣的生动景象，同时，也预示着跨文化交际学科建设的春天已经到来。今天的满园春色，必将迎来明天的累累硕果。

3 全球本土化引发大规模跨国间的合作研究促进着跨文化交际学的发展

全球本土化时代是国与国之间加强文化交流，并在文化交流中促进文化发展的时代。各国文化需要走向世界，世界也需要了解各国文化。多元文化之间的交流以及跨文化交际学科研究的跨国合作，是跨文化交际学科发展的强大推动力量。全球本土化现象本身就是多元文化合作交流的产物，全球本土化趋势的发展又促使多元文化合作交流的趋势进一步增强。中国自20世纪80年代以来持续不断的学习外语热，以及进入新世纪后世界各国的学习汉语热都反映了多样性文化之间加强交流，使全球文化与民族本土文化之间不断融合和互补的趋势。正是在这样的基础上，推动了跨文化交际研究朝着跨国联合攻关的方向发展。

跨文化交际学的研究对象、研究范围以及学科性质等，都决定了这门学科的建设必须依赖于跨国合作研究。跨国合作研究是促进多元文化交流，克服民族文化中心主义的有效途径。跨国合作研究的广度和深度，直接决定着跨文化交际研究的程度和水平。诚然，从国外留学回来的从事跨文化交际研究的学者，对本国文化与别国的文化会有比较深刻的感悟，对跨文化交际学的研究会有很好的帮助。但是，光是依靠他们进行跨国间的文化对比研究还是很不够的。对别国的深层次的文化的习得以及深刻把握，并非一日之功，而需要比较长的时间，特别是一些涉及到宗教信仰、民族风尚、历史传统、国民心理以及价值准则等方面的文化知识，更不是凭短短几年时间在国外的学习就能理解和掌握的。进行跨国间的合作研究，能够有效整合多样性文化的力量，消除跨文化交际研究中的文化偏见，达到合作双赢的目的。因此，在跨文化交际的研究以及学科建设中，只有开展经常性的有专项课题的跨国之间的合作研究，才能推动跨文化交际学理论研究和学科建设的深入。

在全球本土化时代，跨国间进行跨文化交际研究，不但是我国外语界和企业界的需要，是推动跨文化交际科研深入进行的必要环节，也是欧洲、美国以及日本等国家教育界和企业界实施跨国战略的需要。任何民族和国家的经济、政治和文化活动，一旦进入国际领域，就有进行跨文化交际跨国研究的必要。谢里夫·海塔塔在《美元化、解体和上帝》一文中指出："我们称之为跨文化的研究能帮助我们消弭二极世界的对立，帮助我们自下，而不是从上接近实现一个全球性世界。那将是一个人们通过共同学习、工作和研究达到相互了解的全球性世界，而不是一个霸权的、金字塔式的世界。"[2：240] 在2005年10月于北京召开的国际论坛"经济国际化中扩大国际经济、文化和教育的合作"的会议上，德国驻华大使馆公使费华德博士说，德国非常重视跨国文化管理与培训的问题，德国的大学有五十多个跨文化交际方面的课程，它们是从不同的角度，比如经济、语言、心理等方面来探讨这个问题，有些学校是教授管理技巧的，有的是关于咨询的，有的是关于私营领域文化管理的，有的课程是涉及具体的地区、国家的文化问题，有的是涉及跨国文化的交流。但是，德国也面临着一个迫切的要求，那就是进一步加强同亚洲国家，特别是中国的文化交流。有一些研究人员进行了亚洲研究。但是，这是不足够的，不足以能够满足社会的要求，特别是工业和经济领域企业的要求。②美国和日本也是如此，他们的许多跨国公司在产品营销、市场推广、企业文化建设以及信息传播等方面都迫切需要与中国有关专家进行跨文化交际方面的合作研究。这对于增强相互之间的优势互补，推动跨文化交际研究的深入，有效地避免跨文化交际中的矛盾和不必要的误解，都是非常有意义的。可以预见，随着全球本土化趋势的增强以及跨文化交际学科建设的需要，跨国间的交流合作研究将得到进一步发展。跨文化交际研究领域是向全球开放的，跨文化交际的科研机构也将是全球性的。

适应全球本土化或本土全球化趋势，我国关于跨文化交际研究方面的跨国合作，这几年成绩斐然，对跨文化交际学科建设起着积极的作用。在国际跨文化研究学术交流方面既有学校与学校之间的合作交流，又有国家有关部门与国外有关部门

---

② 参见2005年10月14日教育网。

之间的合作交流。在国外举行的国际跨文化交际研讨会与在中国举行的国际跨文化交际研讨会的经常性召开，推动着宏观的研究与微观的研究，整体的研究以及专题的研究不断深入。1995年，首届中国跨文化交际国际研讨会在哈尔滨召开，来自世界20多个国家和地区的几百名学者进行了学术交流和探讨。在这次会议上，中国跨文化交际研究会正式成立了，这是中国跨文化交际研究进入一个有组织、大规模以及与国际对话和交流阶段的重要标志。学会成立以来，跨文化交际的研究工作按照经常化、制度化、规范化和组织化的方式进行，与国际同行之间的合作研究正在向多层次、多角度和纵向的方向发展。可以预见，随着全球本土化趋势的增强，在跨文化交际研究方面，跨国合作研究增强的趋势会愈演愈烈。

4 全球本土化时代的新事物将成为跨文化交际研究的新课题

目前，我国的跨文化交际学的研究取得了很大的成绩，有关著作和论文如汗牛充栋。研究的主要内容涉及跨文化交际与外语教学、跨文化交际与对外汉语教学、跨文化交际能力的培养、跨文化交际与翻译、跨文化交际中的语用失误、非语言交际、词汇的文化内涵、跨文化交际与修辞、经贸领域的跨文化交际、民族之间的跨文化交际等。配合跨文化交际学的研究，还译介了国外大量跨文化交际学方面的著作，同时还译介了国外大量以"跨文化"命名的著作，如跨文化传播、跨文化管理、跨文化市场营销、跨文化心理学、跨文化教育学、跨文化社会学等。国内的一些重点大学在外语教学中，基本上都开设了跨文化交际学课程。有的大学还招收了跨文化交际研究方向的硕士生和博士生。但是，将跨文化交际学置于全球本土化的背景和视域中，直接针对全球本土化带来的一系列新问题展开跨文化交际研究的论著，还寥若晨星。总之，从跨文化交际学科建设的角度看，理论研究的空间还非常巨大，理论研究深入进行的任务还相当艰巨，全球本土化时代的许多新事物需要研究，许多新领域需要拓荒，跨文化交际的研究方法需要大力改进，研究队伍需要加强和充实，研究成果需要进一步走向世界。

在全球本土化时代，存在着一系列需要跨文化交际学深入研究的新课题。笔者认为，最紧迫地需要研究的主要课题有十大方面。

一是对全球本土化概念、实质、规律和发展趋势，以及全球本土化对跨文化交际面临的机遇和挑战的研究。全球本土化化究竟是文化的分裂化，还是文化的同质化？是文化的单一性，还是多元文化主义？是跨文化主义，还是文化的一体化？全球本土化是有利于全球文化发展的馅饼，还是不利于全球文化发展的陷阱？全球本土化对传统的跨文化交际研究究竟带来了哪些新情况和新问题？如何正确对待这些新情况和新问题？必须做出具有说服力的回答。

二是对文化全球化与民族文化本土化双向互动和双向建构辩证关系的研究。文化全球化与本土化的矛盾冲突存在着哪些表现？由什么主要原因引起？文化全球化与民族文化本土化如何才能双向建构和双向互动？双向建构和双向互动的内在机制如何？发展的基本趋势如何？对此，应该通过前瞻性的研究，获得比较清晰的认识。

三是对全球本土化增强多元文化之间合作，扩大世界政治的文化基础的研究。詹姆斯·罗斯诺（James N. Rosenau）在《世界的混乱：变化与继承的理论》中首次提出了"全球文化"（Global Culture）的概念，他认为全球的相互依赖趋势的增强扩大了实践世界政治的文化的基础，加强了国际关系中主权主体和非主权主体之间的合作。相互依赖的加深导致了规范的分享，导致了全球共同体对地域共同体的吸收。[3：348-349]对此，需要作出深入的研究说明。

四是对全球本土化导致的文化的分离化与同质化并存现象的研究。日本学者星野昭吉注意到了文化全球化会带来这一奇特现象，在其《全球政治学——全球化进程中的变动、冲突、治理与和平》中认为："文化全球化意即全球文化的相互依存、相互作用以及文化角色之间的相互交流，它允许分离化与同质化并存"。[4：191]对这一现象以及其蕴涵的内在意义需要从跨文化交际学的视角做出深入说明。

五是对全球本土化促进了文化关系和文化实践的延伸和深化的研究。赫尔德等人在著作《全球大变革——全球化时代的政治、经济与文化》中把文化全球化看作是"文化关系和文化实践的延伸和深化——即人和物的运动有助于在广泛的范围内建立一种共享的文化信念模式。从而有助于在不同地方之间建立一个地方的文化思想影响另一个地方的互动模式。"[5：460] 对于文化全球化促进人的文化关系和文化实践的延伸与深化的表现、路径以及内在机制、发展结果等，都需要在跨文化交际研究中进行深入的阐发。

六是对虚拟世界的跨文化交际研究。网络的发展带来了以网络文化为主体的虚拟世界，跨文化交际从真实世界延伸到了虚拟世界。那么，虚拟世界的跨文化交际有哪些特点？虚拟世界的跨文化交际与实在世界的跨文化交际存在着哪些共性？又有哪些个性特征？虚拟世界跨文化交际中的法律、伦理道德等如何建设？虚拟世界跨文化交际推动全球文化发展的基本趋势如何？对于这些深层次的问题，都需要深入研究。

七是对全球本土化时代强势文化与弱势文化关系的研究。在全球本土化时代，外来强势文化对民族本土文化的冲击究竟有多大？弱势文化在强势文化面前如何保持自己的文化特质？弱势文化如何在跨文化交际中不断地成长壮大？目前，英语文化对非英语国家的影响大大超过了非英语国家文化对英语国家文化的影响，对其他文化的信息传播构成了极大的冲击和威胁。如何认识和预见文化冲突的范围、文化冲突的多样化和更加频繁性？如何认识信息高速公路上的文化多样性问题？如何抵制信息殖民主义？深入研究这些问题，已经很有必要。

八是对全球本土化时代跨文化交际学与各种以"跨文化"命名的学科之间关系的研究。跨文化交际学与各种以"跨文化"命名的学科之间具有哪些互补性和互馈性？如何在它们之间建立起学术成果的共享机制？它们在各自发展中存在着哪些基本规律？都是跨文化交际研究需要说明的问题。

九是对全球本土化时代，跨文化交际过程中因为性别差异、身份差异、地位差异以及年龄差异所导致的文化差异的研究以及全球本土化时代语言和非语言变异以及变异的基本规律、发展趋势的研究。

十是对全球本土化时代跨文化交际能力的研究,如全球本土化时代,跨文化交际能力的价值、跨文化交际能力提高的途径,全球本土化时代跨文化交际对外语教学提出的机遇和挑战等问题的研究。

此外,适应全球本土化时代的特征,在跨文化交际研究中如何进行研究方法的变革,如何将宏观研究与微观研究结合起来,如何将定性分析与定量分析结合起来,如何将理论研究与实际运用结合起来,如何推进跨文化交际学科建设等问题,都是跨文化交际学研究的重大课题。

5 结语

在全球本土化时代,跨文化交际学的研究空间更加宽广、研究对象更加众多、研究任务更加艰巨、研究方法更加多样、研究成果也更有价值。跨文化交际研究的春天已经来临,一路前行,一定会更加姹紫嫣红、美不胜收。

参考文献

弗雷德里克·杰姆逊, (2002),《全球化的文化》,(三好将夫编,马丁译), 南京: 南京大学出版社。

[Jameson, F. & M. Miyoshi (Eds.), (2002). *The cultures of globalization* (Ma, D. Trans.). Nanjing: Nanjing University Press.]

谢里夫·海塔塔, (2002), 美元化、解体和上帝, 载弗雷德里克·杰姆逊, 三好将夫编, 马丁译,《全球化的文化》, 南京: 南京大学出版社。

[Hetata, S. (2002). Dollarization, fragmentation and god. In F. Jameson & M. Miyoshi (Eds.), Ma, D. (Trans.) *The cultures of globalization.* Nanjing: Nanjing University Press.]

詹姆斯·罗斯诺, (1990), 世界的混乱: 变化与继承的理论, 转引自王缉思 (1995),《文明与国际政治》, 上海: 上海人民出版社,第348-349页。

[Rosenau, J. N. (1990). *Turbulence in world politics: a theory of change and continuity.* Cited from Wang, J. S. (1995). *Civilization and international politics* (pp.348-349). Shanghai: Shanghai People's Publishing House.]

星野昭吉, (2000),《全球政治学》(刘小林, 张胜军译), 北京: 新华出版社。

[Hosino, A. (2000). Liu, X. L. & Zhang, S. J. (Trans.). *Global politics: change, conflict, governance and peace in the process of globalization.* Beijing: Xinhua Publishing House.]

赫尔德等, (1999/2001),《全球大变革——全球化时代的政治、经济与文化》(杨雪冬等译), 北京: 社会科学文献出版社。

[Held, D., McGrew, A. Goldblatt, D.& Perraton, J. (1999/2001). *Global transformations: politics, economics and culture* (Yang, X. D. Trans.). Beijing: Social Sciences Academic Press.]

The future of cross cultural communication: Perspectives from 20 years of the IAICS

L. Brooks Hill   Trinity University, USA

Abstract

For the last forty years I have worked in the intersecting fields of intercultural, international, and development communication, and have spent my career devoted to these challenging areas of study (Honna & Hoffer, 2003). Almost twenty years ago I arrived at Trinity University and was recruited into a new interdisciplinary organization devoted to all of my language related interests. Since that time I have served for two terms as President of the International Association for Intercultural Communication Studies (IAICS), served on the Board of Directors for several years, and currently work as the General Editor of the IAICS journal Intercultural Communication Studies. During my forty years in the profession and especially during the last two decades in IAICS, I have contributed to the field while observing some of the areas of cross cultural communication that need more careful research. Based on this lifetime commitment, the following article will channel my experience into suggestions for the future.

The sections of this article will address a cluster of closely related ideas that form three major challenges for our future. The first section assumes a more theoretical perspective and identifies several specific concerns that we must confront to unify our collective efforts and direct them with more synergy toward greater scholarly and practical achievements. The second section serves as a serious caution about the uncritical acceptance of technological innovation as a means of teaching and otherwise applying our knowledge. The third and final section turns our attention to ethnic relations. Throughout the world, poor ethnic relations are causing the disintegration of society. We must apply our knowledge more carefully to the resolution of these concerns.

Overall, this article will synthesize my experience into three general directions for improvement of the study and practice of cross cultural relations. Its central theme will address the primary question of this anthology: How can we better pull together our collective efforts and thereby synergize our potential for a better world?

Perspectives for Scholars and Scholarship[1]

The studies of intercultural, international, and development communication emerged from slightly different traditions with different emphases. Despite ancient origins of intuitive and general considerations of these subjects, they seemed to have originated as areas of systematic study during the twentieth century with the growth of the social sciences, media technology, and world organizations devoted to global concerns. More specifically, intercultural communication emerged from a more interpersonal orientation, fostered in significant ways by the work of Edward T. Hall and his re-orientation of the United States Foreign Service Institute programs after World War II (Leeds-Hurwitz, 1998). Finding an academic home within speech and applied anthropology, it tended to focus on the mutual negotiation of social reality among participants. In contrast, international communication seemed to originate in political science with emphasis on international relations and the new developments in media technology. While these two separate academic disciplines followed somewhat independent paths, they have come closer together with the more extensive and rapid expansion of media technology as a central focus in globalization. The growth of cultural studies over the last three decades has brought these disciplines even closer. The vast area of development communication perhaps originated with attention to the problems with the diffusion of agricultural and public health information. Because of the communication aspects of these problem areas people from applied anthropology and sociology drew to them contributors from communication studies who were interested in the overlapping topics of organizational communication, campaigning and movement studies. Intercultural, international, and development communication are rich sources of information about cross-cultural problems, but instead of benefiting from symbiotic relationships, they have progressed in relatively independent directions with often separate literatures, academic disciplines, and unfortunately rare integration of resources.

The varied development of interests in cross-cultural questions is further Balkanized by the patterns of humanistic studies. The studies of literature, linguistics, and additional areas of anthropology represent substantive considerations of intercultural, international, and development communication, but they are often not well integrated into the more social scientific traditions represented in the preceding paragraph. As a result, many scholars who treat the processes of communication ignore treatments of the artifactual products of the cultures and nations they engage. Granted that the specific interests of each scholar are

---

1 An earlier version of this section appeared in Hill, L. B., Dixon, L. D. & Goss, L. B. (2000). Intercultural communication: Trends, problems, and prospects. Intercultural Communication Studies, 10 (1), 189-194.

important in their own right, they deserve some broader and synergistic integration. My background was primarily in the arts and humanities, but I saw the overlap of my interests with the social sciences and attempted to take a position with a foot in both camps. This has enriched my experience and expanded the perspective of my students. The motivation that encouraged me to make the IAICS my primary professional organization was the attraction of diverse scholars from all over the world to our collective work. Within this framework I came to some useful definitions that honor the differences of these primary areas, but also consider the shared emphases.

We seriously need to settle on some shared definitions that can serve as points of departure to realize more of our collective potential. By keeping these definitions simple and general, they can chart our work together, as well as sustain our relative independence: **Communication** may be defined as the process of symbolically eliciting meaningful responses that facilitate understanding and/or the fulfillment of other purposes. In other words, communication involves the creation, adaptation, and transmission of messages that can facilitate mutual understanding or other possible results. Culture is another process that overlaps, and often coincides, with communication. **Culture** may be defined as the process of (a) knowing and behaving in a manner acceptable to persons who are members of a culture; (b) developing the semantic or cognitive framework to facilitate appropriate knowledge and behavior; and (c) transmitting and/or perpetuating this knowledge, framework, and behavior. Because communication is a sine qua non of society, and society is a major dimension of culture, these three interrelated constructs form an essential dimension of our humanity.

The term *cross cultural communication* has two general uses: In one sense the term refers to any interaction among people from different cultures. In a much more specific sense the term is used in reference to a more methodological concern called comparative perspectives wherein we compare similar phenomena within two different cultures and derive generalizations that exceed the limits of one culture. While the latter has specific use for research methods, the more general term may be even more useful as a vehicle for integrating all of our mutual concerns. *Intercultural communication* comes primarily out of an interpersonal orientation and addresses the mutual negotiation of social reality among participants. Because of the necessity and reality of interpersonal aspects of our globalization, we can no longer neglect these aspects of any communication among peoples around the world, whatever problems we may be addressing. *International communication* comes out of a mass media and political orientation; it addresses information flow between and among nations and other large groups of people. While these areas are constantly in the news and represent the more visible issues confronting us, we must recognize that these concerns subsume the more personal aspects of interpersonal communication. Finally, *development communication* is the use of all means of communication to assist with the development or social improvements of nations and cultures in need. This may well be the bridge that completes the interconnections between interpersonal communication, international communication, and globalization. We can not continue as a world community without spreading our achievements more equitably so that good, rather than evil, dominates the diverse peoples of the world. Our collective success on planet earth will depend on how well we can understand why we communicate interculturally and replace the tendencies to exploit with progress for the common good of us all.

Beyond the broad definitional level of our need for closer collaboration, a few serious limitations of our work also encourage attention. Breadth and diversity are the cornerstones and most distinctive features of IAICS, as we have from its inception tried to pull together people from many disciplines and interests into a single organization dedicated to the improvement of cultural understanding and intercultural relations. Anyone who hears our convention programs and reads our journal should be excited by the diversity of our subject and the methods of our research. Examination of these materials will not only generate excitement, but also some concerns. From our conference programs and my work on the editorial board, I have identified two general categories of concerns; one is methodological and the other substantive. These reactions focus on the work of scholars in IAICS, but these general observations apply more widely.

I offer four reactions to our methods of research:

(1) The rigor of our methods and the quality of our critical assessments are sometimes weak. We need to establish and present more explicit criteria for research quality, and then meet them; this will reveal our commitment to high standards and provide a better basis for comparing and integrating our studies with those of others.

(2) We sometimes neglect theoretical and conceptual concerns. Whenever we can make our theoretical framework explicit we should do so. We should never forget that knowledge is cumulative, and the building blocks are clear concepts. Here again, more explicit treatment of our theoretical foundations and conceptual clarity will facilitate comparison and integration of our work with that of others.

(3) We tend to be excessively anecdotal, sometimes relying too much on the idiosyncratic. Greater attention to the two preceding concerns should correct this tendency.

(4) We are sometimes overly cynical in our work with far more attention to deconstruction, rather than to something more constructive. Essentially, we need to restore a more critical attitude about our methods with greater precision, carefulness, thoroughness, and rigor in our approach to research and its report. Too much of our literature attempts to correct social imbalances by privileging the minority voice; while some of this approach may be desirable as thought pieces, we should not confuse more careful research with elaborated anecdotes.

Regarding the substance of our work, I applaud the increased integration of perspectives and how the scholars of IAICS are filling the gaps created by more rigid academic compartmentalization. Despite these achievements, my reviews of our programs and journal submissions reveal three serious concerns:

(1) We infrequently address real social problems, escaping instead into the cleanliness of academic scholarship. We need to use what we know to help us understand and possibly resolve social concerns. As noted in my 1997 IAICS presidential address, we can certainly help with our understanding of ethnic or co-cultural problems within our own national cultures.

(2) As noted as a more general problem above, we tend to separate international and intercultural concerns. Granted these two areas emerged within different traditions and sets of issues, the realities of our current world strongly encourage us to bring them back together. In our consideration of these interrelated problems we are not filling the gap effectively.

(3) Especially those of us from the developed nations are ignoring the downside of technological innovation. We can not and should not permit our economic advantages to worsen the distance between peoples around the world. We must not ignore the subtle ways that technology can seductively generate counterproductive ethnocentrism. Overall, these concerns reinforce a serious need to remember a major concern of IAICS: to increase the applicability of our work to genuine improvement of the human condition for all peoples.

A primary goal of this first section is an exhortation to those of us who work in the overlapping areas of intercultural, international and development communication, in one or another of the widely divergent possibilities, to formulate a more interdependent agenda for future study. As we reflect on this challenge, several procedural implications for our organization emerge: IAICS can provide a direction for solutions to real social problems. Alone we scholars may be "voices in the wilderness," but together we comprise a set of influential teachers and scholars who can potentially impact our world. Within this sort of mission statement, we must continually work to bring the diverse perspectives together to confront the overwhelming variability of cultures and challenges of intercultural relations. For our organization this means that we will need even more effective communication among our members. To this end we have initiated a new website, which has improved access to our journal, and facilitated the maximum use of our journal articles. We plan to create a "news and notes" section of both our website and journal to encourage greater familiarity among our membership and more collaborative, interdependent research. In addition the conferences that IAICS sponsors every year provide us an opportunity to renew our commitments and expand our potential to address the problems we confront. At each of our twelve conferences we have grown and advanced our collective cause.

Technological Questions for Intercultural Communication Study[2]

Permit me to begin this section with a hypothetical presumption significant to our concerns: How we recognize and treat differences between and among people is the heart, the core, of intercultural relations. If we accept this point of view, then the study of intercultural relations entails four interrelated goals: (1) the objective, non-judgmental detection of differences, (2) the understanding of the source(s) of differences, (3) the tolerant management of differences, and (4) the appreciation of differences in self and group fulfillment and growth. More specifically, intercultural communication addresses the tactics and strategies of message development, adaptation, and transmission as we use our knowledge of human differences to achieve some level of intercultural effectiveness. From my perspective nearly everyone reading these words is interested in intercultural relations, each of us comes to this concern with varied emphases, but whatever our professional label and identity our work contributes to one or more of the goals of intercultural relations. Mine is a very practical communication orientation.

Those of us who teach intercultural relations, from whatever vantage point, recognize the limitations of the traditional classroom context. No matter how hard we work at our instructional approach we can not capture the vitality of the real intercultural experience. Thus, over the years we have developed several supplements for our traditional courses to provide what we have called experiential learning opportunities. Among these are study abroad, various exchange projects, international living dormitories, foreign language exclusive summer sessions, foreign travels, and even exposures to foreign teachers. These supplements are valuable, but often unavailable to many students. So, we have tried to enhance our somewhat static courses with technology. The possible alternatives lead us to the central question of this section: What are the prospects and liabilities for technological enhancement of experiential learning for intercultural effectiveness?

As with most topics of significance, this one also suffers definitional problems.

(1) The first definitional problem involves "instructional technology," which is the new label for the "instructional media" programs of yesteryear. But unlike prior circumstances,

---

2 An earlier version of this section appeared in Hill, L. B. (1998). Technological enhancement of experiential learning for intercultural communication. Cross-Cultural Communication East and West in the 90's (pp. 15-22). San Antonio, TX: Institute for Cross-Cultural Research, Trinity University.

the responsibility for instructional technology is not being relegated primarily to our colleagues in Colleges or Departments of Education. No longer are they expected to consolidate our equipment in a few rooms and cart it to our classes as needed. Instead, the prominence of computers and the need for very special facilities in the recent trends of instructional technology have introduced unusual demands on the subject area adaptation by disciplines; so, we now have many "cooks in the kitchen." But I fear that even with more, varied contributors, we are recreating some of the same problems encountered with the old instructional media centers.

(2) A second set of definitional problems involves our need to distinguish mass media from mediated interpersonal technology. The former typically includes such media as television, video, and film, while the mediated interpersonal technology includes innumerable computer-facilitated interpersonal connections and various other interactive, individualized media. Overall, however, the distinctions involved among these media are not absolute and tend to range on a continuum of personal to impersonal to non-personal with the same media serving different functions at different points on the continuum. So, when we speak of technological enhancement, I am excluding no medium. In fact, I strongly support varied combinations of media. Perhaps most importantly, I am not equating technology with computers, because the tendency to confuse the two is a dangerous threat to contemporary efforts to use instructional technology more effectively. The "cyberspace craze" in the United States illustrates the naive infatuation of many Americans with the unbridled progression of technology. We hope this economically motivated wave of hysteria will soon reestablish strong roots in reality rather than the imaginary projections of virtual reality.

(3) A third and final set of definitional concerns forces us to focus our attention. At the broadest level of this subject area is a concern for the use of technology in any type of instruction; this certainly applies to our interests but is much broader. Current interest with experiential learning in several disciplines also exceeds, but is applicable to, our concerns (Kolb, 1984; Jackson & Caffarella, 1994; Lewis & Williams, 1994). We are very specifically interested in instructional technology in all possible combinations and applications as a potential enhancement of experiential learning of intercultural communication effectiveness (Jackson & MacIsaac, 1994). Were this a book-length project, we would need to examine instructional technology, experiential learning, intercultural communication effectiveness, and ultimately their interrelations. In this less expansive effort, I shall instead consider first some general uses of technology to enhance experiential learning of intercultural communication effectiveness, noting the several advantages of these prospects. Then, I will

consider three current examples, and the preponderance of my discussion will consider the problems with our dependence on technology.

Many studies are now available that assess media appropriateness for intercultural communication and cross-cultural learning. These studies provide many examples of the effective use of video tapes, teleconferencing, freeze-frame telephone, facsimile, e-mail, and video conferencing, and others in teaching intercultural communication to students in varied parts of the world. Overall, the studies find the efforts successful and worth the time, energy, and money invested, but questions usually remain about the degree of success and costs. Whatever the results, the authors seem to believe that these technological enhancements foster student motivation and energize their subsequent study. Most of us have extensive anecdotal support to confirm these tendencies. At a very advanced level, simulation and virtual reality programming provide some fascinating prospects; adventure programs, video games, even music television or MTV are good prospects currently used. At a more basic level, we now are using e-mail in programs between all parts of the world, and cognitive mapping exercises serve to encourage more effective conceptual development of intercultural communication theory and research, as well as applications. A somewhat retrospective collection of efforts falls under the label "distance learning" which is using many of these techniques to reach audiences unable to come for classes at a central location (Lee & Caffarella, 1994).

These current uses of technology range from the fascinating to the mundane, vary widely in costs, and require a diversity of skills to use as instructor and/or student. They do, however, seem to provide some clear advantages. They maximize opportunities for students and teachers who can not afford to travel or to spend large amounts of time away from home. These technological enhancements can certainly motivate and energize students to study cultural variability and intercultural relations. They further expand the number of cultures one can learn about and interact with. It seems without question that at the initial level of cultural sensitivity and intercultural relations, the technological enhancements are successful. What we lack is evidence of their longer term effectiveness, usefulness, and dangers (MacIsaac & Jackson, 1994; Bassett & Jackson, 1994).

Consider three examples of current technological techniques being used to facilitate an experiential approach to intercultural communication effectiveness. The first occurred in my undergraduate course in international communication. While browsing the "net," one of my students encountered a request for interpersonal contact with a student from an eastern European university. Through e-mail they began to discuss the problems with universities in eastern Europe following the demise of communist rule and the collapse of the Soviet Union. This contact led my student to conduct his major project for the course on the topic of computers in higher education in eastern Europe. The results of this experience were exciting for all involved. My student learned first-hand about issues critical to education in another part of the world, developed a working relationship with a student in another culture, and they taught each other a lot about their respective cultures. Although the costs for my student were minimal, the monetary costs for his contact were comparatively large and virtually impossible to reimburse. From this assignment, my student also learned many of the inadequacies of this limited contact. The conclusion for my student and me, however, was that this was an exciting and extraordinary supplement to an otherwise typical university course, and the lessons learned from the foreign student significantly enhanced my student's learning experience. Subsequently, other students in my classes, and as I understand from colleagues around our country students from their classes as well, have used the internet and e-mail to expand their assignments well beyond the limits of regular courses and library constraints. The extent to which this approach serves to enrich the actual experience of another culture is questionable, however, because students are primarily using the technology to gather information, rather than to learn about or increase their skills for intercultural interaction with people from another culture. The simple act of dealing with someone from another culture, however, is a major step in the right direction, and I strongly urge you to encourage your students to work on projects through internet and e-mail with students from other countries if at all possible.

 A second set of examples comes from colleagues at other universities in the southwestern and western United States. They have developed a network of interrelated courses at American and Mexican universities in which video conferencing, supplemented by e-mail, is a primary vehicle for teaching intercultural communication. Through prior arrangements, instructors of courses at American and Mexican universities develop common syllabi with designated sessions to be managed through video-conferencing and direct student interaction. Obviously, this is an expensive prospect with not only substantial monetary costs, but large demands on time to coordinate the activities. Through e-mail many of the logistics are addressed. Similar to other parallel efforts around the world, this project can in time become such a standard operating procedure that the logistical difficulties virtually disappear. If these projects can be supplemented by exchanges and other joint efforts, then the prospects become even more exciting. Here again, costs and logistics are major concerns, and these realities may constrain the potential.

A third and final illustration involves the exchange of video cassettes between students at an American and a Japanese university. Initiated primarily to secure examples of spoken English, these tapes were requested by a Japanese instructor eager to provide her students with opportunities to learn conversational American English. What soon evolved was a desire for these students to address questions and concerns that would encourage greater cultural sensitivity among both groups of students. Obviously, the products did not have to be of professional quality. So, what we did was simply to provide students a video camera, to set up an agenda of selected questions for discussion, and to turn the students loose to enjoy the filmed discussion. We then mailed the tape to the Japanese teacher who played it for her students, and her class reciprocated. The overall effect of this video exchange was the emergence of a very useful learning experience by both groups. We ultimately learned to send a list of questions which our group wanted the other group to discuss, and they would do likewise. In time the students came to know each other and to actually make comments to one of the foreign students during the discussions. This, too, suffered logistical difficulties, but in time we learned to overcome them. The constraints of completing a course during a limited time frame made these exercises less than integral to the course, but still very enjoyable. Current technology makes this sort of project even more feasible. Ultimately we made arrangements for groups of Japanese students to come to our university during their semester break (March) and to stay in the dorms with their counterparts, attend American classes, and simply "hang-out" with the American students. While this arrangement was more expensive, it was a wonderful success.

Most readers could add more cases perhaps with much greater creativity and even more on the cutting edge of technology. These examples serve my purpose, however, much better than a lengthier list of illustrations or more complex cases. From these examples, which in some combination or another are probably very common around the world, we can begin to see some of the problems and shortcomings of the use of technology as aids for experiential learning. No matter the downside, they do serve to energize and excite students, but unless they are carefully used they may create greater problems than they ever address. The popular and scholarly literature is currently replete with considerations of the pitfalls of technology (Wishnietsky, 1994). Because of our very specific focus and time at our disposal, I will summarize and abbreviate these concerns into three interrelated categories: (1) the more obvious problems which confound our use of technology; (2) the less conspicuous, though more insidious, problems, and (3) illustrations of central intercultural communication concepts which will suffer from technological intervention.

Obvious Problems

Perhaps most apparent is the simple lack of available technology and functional skills. Those of us in well developed countries often fail to realize that most of the world does not have access to our technology, and this obviously renders its use for any type of education or training somewhat meaningless. So, whatever its potential value, we can not expect in the near future to benefit from its use in much of the world. Because of the unavailability of technology, very few people are trained in its use or have even considered its potential. What we need at our conferences are sessions to discuss such technological innovations and their potential as a means of anticipating the time when these options do become available. Unfortunately, even those of us in intercultural relations sometimes forget the wide gap between the haves and the have-nots. While the gap may be diminishing, we must learn how to deal with people with and without technological enhancement.

A second obvious problem is similar to those of the old instructional media programs. We often lack systematic integration of our technology into an overall pedagogical approach. To integrate these innovative possibilities successfully will require re-conceptualization of our courses and major alterations of our instructional techniques (Caffarella & Barnett, 1994). Too often, technology is used in an ad hoc fashion, and the primary benefit may be its novelty. Perhaps we should reassess our approach to intercultural communication education, and for at least a major unit in a course, if not the entire course, we must concentrate on an experiential approach which builds on some of the current technology. In my own undergraduate course I currently use a "contact" paper as a term project (Javidi & Hill, 1987) in which students are to establish contact with a foreign student, conduct extensive interviews, and write about the problems of acculturation encountered by that student. How much more valuable that experience might become if a complementary, simultaneous project required contact with a student in another country through mediated interpersonal communication?

A third obvious problem anticipates some later considerations of a more insidious variety. Dependence on technology can lead students into deceptive oversimplification. No matter how carefully set up, the exercises are contrived and shallow. Despite the value of this contact, the likelihood of a deeper and more intense experience is compromised by the intrusion of the media and the class formalities. The greatest danger stems from the potential that students might think they really understand another culture because they have interacted well in this constrained situation. If we do use these teaching techniques, then we need to work carefully to overcome this potential hazard to intercultural effectiveness.

Growing out of the tendency to oversimplification is a threat to one of the major goals of education in intercultural communication. Reliance on technology can lead one to involvement with technology for its own sake. Not only will this infatuation confound our progress in intercultural communication, but it will also compromise another major reason for the study of intercultural relations, namely, its service as a voyage of self-discovery for the student. Just as the US Peace Corps may help other countries deal more effectively with certain real problems, the primary mission of the Peace Corps is not so much to help others, but to use this service opportunity to help the youth of our own country develop a better sensitivity to the world and to increase their level of cosmopolitanism. Similarly, coursework in intercultural communication should also be a journey of self discovery in that students learn about interaction with other cultures in order to learn more about themselves and their own coping behavior regardless of cultural context. Distractions by the media may compromise this critical goal of cultural self-discovery.

Insidious Problems

Much less obvious is what Professor Helen Harrington has called the "essence of technology" or what is happening to us and our students through the subtle use of technology (1993). In her discussion of this essence, Harrington addressed the "illusion of technological neutrality," and explained how nothing so socially pervasive is neutral and how educators must be especially sensitive to the implications of our pedagogical techniques. Among the possible effects are the ways technology can create a counterproductive orientation toward people and simultaneously distract us away from any realization of these consequences.

For example, technology invites a very functional and manipulative perspective. Especially with mediated interpersonal communication, one resolution of problems is simply to turn off the equipment, an option unavailable in the real world. Beyond this illustration, we should note that the mechanistic dimensions of technology invite further a manipulative sense of control over the variables involved, and this subtly developed orientation works counter to the genuine needs of sympathy and empathy which intercultural effectiveness entails. Finally, the real constraints of time and money on the use of technology also invite a strongly functional orientation. Even though these constraints may be minimized, they have become through our socialization somewhat engrained in our behavior and expectations.

When we examine closely the realities of intercultural communication, the experience is clearly dynamic, can only be grasped holistically, and is a very humane activity. In one way or another, each of these essential characteristics is compromised by technology. No matter how many permutations our machines may predict, the potential irrationality of human behavior and the infinite combination of behavioral possibilities can not be captured. Were these purely human activities codifiable, robotics would be much further along than it is. As anyone from an individualistic culture can attest, dealing with someone from a collectivistic culture absolutely requires a holistic conceptualization of their behavior. Technology can provide us a slice of reality, but it can only assist us in capturing the many ingredients. Perhaps most important, technology can never integrate the personal touches, the nuances so critical to understanding the behavior of another person.

Problems with Intercultural Communication Concepts

As a final extension of the preceding discussion, several intercultural communication concepts are unusually difficult to address through technology. Some dimensions of culture fatigue and shock can surface through the use of technology, but the visceral aspects of symbolic disorientation and the individual reactions are lost in the illusion of understanding. Similarly, uncertainty and anxiety can be addressed through technology, but the intensity, the confusion, and the individualized adjustments are here again lost.

A subject which is difficult to address through any techniques is the synchronization of verbal and non-verbal behavior. Whereas technology may help identify aspects, it is inadequate. Closely related to the questions about dynamic, holistic, and humane dimensions of intercultural communication, technology also has trouble helping students to approach the aesthetic harmony and balance of another culture. Although technologically enhanced learning can provide a taste of these concepts, the danger of oversimplification and deception is a central problem.

As anyone who works with intercultural relations can attest, effective intercultural communication is hard work. It requires a constant reception, digestion, and effective utilization of huge amounts of information as we struggle to render explicit those innumerable "taken-for-granteds" of our daily existence, to decipher those qualities in another culture, and to adjust the two systems into a workable milieu. Success requires continual sensitivity and diligence as one functionally learns another culture. To succeed in the long haul will certainly require more than the immediate gratification of technology. Whether we are the student or the teacher, we must wrestle with the real complexities which technology often insidiously conceals.

As a teacher who is willing to use whatever works, I am strongly encouraged by the persuasive allure of current technology and do make frequent use of the possibilities. But I remain concerned with the less obvious pitfalls involved with more extensive dependence on technology. To conclude this section, I would like to provide some statements by three others who share these concerns. In her fascinating discussion of "Networlds: Networks As Social Space," Professor Linda Harasim raised two very penetrating questions: "How does the mediation of computer networks affect human interaction and communication? What are the salient properties of the technology and how do they impact on the communication?"

(1993). Later in her discussion of these questions, she ventured a partial answer: "Global networks enrich our experience and knowledge options but also introduce new and complex issues. Cultural, linguistic, and political factors in global conversations can confound our ability to establish the meaningfulness of the discourse. Place-independence challenges many habits and customs of interpersonal and group communication" (Harasim, 1993). Consistent with her position, I seriously question the uncritical acceptance and utilization of technology for it may deceive more than enlighten us.

In a similar, yet more cynical, vein we all need to be skeptical about the brash claims currently made for technology. As Mander and Harrington remind us:

Since most of what we are told about new technology comes from its proponents, be deeply skeptical of all claims. Assume all technology "guilty until proven innocent."

Eschew the idea that technology is neutral or "value free."

Every technology has inherent and identifiable social, political, and environmental consequences.

In thinking about technology within the present climate of technological worship, emphasize the negative. This brings balance. Negative is positive (Mander, 1991).

In her struggle with the implications of technology for her students and courses, Harrington prudently concludes, ". . . we may not know what we have lost until it is too late" (1993). For those of us working with intercultural communication the dangers may be profound, because effective intercultural relations requires personal contact, interaction with people of diverse cultures, and the preservation, as well as the overcoming, of differences. Technological interpositions can open prospects, may energize our students, and may enhance the prospects for learning, but, regardless of the attractive potential, technology can not supplant the dynamic, holistic, humane personal contact.

The Centrality of Ethnic Relations[3]

Even a casual reader of any major newspaper or news magazine encounters a barrage of ethnic strife from throughout the world, as almost every continent is afflicted with these problems, and few nations enjoy ethnic peace and tranquility. For most of my professional career I have struggled both inside and outside of the classroom with these concerns. In retrospect, however, I must confess that I often escaped direct engagement of these serious problems by treating my subject abstractly or digging ever more deeply into "cleaner" research. Occasionally students would press or push me into the perplexing world of ethnic

---

3 An earlier version of this section appeared in Hill, L. B. (1997). Ethnic relations and the decline of civility. Intercultural Communication Studies, 6 (2), 1-11.

discord, but even then I tried to keep my distance. Motivated by the ravages of ethnic strife at home and abroad, I have begun within the last decade or so to alter my university courses to wrestle with the realities of disintegrating social life around our world. Because of the personal significance of this message to me and because of its potential for others, I would like initially to identify a catalyzing and precipitating factor which strongly motivated my present course of action, and then provide an approach to culture that may better assist our analysis of ethnic problems. From these points of departure, I will introduce a position about the relevance of civility and what we can do to better our world on the basis of our skills, knowledge, and limited opportunities. Most importantly, and perhaps the primary purpose of this section is that I want everyone to develop an enhanced commitment to action; that is to say, I want us to realize that the vision of IAICS is to transcend limitations and to utilize what we know to make our world better for all groups whatever the basis of their differences.

Have you ever noticed the parallel between the chemical processes stimulated by a catalyst and the operations of our mind? We may have many ideas or chemicals floating around, and then something catalyzes intense activity. Such was my state of mind during the spring months of 1996 when Professor Hoffer gently nudged me to specify a title for an upcoming presidential address for IAICS. I drew upon some recent conversations about ethnic problems and our ineptitude at talking about them. So, I tossed him a title and thought that I would simply reflect on it for a while, gathering information from diverse sources as I formulated my position. And then, from a most unlikely source, a catalyst fell into my placid thoughts and energized them with tumultuous intensity. This chemical reaction so stirred my very person that it became the precipitating cause of my present course of action. Let me describe that catalyst for you.

In addition to national and international communication organizations, the USA has four regional associations dedicated to the study of human communication, with each providing an annual convention, a quarterly journal, and several other services. My home state of Texas is aligned with the Southern States Communication Association. With my membership, I receive the Southern Communication Journal. Summer, 1996, was the final issue for Editor Andrew, King of Louisiana State University. In his last issue he provided a short editorial entitled "The Summing Up" (p. 363). Rarely do I read such notes, but fate provided me a few odd minutes before an appointment, and his title caught my eye for no other reason than retiring editors often conclude their tenure with many lessons learned.

King's comments shocked my perennial, yet complacent, optimism. "As I leave my editorship," he wrote, "my most vivid impression of our field's scholarship is of a somber humanism unfamiliarly mixed with nihilism. Perhaps it is only the fin de siècle sense of exhaustion, but the bulk of the manuscripts brought me to the margin of despair." To explain this emotional reaction, he identified two dominant characteristics of the submissions: "The first is that society achieves cohesion through victimage. Many articles featured the serial mugging of groups as the flywheel of social mobilization. Their point was that if Brutus could not destroy others he would destroy himself." The second characteristic was "the necessity and the impossibility of constructing new social visions. The common argument: our contemporary crisis of meaning demands the production and destruction of ideologies at an ever increasing rate. The weaker our social text, the more robust social analysis becomes." He concluded with an ominous warning from the German philosopher Spengler: "There is the dark moment when all concentric forces become eccentric and the dance macabre begins."

Because of their relevance, my reactions to King's editorial deserve a short chronicle. Initially I felt like one of the witches from Shakespeare's Macbeth as I stood before a cauldron of mixed ingredients stirring up some potential evil for my adversaries. Vicariously experiencing King's pain, I lashed out in my thoughts at the deconstructionists who had torn the text from our lives, rendering nothing permanent or sacred except the processes of interpretation. I wanted to thrash the scholars who had made unbridled relativism the ultimate rationalization for "do your own thing" and "anything goes." My critical acuity, as well as my blood pressure, reached a peak as I stirred, and stirred, and stirred my intolerant and unholy ideas. After a few days of this contemplative bitterness, I paused one morning while shaving. In a fleeting moment I perceived the social value of mirrors: the reflection permits us, if we open our eyes widely enough, to see ourselves as others see us. Just as I was looking to others for the causes of our social failures, I had neglected to see how others could similarly place me in this chain of blame. In what ways, I mused, am I in my own modest ways responsible for the disruption, if not destruction, of our social fabric?

The more I pondered my role, the clearer my vision became. With the world struggling with ethnic strife, I wanted to avoid the issues or at least avoid studying or writing about them from the standpoint of my scholarly expertise. I was so captured by a sense of political correctness and cultural sensitivity that I was unable to speak out, thus leaving the forum open to the extremists who never seem to suffer such reticence. With this frustration and momentum, I approached my topic with renewed vigor and an unanticipated eagerness. Even though my topic originated with dim light and little heat, my revitalized interpretation increased the light and heat, resulting in greater clarity and surging passion. With renewed energy, I broached the problem of ethnic discord. Armed only with the tools of scholarship, I launched into the fray.

Culture and Ethnic Relations

As scholars and many other problem solvers tend to do, I started at the most basic level by listing what I can safely assume about my subject: (1) Poor ethnic relations comprise a serious social problem throughout the world. (2) These problems seem to emerge from diverse causes and within widely different contexts. (3) People who address ethnic problems continually identify cultural variables at work, and some extend these problems to panoramic proportions. For example, American political scientist Samuel Huntington (1996) and his disciples argue that conflict among cultural diasporas is rapidly replacing the cold war and its conflict between superpowers as the context for future international relations. (4) Virtually every writer acknowledges more or less that language and communication are variously woven into ethnic conflicts. (5) As a professed expert in language and human communication, with special concern for intercultural communication, I should be able to help with these problems.

From these basic assumptions and observations, I asked, where can I turn? In other places I have written about what it means to assume an intercultural communication perspective toward a subject (1997), but some pieces of the puzzle are still missing. Even with the caveats, my intercultural perspective and inclinations compelled me to examine the cultural dimensions of these social problems more carefully and then to use those insights to help me better conceptualize ethnic discord. This rather personal series of steps have led me to revisit my conception of culture.

Like the notion of meaning, the concept of culture is pervasive and defined variously to fit nearly any and all circumstances. In fact, many scholars have abandoned both concepts as too expansive for theoretical use. I continue to use these two concepts and would draw on an insightful approach to meaning by American philosopher May Brodbeck for a more useful conceptualization of culture (1968, pp. 58-78). In her analysis Brodbeck differentiated levels or categories of meaning by a subscript with $meaning_1$ indicating the object or idea referenced, $meaning_2$ identifying significance or a lawful connection of one term to another, $meaning_3$ referring to intentional meaning, and $meaning_4$ signifying psychological meaning. Without digging into her distinctions, suffice it to say that she used these variations to facilitate use of the concept meaning in the development of theories and discussions about science, and to make far clearer exactly what she was specifying in her subsequent arguments. On a parallel with this line of analysis, I recommend that we differentiate levels of culture which may, in turn, enhance our efforts to conceptualize the problems of ethnic relations.

For many years I have recited to students my definition of culture as a three-part process of (1) knowing and behaving in a manner acceptable to persons who are members of the culture; (2) developing the semantic framework to facilitate appropriate knowledge and behavior, and (3) transmitting and/or perpetuating this knowledge, framework, and behavior. This abstract, behaviorally oriented, cognitive definition has provided a useful point of departure for my students of intercultural communication. Conveniently, I chose to omit "haute couture" and artifactual remains of culture as the business of others who are less concerned with the vicissitudes of culture in the functional, daily ways of life. I was also somewhat aloof from those who would merely list the many ingredients of culture, such as attitudes, values, beliefs, myths, folklore, and many others. My process orientation about culture meshed neatly with my concern for communication processes, and, in turn, permitted me to evade the content of culture. Addressing ethnic relations, however, forced me to confront both the processes and substance of culture, and especially the interrelationship of process and substance. My definition, therefore, needed expanded re-conceptualization, and Brodbeck's approach to meaning suggested a viable way.

As I have read about ethnic conflicts during the last few years, three prominent features of the commentaries have struck me: First, the underlying causes of the problems are varied, but seem to fall into general categories of economic, political, and religious value differences. Poverty, powerlessness, and spiritual deprivation are regular features of such analyses. Second, the writers regularly comment on the language and communication activities of the participants. Whether the varied expressions of position, the latest caption for their cause, or the stages of negotiations, the interactions of the different groups are variously discussed. Third, diagnoses usually address the clash among various dispositions and prejudices growing out of either the values or the interactions. Differences of attitudes, beliefs, misattributions or stereotypes often become the mediating variables between the value differences and actual behaviors. Based on these realistic commentaries, I was led to a three-part conception of culture similar in some ways to Brodbeck's approach to meaning, rather than to my convenient process orientation which seems to capture only a portion of the total concept.

This line of reasoning generated a three dimensional model. Culture with a subscript v (C_v) constitutes the first dimension and embraces core values. The second dimension is culture with a subscript p (C_p) which embraces the mediating predispositions, such as attitudes, beliefs, and stereotypes. The third dimension offers the behavioral operationalizations; here we have culture with a subscript o (C_o), the space where language and communication interface with other aspects of culture most directly. To apprehend this three dimensional model, consider another icon in my life, the golf ball with its core, the surrounding rubber bands, and its cover. Just as golf balls have evolved, so too has our conception of culture evolved in that the core, its surrounding substance, and cover have become more unified into a single ball with far greater dynamics than prior versions.

Like most models, this one can help us analyze problems with the dynamic processes it embraces: Ethnic strife usually emerges from a history of suppression and unequal treatment by one or more groups. If everyone had equivalent resources, power, and spiritual freedom, then I suspect that we could eliminate ethnic strife. But such a circumstance is only a twinkle in the idealist's eye, and we will probably never achieve such equality on earth. Thus the economic, political, and religious causes will remain deeply centered in ethnic conflicts. Because most people acknowledge a more realistic world, the problems shift to the second dimension where value-rooted predispositions displace and complicate the lack of capital, power, and spirituality. Instead of simply asking for more assets, ethnic minorities make impassioned statements of their predispositions until they weave a fabric of injustice which they wear on appropriate occasions. Language and communication enable them to form these perceptions into tangible artifacts with a greater sense of permanence and illusory security until their vision is blurred and distorted. Thus we can use this model to generate questions about all three dimensions and possibly sort out the nature of an ethnic problem and directions for its resolution.

As a student of intercultural communication, my use of this model will emphasize rhetorical analysis, broadly defined as the systematic study of functional symbolic behavior. Within this methodological framework are many thoughtful procedures for the study of language and communication, and in one way or another most of the membership of IAICS conducts rhetorical analysis. More of us simply need to study the discourse of ethnic groups and the groups they engage, sort out the problems of basic cultural values (Cv), relate these problems to the predispositional matrix (Cp), and then study how ethnic groups, other co-cultures, and the overculture tactically and strategically pursue their goals (Co). In this fashion we can potentially identify the salient aspects of each dimension of the problem, and the enhanced conception of culture will keep us continually aware that all of the pieces ultimately integrate. This approach should enable us to present and examine the social fabric objectively, locate the agreements and disagreements, and build a diagnosis and prognosis accordingly. If this approach works as expected, the dialogue about the problem should improve. Unfortunately, no groups really enjoy the social value of mirrors and often resent the careful examination of their actions. In fact, ethnic groups are sometimes so engrossed with an immediate goal that they can not see what they themselves are doing to thwart their long-term efforts. Our work with language and communication can provide a basis for clearer reflection and possibly more thoughtful dialogue.

We may lack the power to rectify problems in the cultural dimension of core values or Cv. We can, however, use language to aid with values clarification, and through our rhetorical analysis we can locate the motivational despair of social inequities. We may define the complaints, weigh their intensity, and determine their level of justification. For this dimension, I suggest four general patterns of value relations: (1) Convergence of values of different groups can lead to the disappearance of conflict and greater homogeneity. (2) Parallel development of differing values can stabilize differences with reasoned agreement to disagree, but with respect for the equity of positions. (3) Divergence of values can result in greater misunderstanding and lessened cooperation through increased separation and segregation. And (4) the denunciation of values of one group by another can deny the opportunity for resolution, contradict reason, and create revolting circumstances. Values clarification through rhetorical analysis of Cv can help us identify the relationship among sets representing different groups, and thus generate a basis for more reasonable approaches to the problems.

The next layer or dimension of ethnic problems concerns Cp, the collective predispositions of one group about other groups. If our initial values clarification at level Cv does not uncover sufficient motivational force for the strife, then predispositions may represent hardened categorizations which do not permit reasonable flexibility. At this level, rhetorical analysis will consider stereotypes of the groups and break them down through careful language analysis. How, for example, does the estranged group label and categorize the other ethnic groups, cocultures, and/or overculture? How are these labels combined or configured to create myths and storylines about their intergroup relations? Do these rhetorical categorizations generate subversive themes and chains of destructive characterizations? Are they susceptible to legitimate consideration or do they instantly enflame opposition? Answers to these questions may provide some control over abusive predispositions if we can bring them up for public scrutiny and objective consideration. If we are unable to subject them to legitimate scrutiny, then they will function as subversive stereotypes inimical to reasonable consideration and to improvements in intercultural relations. The central problem at this level is defensive unwillingness to examine in public our predispositions about other groups of people. More open consideration is prerequisite for checking the counterproductive outcomes of this dimension of culture.

The third and most encompassing dimension of culture is the behavioral operationalization or Co. Here the collective behaviors of the ethnic groups are formed into tactics and strategies for pursuit of their goals and objectives. If our values clarification is thorough, it should lead to clear coordination of goals and strategy. If the values analysis is ambiguous or vague, then the goals may float without a definite tethering point, or, worse yet, vary with the faddishness of more fickle predispositions. The latter scenario will result in tactics confused with strategies and no clear strategic development. In many ways this becomes a volatile, dangerous combination that is conducive to ready manipulation by articulate participants who for whatever reason thrive and often survive on confrontation. The Co level is most observable and any rhetorical analysis can piece together the patterns of action, but without the underlying causes from Cv and Cp, the determination of strategic possibilities is weakened. Whatever anyone does to correct the situation exclusively at the Co level will likely fail, but through this analysis the grounds for addressing problems at Cv or Cp can develop. What our scholarship must achieve is realistic depiction of these rhetorical behaviors and the opportunity to break down the conflict into manageable proportions.

Throughout this profile of cultural analysis emerges a central argument: culture, language, and/or communication are rarely the cause of ethnic problems. They are all, however, concomitant manifestations of human difficulty, and, as such, become a vital source of data for the analysis of these problems. Just as they are not a primary cause of ethnic conflict, they are also not a solution, but because of their concomitance they become essential propaedeutics for problem solution. In other words, our rhetorical analysis can help us describe and analyze ethnic problems and create a perspective which will permit us to contribute toward the healing of this social disease. We should never, however, imagine that our approach is the answer. We can best serve to elucidate and frame the problems for those people with greater social power to resolve them. Our greatest value may well center on identification of the dimensions of the problems and the interrelationships among the various levels of rhetorical behaviors. To achieve our potential contribution, we must develop ways to call more attention to our analyses.

Ethnic Relations and Civility

During a presentation at Trinity University (2/21/97), David Maybury-Lewis, the prominent American anthropologist and internationally renowned cultural activist, accented the importance of addressing ethnic relations. "If ethnicity is not accommodated in modern society," he argued, "it will poison it." Drawing upon his personal experiences, he noted the "growing tendency to recognize ethnic legitimacy" as "countries throughout Latin America are classifying themselves as pluri-ethnic rather than mestizo" and governments are shifting away from policies of killing off these ethnic groups through genocide or total assimilation to programs of recognition and inclusion. This shift, he explained, seems based on the realization that "ethnic conflict does not come from expression of ethnicity, but rather from the suppression of ethnicity."

In other parts of the world, ethnicity is not only recognized, but variously celebrated. Yet, even at this more positive end of the continuum of ethnic viability, relations among ethnic groups and with the dominant over-culture are problematic. In these situations, such as the USA now represents, ethnicity has become more than a matter of recognition and respect for one's diversity. It has become a political instrument for social engineering as groups employ their ethnicity to secure whatever they may from the existing power structure. Unfortunately, in the process of this legitimate employment of ethnic identity our ineptitude at discussing the issues and rhetoric of this ethnic gamesmanship is diminishing the constructive vitality of ethnic diversity and exacerbating the problems of ethnic conflict (Hill & Lujan, 1983 and 1984). Somewhere between the genocidal policies toward ethnic groups and the rampant abuse of ethnicity lies a more reasonable approach to the positive development of ethnic identity and relationships among all groups. Creating an environment where we may achieve such balance is where civility and our potential intervene.

In another speech at Trinity University, former US Senator Bill Bradley examined what he perceived as the primary political issues facing our nation (3/4/97). Among these was our problem with ethnic relations. He offered a very simple solution, or at least a first step toward solution of this problem: "We've got to talk to each other," he observed, and then he extended this simple idea into a number of challenges. He made quite clear that the USA, as the remaining superpower on the stage of global politics, can not lead the world without moral quality; so, we must treat each other equitably and fairly and thus set a model for other countries. How can we hope to guide the world, I was stimulated to wonder, when we are so tongue-tied in dealing with our own circumstances? As some of you probably know, the US congress has actually held retreats to address the decline of civility in the operation of our own government. They seemed to recognize that restoration of civility was a first step in overcoming the gridlock of ineptitude undermining reasoned discourse about our national policies and agenda.

As scholars and teachers we are in positions to advance the cause of civility which may permit us to open perspectives about ethnic problems and to create opportunities for their resolution. To realize this prospect requires us to examine the concept of civility, what it entails, how we can nurture it, and how on the basis of its revitalization we can advance our rhetorical/cultural approach to ethnic discord. For help with this task, and quite predictably, I turned to a colleague for help. Colin Wells, a distinguished British professor of Classical Studies, guided me through the historical evolution of the Latin concept of civility: In his biography of the Emperor Claudius, Seutonious noted how being restrained and unassuming (civilis) Claudius refused the title of Emperor; that is, he refused to be so-called, preferring to be called first citizen (princeps). The Oxford Latin Dictionary quotes this passage and translates civilis here as "suitable to a private citizen, unassuming, unpretentious." Focusing on this idea of civilis princeps, British classicist Andrew Wallace-Hadrihl discusses civilitas or civility, and defines the concept as "the conduct of a citizen among citizens" or the politeness and consideration due to one's social equals (1982). He further noted that "... it is not until the second century A.D. that an abstract noun is formed: the ideal can be described as civilitas" (p. 43). From this historical vantage point, we can understand how civility came to imply a set of behaviors which make a leader good or bad in relation to the people governed.

On the contemporary scene, we understand the concept to embrace these two ancient dimensions, but it has become generalized beyond the behavior of emperors to include the populace as well. On the one hand, the concept refers to the performance of our duties as citizens, and, on the other hand, to an ethical code of behavior appropriate to good citizenship. Thus civility refers to our assumption of citizenship and behaving toward each other in a civil manner which translates as affable, courteous, differential, gracious, polite, and respectful. If we further translate these synonyms for civil behavior, they collectively imply avoidance of rudeness toward others, the observance of social requirements, and a positive, dignified, sincere, and thoughtful consideration of others (Random House Dictionary). As we incorporate these qualities into codes of habituated behavior, we refer to civilized people forming themselves into civilizations. Obviously, civility is closely related to the reasonable consideration of problems between groups of people.

Because civility is expressed symbolically, our rhetorical analyses can become indispensable for the operationalization of guidelines. Simply reflect on the expanding literature about the idea of "face" and how people in different cultures engage in face-saving interactions that create more civil situations for the resolution of personal concerns. What we need to do with this example and hundreds of others which come from our research is to teach our students the relevance of such principles for effective citizenship and the use of these guidelines in the actual treatment of ethnic problems. At no time in our history is this task more compelling; we must prepare our students for lives of civility and give them the instruments of respect, rather than the weapons of destruction which come from the neglect of civility. To meet this challenge would only require modest alterations of our scholarship and teaching strategies. We can easily shift our attention to the broader implications of our work for enhanced intercultural communication and more cooperative ethnic relations.

When I began research on the topic of this section, I had a genuine, but somewhat modest, commitment to this subject. The despair reflected in an editor's postscript catalyzed my behavior well beyond what I expected to do on this occasion. For the past few months I have been unable to extricate myself from this topic. I sincerely hope that my comments will serve to catalyze each of you to transcend the boundaries among our disciplines and nations and join in the vision of IAICS to use our skills and knowledge to make our world a better place for all groups of people. What began for me as a sojourn into an interesting subject has passed the point of no return. My work with intercultural communication has attained a new focus which will help my students and me to become more civilized in a world of interdependent people.

As we enter a new century on Western calendars and reflect on the lessons learned from the past, I hope that we will see the importance of pulling together the best of the East and West in a broader remedy for the diseases of social disintegration. Among the possibilities are two prominent schools of thought. From the West and our individualistic orientation come the concepts of dialogue and self worth. From the East and their collectivistic orientation come the concepts of social order and community. If we can integrate these two orientations, we will have the basis for a new millennium created from the strengths of our different orientations. One of the greatest pitfalls along this integrative path will be ethnic instability. If we can use our potential for rhetorical analysis, perhaps we can enhance our leadership in describing the problems more usefully and creating approaches which foster reasoned consideration of the confounding differences. My suggestions may not be the answer, but they may stimulate some of you or some of your students to improve on these ideas and determine ways to enhance our role in the analysis and resolution of these problems. Unlike the manuscripts of the editor I mentioned, I have a vision of a better future, a vision that transcends the boundaries of our disciplines and nations and that includes our collective scholarship in making this a better world. Will you join IAICS and me in this challenge?

Conclusion

I was honored by the invitation to contribute to this book. Having spent my entire professional career in the study and application of intercultural, international, and development communication, I sincerely believe that I have something valuable to contribute for those who hold the future in their hands. As the preceding sections indicate, we have three major challenges that we must ultimately address: (1) We need to pull together the widely varied groups of people who work in these areas and concentrate on better systemization of our collective work. With this improved synergy, we can generate a much more powerful influence. (2) We need to be cautious about excessive commitment to technology, rather than personal interaction, as we deal with the "people problems" of our world. We should never neglect the downside of any technology in human affairs. (3) Finally, we need to focus our attention on ways to resolve the most threatening social disease we have ever confronted. As our world grows in population and technology brings us closer together, we must be constantly vigilant about the threats of poor ethnic relations. We can valuably contribute to the dialogue about these problems and the results of improved dialogue may bring our collective work into better focus. Overall, better synergy of our efforts will lead to greater potential for the use of our ideas and research in coping with the serious problems that confront our world.

References

Bassett, D. & Jackson, L. (1994). Applying the model to a variety of adult learning situations. In L. Jackson & R. Caffarella, (Eds.), *Experiential learning: A new approach. New directions for adult and continuing education, No. 62*, summer. San Francisco, CA: Jossey-Bass.

Bradley, B. (3/4/97). *America: the path ahead.* Speech delivered at Trinity University, San Antonio TX.

Brodbeck, M. (1968). Meaning and action. In M. Brodbeck, (Ed.), *Readings in the philosophy of the social sciences* (pp. 58-79). London, England: Collier-Macmillan.

Caffarella, R. & Barnett, B. (1994). Characteristics of adult learners and foundations of experiential learning. In L. Jackson & R. Caffarella, (Eds.), *Experiential learning: A new approach. New directions for adult and continuing education, No. 62,* summer. San Francisco, CA: Jossey-Bass.

Harasim, L. M. (1993). *Global networks: Computers and international communication.* Cambridge, MA: MIT Press.

Harasim, L. M. (1993). Networlds: Networks as social space. In L. M. Harasim, (Ed.), *Global networks: Computers and international communication.* Cambridge, MA: MIT Press.

Harrington, H. L. (1993). The essence of technology and the education of teachers. *Journal of Teacher Education, 44* (1), 5-15.

Hill, L. B., Long L., & Cupach, W. (1997). Aging and the Elders from a cross-cultural communication perspective. In Hana S. Noor Al-Deen, (Ed.), *Cross- Cultural communication and aging in America* (pp. 5-22). Hillsdale, NJ: Erlbaum.

Hill, L. B. & Lujan, P. (1983). The Mississippi choctaw: A case study of intercultural games. *American Indian Culture and Research Journal, 7,* 29-42.

Hill, L. B. & Lujan, P. (1984). Symbolicity among Native Americans. *Journal of Thought, 19* (3), 109-121.

Honna, N. & Hoffer, B. L. (2003). L. Brooks Hill — A professional overview. *Intercultural Communication Studies, 12* (2), 181-185.

Huntington, S. (1996). *The clash of civilizations and the remaking of world order.* Old Tapper, NJ: Simon and Schuster.

Jackson, L. & Caffarella, R. (1994). *Experiential learning: A new approach. New directions for adult and continuing education, No, 62,* summer. San Francisco, CA: Jossey-Bass.

Jackson, L. & MacIsaac, D. (1994). Introduction to a new approach to experiential learning. In L. Jackson & R. Caffarella, (Eds.), *Experiential learning. A new approach. New directions for adult and continuing education, No. 62,* summer. San Francisco, CA: Jossey-Bass.

Javidi, M. & Hill, L. B. (1987). International students and intercultural communication instruction. *Journal of Thought, 22* (4).

King, A. (1996). The summing up. *The Southern Communication Journal, 41,* 363.

Kolb, D. (1984). *Experiential learning: Experience as the source of learning and development.* Englewood Cliffs, NJ: Prentice Hall.

Lee, P. & Caffarella, R. (1994). Methods and techniques for engaging learners in experiential learning activities. In L. Jackson and R. Caffarella, (Eds.), *Experiential learning: A new approach. New directions for adult and Continuing education, No. 62,* summer. San Francisco, CA: Jossey-Bass.

Leeds-Hurwitz, W. (1990). Notes in the history of intercultural communication:

The foreign service institute and the mandate for intercultural training. *The Quarterly Journal of Speech, 76*, 262-281.

Lewis, L. & Williams, C. (1994). Experiential learning: Past and present. In L. Jackson & R. Caffarella, (Eds.), *Experiential learning: A new approach. New directions for adult and continuing education, No. 62*, summer. San Francisco, CA: Jossey-Bass.

MacIsaac, D. & Jackson, L. (1994). Assessment processes and outcomes: Portfolio construction. In L. Jackson & R. Caffarella, (Eds.), *Experiential learning: A new approach. New directions for adult and continuing education, No. 62*, summer. San Francisco, CA: Jossey-Bass.

Mander, J. (1991). *In the absence of the sacred: The failure of technology and the survival of the Indian nations. San Francisco*, CA: Sierra Club Books.

Maybury-Lewis, D. (2/21/1997). *Indigenous peoples and the 21st Century*. Speech delivered at Trinity University, San Antonio TX.

Random house Dictionary. (1967). "Civility," "Civil," "Civilized," and "Civilization." *The Random House Dictionary of the English Language* (The Unabridged Edition). New York, NY: Random House.

Wallace-Hadrill, A. (1982). Civilis princeps: Between citizen and king. *Journal of Roman Studies, 72*, 32-48.

Wishnietsky, D. (1994). *Assessing the role of technology in education.* Bloomington, IN: Phi Delta Kappa.

Theorizing about intercultural communication: Dynamic semiotic and memetic approaches to intercultural communication

Gu Jiazu   Nanjing Normal University

Abstract

The author fully supports Gudykunst's view concerning theorizing about intercultural communication and ventures that the present approaches to intercultural communication seem inadequate. The author, therefore, puts forward ways and means to intercultural communication, of which semiotic and memtic approaches prove to be more theoretically acceptable.

Theorizing About Intercultural Communication

As pointed out by Gudykunst in his Theorizing About Intercultural Communication (2005), Theorizing about communication and culture has made tremendous progress in the last 20 years. Such theorizing about intercultural communication was evidenced particularly by the publication of Communicating With Strangers (1997) by William Gudykunst and Young Yun Kim, which markedly changed the tradition of intercultural communication and highlighted the importance of theorizing in intercultural communication scholarship. In spite of the general progress in the past 20 years in theorizing about intercultural communication so far as this discipline is concerned, we have to admit that we are confronted with lots of problems to be solved.

Problems with Theorizing about Intercultural Communication
Imbalance in the Production of Indigenous Theories

The past 20 years' intercultural communication scholarship has witnessed the striking imbalance in the production of indigenous theories. Unfortunately, we have found that " the vast majority of the theories were born in the United States" (Gudykunst, 2005, p. 25), which was attributed by Gudykunst to the fact that "developing theories is not emphasized in many cultures" (p.25). It is particularly true in a culture like ours in which people generally appeal to history, tradition and authority and seldom think of theorizing about a discipline such as intercultural communication. "There is , nevertheless, a need for indigenous theories developed by scholars outside the United States"(Gudykust, 2005, p. 25). It is extremely important for scholars in our culture to speed up the process of producing theories with our own cultural characteristics, making indigenous theories in its true sense of the word.

The Lack of New Approaches to Theorizing about Intercultural Communication

While acknowledging the achievement of the past intercultural communication scholarship, I venture to say that the past scholarship seems to be largely limited to sociological, anthropo-linguistic, psychological, socio-psychological, and philosophical approaches which I admit, are useful and effective, particularly necessary in its initial period of development. However, after the lapse of about 50 years ever since the publication of *Silent Language* by Edward Hall in 1959, these approaches do not seem adequate in meeting the needs of the discipline's further development. Moreover, a lot of such approaches seem static, rather than dynamic. It is, therefore, imperative that we should resort to some other disciplines such as semiotics and memetics .

Dynamic Semiotic Approach to Intercultural Communication

Intercultural communication, in its final analysis, is a semiotic activity, dealing with sign exchanges through sign transmissions in a much more complicated dynamic manner than interpersonal communication in an intraculure. Many semiotic theories given by classic semoitians or contemporary semiotic scholars can explain intercultural communication phenomena better than those borrowed from other disciplines, at least more theoretically acceptable.

The Essence of Dynamic Semiotics

Dynamic semiotics advocates that everything changes. With the theories about the division between synchronic and diachronic linguistics, the division between variability and invariability of the sign, and the division between static and evolutionary linguistics (Saussure, 2001, pp.81,74,76) and Peirce's theory that every thought is a sign and life is a train of thought (Peirce,5.313-314), Jakobson's theory about every piece of information being a sign, and Bakhtin's theory about the whole system of ideology being formed by signs. In short, signs are dynamic and signs are living and changing all the time.

Exemplification: Dynamic Semiotic Analysis of Stereotypes in Intercultural Communication

As mentioned above, intercultural communication is a sign transmission movement; it is, therefore, justified to refer to semiotic theory in interpreting intercultural communication phenomena, consequently making intercultural communication theory more adequate. Take, for example, the explanation of stereotypes. Tajfel defines "stereotypes as "certain generalizations reached by individuals" (in Gudykunst,1997, p.113). After introducing various theories about stereotypes by many different scholars and after giving a lot of social and psychological analyses to reducing stereotypes, the author does not seem to be self-confident so far as the reduction of stereotypes is concerned.

Semiotically speaking, as signs are both static and dynamic (or evolutionary), any stereotypes may be true to life for a certain period of time, but we have to remember that, as signs are evolutionary, and they are changing all the time, no generalization can always remain reliable. Likewise, no stereotypes can remain unchanged. Our stereotypes are multidimensional images. Vassiliou et al. (1972) contended that stereotypes vary along six dimensions. Take, for example, the use of "Miss"(小姐) in Chinese, which was regarded as respectable by many in the past, is now on many occasions derogatorily used as "prostitute." However, the use of "Miss" may be acceptable in certain occupations in China, particularly with waitresses in restaurants in certain areas.

The change of stereotypes is, therefore, semiotically inevitable no matter how long it takes and no matter what kind of stereotype it belongs to. This is true with other intercultural communication phenomena. Take for example, the assimilation of cultural concepts. In the previous years, some Chinese young people seemed to accept the Western concept of DINK (double income, no kid) and much of the discussion concerning DINK was heatedly carried on in Chinese media and a lot of Chinese young couples followed the suite. However, things seem to change, a lot of young couples who originally followed DINK for years, have now changed their attitudes and they prefer to have babies now although some others still adhere to their DINK choices.

Memetic Analysis of Intercultural Communication

The rise of Memetics towards the Turn of the Century

The publication of *The Selfish Gene, The Meme Machine, The Selfish Meme*, etc. marked the rise of memetics towards the turn of the century. Memetics analyses from biological point of view how imitation produces memes, and promotes the spreading of information, and the development of human brains through selection, which, in turn, promotes the replication of memes. Consequently, meme transmission causes the formation of culture , cultural evolution and language, forming a triangular relation of brains (providing cognitive and psychological conditions), language and memes (formed by memetic imitation and transmission).

Imitation as the main content of intercultural communication

According to memetic theory, imitation or copying is human specific and humans do it naturally: "We do copy each other all the time and we underestimate what is involved because imitation comes so easily to us. When we copy each other, something, however intangible, is passed on. That something is the meme. And taking a meme's eye view is the foundation of memetics" (Blackmore, 1999, p.52). In the meantime, memetic theory emphasizes the importance of selection in the process of imitation. In other words, humans do not imitate others blindly, their imitation is based on selection and human selection has its own criterion: The anthropologist William Durham claims "that organic and cultural selection work on the same criterion — that is, inclusive fitness — and are complementary" (Blackmore, 1999, p.35).

The law of imitation can be applied in every aspect of human culture and it is particularly applicable to intercultural communication. As a matter of fact, the whole process of intercultural communication is the process of imitation and selection. For example, we can hardly say many intercultural communication phenomena such as the adaptation process of enculturation to assimilation through deculturation and acculturation can be achieved without the memetic process of imitation and selection. On the other hand, from memetic point of view, cultural fitness and adaptation possibility provide the condition to strengthen the transmission of memes, and consequently promote the further development of intercultural communication. Many other phenomena such as anxiety, uncertainty or even conflict one might encounter in intercultural communication can also be accounted by memetic theory either as the process of imitation and selection or the result of such behavior as the feeling of anxiety and uncertainty is very often caused by stereotypes and stereotypes are formed through the spreading of memes, which eventually becomes, in lippman's term, "pictures in our heads" (Gudykunst, 1997, p. 112).

Criteria for Memetic Selection as the Main Psychological Process in Intercultural communication

A. Internal criteria for memetic selection in intercultural communication: A. fidelity; B. fecundity; C. longevity

Memetically, there are three criteria for good quality replicator (meme): fidelity, fecundity, and longevity. "This means that a replicator has to be copied accurately, many copies must be made, and copies must last a long time — although there may be trade-offs between the three (Blackmore, 1999, p. 58). If memetic criteria can be applied everywhere, it should be noted that they are perhaps most applicable to intercultural communication, particularly in the perspective of determining whether intercultural communication is a success or not and in the perspective of measuring the quality of cultural adaptations and assimilation. Take loanwords for example. The formation of loanwords is the outcome of intercultural communication, and they serve as indicators of cultural assimilation and adaptation, and the quality of loanwords must be tested by above-mentioned criteria: fidelity, fecundity, and longevity, This means the loanwords must be true to the original ones in target languages in terms of meaning and pronunciation and they must be used widely and continue to be used for a long period of history. Similarly, the assimilation and adaptation of foreign cultural habits, customs and concepts can be tested by the same memetic criteria.

The above criteria for the quality of memes in intercultural communication are used only from internal point of view, that is, from memes themselves. One nation's good memes, however, may not be assimilated and adapted by others, and on the other hand, one nation's bad memes may not be refused to accept by others although good quality memes in intercultural communication can be in the long run more easily assimilated and adapted by others. In other words, cultural assimilation and adaptation are determined not by internal factors of memes, but also by external factors, that is, human cognitive and emotional preferences.

B. External criteria for memetic selection in intercultural communication: human's cognitive and emotional preference

Different from behaviorist and mentalist schools, memetic theory advocates the unity of memes, language and brain. As to the function of brains, Blackmore makes the following observation:

If a meme can get itself successfully copied it will. One way to do so is to command the resources of someone's brain and make them keep on rehearsing it, so giving that meme a competitive edge over memes that do not get rehearsed. Memes like this are not only more likely to be remembered, but also to be "on your mind" when you next speak to someone else. If we take stories as an example, a story that has great emotional impact, or for any other reason has the effect that you just cannot stop thinking about it, it will go round and round in your head. This will consolidate the memory for that story and will also mean that, since you are thinking about it a lot, you are more likely to pass it on to someone else, who may be similarly affected (Blackmore, 1999, pp. 40-41).

The above passage vividly reveals the importance of human brain in making memetic selection as the use of human brain will surely involve cognitive and emotional factors in many issues of intercultural communication such as adoption of value orientations, individualism or collectivism, ways in interpreting messages and making intercultural transformation, all of which are more or less influenced by human cognitive and emotional preferences. This explains why some memes are copied and some others are rejected in intercultural communication apart from the internal reasons for meme transmission and duplication.

Memetic and Semiotic Criteria for Successful Intercultural Communication

Successful intercultural communication is semantically and mimetically judged by the quality and quantity of foreign memes (foreign material and spiritual signs) stored in native culture as a result of memetic imitation, selection, assimilation and adaptation. In measuring the degree of success in intercultural communication, we should admit that certain signs(memes) are overt, while the majority of signs (memes) indicating the success in intercultural communication are covert. For example, strengthening of friendship and change of concepts as a result of intercultural communication can hardly be statistically measured, yet such activities must have left signs in both material objects and spiritual traces such as loan words in different cultures. The quality and quantity of loan words are often said to be a wind vane indicating the frequency and success of intercultural communication. A marked increase of loan words in Chinese language ever since the beginning of reform in late 1970's, for instance, vividly reveals the rapid growth of intercultural communication between Chinese and foreigners and huge success in it. This increase of loanwords in Chinese, in the meantime, reveals the change of Chinese national mentality towards their openness to the outside world, a sort of change in collective emotion towards foreigners. The success of intercultural communication, therefore, can be semantically and mimetically judged in spite of seemingly difficulties in observation.

Conclusion

If Edward Hall was the founder of intercultural communication studies and William Gudykunst and others are the pioneers in theorizing about intercultural communication, then what is the role of others who are equally interested in the study of intercultural communication? My answer to the question is that we should first of all encourage theorizing about our discipline, without which no one can say intercultural communication is an independent discipline; secondly, in theorizing about our discipline, we should resort to as many other disciplines as possible, including semiotics and memetics.

(Taken from China Media Research, April 2008/Vol.4 No.2, U.S.A.)

References

Blackmore, S.(1999). *The meme machine*. New York: Oxford University Press.
Gudykunst, W. B. (2005). *Theorizing about intercultural communication*. Thousand Oaks:Sage.
Gudykunst,W. B. & Kim,Y. Y.(1997). *Communicating with strangers: An approach to intercultural communication*. New York: The McGraw-Hill Companies, Inc.
Hall, E.T. (1959). *The silent language*. New York: Anchor Books.
Saussure, F.(2001). *Course in general linguistics*. Beijing: Foreign Language Teaching and Research Press.
Vassiliou, V. (1972). Interpersonal contact and stereotyping. In Triandis, H., (Ed.), *The Analysis of Subjective Culture* (pp 89-115). New York: Wiley.

CULTURAL IDENTITY AND INTERCULTURAL COMMUNICATION

The influence of culture and strength of cultural identity on individual values in Japan and the United States

William B. Gudykunst California State University, Fullerton, USA
Tsukasa Nishida Nihon University, Japan

Abstract

Two studies were conducted using data from Japan and the United States to examine the influence of the interaction between culture and strength of cultural identity on individual-level individualistic and collectivistic values. In the first study, culture and strength of cultural identity interacted to influence four values (freedom, pleasure, social recognition, and self-sacrifice). In the second study, culture and strength of cultural identity interacted to influence three values (being independent, having harmony, and accepting traditions). The results suggest that strength of cultural identity must be taken into consideration in order to understand values that members of a culture hold.

Introduction

Values are an important aspect of human behavior. Rokeach (1972) suggests that people have values if they have enduring beliefs "that a specific mode of conduct or end-state of existence is personally or socially preferable to alternative modes of conduct or end-states of existence" (pp. 159-160). Ball-Rokeach, Rokeach, and Grube (1984) argue that values are the central core to individuals' personalities and have a direct effect on behavior. They contend that values serve as the major component of the personality that helps individuals maintain and enhance their self-esteem.

Individuals learn their values through the socialization process. Individuals' behavior is affected by cultural values and the individual values they hold. Cultural values provide broad guidelines about what are acceptable means for achieving end-states in different situations and influence cultural norms and rules. Individual values provide specific guidelines for behavior across situations (Feather, 1990). Feather (1995) demonstrated that the values individuals hold are linked to the valences they attach to different behaviors. Gudykunst, Matsumoto, Ting-Toomey, Nishida, Kim, and Heyman (1996) demonstrated that individual-level values affect communication styles across cultures.

One way to study cultural values is by focusing on cultural individualism-collectivism (I-C). I-C is the major dimension of cultural variability isolated by theorists across disciplines (e.g., Hofstede, 1980; Ito, 1989b; Kluckhohn & Strodtbeck, 1961; Triandis, 1988, 1990, 1995). Schwartz and his associates (e.g., Schwartz, 1992, 1994a, 1994b; Schwartz & Bilsky, 1987, 1990) and other theorists (e.g., Chinese Culture Connection, 1987) have isolated values associated with cultural I-C. The values that are predominant in a culture influence the values that individuals learn, but individual value structures can be different from cultural value structures (see Schwartz, 1992; 1994b).[1]

There are many factors that can influence whether people from individualistic and collectivistic cultures hold individual-level individualistic or collectivistic values. One important factor is whether people identify strongly or weakly with being members of their cultures. People who strongly identify with their culture should hold individual values that are consistent with cultural-level values, while people who do not strongly identify with their culture probably hold some individual values that are inconsistent with cultural-level values.

Two cultures where there are clear differences in cultural-level values based on I-C, and where there are inconsistent results regarding individual-level values are Japan and the United States (Gudykunst & Nishida, 1994). The purpose of this paper is to present data from two studies in the United States and Japan on the extent to which strength of cultural identity interacts with culture to influence the individual-level values people hold.

Individualism-Collectivism and Values

In order to explain individual behavior within and across cultures, it is necessary to understand how I-C operates at the cultural- and individual-levels. In this section, we will overview I-C values at the two levels of analysis.

Cultural Level

Individualistic cultures emphasize the goals of the individual over group goals, while collectivistic cultures stress group goals over individual goals (Triandis, 1988, 1990, 1995). In individualistic cultures, individuals assume responsibility for themselves and their

---

1. Schwartz (1992), for example, points out that power and authority at the cultural level are given priority in collectivistic cultures, but they tend to serve individual interests at the individual level; loyalty and responsibility at the cultural level are given priority in individualistic cultures, but they serve collective interests at the individual level.

immediate family only.² In collectivistic cultures, individuals belong to collectivities or ingroups which look after them in exchange for the individuals' loyalty (Hofstede, 1980). Ingroups are "groups of people about whose welfare one is concerned, with whom one is willing to cooperate without demanding equitable returns, and separation from whom leads to discomfort or even pain" (Triandis, 1988, p. 75). Triandis (1988) contends that ingroups are more important in collectivistic than individualistic cultures. Lebra (1976), for example, points out that collectivism "involves cooperation and solidarity, and the sentimental desire for the warm feeling of ittaikan ("feeling of oneness") with fellow members of one's group" (p. 25) and that this feeling is shared widely in Japan.

Most scholars agree that the United States is an individualistic culture and Japan is a collectivistic culture (see Gudykunst & Nishida, 1994).³ Critiques of the group model of Japanese society (e.g., Befu, 1980a, 1980b), however, suggest that acceptance of this model with its emphasis on harmony and giri (voluntary feelings of obligation) leads scholars to overlook Japanese "personhood" (e.g., concepts such as seishin or jinkaku).⁴ Befu (1980b), for example, argues that seishin deals with "individuals qua individuals." Befu (1980a, 1980b) believes that the group model (collectivism as used here) can explain public matters, but not private matters. This contention is supported by two studies of value orientations in Japan. Caudill and Scarr (1961) and Nishida (1981) found that while collaterality predominates in Japan, the value orientation (collaterality, lineality, individualism) individuals select depends on the specific sphere of life being examined.⁵

Hamaguchi's (1980) research suggests that Japanese working in corporations who were born before World War II clearly are collectivistic (or contextualists to use his term). There appear to be trends for younger Japanese, however, to be more individualistic. Miyanaga

---

2   If there is a conflict between individual values and family values, high individualists probably will follow their own values.
3   While these terms are not heavily value laden in the United States, the translations of both terms are value laden in Japan. Ito (1989b), for example, points out that Japanese scholars do not use the translation of the term collectivism, *zentaishugi*, because it often is used to refer to dictatorial political systems. Rather, they use terms like group oriented (*shudanshugi*; Nakane, 1970), contextualism (*kanjinshugi*; Hamaguchi, 1980), or inter-individualism (*saijinshugi*; Ito, 1989a). Ito (1989b) also points out that the term used for individualism in Japanese, *kojinshugi*, has negative connotations (e.g., selfishness).
4   See Mito (1991), Murakami (1983), and Yamazaki (1990) for recent discussions of Japanese individualism.
5   Caudill and Scarr (1961), for example, found that collaterality predominates in Japan for family/work relations (Kluckhohn & Strodtbeck's, 1961, question R3) and personal property inheritance (R6), while individualism predominates for choice of delegates (R4) and wage work (R5). Nishida (1981) found that collaterality predominated for choice of delegate (R4), bridge building (R1), and wage work (R5), while individualism predominated in family/work relations (R3), property inherence (R6), and land inheritance (R7).

(1991) also points out that there has been a growing individualism among people on the periphery of Japanese culture (e.g., artists, people in the fashion industry, people in small businesses) since the end of the war. She sees this "dropping out of established groups for the purpose of self-realization" as a form of "passive individualism" (p. 4).

Focusing only on the individualistic tendencies in the United States leads scholars to overlook collectivistic aspects of the culture (e.g., Bellah, Madsen, Sullivan, Swidler, & Tipton, 1985; Kluckhohn & Strodtbeck, 1961; Nishida, 1981; Waterman, 1981; Wuthnow, 1991). Kluckhohn and Strodtbeck, for example, point out that while individualism predominates in the United States, collaterality and lineality (two forms of collectivism) also affect behavior. Nishida found that while individualism predominates overall in the United States, the value orientation (individualism, collaterality, lineality) individuals select depends on the specific sphere of life being examined.[6]

Hofstede and Bond (1984) isolated cultural dimensions of values using data from the Rokeach (1973) value survey. They observed a value function consisting of salvation and an exciting life that correlated with Hofstede's (1980) individualism dimension at the cultural level.

Schwartz (1994b) isolated cultural-level values associated with I-C. He suggests that conservatism is related to collectivism. Conservatism is the culture-level value type that focuses on "those values likely to be important in societies based on close-knit harmonious relations, in which the interests of the person are not viewed as distinct from those of the group" (p. 101). Intellectual and affective autonomy are related to individualism. These values are those "likely to be important in societies that view the person as an autonomous entity entitled to pursue his or her individual interests and desires. Two related aspects of autonomy appear to be distinguishable: a more intellectual emphasis on self-direction and a more affective emphasis on stimulation and hedonism" (p. 102). Schwartz's study did not reveal differences between Japan and the United States on conservatism (US=3.90, J=3.87). There was a small difference on affective autonomy in the expected direction (US=3.65, J=3.54), but the difference in affective autonomy was opposite the expected direction (US=4.20, J=4.68).

The Chinese Culture Connection (1987) examined cultural values from a Chinese perspective. In their study of Chinese respondents in 21 cultures, they isolated a social integration factor that correlated with collectivism in Hofstede's (1980) data. This factor included values such as tolerance of others, harmony with others, non-competitiveness, filial piety, respect for tradition, and observation of rites and social rituals. Japan had a

---

6   Nishida (1981) found the same pattern for North Americans as for the Japanese (see previous note).

higher score (4.97) on this dimension than the United States (2.84).

I-C at the cultural level has been used widely to explain cultural differences in different types of behavior (see Triandis, 1990, for a summary). Kashima (1989), however, points out that there are problems with using dimensions of cultural variability to explain individual level behavior. One area where there are problems is the area of developing causal explanations; it is impossible to test causal explanations of behavior based on cultural level explanations (e.g., culture cannot be controlled in an experiment). The second area where there are problems is in mapping individualistic and collectivistic cultures. Hofstede (1980) and the Chinese Culture Connection (1987) present cultural level scores regarding various dimensions of cultural variability, including I-C. When specific samples are collected, however, they do not necessarily correspond with the cultural level scores. To illustrate, when college students are sampled in Japan and the United States, the Japanese college students often are more individualistic than the college students in the United States (Triandis et al., 1988). I-C at the individual level, therefore, must be taken into consideration.

Individual Level

There are at least three related, but distinct ways to conceptualize I-C at the individual level: as personality characteristics (e.g., idiocentrism-allocentrism; Triandis et al., 1985), as value differences (e.g., Schwartz & Bilsky, 1987), and as self construals (e.g., Markus & Kitayama, 1991). Our focus here is on individualistic and collectivistic values.

The influence of cultural I-C on individuals' behavior is mediated by their values (Gudykunst et al., 1996). Cultural-level values based on I-C have a direct influence on behavior (e.g., through the norms and rules of the culture), but there is also an indirect effect through the socialization process when people learn individual values. While there generally is consistency between cultural and individual values, there are differences (Schwartz, 1994b).

Schwartz (1992) isolates 11 motivational domains of individual values. Value domains specify the structure of values and consist of specific values. Schwartz argues that the interests served by the 11 value domains can be individualistic, collectivistic, or mixed. The value domains of stimulation (e.g., exciting life), hedonism (e.g., pleasure), power (e.g., authority), achievement (e.g., social recognition), and self-direction (e.g., independent) serve individual interests; the value domains of tradition (e.g., respect for tradition), conformity (e.g., self-discipline), and benevolence (e.g., helpful) serve collective interests; and the value domains of security (e.g., social order), universalism (e.g., equality), and spirituality (e.g., inner harmony) serve mixed interests. Schwartz (1990) contends that individuals hold both individualistic and collectivistic values and that they are not necessarily in conflict.

There have been numerous studies of values in Japan and the United States (e.g.,

Berrien, 1966; Berrien, Arkoff, & Iwahara, 1967; Caudill & Scarr, 1961; Kikuchi & Gordon, 1968, 1970; Gudykunst et al., 1996; Nishida, 1981; Rokeach, 1973; Triandis, 1972). Triandis, for example, discovered that Japanese value serenity, aesthetic satisfaction, contentment, self-confidence, responsibility, peace, and good adjustment. US Americans, in contrast, valued individual progress, self-confidence, status, serenity, achievement, and joy. Rokeach found that US Americans value materialistic achievement more than Japanese, but Japanese valued hedonism more than US Americans. More recently, Gudykunst et al. observed that there are no differences in individualistic values between their US American and Japanese samples (US=5.85, J=5.80), but the Japanese sample held more collectivistic values than the US American sample (US=4.77, J=5.02).

The results of the studies of individual level values in Japan and the United States, as well as other cultures, do not consistently fit the expected patterns given the cultural-level individualistic and collectivistic tendencies of the cultures (see Zavalloni, 1980, for summaries of numerous studies). One reason that the findings are not consistent with the general cultural values is that the socialization process is not deterministic; some people become individualists in collectivistic cultures, and some people become collectivists in individualistic cultures. One potential explanation for this is cultural changes taking place in different sphere of the two cultures (see earlier discussion of cultural I-C).

There is an alternative explanation that might explain why some Japanese do not hold collectivistic values; that is, people who tend to be individualistic do not identify strongly with the Japanese culture. Similarly, people who tend to hold collectivistic values in the United States may not strongly identify with the culture of the United States. We discuss strength of cultural identity in the next section.

Strength of Cultural Identity and Individual Values

Cultural identity is one of many social identities individuals have. Social identities are those parts of an "individual's self-concept which derives from his [or her] knowledge of his [or her] membership in a social group (or groups) together with the value and emotional significance attached to that membership" (Tajfel, 1978, p. 63). Social identities can be based on demographic categories (e.g., nationality, ethnicity), membership in formal or informal organizations, the roles individuals play, vocation, or membership in stigmatized groups. Social identities influence behavior (including the use of language and communication behaviors) when they are activated (see Abrams & Hogg, 1990, for evidence).

Billig (1995) argues that our national cultural identities are "flagged" in the mass media through the use of symbols and habits of language. Symbols and language usage remind individuals of their culture, but they operate mindlessly (i.e., beyond conscious awareness). Berry (1980) points out that cultural identity provides a frame of reference for how individuals define themselves, and it also provides "a frame of reference for ordering social relationships" (p. 258). He proposes a model that combines cultural and ethnic identities to define how individuals fit into their culture (i.e., individuals are categorized as integrated, assimilated, separated, or marginal; see also Berry, 1990, for a discussion of the model).

The majority of research on cultural identity has used it as a factor to explain how people respond to living in multicultural contexts (e.g., Berry, 1980, 1990; Betancourt & Lopez, 1993), as well as how individuals respond in new cultural contexts (e.g., Kosmitzki, 1996). Zavalloni (1972, 1975) suggests that social identities (including cultural identity) that individuals activate affect the values they hold across cultures.

The strength of individuals' cultural identities should influence the individual values people hold. Strength of cultural identity involves the degree to which individuals identify with being members of their cultures. Stated differently, it includes the importance individuals place on being members of their culture and the centrality cultural membership has in defining who they are. It appears reasonable to assume that strength of cultural identity should interact with culture to influence the individualistic and collectivistic values people hold. To illustrate, students in Japan and the United States who strongly identify with their cultures should hold different values than those who do not strongly identify with their cultures. Students in Japan who strongly identify with their culture should hold collectivistic values, while students who do not strongly identify might hold individualistic values. Students in the United States who strongly identify with their culture, in contrast, should hold individualistic values, while those who do not strongly identify might hold collectivistic values.

Data from two studies were used to test the predictions regarding cultural identity outlined here. Given that both studies test the same predictions, the results for each study will be presented and then the findings will be discussed.

Study I

Methods

Respondents. Three hundred and sixty-four students in Japan and the United States served as respondents: 210 (104 males and 94 females, 12 people did not identify their sex) from a large southwestern university in the United States and 164 (68 males and 94 females, two did not identify their sex) from a moderate-sized private university east of Tokyo in Japan. The average age of the Japan sample was 20.56 years (SD=1.50), while the average age of the United States sample was 21.96 years (SD=3.98).

Measurement. All measures were contained in a questionnaire booklet that was constructed in English and translated into Japanese (with back translation).[7] Strength of cultural identity was based on a three semantic differential type items (with a six point response scale): Being a member of my culture is (1) not important to my self-definition — important for my self-definition, (2) does not define me — defines me, and (3) not central to who I am-central to who I am. Reliability (alpha) was .76 in the United States sample and .73 in the Japan sample. The three items were averaged within cultures and a median split was used to define weak and strong identification (US median=4.33, Japan median=3.50).

Eight values derived from Rokeach's (1973) value survey were utilized in the present study: (1) "cooperation; i.e., working together with others," (2) "freedom; i.e., independence, free choice," (3) "obedience; i.e., doing what parents, bosses direct," (4) "pleasure; i.e., an enjoyable fun life," (5) "self-sacrifice; i.e., altruism, helping others at a cost," (6) "self-reliance; i.e., independence from others," (7) "equality; i.e., brotherhood or equal opportunity for all," and (8) "social recognition; i.e., respect, admiration from others." A six-point response scale was used: not at all important (1) — very important (6).

Results

Multivariate analysis of variance (MANOVA) was used to test the predictions. The eight values were the dependent measures, while culture (Japan vs. United States) and strength of cultural identity (weak vs. strong; abbreviated ID below) were the independent variables.

The culture X strength of cultural identity multivariate interaction was significant (Wilk's lambda=.95, $F[8,327]=1.96$, $p<.05$). Four univariate tests were significant or approached significance: freedom ($F[1,334]=3.60$, $p=.06$, $eta2=.01$), pleasure ($F[1,334]=6.63$, $p<.01$, $eta2=.02$), self-sacrifice ($F[1,334]=3.06$, $p=.08$, $eta2=.01$), and social recognition ($F[1,334]=4.15$, $p<.05$, $eta2=.01$).[8] Respondents in the United States who identified strongly with their culture had higher scores for freedom (M=5.48) than those who identified weakly with the culture (M=5.30; $t=1.80$, $p<.05$), while the opposite pattern (but non-significant) emerged in the Japanese sample (weak ID=5.36, strong ID=5.22, $t<1$, p=ns). US Americans who identified strongly with their culture had a higher mean for pleasure (M=5.50) than those who weakly identified with their culture (M=5.16, $t=3.40$, $p<.05$), while the pattern in the Japanese sample was the opposite but not significant (weak ID=5.27, strong ID=5.16, $t<1$, p= ns). A similar pattern emerged for social recognition in the

---

[7] We want to thank Yoko Nadamitsu and Jiro Sakai for their assistance in translating and coding the data from this study.

[8] Cramer and Bock (1966) point out that univariate tests that approach significance should be interpreted if the multivariate test is significant.

United States (weak ID=4.67, strong ID=5.08, t=2.93, p<.05), but there was little difference by strength of identification in the Japanese sample (weak ID=4.51, strong ID=4.57, t<1, p=ns). For self-sacrifice, the Japanese respondents who identified strongly with the culture had a higher score (4.09) than those who had weak identification (3.69, t=2.0, p<.05). There was little difference in self-sacrifice by strength of identification in the United States sample (weak ID=4.39, strong ID=4.31, t<1, p=ns).

The multivariate main effect for strength of cultural identity was not significant (Wilk's lambda=.97, F[8,327]=1.25, p=ns). The multivariate main effect for culture was significant (Wilk's lambda=.84, F[8,327]=7.69, p<.001). Three of the univariate tests were significant: self-sacrifice (F[1,334]=12.95, p<.001, eta2=.04), self-reliance (F[1,334]=25.98, p<.001, eta2=.08), and social recognition (F[1,334]=7.55, p<.01, eta2=.02). The means in the United States sample were higher than the means in the Japan sample for self-sacrifice and social recognition. The mean for self-reliance was higher in the Japan sample than in the United States sample. The results for self-sacrifice and self-reliance are inconsistent with cultural values in Japan and the United States. Means are presented in Table 1.

Table 1 Means of the Variables in Study I

	Japan		United States	
	Weak	Strong	Weak	Strong
Cooperation	4.72	4.90	4.76	4.99
Freedom	5.36	5.22	5.30	5.48
Obedience	3.83	4.01	3.80	4.21
Pleasure	5.27	5.16	5.16	5.50
Self-sacrifice	3.69	4.09	4.39	4.31
Self-reliance	5.35	5.28	4.76	4.74
Equality	5.21	5.22	5.24	5.19
Social recognition	4.51	4.57	4.67	5.08

Study II

Methods

Respondents. Four hundred and thirty-two college students from Japan and the United States served as respondents in the study: 247 (109 males, 137 females, with one unidentified) students from a moderate-sized university on the west coast in the United States and 185 (89 males, 95 females, one unidentified) from a moderate-sized university east of Tokyo in Japan. The average age of the United States sample was 22.16 (SD=5.31), while the average age of the Japanese sample was 21.04 (SD=5.55).

Measurement. The measures were contained in a questionnaire booklet that was constructed in English and translated to Japanese (with back translation).[9] Strength of cultural identity was measured the same as in Study I, except that a seven point response scale was used instead of a six point scale as in Study I. Reliability was .75 in the United states sample and .72 in the Japan sample. The medians were 4.33 in the United States sample and 4.00 in the Japanese sample.

Ten values were adapted from Schwartz's (1990) description of individualistic and collectivistic values: (1) "obtaining pleasure or sensuous gratification," (2) "restraining my behavior if it is going to harm others," (3) "being successful by demonstrating individual competency," (4) "preserving and enhancing the welfare of others," (5) "being independent in thought and action," (6) "safety and stability of people with whom I identify," (7) "obtaining status and prestige," (8) "harmony in my relations with others," (9) "having an exciting and challenging life," and (10) "accepting my cultural and religious traditions." A seven-point response scale was used: not at all important (1) — extremely important (7).

Results

The data were tested using MANOVA. Culture (Japan vs. United States) and strength of cultural identity (weak vs. strong) were treated as independent variables. The ten individualistic and collectivistic values were the dependent variables.

The culture X strength of cultural identity multivariate interaction was significant (Wilk's lambda=.95, $F[10,408]=2.30$, $p<.01$). Three values were significant or approached significance: being independent ($F[1,417]=8.62$, $p<.01$, $eta2=.02$), having harmony ($F[1,417]=2.19$, $p=.10$, $eta2=.01$), and accepting traditions ($F[1,417]=3.50$, $p=.06$, $eta2=.01$). Examination of the mean scores indicates that for being independent the Japanese mean for the weak identification group was higher (5.45) than for the strong identification group (4.83, $t=3.11$, $p<.05$), while the means for the two groups in the United States sample were about the same (weak ID=5.98, strong ID=5.93, $t<1$, $p=ns$). For harmony and accepting traditions, the mean in the Japanese sample for the strong identifiers was higher (harmony=6.30, traditions=4.43) than for the weak identifiers (harmony=6.07, traditions=3.73; harmony $t=1.85$, $p<.05$, traditions $t=2.50$, $p<.05$). The means for both variables were approximately the same in the weak (harmony=6.27, traditions=5.01) and the strong (harmony=6.18, traditions=5.13) identification conditions in the United States sample (harmony $t<1$, $p=ns$, traditions $t<1$, $p=ns$).

---

9 We want to thank Jiro Sakai for his assistance in translating the questionnaire and Seiichi Morisaki and Lori Reisig for their assistance in coding the data for the study.

The multivariate main effect for culture was significant (Wilk's lambda=.57, $F[10,408]=29.73$, $p<.001$). Six univariate effects were significant: obtaining pleasure ($F[1,417]=142.38$, $p<.001$, eta2=.25), preserving others' welfare ($F[1,417]=31.90$, $p<.001$, eta2=.07), being independent ($F[1,417]=36.12$, $p<.001$, eta2=.08), safety ($F[1,417]=6.44$, $p<.01$, eta2=.02), exciting life ($F[1,417]=64.98$, $p<.001$, eta2=.13), and accepting traditions ($F[1,417]=28.61$, $p<.001$, eta2=.06). The means for all of the variables except obtaining pleasure were higher in the United States sample than in the Japan sample. The results for preserving others' welfare, obtaining pleasure, and accepting traditions were not consistent with the cultural-level values in Japan and the United States. Means are presented in Table 2.

Table 2 Means of the Variables in Study II

	Japan		United States	
	Weak	Strong	Weak	Strong
Obtaining pleasure and sensuous gratification	6.60	6.58	5.38	5.33
Restraining my behavior if it is going to harm others	6.00	5.86	5.87	5.77
Being successful by demonstrating my individual competency	5.85	6.05	5.80	6.03
Preserving and enhancing welfare of others	4.52	4.77	5.48	5.41
Being independent in thought and action	5.45	4.83	5.93	5.99
Safety and stability of people with whom I identify	5.48	5.43	5.72	5.84
Obtaining status and prestige	4.93	5.13	4.81	5.30
Having harmony in my relations with others	6.07	6.30	6.27	6.18
Having an exciting and challenging life	4.90	4.88	5.99	6.02
Accepting my cultural and religious traditions	3.73	4.43	5.02	5.14

The multivariate main effect for strength of cultural identity was significant (Wilk's lambda=.93, $F[10,408]=3.18$, $p<.001$). Four univariate effects were significant or approached significance: being successful ($F[1,417]=3.04$, $p=.08$, eta2=.01), being independent (F[1,417]=5.60, p<.05, eta2=.01), obtaining status (F[1,417]=6.11, p<.05, eta2=.01), and accepting traditions (F[1,417]=8.27, p<.01, eta2=.02). The means for being independent and accepting traditions were lower for weak identifiers than for strong identifiers. The means for being successful and obtaining status, in contrast, were higher for strong identifiers than for weak identifiers.

Discussion

The purpose of the present research was to determine the extent to which strength of cultural identity interacts with culture to influence individual-level individualistic and collectivistic values. The data from both studies indicate that culture interacts with strength of cultural identity to influence individual-level individualistic and collectivistic values. Specifically, the present data suggest that if the values of freedom, pleasure, social recognition, self-sacrifice, being independent, harmony, and accepting traditions are studied at the individual level, strength of cultural identity must be taken into consideration. All of the interaction effects that emerged in the present study were consistent with expectations based on cultural I-C in Japan and the United States. To illustrate, respondents who strongly identify with the Japanese culture valued harmony and accepting traditions more than respondents who did not identify strongly with the Japanese culture or respondents from the United States.

With the exception of three values (social recognition, being independent and exciting life), the results for the main effect of culture on values in the two studies were not consistent with expectations based on cultural I-C values in the two cultures. The Japanese respondents were more self-reliant, more pleasure seeking, less self-sacrificing, less interested in preserving others' welfare, less accepting of traditions, and less safety oriented than the United States respondents. The patterns for social recognition, being independent and exciting life, however, were consistent with expectations (i.e., scores for United States respondents were higher than scores for Japan respondents on these three values). The present data clearly indicate that respondents in the United States and Japan hold individualistic and collectivistic values. Further, the present study suggests that individual-level values often are not consistent with cultural-level values when only culture is used as an independent variable.

There are three major implications of the present study. The first implication is that strength of cultural identity is an important factor that can not be ignored when studying variability in communication across cultures. People's personality, the way they conceive of themselves, and the values they hold are influenced by the socialization process. While many (probably most) members of a culture learn patterns that are consistent with cultural-level tendencies, not all members of the culture learn patterns consistent with the cultural-level tendencies. Strength of cultural identity provides one way of differentiating people who behave in ways that are consistent with the general cultural-level tendencies.

The second implication of the present study involves the importance of including individual-level factors that mediate the effect of cultural-level variability (e.g., cultural I-C) on communication in future research. To illustrate, Gudykunst et al. (1996) argues that while cultural I-C has a direct effect on communication (e.g., through communication rules used in a culture), personality orientations, self-construals, and individual values also mediate the influence of cultural I-C on communication. Both cultural-level and individual-level values may influence communication in the same situation. Since cultural-level and individual-level values are not necessarily consistent, both must be taken into consideration to understand communication across cultures.

The third implication of the present study involves the way researchers demonstrate that their samples are representative of the cultural tendencies (e.g., cultural I-C) under study. Triandis and his associates (1988) suggest that college students in Japan may not provide an adequate sample if researchers are trying to test the effects of collectivism on individuals' behavior. The present research suggests that demonstrating whether samples are individualistic or collectivistic can not be accomplished by simply assessing individual-level values. The present data indicate that individuals' strength of cultural identity interacts with their cultural background to influence their individualistic and collectivistic values.

It is critical that future research make very specific predictions regarding the linkages between the cultural and individual-level aspects of I-C and individuals' behavior (e.g., cultural-level: strong identifiers in cultures which value conservatism will follow cultural rules more than strong identifiers in cultures which do not value conservatism; individual-level: the more individuals value being independent, the more they will self-disclose with members of outgroups). Isolating very specific relationships between particular aspects of I-C at the cultural level and at the individual level to individuals' behavior is necessary to understand the influences of the cultural- and individual-levels of analysis on communication.

References

Abrams, D., & Hogg, M., (Eds.). (1990). *Social identity theory: Constructive and critical advances*. London: Springer-Verlag.

Ball-Rokeach, S., Rokeach, M., & Grube, J. (1984). *The great American values test*. New York: Free Press.

Befu, H. (1980a). A critique of the group model of Japanese society. *Social Analysis*, 5/6, 29-43.

Befu, H. (1980b). The group model of Japanese society and an alternative. *Rice University Studies*, 66, 169-87.

Bellah, R., Madsen, R., Sullivan, W., Swidler, A., & Tipton, S. (1985). *Habits of the heart: Individualism and commitment in American life*. Berkeley: University of California Press.

Berrien, F. (1966). Japanese and American values. *International Journal of Psychology, 1*, 129-42.

Berrien, F., Arkoff, A., & Iwahara, S. (1967). Generation difference in values: Americans, Japanese-Americans, and Japanese. *Journal of Social Psychology, 71*, 169-76.

Berry, J.(1980). Social and cultural change. In H. Triandis & R. Brislin, (Eds.), *Handbook of cross-cultural psychology, Vol. 5*, 211-79. Boston: Allyn & Bacon.

Berry, J. (1990). Psychology of acculturation. In R. Brislin, (Ed.), *Applied crosscultural psychology* (pp. 232-53). Thousand Oaks, CA: Sage.

Betancourt, H., & Lopez, S. (1993). The study of culture, ethnicity, and race in American psychology. *American Psychologist, 48*, 629-37.

Billig, M. (1995). *Banal nationalism*. London: Sage.

Caudill, W., & Scarr, H. (1961). Japanese value orientations and culture change. *Ethnology, 1*, 53-91.

Cramer, E., & Bock, R. (1966). Multivariate analysis. *Review of Educational Research, 36*, 604-17.

Feather, N. (1990). Bridging the gap between values and action. In E. Higgins & R. Intercultural Sorrentino, (Eds.), *Handbook of motivation and cognition Vol. 2* (pp. 151-92). New York: Guilford.

Feather, N. (1995). Values, valences, and choice. *Journal of Personality and Social Psychology, 68*, 1135-51.

Gudykunst, W. B., Matsumoto, Y., Ting-Toomey, S., Nishida, T., Kim, K. S., & Heyman, S. (1996). The influence of cultural individualism-collectivism, self construals, and individual values on communication styles across cultures. *Human Communication Research, 22*, 510-43.

Gudykunst, W. B., & Nishida, T. (1994). *Bridging Japanese/North American differences*. Thousand Oaks, CA: Sage.

Hamaguchi, E. (1980). *Nihonjin no rentaiteki jiritsusei: Kanjinshugi to kojinshugi* (Japanese connected autonomy: Contexualism and individualism) *Gendai no Esupuri* (Contemporary Spirit), *160*, 127-43.

Hofstede, G. (1980). *Culture's consequences*. Beverly Hills, CA: Sage.

Hofstede, G., & Bond, M. H. (1984). Hofstede's culture dimensions: An independent validation using Rokeach's value survey. *Journal of Cross-Cultural Psychology, 15*, 417-33.

Ito, Y. (1989a). A nonwestern view of the paradigm dialogues. In B Dervin, L. Grossberg, B. O'Keefe, & E. Wartella, (Eds.), *Rethinking communication* (pp. 173-7). Newbury Park, CA: Sage.

Ito, Y. (1989b). Sociocultural backgrounds of Japanese interpersonal communication style. *Civilizations, 39*, 101-27.

Kashima, Y. (1989). Conceptions of person: Implications in individualism/collectivism research. In C. Kagitcibasi, (Ed.), *Growth and progress in crosscultural psychology* (pp. 104-12). Amsterdam: Swets & Zeitlinger.

Kikuchi, A, & Gordon, L. (1966). Evaluation and cross-cultural application of a Japanese form of the survey of interpersonal values. *Journal of Social Psychology, 69*, 185-95.

Kikuchi, A, & Gordon, L. (1970). Japanese and American personal values. *International Journal of Psychology*, 5, 183-7.

Kluckhohn, F., & Strodtbeck, F. (1961). *Variations in value orientations*. New York: Row, Petersen.

Kosmitzki, C. (1996). The reaffirmation of cultural identity in cross-cultural encounters. *Personality and Social Psychology Bulletin, 22*, 238-48.

Lebra, T. (1974). *Japanese patterns of behavior*. Honolulu: University of Hawaii Press.

Markus, H. R., & Kitayama, S. (1991). Culture and the self: Implications for cognition, emotion, and motivation. *Psychological Review, 98*, 224-53.

Mito, T. (1991). *Ie no ronri* (The theory of ie) (two vols.). Tokyo: Bunshindo.

Miyanaga, K. (1991). *The creative edge: Emerging individualism in Japan*. New Brunswick, NJ: Transaction Books.

Murakami, Y. (1983). *Shinchukantaishu no jidai* (The age of the new middle masses). Tokyo: Chuokoronsha.

Nakane, C. (1970). *Japanese society*. Berkeley: University of California Press.

Nishida, H. (1981). Value orientations and value changes in Japan and the United States. In T. Nishida & W. Gudykunst, (Eds.), *Readings on intercultural communication* (pp. 35-59). Tokyo: Geirinshobo.

Rokeach, M. (1972). *Beliefs, attitudes, and values.* San Francisco: Jossey-Bass.

Rokeach, M. (1973). *The nature of human values.* New York: Free Press.

Schwartz, S. (1990). Individualism-collectivism: Critique and proposed refinements. *Journal of Cross-Cultural Psychology, 21*, 139-57.

Schwartz, S. (1992). Universals in the content and structure of values. In M. Zanna, (Ed.), *Advances in experimental social psychology Vol. 25*, (pp. 1-65). New York: Academic Press.

Schwartz, S. (1994a). Are there universal aspects in the structure and content of values? *Journal of Social Issues, 50* (4), 19-45.

Schwartz, S. (1994b). Beyond individualism-collectivism: New cultural dimensions of values. In U. Kim, H. Triandis, C. Kagitcibasi, S. Choi, & G. Yoon, (Eds.), *Individualism and collectivism: Theory, method, and application* (pp. 85-121). Newbury Park, CA: Sage.

Tajfel, H. (1978). Social categorization, social identity, and social comparisons. In H. Tajfel, (Ed.), *Differentiation between social groups* (pp. 61-76). London: Academic Press.

Triandis, H. C. (1972). *The analysis of subjective culture.* New York: Wiley.

Triandis, H. C. (1988). Collectivism vs. individualism. In G. Verma & C. Bagley, (Eds.), *Cross-cultural studies of personality, attitudes and cognition* (pp. 60-95). London: Macmillan.

Triandis, H. C. (1990). Cross-cultural studies of individualism-collectivism. In J. Berman, (Ed.), *Nebraska Symposium on motivation. Vol. 37*, (pp. 41-133). Lincoln: University of Nebraska Press.

Triandis, H. C. (1995). *Individualism & collectivism.* Boulder, CO: Westview.

Triandis, H. C., Bontempo, R., Villareal, M., Asai, M., & Lucca, N. (1988). Individualism-collectivism: Cross-cultural perspectives on selfingroup relationships. *Journal of Personality and Social Psychology, 54*, 323-38.

Triandis, H. C., Leung, K., Villareal, M., & Clack, F. (1985). Allocentric versus idiocentric tendencies. *Journal of Research in Personality, 19*, 395-415.

Waterman, A. (1981). Individualism and interdependence. *American Psychologist, 36*, 762-73.

Wuthnow, R. (1991). *Acts of compassion: Caring for others and helping ourselves.*

Princeton: Princeton University Press.

Yamazaki, M. (1990). *Nihonbunka to kojinshugi* (Japanese culture and individualism). Tokyo: Chukoronsha.

Zavalloni, M. (1972). Social identity: Perspectives and prospects. *Social Sciences Information, 12* (3), 65-91.

Zavalloni, M. (1975). Social identity and the recoding of reality. *International Journal of Psychology, 10*, 197-217.

Zavalloni, M. (1980). Values. In H. Triandis & R. Brislin, (Eds.), *Handbook of cross-cultural psychology Vol. 5*, (pp. 73-120). Boston: Allyn and Bacon.

Beyond cultural identity[1]

Young Yun Kim   University of Oklahoma, USA

Abstract

This theoretical essay takes a critical look at the views of cultural identity prevalent in contemporary American public discourse. The author finds it particularly problematic that cultural identity is commonly conceived as a fixed and exclusive entity with an inherently positive moral imperative. An alternative, dynamic view is thus presented emphasizing continuing development beyond the perimeters of one's ascribed or primary cultural identity.

In this approach, the concept of "intercultural identity"[2] is employed as an extension of, and a counterpoint to, cultural identity. Grounded in an open systems perspective, the identity development beyond one's primary culture is explained in terms of the internal stress-adaptation-growth dynamic, a psychological response to the challenges of interfacing with differing cultural identities. Such intercultural challenges are described as the very force that "pushes" an individual in the direction of greater intercultural learning, perceptual refinement, and a self-other orientation that is at once individuated and universalized.

The Polemics of Cultural Identity

About two years ago, the Cincinnati school district instituted a discipline code that provides stiff penalties for students who disrupt classes and who endanger others. This code was challenged by a claim that it would disparately affect African-American students. An impending court settlement requires that schools keep records of the racial and gender identities of the teachers referring students for disciplinary action and the same identities of

---

1 Throughout this essay, the term "cultural identity" is used broadly as a generic term and can be used interchangeably with other terms commonly used in both international and domestic contexts such as "national," "ethnic," "ethnolinguistic," and "racial" identity, or more generic concepts such as "social" and "group" identity.
2 The term "intercultural identity" is employed exchangeably with related terms such as "interethnic identity," "interracial identity," "intergroup identity," "multicultural identity," "meta-identity," "transcultural identity," "species identity," and "universal identity."

the students. These records are to help decide whether a teacher should get a pay increase or further training in classroom management–or should be terminated. This court settlement, if approved, threatens to seriously compromise the way the code is enforced. Albert Shanker, President of the American Federation of Teachers, raises the following concerns in The New York Times (January 16, 1994, Editorial/Letters Section).

What standards will be used in interpreting the records? Will it be OK for a black teacher to refer a black child for disciplinary action but not for a white teacher–even if it's the same offense? Will a white female teacher who mainly refers African-American boys be in trouble while a black male teacher doing the same will be all right? Will kids of different races who break the same rules be dealt with differently? Might a quota system be set up that establishes how many kids in different race groups can be disciplined for a given offense in a given year? (p. 7)

The problems with approaching school discipline based on racial and gender identities are obvious. The mere fact that there is a disparity between referrals of white and black students does not mean there is discrimination. The question must be whether a particular teacher is justified in referring a particular student for discipline, and we can not answer this question by looking at the races. If the court accepts this settlement, teachers will most likely think twice before referring a student for discipline. As Shanker puts it, "This settlement is like telling teachers, the more students you turn in, the harder time we will give you. And, incidentally, your referrals had better be racially balanced" (p. 7).

This story is but one of the many dominating contemporary American social discourse. It directly points to the prevalence of the misguided idea of group identity that channel public attention away from the real issues to be dealt with. The United States–a unique construction organized by free, democratic principles that transcend a monolithic tribal ancestral and territorial condition–has never before seen so many claims pushing identity and differences. The seemingly innocent banner of cultural identity (or related labels such as racial and ethnic identity) is now a compelling "sore spot" for many Americans, frequently galvanizing them into "us-against-them" posturing. The traditional American "melting pot" ideal is threatened in the midst of the fractious landscape of the identity politics discussed in a spate of recent books such as The Disuniting of America (Schlesinger, 1992), Race (Terkel, 1992), The Racial Crisis in American Higher Education (Altbach & Lomotey, 1991), Race Matters (West, 1993), Culture of Separation (Bellah et al., 1985), and Culture of Complaint (Hughes, 1993), to name only a few.

The exacerbated division between the "right" and "left" of the American political spectrum is embroiled in the bickering about "political correctness" (PC)-an unfortunate offshoot of "multiculturalism." Indeed, much mud has been stirred up by the linkage of the two. Radicals in both ideological camps seem stuck in the defensive "victim" mode, orating about a wildly polemical "separatism" and denying the value, even the possibility, of a truthful dialogue. On the one hand, the radical left advocates a fortification of minority identities with angry outcries about "victimizations" and "entitlements." The radical right has its own form of PC–what Robert Hughes calls "Patriotic Correctness'–equally designed for protecting its vested interest in dividing the American polity by creating scapegoats and hate-objects. As such, we now hear from some radical conservatives promises for a "culture war" to "take our culture back." Although considerably toned down, the identity polemic of the extreme right has a startling resemblance to the bigotry vivid in the fatwa pronouncement of the Iranian mullahs against a live writer, Salman Rushdie, for "blasphemy" against Islam.

Thus extremes meet. Radical liberals and conservatives find themselves in a destructive game of confrontation. In Robert Hughes's (1993) words, they are now "locked in a full-blown, mutually sustaining folie a deux , and the only person each dislikes more than the other is the one who tells both to lighten up" (p. 79). In these highly charged polemics of cultural identity, the traditional American genius for finding a consensus for resolving problems through constructive debates and compromises is in danger of extinction. Absent in the confrontational discourse, too, are the main ideals of multi-culturalism itself, that is, people with different roots can co-exist, that they can learn from each other, and that they can and should look across and beyond the frontiers of race and ethnicity (as well as gender and other social categories) without prejudice or illusion, and learn to think against the background of an integrated society of true multiculturalism. Most importantly, the current polemics seem to deny the fact that some of the most interesting things in American history have happened, in fact, at the interface of various cultural roots.

Academic Approaches to Cultural Identity

Systematic investigations of cultural identity can be traced back to psychologist Erik Erickson's (1950; 1968) important early theoretical framework. Erickson's theory places identity at the "core" of the individual and yet also in the core of his or her "common culture." Erickson further views the process of identity development as one in which the two identities–of the individual and of the group–are merged and integrated into one. Other investigators have since echoed Erickson's conception and have articulated similar presumptions about cultural identity. F. Yinger (1986), for instance, describes ethnic attachment as the person's "basic identity" formed during the earliest periods of socialization, and that strengthens the individual's self-esteem. Further elaborations of identity have been made in social identity theory (Tajfel, 1974, 1978; Turner, 1975) and many experimental studies based on the theory (e.g., Giles & Bourhis, 1976; Giles & Saint-Jacques, 1979). A dominant feature of the social identity theory is the presumed value and emotional significance attached to group identity and its close relationship to self-identity, self-esteem, and outgroup behavior (Brewer Miller, 1984; Turner & Giles, 1981).

Taken as a whole, existing conceptions of cultural identity are clearly based on a presumption of inherent positivity. An implicit agreement exists in the literature concerning a moral value attached to the idea of cultural identity. No matter that the presumed linkage between cultural identity and self-esteem has been found inconclusive in empirical studies (Phinney & Rosenthal, 1992). The predominant belief among social scientists appears to be that identity boundaries are something everyone feels, and ought to feel, reluctant to change or compromise and that the cultural homogenization of a society would lead to a debasement of an individual with a minority ethnic background. Such appears to be the case, for example, with Jean Phinney's (1989) description of ethnic identity development. In presenting the model, Phinney strongly emphasizes the critical importance of achieving a commitment to one's ethnic identity and thus implies that not achieving such a commitment would result in a significant detriment to the individual's psychological and social functioning. Interestingly, the importance placed on maintaining a cultural identity among ethnic minorities is seldom extended to white ethnics in the United States.

Undeniably, the exclusive assignment of positive values to cultural identity oversimplifies the reality. It overlooks the "dark side" of cultural identity abundantly witnessed in the contemporary American society–the tendencies of collective self-glorification and outgroup denigration. An insufficient amount of attention has been given to the apparent association between strict adherence to a single cultural identity and distrust of other groups or separatist sentiments. Yet, the notion of intrinsic "goodness" in cultural identity continues to prevail, widely shared by a broader mass of journalists, politicians, and some segments of the general population.

The positive bias in academic approaches to cultural identity has been intensified by the tendency among social scientists to exaggerate the exclusivity of cultural identity. A person is viewed to "belong to" one and only one cultural identity: If someone sees himself or herself, or is seen by others, as a Mexican-American, then this person's identity is viewed to exclude all other identities. This tendency of an "all-or-none" and "either-or" conception glosses over the fact that many people's identities are not locked into a single, uncompromising category but incorporate other identities as well. Particularly in the United States, 30-70% of Blacks, virtually all Latinos and Filipinos, the majority of American Indians and Native Hawaiians, as well as a significant proportion of White-identified persons are of multiracial-multiethnic origins (Root, 1993, p. 9).

Related, the common conceptions of cultural identity often exaggerate uniformity among the individuals who are associated with a particular group. Researchers have tended to lump together all individuals identified as "belonging" to a particular group and portray them as though they were a homogeneous group with identical characteristics. In Two Nations (1992), for example, the author Andrew Hacker describes the contemporary Black as someone who is marginal, separate, and victimized in the White world, despite the many contrary statistics presented in this book. Uniformities of a cultural group such as this are, of course, far from being accurate and tend to perpetuate the impasse of preconceived categories and stereotypical generalizations, thereby preventing a more accurate understanding of the complex relationship between the individual and the group.

The fact frequently put aside in recent academic investigations is that, even with a common cultural background, individuals vary significantly in the intensity of identification with and commitment to collective experiences and goals as well as in the degree to which their daily activities and accomplishments are bound up with their membership to that group. It has been further forgotten that many people's experience of cultural identity is thus filled with a dynamic set of social-psychological processes that allow a trade-off among multiple group identities or a merger thereof into a single selfhood. Findings from a recent survey of Hispanic Americans (Garza et al., 1992) remind us of such complexities in cultural identity. The study, for example, shows that the majority of Hispanic Americans feel at least as close to Anglos as they do to members of the other Hispanic groups. Despite the strong fear expressed by those who adhere to identity maintenance at any cost, the study further indicates that a large majority of Hispanics are moving toward mainstream American culture and that 60% or more say the purpose of bilingual education is to learn both languages, and less than 10% believe it is exclusively "to maintain the Spanish language/culture." The majority of those surveyed further indicates their loyalties toward the United States as a whole expressing very strong "love" and "pride" for the country.

An additional misnomer in the current academic conceptions of cultural identity is found in the exaggerated presumption of its permanence: Once an Italian-American, always an Italian-American. Even theories that describe the developmental process of cultural identity (Erikson, 1950, 1968; Phinney, 1989; Phinney, Lochner & Murphy, 1990; Phinney Rosenthal, 1992) have not addressed the phenomenon of identity development beyond the formation of the primary identity during the formative years. Phinney's (1989) description of the identity development of minority adolescents, for instance, identifies three stages: (1) the stage of "an unexamined ethnic identity" during which the adolescent remain largely passive in reacting to ethnic images and stereotypes; (2) the stage of "exploration" of what it means to be a member of a specific ethnic group in society, which is equivalent to the identity crisis or moratorium described by Erikson (1968); and (3) the stage of "resolution," in which the adolescent develops "an achieved ethnic identity," and "makes a commitment to a particular way of being a member of [his or her] group" (Phinney, 1989, p. 41). While this conceptualization helps us to understand minority adolescents" struggle to "finally obtain a secure sense of themselves as ethnic group members" (p. 42), it fails to account for the fact that, for many of these adolescents, identity development reaches beyond the attainment of "a secure sense" of their ethnic selves. This limited perspective discounts the extensively documented fact that immigrants and their offspring undergo assimilative changes over time and across generations (See Kim, 1988, for a review of pertinent literature).

The prevailing academic conceptions examined above clearly reflect an ideological tilt toward pluralism with a slight tinge of the separatist notion, as noted by Thomas Pettigrew (1988) and Eugene Roosens (1989). The literature tends to espouse an idea that cultural identity must not be negotiated or changed and that any change in an individual's original identity is undesirable and opposed to a healthy existence. Pettigrew (1988) goes even further in concluding that:

To many, talk of mosaics and quilts to emphasize the autonomous nature of identity and its relationships among cultural identities is both an attempt to describe the way America is headed and an effort to hurry it along. (p. 19)

A Systems Approach to Identity

Reiterating Alfred Korzybski's (1958; 1933) General Semantics principle, "the map is not the territory," Harry Weinberg (1987) points out that when our conceptual tools do not fit the empirical reality, when we act as though our inferences are factual knowledge, "the inevitable result is frustration and an ever-increasing tendency to warp the territory to fit our maps" (p.29). We now need to acknowledge the common misconception that a person's cultural reach is categorically fixed forever by whatever slot into which one is born and raised. In so doing, we need to suspend the prevailing notion that such occurrences would necessarily involve "throwing away" or "being disloyal to" one's original identity. We need, instead, to address what has been conspicuously shunned in current academic approaches to cultural identity, and recognize the contentiousness of the claims of identity in the contemporary political landscape. We must further pay greater attention to a form of identity that allows a greater flexibility and openness toward differing cultural identities. To do so, we need to pay as much attention to where two or more identities touch and join one another as to where they separate and diverge, and to investigate what such an interface does to the human personality, or more specifically, the construction, negotiation, expansion, and transformation of identities–a kind of traditional American common sense.

To move in this new direction requires us to examine the experiences of numerous everyday folks who recognize that the boundaries of a cultural identity are seldom impermeable, engage in cultural cross-borrowing, and understand that cross-borrowing of identities is often an act of appreciation that leaves neither the lender nor the borrower deprived, symbolically or otherwise. Among such individuals is Mary Catherine Bateson, author of Composing a Life (1989), whose insight touches on the complexity and richness of her own identity:

I had spent my senior year of high school in Israel and had come back to the United

States to start college with a deep sense of dividedness, of having first found a new sense of myself in Israel and then having left that clarity behind. The new task was to combine and translate, to put an American gentile identity with my Israeli experience and to use my college education to shape them into some new whole....Each of us has repeatedly had to pose the question of who we are. (p. 212-213)

Sandra Kitt is another one of the many Americans whose personal experiences and views challenge the prevailing academic notions about cultural identity. She felt strongly enough to write to the editor of The New York Times Magazine (April 29, 1992) in response to an earlier article on "cultural baggage':

I've been fighting ethnic labels since I was 12 or 13, and decided that only I had a right to define myself. It was a lonely position to take. I am not almost WASP. I am African-American. I'm also part Cherokee from both sides of my family. But so what?....I've taken risks with my life that only I am responsible for, and I have reaped substantial rewards for daring to be myself and not just different. (p. 10)

Yet another person named A. J. Nagel reacted similarly to a different story about cultural identity in The Tulsa World (April 17, 1992, Section. A) and wrote the following letter to the editor:

I am an American with a German name. My forbears have lived as loyal U.S. citizens for 150 years. Am I a German-American? I have some Cherokee blood also. Am I a Native-American? It makes little sense to refer to a group or an individual by the use of such titles. We are all Americans and as such should have equal opportunities. Along with those opportunities goes the acceptance of responsibility. The United States has enough problems without injecting background and race. This country was built and became great by the efforts of all. Why inhibit its growth and existence by separating its citizens into fractions? (p. 16)

Identity Interface and Transformation

A metatheoretical foundation for the present conception of identity is found in the General Systems perspective, which views a person as an "open system" that evolves throughout life (Bertalanffy, 1968; Ford & Lerner, 1992; Ruben & J. Kim, 1975; Slavin & Kriegman, 1992). Plasticity–the ability to learn and change through new experiences–is considered one of the most profound characteristics of the human system and, indeed, the very basis upon which individuals acquire a cultural identity. Born into this world knowing literally nothing of what is needed to function acceptably in a given society, and through continuous interaction with various aspects of the cultural "data field," adaptive human minds undergo a progression of changes, in each of which some of the new concepts, attitudes, and behaviors are "programmed" into them forming a sense of identity.

Accordingly, the systems perspective on human life is dynamic and evolutionary. It offers the insight that human beings are equipped with the capacity to maintain an overall integrity despite the continual instability, and that such systemic integrity is possible because of an open system's capacity to evolve, that is, to develop new forms of relating to a given milieu. The concept of autopoisis (Maturana & Varula, 1975, cited in Jantsch, 1980, p. 7) points to this tendency of humans to continuously renew themselves and to regulate this process in such a way that the overall integrity of the structure is maintained. This autopoitic property, in turn, reflects the self-reflexiveness of the human mind that reviews, anticipates, generalizes, analyzes, plans, and thereby transform itself. Erich Jantsch (1980) reflects all of these human capacities when he describes humans as "self-organizing': "We live, so to speak, in co-evolution with ourselves, with our own mental products" (p. 177).

Based on the above premises, this writer attempts to explain the identity development beyond culture by using a new concept, "intercultural identity." As a counterpoint and an extension of the term "cultural identity," this new concept helps us shift our primary attention temporarily from the question of "who we are" to the question of "whom we may yet become." Just as a cultural identity serves as a psychological linkage between a person and a specific biological and/or social community, an intercultural identity can be also viewed as a linkage between a person and more than one such community. The meaning of intercultural identity further includes a vital component of an emotional identification of oneself that is not limited to one's own social group but to other cultures as well, thereby projecting an outlook that is not locked into a parochial group interest but, instead, one in which one sees and identifies with others" perspectives. As Peter Adler (1982) describes it, the intercultural identity can be viewed to be based, not on belongingness which implies either owning or being owned by culture, but on a style of self consciousness that is capable of negotiating ever new formations of reality. He is neither totally a part of nor totally apart from his culture; he lives, instead, on the boundary (p. 391).

The phenomenon of identity development beyond the ascribed or primary cultural perimeters is closely linked with intercultural communication activities. Through face-to-face or mediated forms of communication, intercultural interfaces often present a multitude of challenges, including those that force people to confront and re-assess their own identity as well as the taken-for-granted practices of thinking, feeling, and acting associated with the identity. The severity of challenges to one's cultural identity would be a function of the severity of cultural difference and incompatibility presented by the other person's cultural identity (Sarbaugh, 1979). Severe or not, however, few people living in a society of multitudes of cultural identities such as the United States can escape what Dean Barnlund (1989) has described as "the paradox of closeness': Faced with the new reality of both the physical and informational closeness of the cultural other, the involved communicators must redefine the universe around them and, more importantly, redefine themselves, their own identity, in relationship with the cultural others. As Jantsch (1980) points out,

Communication between autopoietic systems includes the possibility of the self-organization of knowledge by mutual stimulation of the exploration and extension of the cognitive domain. A true dialogue is never the exchange of readily available knowledge, but also active organization of knowledge which was not in the world before. (p. 206)

Indeed, the popular concept "culture shock" (Oberg, 1960) essentially points to reactions to such intercultural stress or, as Janet Bennett (1977) describes it, "a natural consequence of the state of a human organism's inability to interact with the new and changed environment in an effective manner" (p. 46). (See Furnham & Bochner, 1986, for a detailed discussion of culture shock) A more pointed linkage of culture shock to identity crisis is made in the term, "self-shock" (Zaharna, 1989), or the ubiquitous tension between the individual's own internal strengths and imbalances, and the supportive or stress-producing nature of the environment.

What both concepts do not readily reveal, however, is the fact that the "shock" experiences are generally followed by a profound learning experience leading to a high degree of self-awareness and personal growth (Adler, 1975, 1987/1972). As explained by this writer elsewhere (Kim, 1988; Kim & Ruben, 1988), individuals as open systems experience a state of disequilibrium or stress in the face of challenges, followed by a struggle to regain an equilibrium. Stress, as such, is viewed as a manifestation of a generic process, a temporary personality disintegration or a sequence of "symmetry breaks" (Jantsch, 1980, p. 79). Stress occurs whenever the capabilities of an open system are not totally adequate to the demands of the environment, as is likely to be the case when a person is confronted by a person or an event whose cultural identity threatens his or her own.

Yet, no autopoietic human structure can stabilize itself forever by defense activities only. In time, most people manage to regain an equilibrium through an adaptive process of making adjustments in the existing internal structure so as to maximize the "functional fitness" (Kim, 1988) between them and the challenges at hand. Here, it is the very stress that "pushes" an individual to restructure his or her existing conditions and thereby realize an increased adaptation to the external challenge. As Jantch puts it (1980),

> The higher the resistance against structural change, the more powerful the fluctuations that ultimately break through, and the richer and more varied are the unfolding of mind. (p. 255)

This seemingly paradoxical principle suggests the unity in which stress and adaptation are inseparable. Stress is part-and-parcel of the intercultural transformation cycle, as individuals strive to regain their inner balance and make themselves better equipped to face the demands and opportunities of the intercultural reality. This process continues as long as they are in communication with, and are challenged by, the milieu in which they must function. As such, the interrelateness of stress and adaptation describes the process of organizing and reorganizing oneself–the process that, in the context of intercultural interface, involves the continual reinventing of oneself beyond the parameters of the original cultural identity. In the moment of calm and relaxation, the process of what may be called the "inner alchemy," or the restoration of inner cohesiveness, takes place. As the "old" person breaks up, new cultural knowledge, attitudes, and behavioral elements are incorporated, ever so subtly and gradually, into an enactment of growth–an emergent "new" person at a higher level of integration. Here, the symmetry between the inner and the outer world is broken, but is still present in the ecological relations of the organism with its environment.

The stress-adaptation-growth dynamic underlies a cyclic and continual process of identity transformation as illustrated in Figure 1 on the next page. It lies at the heart of identity development in the forward-upward movement of a cycle of "draw-back-to-leap" in the direction of more intercultural adaptation and growth. Each stressful experience is responded to with a draw back," which then activates one's adaptive energy to "leap forward." The shifting between the breakup of the old internalized cultural system and the creation of a new system enables the individual to be better adapted to subsequent intercultural encounters. Here, intercultural stress is the internal resistance of the human organism against its own cultural evolution.

The above conception of identity development as a dynamic, dialectic process enables us to understand seemingly paradoxical statements so common in many cultural injunctions such as, "The greatest gain is in the giving" and "One finds oneself by losing oneself." As Chuang Tzu, in Great and Small, wrote:

> Consequently, he who wants to have right without wrong,
> Order without disorder,
> Does not understand the principles
> Of heaven and earth.
> He does not know how
> Things hang together.

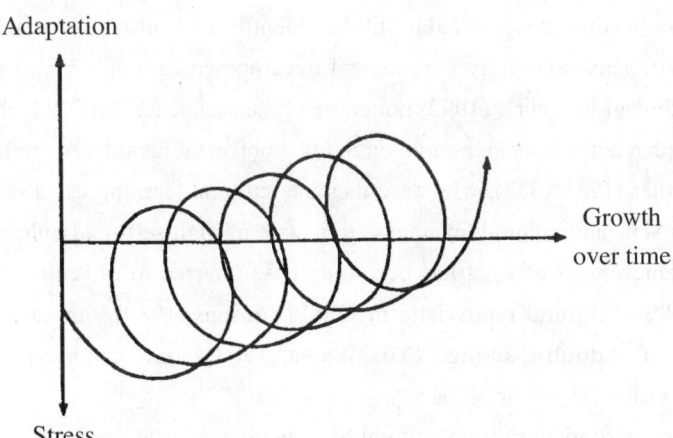

Figure 1 Stress-Adaptation-Growth Dynamics of Adaptive Transformation
(Source: Kim 1988, p. 56)

The dialectics of push and pull in the evolution of human psyche has been also explained by anthropologist Edward Hall's (1976) idea of "identity-separation-growth dynamism." In addition, psychologist Sydney Jourard (1974) describes the same phenomenon in terms of "integration-disintegration-reintegration':

Growth is the dis-integration of one way of experiencing the world, followed by a reorganization of this experience, a reorganization that includes the new disclosure of the world. The disorganization, or even shattering, of one way to experience the world, is brought on by new disclosures from the changing being of the world, disclosures that were always being transmitted, but were usually ignored." (p. 456)

The spiral of the shaping and reshaping of identity gradually brings about more skillfulness in the very activities of learning to become a part of a new, larger human community. In this spiral, the consequence of intercultural interaction is the creation of new mental constructs. This is not to suggest that the old constructs will disappear, nor that a gradual and partial acquisition of each other's initial cultural constructs will not take place. It only means that the new constructs constitute a decisive transformational element.

As such, intercultural identity transformation is manifested in the progressive attainment of a self-other orientation that is individuated. This means that, as an individual's cultural identity evolves toward increasing interculturalness, that person's definition of self and others become increasingly less restricted by rigid cultural and social categories. Instead, the person's perceptual orientations become broadened and enriched by an increased ability to "particularize" his or her perception of each communicative event in the context of a specific situation.

Simultaneously, this perceptual refinement toward individuation reflects a development of a universalized self/other orientation, which enables the individual to broaden his or her orientation beyond any particular cultural identity and ultimately reach the level of humanity itself. This seemingly paradoxical development in one's identity is generally consistent with Paul Ricoeur's (1992) notion of a "transcendental ego," which is associated by Ricoeur with a non-personal, non-cultural, but a universal identity. A similar observation is made by Adler (1987/1972), who describes intercultural learning as "a movement from a state of low self- and cultural awareness to a state of high self- and cultural awareness" (p. 15) –an achievement of what has been otherwise referred to as "cultural reflexibility" (Roosens, 1989), "cultural relativistic insight" (Roosens, 1989), "moral inclusiveness" (Opotow, 1990), "double-swing" (Yoshikawa, 1988), and "double-perspective" or "stereoscopic vision" (Rushdie, 1991).

The evolution of identity from cultural to intercultural further resembles the attainment of the characteristics of what Abraham Maslow (1954) called the "self-actualizing" individuals: (a) more efficient perception of reality and more comfortable relations with it; (b) acceptance of self and others; (c) spontaneity and naturalness (i.e., they have "codes of ethics that are relatively autonomous and individual rather than unconventional'); (d) problem-centered rather than ego-centered; and (e) continuous freshness and appreciation (pp. 232-234). In addition, the present conception of intercultural identity suggests a close linkage to what Linda Harris (1979) referred to as an "optimal level of communication competence'–the maximum capacity to communicate with individuals who are significantly different or incompatible, and to make deliberate choices of actions rather than having them simply being dictated by the normative courses of action in a given culture.

Identity development beyond culture, as has been described above, is not to be viewed as the product of aberration but the expression of the normal people in the act of "liberating" themselves from the hidden grips of their own psychocultural "status quo." The specific attributes of increased individuation and universalization, along with a heightened moral inclusiveness and communicative competence, are most incisively articulated by Glenn Louri (1993), a Black American scholar of English Literature.

I have often experienced this dissonance between my self-concept and the socially imputed definition of who I am supposed to be. I have had to confront the problem of balancing my desire not to disappoint the expectations of others–both whites and blacks, but more especially blacks–with my conviction that one should strive to live life with integrity....I no longer believe that the camaraderie engendered among blacks by our collective experience of racism constitutes an adequate basis for any person's self-definition....The most important challenges and opportunities that confront me derive not from my racial condition, but rather from my human condition. I am a husband, a father, a son, a teacher, an intellectual, a Christian, a citizen. In none of these roles is my race irrelevant, but neither can racial identity alone provide much guidance for my quest to adequately discharge these responsibilities. The particular features of my social condition, the external givens, merely set the stage of my life, they do not provide a script. That script must be internally generated, it must be a product of a reflective deliberation about the meaning of this existence for which no political or ethnic program could ever substitute....The expression of my individual personality is to be found in the blueprint that I employ to guide this project of construction. The problem of devising such a plan for one's life is a universal problem, which confronts all people, whatever their race, class, or ethnicity. By facing and solving this problem we grow as human beings, and give meaning and substance to our lives. (pp. 7-10)

Stricture and Freedom in Identity Development

At this time, let us note that the theoretical description and explanation presented in this essay are of a general nature, and that the degree to which intercultural identity development actually occurs in specific people would depend on combinations of many forces, some external and some internal (Kim, 1989; 1994). Among more salient external factors are the conditions of the societal environment such as the historical and institutionalized subjugation of one group by another. Under such conditions of systemic inequity, the prejudice and discrimination directed against members of a particular ethnic background may constrain their full participation in intercultural communication activities and thus interfere with an intercultural identity development. The self-definitions of the members of a historically discriminated group may be dramatically inconsistent with the identity reflexively imputed to them by others. This lack of social confirmation for their subjective self-definitions may leave them uncertain about who they really are, compelling them to find emotional refuge in a rigidified ethnic identity. People in this situation are likely to avoid opportunities for positive intercultural experiences.

Internally, the limits of an individual's identity development can be found where the balance between the stress engendered by intercultural challenges and the adaptive capacity that a given person is capable of mustering up. This means that, in the process of intercultural identity development, the aim must be to strike a balance between stress and adaptation, or between novelty and confirmation (Jantch, 1980, p. 139). The optimal point of such balance varies from person to person. Not everyone is sufficiently open-minded or motivated to be influenced by the challenges of intercultural interface. Some, by innate temperament, may be extremely susceptible to ill effects from such situations. Others may try to alleviate the fear of cultural strangers by retreating into their own cultural identity or aggressively asserting it.

As such, identity development beyond one's primary culture must be considered ultimately "the gift of the individuals" (Steele, 1990, p. 171). The power and responsibility for change rests in each person, who can either obstruct or facilitate his or her own transformation. To most people, adaptation to intercultural challenges is something that is desirable (Cornell, 1988; Kim, 1988). Contrary to the embittered polemics of ethnic politics among political extremists, the common wisdom of most Americans is one of pragmatic accommodation and the reconciliation of divergent identities for the common good. Such is clearly the case in the experiences of the persons whose testimonials presented earlier in this essay helped illuminate the reality of intercultural identity development: Mary Catherine Bateson, Sandra Kitt, A. J. Nagel, and Glenn Louri. All of them proclaim the value of an intercultural personhood in their respective writings and provide witness to the spirit of affirmation of differing identities. These and numerous others who have achieved varying levels of intercultural identity serve as the sustaining core or "cross-links" (Molina, 1978) of multicultural communities. They provide the hub and glue of the moral infrastructure that helps to hold together groups in conflict, to facilitate individual freedom, and to discourage excessive claims for social categories.

The evolutionary conception of identity presented in this essay, then, projects a personhood that is profoundly humanistic. It points to a sensible existence in the face of a multitude of divergent cultural identities. Both individuated and universalized, intercultural identity allows for ever-widening circles of self-other definition without diminishing one's cultural root. The concept of intercultural identity further discourages the obsessive adherence to the rigid categorization of people, exclusive loyalty based on past group affiliations, and fragmentation of the American society into many islands of cultural "interest groups."

In the end, the system's principles underlying the present conception of identity remind us of "the ultimate resource of human intelligence" (Boulding, 1985, p. 206)–our creative, adaptive capacity. It instructs us that, indeed, each of us can discover the shape of our own identity along the way, rather than insisting on the one already defined by birth and the scripts prepared by others. In Jantsch's (1980) words: "To live in an evolutionary spirit means to engage with full ambition and without any reserve in the structure of the present, and yet to let go and flow into a new structure when the right time has come" (underline added, pp. 255-6). The "right time" is now.

This article is an updating of a keynote address delivered at the 4th International Conference on Cross-Cultural Communication, San Antonio, Texas, March 24-28, 1993.

References

Adler, P. (1975). The transition experience: An alternative view of culture shock. *Journal of Humanistic Psychology, 15* (4), 13-23.

Adler, P. (1982). Beyond cultural identity: Reflections on cultural and multicultural man. In L. Samovar & R. Porter, (Eds.), *Intercultural communication: A reader* (pp. 389-408). Belmont, CA: Wadsworth.

Adler, P. (1972/1987). Culture shock and the cross-cultural learning experience. In L. Luce & E. Smith, (Eds.), *Toward internationalism* (pp. 24-35). Cambridge, MA: Newbury.

Altbach, P., & Lomotey, K. (1991). *The racial crisis in American higher education.* Ithaca, NY: State University of New York Press.

Barnlund, D. (1989). *Communication styles of Japanese and Americans: Images and realities.* Belmont, CA: Wadsworth.

Bateson, M. (1989). *Composing a life.* New York: Plume.

Bellah, R., et al. (1985). *Habits of the heart: Individualism and commitment in American life.* Berkeley, CA: University of California Press.

Bennett, J. (1977). Transition shock: Putting culture shock in perspective. In N. Jain, (Ed.), *International and Intercultural Communication Annual, 4*, 45-52.

Bertalanffy, L. (1968). *General systems theory: Foundations, developments, applications*. New York: Braziller.

Boulding, K. (1985). *The world as a total system*. Newbury Park, CA: Sage.

Brewer, M., & Miller, N. (1984). Beyond the contact hypothesis: theoretical perspectives on desegregation. In N. Miller & M. Brewer, (Eds.), *Groups in contact: The psychology of desegregation* (pp. 281-302). New York: Academic Press.

Cornell, S. (1988). *The return of the native: American Indian political resurgence*. New York: Oxford University Press.

Erikson, E. (1950). *Childhood and society*. New York: W. W. Norton.

Erikson, E. (1968). *Identity, youth and crisis*. New York: W. W. Norton.

Ford, D., & Lerner, R. (1992). *Developmental systems theory: An integrative approach*. Newbury Park, CA: Sage.

Furnham, A., & Bochner, S. (1986). Culture shock: Psychological reactions to unfamiliar environments. London: Mathuen.

Garza, R., et al. (1982). *Latino voices: Mexican, Puerto Rican and Cuban perspectives on American politics*. Boulder, CO: West view Press.

Giles, H., & Bourhis, R. (1976). Voice and social categorization in Britain. *Communication Monographs, 43*, 108-114.

Giles, H., Saint-Jacques, B. (1979). *Languaqe and ethnic relations*. New York: Pergamon Press.

Hacker, A. (1992). *Two nations: Black and white, separate, hostile, unequal*. New York: Charles Scribner's Sons.

Hall, E. (1976). *Beyond culture*. New York: Doubleday.

Harris, L. (1979). *Communication competence: an argument for a aystemic view*. Paper presented at the annual conference of the International Communication Association, Philadelphia. May.

Houston, J. (1981). *Beyond mansamar: A personal view on the Asian-American womanhood*. Lecture given to Governors State University (audio recording). University Park, IL. May.

Hughes, R. (1993). *Culture of complaint: The fraying of America*. New York: Oxford University Press.

Jantsch, E. (1980). *The self-organizinq universe: Scientific and human implications of the emerging paradigm of evolution*. New York: Pergamon.

Jourard, S. (1974). Growing awareness and the awareness of growth. In B. Patton & K. Giffin, (Eds.), *Interpersonal communication*. New York: Harper & Row.

Kim, Y. (1988). *Communication and cross-cultural adaptation*. Clevedon, England:

Multilingual Matters.

Kim, Y. (1989). Explaining interethnic conflict. In J. Gittler, (Ed.), *Annual review of conflict knowledge and conflict resolution, volume 1* (pp. 101-125). New York: Garland.

Kim, Y. (1994). Interethnic communication: The context and the behavior. In S.Deetz, (Ed.), *Communication yearbook 17* (pp. 511-538). Newbury Park, CA: Sage.

Kim, Y., & Ruben, B. (1988). Intercultural transformation: A systems theory. In Y. Kim & W. Gudykunst, (Eds.), *Theories in intercultural communication* (pp. 299-321). Newbury Park, CA: Sage.

Korzybski, A. (1933/1958). *Science and sanity*. (4th, ed.), Lakeville, CN: The International Non-Aristolelian Library Publishing Co.

Louri, G. (1993). Free at last? A personal perspective on race and identity in America. In G. Early, (Ed.), *Lure and loathing* (pp. 1-12). New York: Allen Lane/ Penguin.

Maslow, A. (1954). *Motivation and personality*. New York: Harper & Brothers.

Molina, J. (1978). Cultural barriers and interethnic communication in a multiethnic neighborhood. In E. Ross, (Ed.), *Interethnic communication* (pp. 78-86). Athens, GA: The University of Georgia Press.

Oberg, K. (1960). Cultural shock: Adjustment to new cultural environments. *Practical Anthropology, 7*, 170-179.

Opotow, S. (1990). Moral exclusion and injustice: An introduction. *Journal of Social Issues, 46* (1), 1-20.

Pettigrew, T. (1988). Integration and pluralism. In P. Ratz & D. Taylor, (Eds.), *Eliminating Racism* (pp. 19-30). New York: Plenum.

Phinney, J. (1989). Stages of ethnic identity development in minority group adolescents. *Journal of Early Adolescence, 9*, 34-49.

Phinney, J., Lochner, B., & Murphy, R. (1990). Ethnic identity development and psychological adjustment in adolescence. In A. Stiffman & L. Davis, (Eds.), *Ethnic issues in adolescent mental health*. Newbury Park, CA: Sage.

Phinney, J., & Rosenthal, D. (1992). Ethnic identity in adolescence: Process, context, and outcome. In G. Adams, T. Gullotta, & R. Montemayer, (Eds.), *Adolescent identity formation* (pp. 145-172). Newbury Park, CA: Sage.

Ricoeur, P. (1992). *Oneself as another*. Chicago: University of Chicago Press.

Roosens, E. (1989). *Creating ethnicity: The process of ethnogenesis*. Newbury Park, CA: Sage.

Root, M. (1993). Within, between, and beyond race. In M. Root, (Ed.), *Racially mixed people in America* (pp. 3-11). Newbury Park, CA: Sage.

Ruben, B., & Kim, J. (1975). *General systems theory and human communication*. Rochelle Park, NJ: Hayden Books.

Rushdie, S. (1991). *Imaginary homeland*. New York: Penguin Books.

Sarbaugh, L. (1979). *Intercultural communication*. Rochelle Park, NJ: Hayden.

Schlesinger, A., Jr. (1992). *The disuniting of America: Reflections on a multicultural society*. New York: W. W. Norton.

Slavin, M., & Kriegman, D. (1992). *The adaptive design of the human psyche*. New York: Guilford.

Steele, S. (1990). *The content of our character: A new vision of race in America*. New York: Harper Perennial.

Tajfel, H. (1974). Social identity and intergroup behavior. *Social Science Information, 223* (2), 96-102.

Tajfel, H. (1978). Social categorization and social discrimination in a minimal group paradigm. In H. Tajfel, (Ed.), *Differentiation between social groups*. London: Academic.

Terkel, S. (1992). *Race: How blacks and whites think & feel about the American obsession*. New York: The New Press.

Turner, J. (1975). Social comparison and social identity: Some prospects for intergroup behavior. *European Journal of Social Psychology, 5*, 5-34.

Turner, J., & Giles, B. (1981). *Intergroup behavior*. Chicago: University of Chicago Press.

Weinberg, H. (1959/1987). *Levels of knowing and existence: Studies in general semantics*. Englewood, NJ: Institute of General Semantics.

West, C. (1993). *Race matters*. Boston, MA: Beacon Press.

Yinger, J. (1986). Intersection strands in the theorisation of race and ethnic relations. In J. Rex & D. Mason, (Eds.), *Theories of race and ethnic relations* (pp. 20-41). New York: Cambridge University Press.

Yoshikawa, M. J. (1988). Cross-cultural adaptation and perceptual development. In Young Y. Kim & William B. Gudykunst, (Eds.), *Cross-cultural adaptation: Current approaches* (pp. 140-148). Newbury Park, CA: Sage.

Zaharna, R. (1989). Self-shock: The double-binding challenges of identity. *International Journal of Intercultural Relations, 13* (4), 501-525.

Ricoeur, P. (1992). *Oneself as Another*. Chicago: University of Chicago Press.

Roosens, E. (1989). *Creating ethnicity: The process of ethnogenesis*. Newbury Park, CA: Sage.

Root, M. (1993). Within, between, and beyond race. In M. Root, (Ed.), *Racially mixed people in America* (pp. 3-11). Newbury Park, CA: Sage.

Ruben, B., & Kim, J. (1975). *General systems theory and human communication*. Rochelle Park, NJ: Hayden Books.

Rushdie, S. (1991). *Imaginary homeland*. New York: Penguin Books.

Sarbaugh, L. (1979). *Intercultural communication*. Rochelle Park, NJ: Hayden.

Schlesinger, A., Jr. (1992). *The disuniting of America: Reflections on a multicultural society*. New York: W. W. Norton.

Slavin, M., & Kriegman, D. (1992). *The adaptive design of the human psyche*. New York: Guilford.

Steele, S. (1990). *The content of our character: A new vision of race in America*. New York: Harper Perennial.

Tajfel, H. (1974). *Social identity and intergroup behavior. Social Science Information, 223* (2), 96-102. 1978 Social categorization and social discrimination in a minimal group paradigm. In H. Tajfel, (Ed.), *Differentiation Between Social Groups*. London: Academic.

Terkel, S. (1992). *Race: How blacks and whites think & feel about the American obsession*. New York: The New Press.

Turner, J. (1975). Social comparison and social identity: Some prospects for intergroup behavior. *European Journal of Social Psychology, 5*, 5-34.

Turner, J., & Giles, B. (1981). *Intergroup behavior*. Chicago: University of Chicago Press.

Weinberg, H. (1959/1987). *Levels of knowing and existence: Studies in general semantics*. Englewood, NJ: Institute of General Semantics.

West, C. (1993). *Race matters*. Boston, MA: Beacon Press.

Yinger, J. (1986). Intersection strands in the theorisation of race and ethnic relations. In J. Rex & D. Mason, (Eds.), *Theories of race and ethnic relations* (pp. 20-41). New York: Cambridge University Press.

Yoshikawa, Muneo Jay (1988). Cross-cultural adaptation and perceptual development. In Young Y. Kim & William B. Gudykunst, (Eds.), *Cross-cultural adaptation: Current approaches* (pp. 140-148). Newbury Park, CA: Sage.

Zaharna, R. (1989). Self-shock: The double-binding challenges of identity. *International Journal of Intercultural Relations, 13* (4), 501-525.

Construction of intercultural identity — A two-directional extension model

建构跨文化认同的路径——双向拓展模型

戴晓东
上海师范大学

Abstract

Intercultural identity transcends traditional sense of identity, and whose unique qualities lie in its openness to cultural others, the recognition and appreciation of differences, the potential to integrate diverse cultural elements into a coherent whole, as well as the ability to achieve self-transformation and mutual growth. This paper firstly reviews previous researches; secondly, it puts forward a Two-Directional Extension Model; and finally explains its theoretical assumptions and the basic connotations. It is argued that extending cultural identity provides communicators an effective way to construct intercultural identity. Extension toward particularity makes cultural identity more inclusive to ingroup members; extension toward human universals turns it more open to cultural others. The construction of intercultural identity does not lead to the removal of cultural boundaries, but rather the stretching of cultural domains and the ontological openness of cultural identity. In constructing intercultural identity, communicators develop more sharing and produce wider space for intercultural dialogues. The construction process mainly involves three interrelated aspects: the deepening of interculturality, the transformation of local framework of meaning, and the shift of communication ethics.

人类生活的世界是联系与独立并存，同质与异质杂糅的世界。跨文化空间构成最为广阔、最富活力和创造性的对话场所。全球化进程中，世界文化之间的联系不断加强。它们相互渗透、相互激荡，渐渐融为一体，使原有的文化边界日趋淡化，有力地促进了跨文化认同的发育与生长。跨文化认同体现了交际者对他者开放、勇于探索新的可能，以及愿意在差异中相互协商、寻求共识、实现自我更新和文化创造的独特品格。分析建构跨文化认同路径的文献并不多见。本文拟对现有论述跨文化认同的文献作简要回顾和批判，同时提出双向扩展模型，阐释其理论依据和基本内涵。

1 现有三种路径的评述

Peter S. Adler、吉川（Muneo J. Yoshikawa）和金荣渊（Young Yun Kim）等学者曾探讨过建构跨文化认同的途径问题。Adler（1985）认为，跨文化认同的建构是人们摆脱特定的民族或集体身份的束缚，自由地跨越文化边界，成为不再隶属于任何文化群体的、介于不同文化之间的多元文化人或世界主义者的过程。Adler的论断反映了那种"居无定所，四海为家"的世界主义者的认同方式。多元文化人似乎为人们超越单一文化认同观提供了一种可行的选择。然而稍加审视，我们就会发现，世界主义者同时介入多种文化，但并没有成为其中任何一个群体的成员，实际上是无家可归的流浪儿。这种认同方式忽略了文化的历史传承性和社会依附性。文化一旦离开了它赖以存活与生长的历史传统和社会土壤就会失去活力。世界主义者的文化认同缺乏现实根基，在本质上是虚幻的，既不可能稳定地延续，更无法深层次地满足人们的社会归属感。

依据吉川的观点，建构跨文化认同是塑造文化中介人（man of inbetweenness），打造联合式身份（identity-in-unity）的过程；联合式的身份使交际者不仅能够从文化相似方面，而且能从文化差异上汲取养分，无拘无束地穿梭于自我与他者之间，不受任何羁绊（Yoshikawa, 1988）。吉川的理论导源于出世的佛教思想，他对跨文化认同的解读忽略了世界文化发展的非对称性和不平衡性。人们为了生存和赢得成功，建构积极的社会身份，必须明确地认同某个特定的文化群体。同等、不带任何歧视地认同于两个或数个文化群体可以让人们在意念层面上超越文化界限，但却难以面对严酷的现实。易言之，联合式认同不具备可操作性。

比较而言，金荣渊的论断更为现实。在她看来，跨文化认同建构的过程是交际双方作系统性文化调整、消弭排斥性认同、吸纳新的文化元素、不断回归自我、融入人类共同体的发展过程（Kim, 2001）。金荣渊的论断演示了交际者在跨文化调整中自我反省，逐步跨越文化藩篱，领悟人类共性的进程。她意识到多元文化人的脆弱，承认文化更新并不意味着原有传统的抛弃；在大多数情形中，交际者是在立足本土文化基础上，拓宽视野，推陈出新，发展出能够整合不同文化元素的跨文化认同。金氏的观点比Adler的温和与全面，更容易让人接受，但她提出的通过认同的"个体化和普遍化"（individualization and universalization）来建构跨文化认同的路径，在逻辑上有严重的漏洞。金氏的理论虽然强调交际者原有文化的重要性，承认跨文化认同是文化认同的延伸；但在逻辑上，它与Adler提出的世界主义殊途同归，皆希冀通过消除文化边界与文化差异来实现文化超越和跨文化认同的建构。

在理想状态下，当个体认同和世界认同取代族群、社群等地方性认同，文化歧视和偏见将不复存在，每个文化成员最终将在普遍的人性中实现统一。然而，文化认同根植于历史传统，受制于具体的社会环境，所表达的乃是每个集体共同的想象、意愿和选择。它允许其成员有一定的变异，但同时也要求他们具备相当程度的同一性。一旦文化认同彻底地个体化或普遍化，文化主体随即被虚化，集体归属的意义便不复存在，文化认同因此也就失去了根本的依托。认同形成的过程是自我的同一性与连续性渐次发展的过程，涉及个性与集体属性之间的相互协调和磨合；文化内部的同一性以及它与外部的差异性构成认同的两个相辅相成、缺一不可的方面。在此意义上，多元、宽容的集体认同也须有一定具体的形态和相对明确的界限。在现今的文明中，人们还未找到能够让个体健康地发展的、容纳一切差异的普遍化的认同形式（Erikson, 1968: 299）。文化的差异是无法消除的，其范畴的划分有内在的合理性。倘若我们人为地解除它，替代性的范畴就会出现（Brewer & Gaertner, 2004: 307）。世界早已被不同的地理环境、语言、社会制度和生活经验等划分为不同的文化区域，人们可以跨越自身的文化边界，但不能彻底打破文化的地域性，更不会仅仅满足于世界公民身份，不再追问自己特定的集体归属。现实表明，在世界日益统一的全球化时代，"追求独特的文化身份正成为一种普遍的风尚"（Robertson, 1992: 211）。持久、良性的跨文化认同不仅要具备坚实的社会基础，而且要有高度的开放性、包容性和广阔的文化视野。在此意义上，文化认同的拓展为我们建构跨文化认同提供了另一种思路。

2 双向拓展模型的理论依据

文化是历史地传承下来的符号、意义和规范系统。同一个文化群体的成员之所以能够建立社会认同，是因为他们拥有共享的生活、共同的价值规范与社会目标以及共同的意义框架。在跨文化交际中，文化重叠的累积与扩展使不同文化成员的生活经验产生共时性和交互性。随着文化间关系的不断深入，他们分享的经验与知识也在与日俱增，原本各自独立的意义框架就会渐渐交汇和贯通。当交际者超越自我中心主义，以平等的姿态欣赏其他文化之时，跨文化认同就会悄然而生。本文在上述几位学者的研究基础上，围绕文化间性这个核心概念提出双向扩展模型。

文化的拓展与延伸是人类完善自我，增进共同点的基本手段之一（Hall, 1976）。延展文化身份，既包容个体与亚文化群体，同时又寻求人类的共识，同样是建构跨文化认同现实可行的途径。文化认同的双向拓展由两个互为表里、相反相成的向度构成：其一是面向独特性的扩展；其二是面向普遍性的扩展。向独特性方向拓展，意味着亚文化群体或个人的特性与行为方式不断被吸纳与整合进来，文化认同对内变得更为多元与宽容；向普遍性方向拓展，意味着其他文化的思想或风习被源源引进和消化，文化间性渐渐累积、深化，人类共识逐步增加，文化认同对外变得更为开放和更具反思性。

双向拓展模型

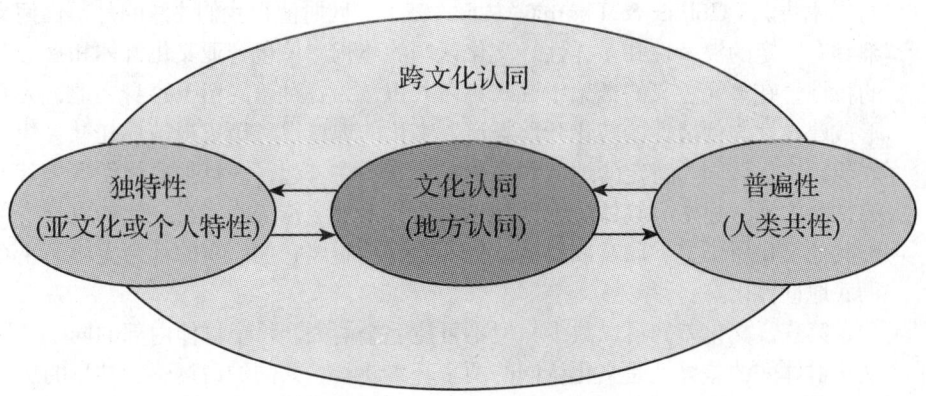

从表面上看，双向拓展模型似乎与金荣渊的思路非常接近，但实际上两者运作的逻辑大相径庭。双向拓展模型把文化认同视为身份拓展的基础，它不是要去除文化边界，而是要扩展它的界域，提高它的柔韧性和开放性，使不同的文化能够有更多共享的空间和更为广阔的沟通平台。跨文化交际的目的不在于文化调整、适应或同化，而在于彼此通过真诚、平等的协商，发现生活的真谛，相互取长补短，共同改造世界并推动人类的发展。双向拓展模型的理论依据大体如下：

第一，文化认同构成跨文化认同的基底，任何形式的跨文化认同都必须依托文化认同的支撑。文化发源于特定的地域，并且在地方社会的滋养下发育、生长和传播。跨文化认同只有立足于地方文化才能获得稳固的基础与发展的潜力。世界公民认同与任何特定的时间和地点相分离，拒绝在历史中对自己加以定位，排除了一切地方社会情感；多元文化主义同时介入多种文化，但却不明确地归依于任何特定的社群。这类认同缺乏扎实的历史根基和丰厚的社会土壤，既暧昧又脆弱，不仅无法获得强大的社会亲和力，也难以开拓良性的跨文化关系（史密斯，2000）。

第二，文化认同根植于人类的历史传统，被特定的社会环境所塑造，既有其理性的层面，又受到非理性的、情感的因素的影响；它是多元的统一，既不能被完全化约为个人特性，也不能彻底升华为普适性的原则或观念。文化认同是特定社会群体在其历史实践中不断交流、互动和沟通而形成的集体共识。建构文化共识的过程一方面受到传统因素的影响，另一方面又受到现有社会机制的制约。一般情形下，占据主导地位团体的观念将成为主流价值，其他处于次要或附属团体的观念往往在文化博弈中被主流社会同化或整合。文化认同表达了集体的价值取向和情感归依，其中冷静、理性的选择和冲动、狂热乃至宿命论式的依恋相互交织在一起，无法仅仅从理性主义的视角来理解它的建构过程。跨文化认同的建构不应回避情感问题，对某些非理性的观念与行为要给予适当的宽容。

文化认同建立在社会个体的观念和行为模式之上，但它形成后便独立于个体成员，按照自身的逻辑运作和发展（see Tajfel, 1978; Turner, 1982），其本质体现在主体间性（intersubjectivity）——通过社会个体相互交流、相互沟通而形成的集体共识（Collier & Thomas, 1988:105）。同时值得我们注意的是，任何文化都具有一定的混杂性和多样性。文化认同的建构应该包容亚文化群体和社会个体的特性，在多元主义的框架中寻求集体共识，为各种差异留下容身之地，为它们形成建设性与创造性的转化开辟渠道。文化的地域性、历史根植性和社会建构性表明，文化认同与特定的地域和历史经验联系在一起，一旦抽象化便失去其丰富的社会内涵，那些与具体的地理环境以及特定社会传统联系在一起的成分，可以被其他文化所借鉴、欣赏或移植，但不能完全脱离它们原有的社会土壤而生存，彻底地世界化。

第三，文化差异可以减少，但不可能完全消失。每个群体内部的同一性以及文化群体间的差异性是文化认同的两个基本要素。共同的命运感、共享的历史记忆、意义框架、价值观念以及共有的行为模式为集体意识和集体行动的产生奠定了基础；文化群体自身的统一性及其它与其他群体的差异为文化主体性的确立提供了必要条件。文化认同的两个方面相互依赖、相互促进、相反相成。人们应该从地理、历史和社会的多重维度来解读文化差异，理解它们的合理性和不可替代的价值。大千世界，林林总总，自然地划分为不同的区域和范畴，各奉其责、各得其所。交际者可以通过不断地交往，增进共识，超越那些人为的、不合理的界限，但永远也不能彻底地消除文化之间的差异。

第四，跨文化经验的积累和互惠性跨文化关系可以帮助交际者摆脱中心主义的束缚，培养他们的跨文化意识。"族群中心主义（ethnocentrism）是跨文化交际活动最显著的特征之一"（Samovar et al., 2000: 46）。交际者在经历了一系列的跨文化交往之后，其跨文化经验与知识逐步增加，自我中心的倾向渐渐淡化，缓慢地向族群相对化（ethnorelative）的文化定位转变（Bennett, 1993; Berry, 2005）。跨文化经验的积淀有助于人们克服文化偏见，减少陈见与误解。很多偏见与误解是因交际双方缺乏基本的接触与了解。跨文化交往可以使不同文化的成员相互熟悉、知己知彼，更为真切地认识对方，更为客观地理解对方，不再完全以自己的价值体系论断是非、以单一的标准评价他人。一旦双方能够从更为开阔的跨文化视野来界定自我与他人，良性的跨文化关系便有可能建立起来。良性、互惠的跨文化关系主要体现在反思性的思维、沟通式的理解和深层次的互动上。由此，交际者能够相互取长补短，共生共赢。

第五，地方性意义框架构成历史与社会事实（Grace, 1987），不能彻底地颠覆和清除，但能加以扩展和更新。特定文化的意义框架乃是社会成员相互交流，并且经过历史的传承、淘汰和再创造而形成的产物。它具有系统性、客观性和稳定性等特点，留存于集体记忆里，应用于地方的日常交往中，既不以社会个体的意志为转移，也无法像物理装置一样机械、彻底地清除。恰恰相反，它是交际者获得自我理解和跨文化沟通能力的基础。地方意义框架相对封闭，但同时也呈现一定的开放性——不同文化彼此沟通，进行器物交换、技艺的切磋和观念的借鉴，从而产生文化重组和增值的特性（冯天瑜，2006: 82）。亚文化元素和个人特性同样可以通过这个开放机制不断地进入地方社会系统，丰富它的文化内容。随着跨文化交往的增加和深化，新的知识和观念源源地被吸收进来，地方文化内涵随之日益丰盈。地方意义框架的扩展增加了文化重叠，提高了不同系统之间的通约性。文化通约性的提高为跨文化协商的展开、文化间性的延伸以及跨文化协议的达成铺平了道路。

第六，在推进文化反思，促进健康、良性的跨文化关系过程中，适当的文化张力是必要的。跨文化认同的建构并不能够消除差异与冲突，但它能够缓解矛盾，使文化纷争变得更易调和与掌控，使交际者获得有建设性的转化的潜力。和谐固然是实现跨文化沟通的最佳途径，但处于可管理范围内适度的文化张力也是不可或缺的。它在打破自我封闭和中心主义壁垒的过程中可以起到不容忽略的积极效用。文化系统具有自我平衡的趋向，在缺乏外部冲击的情况下，容易失去活力，陷入停滞或休眠状态。适度的跨文化张力迫使交际双方不断进行自我反思，敦促他们改变单一的思维模式，在相互批评中认识到自身的缺陷与力量所在，在有益的竞争中推陈出新，建构各自积极的文化身份（positive identity），协同发展。

3 双向拓展文化认同的基本内涵

拓展文化认同，建构跨文化认同主要涵盖3个基本层面：文化间性的深化、地方意义框架的更新以及交际伦理的重建。跨文化认同的建构始自文化间性的开拓。L. E. Sarbaugh（1988）曾辨析出7个层次的文化间性来显示文化间的关系，它们从完全相同到完全不同构成了文化间性连续流（interculturalness continuum）。Sarbaugh主要关注文化之间的相似性。实际上，文化间性的内涵是很丰富的。它体现了文化之间的联系程度；既反映了文化的接近程度，也反映了文化的互动频率、深度和范围；既涵盖文化的重叠与相似性，也包括文化的差异以及似是而非的灰色地带；既包括文化的共生与互补，也包括它们之间的矛盾和张力。文化间性的扩展和深化可以减少文化差异带来的负面效应，为跨文化互动关系的建立奠定基础，为相互沟通、相互借鉴与共同发展开辟渠道。寻找共同的话题、商讨交往的意义、分享经验与知识以及协调双方的目标是发展文化间性的基本手段。

跨文化认同的建构首先有赖于文化间性的扩展与深化。人类拥有相似的生物禀赋，居住在大体相似的自然环境中，面临着在本质上较为相似的生活需求。然而，这些联系远不足以使来自不同文化的人们建立起和睦的关系。人们第一次遇到其他文化成员时，常常把他们当作"陌生人"。因为，他们虽然"在物理空间上感到邻近，但在思维空间上却觉得疏远"（Gudykunst & Kim, 2003: 23）。陌生感造成文化上的疏远与隔阂，使交际者产生紧张、焦虑、不安甚至震惊等不良的心理反应，导致交际的受阻或失败。人们置身于异文化环境中，总要面对诸多的不确定性，产生相应的不安全感。当他们觉得一片茫然、无所适从时，往往会采取退缩或回避的策略，交际进程随时都有可能中止。文化间性的存在使交际者有似曾相识的感觉，戒备心理和恐惧感相应地得到缓解，双方容易建立起基本的互信。随着文化间性的不断深化，交际者渐渐了解和熟识对方，有可能排除多余的顾虑，协力推进交往的进程。彼此熟悉与信赖是展开对话、商讨共识以及达成跨文化协议的前提。

文化间性的发展不仅能够促进跨文化关系的建立，而且还能够提高文化通约性。每个文化都有其独特的核心价值以及表征这些价值的符号系统。它通过自己特有的划分事物范畴的方式建构起相对封闭、独立的意义体系。对于文化而言，经验的范畴化至关重要。范畴化涉及经验的简化和抽象等过程。它使原本杂乱无序的世界变得有条理，使原本变化莫测、数不胜数的现实情形有了相应的界域，处于可以掌控的范围之内。不仅如此，经验的范畴化还使意义的建构和解读有了较高的可预测性，社会交际随之成为可能（Ellis, 1993）。然而，范畴化是一个社会过程。来自不同社会的人们往往依据自己的经验区分事物，赋予它们不同的价值（Goodenough, 2001）。他们虽然看到同一个事物，谈论同一个生活经验，但由于其划分世界的方式以及由此而形成的意义体系不尽相同，因而常常有大相径庭的理解，难以相互沟通。在跨文化交际中，人们始终面临如何增进文化通约性的问题。

当文化间的联系加强后，交际者虽然来自不同的文化，但其共享的经验会不断增加。共享经验的增加不能彻底跨越文化鸿沟，但它将有力地减少文化空白，为相互沟通扫除障碍。随着共有生活经验的增加，文化范畴的交叉与重叠也会相应地提高，意义的转换与翻译日趋简易、便捷。文化相对主义和语言相对论都断言不同语言或文化系统之间缺乏通约性。它们的观点建立在静止、孤立地看待各个语言与文化系统的立场之上。在一个具有高度共享性的跨文化交际中，人们接触的事物，谈论的话题，理解问题与思考的方式比较接近，相互之间沟通能力显著提高，原有语言或文化上的障碍已经不再无法逾越。如果说，同一个文化语境是社会交往与沟通的根本要素，那么文化间性的发展则构成跨文化理解的关键所在。

建构跨文化认同的第二个方面涉及意义框架的更新。意义框架的扩展与转变是深化跨文化关系的必要环节。人类生活是群居性生活，语言的学习和使用构成主体间性的核心（Prus, 1996: 10）。共同的语言和共享的意义参照框架为社会成员之间的沟通与理解提供了保障。地方性解读（local interpretation）具有丰富的文化内涵，比抽象、一般化的理解更能准确地表达文化身份（Geertz, 1983）。然而，地方性解读在跨文化交际中往往缺乏高度的文化通约性，常常造成沟通上的困难，甚至导致交际失败。在跨文化交际中，交际者之所以时常造成误解，是因为他们来自不同的社会，有着各自独特的历史经验和迥异的意义框架。意义框架的拓展意味着交际者主动吸纳其他文化、亚文化抑或某些有价值的个人的思想与行为模式，不断地丰富自己的文化范畴，压缩真空地带。意义框架的转变意味着交际者不仅仅以地方标准或从地方语境解读意义，常常从其它文化的角度理解问题，并且在自我反思和相互协商的基础上作更为客观、公正的判断，发展跨文化解释框架。跨文化意义框架拓展了交际者的视野，使不同文化的成员更容易关注共同的事物，找到一致的目标；随着不同解释视角的交叉与融合，他们更有可能跨越文化差异的樊篱，通力合作，一道建构生活的意义，进一步拓展文化间性。

首先，跨文化意义框架不拘泥于地方性文化范畴，使文本或话语的解读打破原有的文化界限，变得更为开放和多元化。意义解读的开放性是拓展文化视野、增进跨文化沟通的起点。意义解读的多元化，以及与之俱来的文化反思机制不仅能够有效地改善文化通约性，而且为交际者相互学习、取长补短，以及在此基础上推陈出新增添内在的动力。其次，它强调在对话和协商中共同建构意义，提高了文化共识形成的可能性，深化了文化间性。文化共识的达成固然不一定很顺利，往往涉及持久的磋商、辩论和争议。但平等的对话和共同的参与使双方共享的经验逐步累积，相互了解日益加深，更容易达成协议。随着共识的不断增加，跨文化交际者之间的默契渐渐形成，其行为的协调性因此能够得到改善。相互沟通与协调标志着跨文化关系进入良性发展阶段。它为双方积累更多的共识，采取更为一致的行动，建立更深层次的跨文化关系铺平了道路。

Thomas Kuhn（1970: 111）指出，范式的转换实质上是世界观的改变。超越文化认同，建构跨文化认同需要交际者改变传统观念，发展新的交际伦理。文化普世主义和文化相对主义虽然从不同的侧面反映了社会现实，但均失之偏颇，过于极端。普世主义认为，人类拥有内在、普遍、共有的理性；交际伦理是非历史、非文化的，普遍性的原则与规范应该被理解为绝对的真理，凌驾于个人、文化和历史之上；文化之间的差异仅仅是表面的，在深层次上人类心灵具有不容置否的统一性（Foley, 2001）。相对主义认为，不同的文化以不同的方式划分范畴、解读世界；每个文化都同样有效地表达了真理，只有把它们放到特有的语境中，才能理解它们；适用于所有文化的普遍的标准是不存在的，人类没有共同行动的基础。导源于实用主义哲学的建构主义为我们重塑交际伦理提供了新的理论依据。

建构主义者承认人类具有交往理性，以及参与不同的文化活动、理解不同视角的能力。他们认为，一切文化价值或文化规范都是社会的建构，没有什么既定的普遍性，也不存在什么一成不变的特殊性。那种把身份固定化、基要化（essentialized）的观念是站不住脚的，人们应该把认同的建构看作开放、随语境变化而变化的进程。来自不同文化的交际者虽然不能在无需努力的情况下获得共享的价值观，形成统一的视角，实现相互沟通，但他们能够通过对话取得共识，能够借助自我反思、批判性思维和创造性的文化整合，建立更为宽广、且为交际双方所共享的意义框架（Evanoff, 2004）。在建构主义视野中，文化差异并非交际的主要障碍，恰恰是建设性对话的有利因素，而人类的共性则成为交际者不断努力追求的目标。

建构主义伦理观对普世主义与相对主义的超越主要体现在以下三点：第一，突出了人建构社会的能力；第二，揭橥了跨文化空间；第三，把人类的普遍历史与特殊历史有机地结合到一起。从第一个方面看，普世主义认为，人类发展有着既定、统一的路径；文化相对主义虽然肯定了人类发展进程的多样性，但却断言人们无法改变各个文化彼此独立、难以沟通的现实，两者都对人能否改变现实持怀疑的态度。人类不仅仅被动地适应环境，他们能够在物理现实之外，按照自己对世界的理解与界定，建构出社会现实，并且对之作积极的回应（Charon, 1998: 42-43）。社会现实是人们相互协商、相互沟通和相互影响的产物，在一定意义上随着人们的观念和语境的变化而变化（Searle, 1995）。它制约着人们的行为，但同时也被人们不断地建构。社会现实的变异性和可塑性表明，既没有放之四海皆准的普遍性社会法则，也不存在亘古不变、难以更改的社会状态。人类内在的统一并不能排除社会发展的多样性；文化的多元化也并不意味着不同文化的成员永远不能实现沟通与统一。建构主义寻求共识，但把共识的达成看作开放的进程；它承认差异，但相信人们具有超越差异和实现相互理解的潜力。由于建构主义没有既定的文化预设，强调社会变化的可能性和必然性，人的能动性和创造力因此而得到了彰显与强化。

从第二个方面看，普世主义注重人类文化的共性，相对主义强调其多样性，两者从不同的侧面忽略了跨文化空间。世界从未实现完美的统一；但也不曾瓦解为彼此孤立、互不联系的社群。粗略地回顾一下人类文化交流的历史，我们就可以发现这样一个基本事实：一方面，人们经过长时间的交往，积累了诸多共识，但同时又有很多充满争议、留待协商的问题；另一方面，尽管人们一再表示跨文化沟通的困难，但他们却不断地跨越差异，形成越来越多的共识。建构主义捕捉到共识与差异并存、交叉与平行同在的文化现实。它相信人类的共性，但拒绝接受任何既定的共性；它承认每个文化的特殊性，但拒绝把它们本质化。在建构主义者看来，不同的文化虽然有各自独特的价值规范，但它们不仅可以通过交流建立跨文化关系，而且可以通过协商达成跨文化协议，造就跨文化认同。建构主义对跨文化空间的揭示极具重要意义。它为不同文化以及文化内部群体之间如何以更现实、更有效的模式进行交往提供了新的启示。杜维明指出："位于毫无个性的普世主义和民族沙文主义之间有着开阔的跨文化对话场所"（Tu, 2001: 67）。在跨文化空间中，文化差异的张力与人类共性的合力相对平衡，两者形成了良性的互动关系，文化交流非但最具活力，也最富有创造性（周宁，2007）。

从第三个方面看，普世主义肯定了人类发展的统一性，但却没有对特定文化的发展过程给予应有的重视；相对主义肯定了各个文化自身发展的历程，但却否认它们之间存在统一性；两者都在某种意义上割裂了人类的普遍历史以及每个文化特殊的历史。人类发展是普遍性与特殊性辩证统一的进程：普遍性法则需要借助特定的文化、以特定的形式才能付诸实践，同时每个特定形式的文化实践只有在普遍性法则的规约下才能避免自我迷失，才能与其它文化有效地沟通，健康地发展。文化演进的统一性表现在诸多方面。例如，詹姆斯·乔治·弗雷泽曾在其经典之作《金枝》中提出，人类心智的发展经历了三个有普遍意义的阶段，即巫术阶段、宗教阶段和科学阶段（转引自：夏建中，1997: 21）；Carol Gilligan指出，人的交际伦理从关心自己向关心他人，再向既关心自己又关心别人的成熟阶段渐次进展（quoted in Elliott, 1997: 77）。承认人的理性以及人类历史的普遍性，并非等于否定文化发展的特殊性。由于环境的不同、偏好的差异、以及发展进程的不均衡与变异等因素，每个文化与其它文化既有共通之处，同时又呈现出各自的特点。人类学家露丝·本尼迪克特（1988）在其代表作《文化模式》中剖析到，一种文化在无穷的可能性里只能选择其中的一些；这种选择有其自身的价值取向，它经过不断的筛选、整合和抽象，逐步形成稳定的文化模式。建构主义立足于动态、开放的文化观念，有着更广阔的文化视野。它侧重不同文化的互动，力求在差异中建构共识，同时在建立共识的基础上促进各个文化的发展，使人类的普遍历史和特殊历史得到了较好的整合。

4 结论

跨文化认同取"和而不同"之中庸之道，力图在差异中建构共识，在协商和整合中实现超越，为我们改善跨文化关系开辟了新的可能。建构跨文化认同的路径既不在于投入世界主义或多元文化主义者的怀抱，也不在于抛弃集体属性，彻底地回归个人，而在于拓展原有的文化身份，以开放的姿态参与其他文化成员的社会生活，协同发展。文化认同的双向拓展使认同本体对内变得更为多元与宽容，对外变得更为友善和开放。跨文化认同的建构始自文化间性的扩展，然后经过意义框架更新的中间环节，最终完成于交际伦理的转变。文化间性的扩展可以填补文化空白，减少文化差异带来的负面效应，为跨文化关系的建立奠定基础。意义框架的更新是交际者进行自我反思，推进跨文化关系的必由之路。跨文化的意义框架拓展了交际者的视野，使他们能够更有效地沟通，并且在此基础上建构双方共享的意义，进一步深化跨文化关系。超越文化认同需要新的交际伦理。承认人的交往理性，强调文化互动过程，不懈追求人类共识的建构主义为交际者跨越文化樊篱，实现自我更新提供了更合理的选择。跨文化空间具有高度的开放性和巨大的创造潜力，在跨文化研究中有着不容忽略的重要性。本文提出的双向拓展跨文化认同模型仅仅初步探讨了这一重要领域很小的一部分，诸如跨文化认同的运作机制以及它的转化潜力等一系列问题有待于今后作进一步的分析与研究。

参考文献

Adler, P. S. (1985). Beyond cultural identity: reflections on cultural and multicultural man. In L. A. Samovar & R. E. Porter, (Eds.), *Intercultural communication: A reader*. Belmont: Wadsworth Publishing Company, pp. 410-425.

Brewer, M. B. & Gaertner, Samuel L. (2004). Toward reduction of prejudice: Ingroup contact and social categorization. In Mrilynn B. Brewer & Miles Hewstone, (Eds.), *Self and social identity*. Malden: Blackwell Publishing Ltd., pp. 298-318.

Bennett, M. (1993). Towards ethnorelativism: A development model of intercultural sensitivity. In M. Paige, (Ed.), *Education for the intercultural experience.* (second edition), Yarmouth: Intercultural Press. pp. 21-70.

Berry, J. W. (2005). Acculturation: Living successfully in two cultures. In *International Journal of Intercultural Relations, 29*, 697-712.

Charon, Joel M. (1998). *Symbolic interactionism: An introduction, an interpretation, an integration.* Upper Saddle River: Prentice-Hall, Inc..

Collier, Mary J. & Thomas, Milt. (1998). Cultural identity: An interpretive perspective. In Y. Y. Kim & W. B. Gudykunst, (Eds.), *Theories in intercultural communication.* Newbury Park: Sage Publications, pp. 99-120.

Elliott, Deni. (1997). Universal values and moral development theories. In Clifford Christians & Michael Traber, (Eds.), *Communication ethics and universal values.* Thousand Oaks: Sage Publications.

Ellis, John M. (1993). *Language, thought, and logic.* Evanstom: Northwestern University Press.

Erikson, Erik. (1968). *Identity, youth, and crisis.* New York: Norton.

Evanoff, Richard J. (2004). Universalist, relativist, and constructivist: Approaches to intercultural ethics. *In International Journal of Intercultural Relations, 28*, 439-458.

Foley, William. (2001). *Anthropological linguistics: An introduction.* Beijing: Foreign Language Teaching and Research Press.

Geertz, Clifford. (1983). *Local knowledge: Further essays in interpretive anthropology.* New York: Basic Books, Inc., Publishers.

Goodenough, Ward H. (2001). Category. In Alssandro Duranti, (Ed.), *Key terms in language and culture.* Malden: Blackwell Publishers Inc., pp. 19-20.

Grace, George W. (1987). *The linguistic construction of reality.* New York: Croom Helm.

Gudykunst, William B. & Kim, Young Yun. (2003). *Communicating with strangers: An approach to intercultural communication* (fourth edition). New York: The McGraw-Hill Companies, Inc,.

Hall, E. T. (1976). *Beyond culture.* New York: Anchor Books.

Kim, Young Yun. (2001). *Becoming intercultural: An integrative theory of communication and cross-cultural adaptation.* Thousand Oaks: Sage Publications, Inc..

Kuhn, Thomas S. (1970). *The structure of scientific revolution.* Chicago: Chicago University Press.

Prus, Robert. (1996). *Symbolic interactionism and ethnographic research: Intersubjectivity and the study of human lived experiences.* Albany: State University of New York Press.

Robertson, Roland. (1992). *Globalization: Social theory and global culture.*

Thousand Oaks: Sage Publications, Inc..

Sarbaugh, L. E. (1988). *Intercultural communication*. New Brunswick: Transaction Books.

Samovar, L. A. et al. (2000). *Communication between cultures*. Shanghai: Shanghai Foreign Language Education Press.

Searle, John R. (1995). *The construction of social reality*. New York: The Free Press.

Tajfel, Henri. (1978). *Differentiation between social groups*. New York: Academic Press Inc..

Tu, Weiming. (2001). The context of dialogue: Globalization and diversity. In giandomenico picco et al, (Ed.), *Crossing the divide: Dialogue among civilizations*. South Orange: Seton Hall University, pp. 51-96.

Turner, John C. (1982). Toward a cognitive redefinition of the social group. In H. Tajfel, (Ed.), *Social identity and intergroup relations*. London: Cambridge University Press, pp. 15-40.

Yoshikawa, Muneo Jay. (1987). Cross-cultural adaptation and perceptual development. Y. Y. Kim & W. B. Gudykunst, (Eds.), *International and Intercultural Communication Annual, Vol. XI*, pp. 140-148.

本·尼迪克特,(1988),《文化模式》,(王炜等译),北京: 生活·读书·新知三联书店出版。

[Benedict, Ruth. (1988). *Patterns of culture* (Wang Hui et al Trans.). Beijing: Shenghuo-Dushu-Xinzhi Joint Publishing Company.]

冯天瑜,(2006),《文化守望》,武汉: 武汉大学出版社。

[Feng, T. Y. (2006). *Cultural watcher*, Wuhan: Wuhan University Press.]

史密斯、龚维斌等译,(2002),《球化时代的民族与民族主义》,北京: 中央编译出版社。

[Smith, A. D. (2002). *Nations and nationalism in a global era*. Beijing: Central Compilation & Translation Press.]

夏建中,(1997),《文化人类学理论流派: 文化历史的研究》,北京: 中国人民大学出版社。

[Xia, J. Z. (1997). *Perspectives of cultural anthropology*. Beijing: China Renmin University Press.]

周宁,(2007),走向"间性哲学"的跨文化研究,《社会科学》,第10期,第162-168页。

[Zhou, N. (2007). Cross-culture study marching to intersubjectivity philosophy. *Social Sciences in China*, 10, 162-168.]

DISCOURSE STUDIES
IN CULTURAL CONTEXTS

On bian (change): A perpetual discourse of *I Ching*

Guo-Ming Chen   University of Rhode Island, USA

Abstract

What is the fundamental principle of the universe? The question has preoccupied the mind of Chinese elites for centuries. The answer can be found in the discourse on the concept of bian (change), which is the central theme of I Ching or the Book of Changes. This essay, based on the discourse of I Ching, aims to demystify the concept of bian from the following aspects: the attributes of change, the principle of change, the forces of change, the forms of change, and the outcome of change. Through the analyses, the author wishes to identify various change-oriented patterns of expressions that contribute to constructing the deeply ingrained change discourses in Chinese intellectual tradition.

Introduction

As an unalterable rule, change dictates the fundamental principle of the universe. Chinese sages used to say that change itself is the only constant phenomenon of the universe. Like the coming and going of the four seasons, the succession of day and night, the periodical ebb and flow of tide, the blooming and withering of flowers, and the cycle of birth, aging, sickening, and death, everything is flowing like a running river. While East and West are different in their ways of approaching intellectually the concept of change, they are similar in recognizing the nature of change of the universe.

In Chinese intellectual pursuit, the concept of change was mainly stipulated in the ancient Chinese writing, *I Ching* or the *Book of Changes*. The concept of change not only gives I Ching its name but also formulates its system of thought. Etymologically, before being applied to I Ching, the Chinese character I (易) had three meanings (Li, 1987; H. Wilhelm, 1960). First, I parallels "lizard" with the top side being likened the round head of the lizard, and the bottom part similar to lizard's legs. In addition, both I and lizard have the same pronunciation. It is said that lizard changes its skin color several times a day. Thus, I receives its semantic meaning of change, which shows the mobility and changeableness nature of a lizard.

Second, structurally, I is comprised of "sun" and "moon." The sun represents the nature of *yang*, and moon the nature of *yin*. Together, the interaction of sun and moon comes to the emphasis of *yin* and *yang* in *I Ching*. Finally, in Chinese ancient oracle-bone writing the phrases "*I ru*" (alternating sun) and "bu I ru" (unalternating sun) were found often. The "I" in the phrases means alternation or transformation which is suitable for being used to explain the changeable nature of trigrams and hexagrams in *I Ching*.

Change as a fundamental principle of the universe forms ontological assumptions of the Chinese philosophy and was further developed into a set of guidelines for Chinese beliefs and behaviors. "Change discourse" naturally became the central focus in early Chinese discursive practices. For example, according to the *Great Treatise* in *I Ching*:

The Changes is a book from which one may not hold aloof. Its *tao* is forever changing. Alteration, movement without rest, flowing through the six empty places; rising and sinking without fixed law, firm and yielding transform each other. They can not be confined within a rule; it is only change that is at work here. (Zhu, 1974, p. 112)

The "six empty places" refer to the six lines (*yao*) of a hexagram which stipulate the patterns, directions, and principle of change. The movement from the bottom line up to the top line symbolizes the change of a specific situation. *I Ching* proposes 64 hexagrams, in which each contains six lines with totally 384 representing all the possible situations of the universe. The first or the bottom line indicates the foundation of change; the second line is the sprouting period which indicates the formation of a change of things; the third line is the embodiment indicating the concretizing stage of change; the fourth line is like the leaves of a tree, indicating the strong growth of change; the fifth line is the blooming period, indicating the flourishing of change; and the sixth or top line is the fruit, indicating the fullness of change which implies a stage of transformation to another cycle.

The developmental discourse of change was also shown in the Doctrine of the Mean (see Zhu, 1978), when explaining the nature of cultivating a particular goodness based on a sincere or honest mind:

As there is sincerity, there will be its expression. As it is expressed, it will become conspicuous. As it becomes conspicuous, it will become clear. As it becomes clear, it will move others. As it moves others, it changes them. As it changes them, it transforms them. (Chan, 1963, p. 108)

In addition, the similar discourse appears in the *Great Learning*, in which the developmental change into the state of highest good is stipulated:

Only after knowing what to abide in can one be calm. Only after having been calm can one be tranquil. Only after having achieved tranquility can one have peaceful repose. Only after having peaceful repose can one begin to deliberate. Only after deliberation, can the end be attained. (Chan, 1963, p. 86)

Although these discourses resemble in its six stages of change, they do not imply a fixed order of transformation. Instead, they indicate that change is an orderly, non-chaotic but dynamic process of movement. In other words, from the humanistic perspective, the dialectical nature of change always reveals a trace and track, and that can be detected through learning and observation. It is on this basis that a possibility is open for human beings to regulate change so that a proper space for the self can be established, the value of life can be developed, the meaning of living can be unfolded, and therefore a human being can be parallel and integrated with heaven and earth as the three sides of a triangle.

According to *I Ching*, the formation of change relies on the dialectical interaction of *yin* and *yang*, the two opposite but complementary forces of the universe, with *yin* representing the attributes of yieldingness and submissiveness and *yang* representing unyieldingness and dominance. As Chen (2001) indicated, the pushing and pulling of the two forces makes the universe "forever changing — alteration, movement without rest, and flowing, rising, and sinking without fixed law" (p. 56). Thus, in order to bring continuity into the process of change, Chinese philosophers generated three ontological assumptions that were used to achieve the goal (Chai & Chai, 1969; Chen, 2001): (a) the universe is a great whole in which all is but a transitional process, with no fixed substance of its substratum; (b) the transforming process of the universe does not proceed onward, but revolves in an endless cycle; and (c) there is no ending for the transforming process of the universe. This discourse of endless, cyclic, and transforming movement of change continues to influence the philosophical discourse and its assumptions never cease to affect Chinese behaviors in the contemporary Chinese world.

The purpose of this essay is to continue this line of discourse by attempting to explore the essence of change from five perspectives: the attributes of change, the principle of change, the forces of change, the forms of change, and the outcome of change.

The Attributes of Change

As indicated previously, change is embedded in the dialectical interaction of the two opposite but complementary forces, *yin* and *yang*. Each of the two forces represents a self-changing system which itself develops an internal transforming process, and it is the interaction of the two forces that forms a complete and holistic system of change. Thus, in the *Great Treatise*, it says "The successive movement of *yin* and *yang* constitutes the Way (Tao)" (Zhu, 1974, p. 95). Here the yin refers to the dark and yang the light; they are two primal powers of nature which also include the notion of the two polar forces, positive and negative, of the universe. Since the primal powers of nature never cease to move, the cycle of movement continues uninterruptedly and is constantly regenerated in a state of tension which keeps the powers in motion and causes them to unite into a dynamic system of transformation. Therefore, "Changes mean production and reproduction" (p. 96).

As the attributes of change, *yin* and *yang* are also represented by hexagrams *kun* and *qian* separately, "Therefore they called the closing of the gates the Receptive (i.e., *kun*), and the opening of the gate the Creative (i.e., yang). The alternation between closing and opening they called change" (p. 103). In addition, "When yin and yang are united in their character, the weak and the strong attain their substance. In this way the products of Heaven and Earth are given substance and the character of spiritual intelligence can be penetrated" (p. 110). In other words, through the interfusion and interpenetration of yin and yang, changes "disclose things, complete affairs, and encompass all ways on earth" (p. 102).

The union of the opposite forces of *yin* and *yang* genders a holistic harmony that becomes the golden rule of change and the ultimate goal *I Ching* pursues. As specified in *qian* hexagram, the way of *qian* works "through change and transformation, so that each thing receives its true nature and destiny and comes into permanent accord with the Great Harmony: this is what furthers and what perseveres" (p. 3). The equilibrium of the two opposite forces is named *zhong* (centrality) which has become an everlasting subject of Chinese discourse (Chen, 2006; Wang, 1982; Xiao, 2003; Xu, 1994).

Apply to the human world, a person's mind is said to be in the state of "*zhong*" when there are no stirrings of pleasure, anger, sorrow, or joy; when the mind is stirred and one can act in his due degree, it is said to be in the state of "harmony" (*he*). Hence, the Doctrine of the Mean states that:

This *zhong* is the great root from which grows all the human acting in the world, and harmony is the universal path which they should pursue. Let the states of *zhong* and harmony exist in perfection, and a happy order will prevail throughout heaven and earth, and all things will be nourished and flourish. (see Legge, 1955, pp. 2-3)

Holding the *zhong* or embracing the great harmony not only dictates all schools of Chinese thought, but also is the cardinal criterion of Chinese behaviors (e.g., Chen, 2001, 2002; Chen & Chen, 2002; Huang, 1999-2000; Yang, 1989).

The Principle of Change

The interdependent existence of *yin* and *yang* and their interaction leading to a great whole reveal that change is an occasion for relativism (Cheng, 1987). Independently, *yin* and *yang* are a closed system separately, in which internal change is manifested by its self-absorbed and self-collected nature. However, reality is revealed through the interaction of the two forces, which indicates that everything is "a synthetic unity of *yin* and *yang* in various stages of their functioning" (p. 34). In other words, change is defined by the dialectic transformation of *yin* into *yang* and vise versa. The totality of *yin* and *yang* that forms the reality is symbolized by *Tai Chi* (the Great Ultimate. See Figure 1) in *I Ching*. It is the whole of Tai Chi in which the black area represents *yin* and white area *yang*, from which the myriad are originated. Thus, everything must be composed of *yin* and *yang*.

Figure 1. Tai Chi

Yin, yang, and the interaction of the two forces to complete the reality reflect three principles of change: straight forward, capacious, and cyclic.

First, change is straight forward. This refers to the internal nature of the *qian* hexagram. As described in *Great Treatise*, "In a state of rest the Creative (i.e., *qian*) is one, and in a state of motion it is straight; therefore it creates that which is great" (Zhu, 1974, p. 96). The straight forward movement of *qian* is symbolized by a solid or unbroken line (—), corresponding to Heaven, ceaselessly moving ahead without interruption like the endless extension of time. The creative power of *qian*'s movement in a straight forward direction characterized by dynamic greatness produces the quality of change (R. Wilhelm, 1990). The movement of *qian* is then "firm and strong, moderate and correct" (Zhu, 1974, p. 6). Only through the nature of being firm and strong, can the *qian* continuously move ahead; and through being moderate and correct, can the movement be stably forwarded (Wang, 1970).

Second, change is capacious. This refers to the internal nature of the *kun* hexagram. The Great Treatise says, "The Receptive (i.e., *kun*) is closed in a state of rest, and in a state of motion it opens; therefore it creates that which is vast" (Zhu, 1974, p. 96). The open and vast movement of *kun* is symbolized by divided lines (— —), corresponding to Earth, ceaselessly moving around without interruption like the endless expansion of space. The producing power of *kun*'s movement in an open manner characterized by dynamic vastness produces the quantity of change (R. Wilhelm, 1990). The movement of *kun* is then "gentle but firm, still but square" (Zhu. 1974, p. 10). Only through the nature of being gentle and yielding, can the kun continuously moves around; and through its perseverance, can the movement be strongly furthered.

Finally, change is cyclic. Because it takes a synthetic unity of *yin* and *yang* to complete the reality of existence, the on-going opposition and cooperation of the two forces leads to a dialectical and cyclic movement of the universe. As the Great Treatise indicates:

When the sun goes, the moon comes; when the moon goes, the sun comes. The Sun and moon alternate; thus light comes into existence. When cold goes, heat comes; when heat goes, cold comes. Cold and heat alternate, and thus the year completes itself. The past contracts. The future expands. Contraction and expansion act upon each other; hereby arises that which furthers. (Zhu, 1974, p. 108)

The movement of *Tai Chi* itself is cyclic. Reflected in hexagrams, each of them as well forms an internal small-scale cyclic transformation such as qian and kun. Expanded to the whole 64 hexagrams in *I Ching*, together they form a large-scale cyclic movement (Liu, 1990; Wang, 1957). Thus, "No plain not followed by a slope. No going not followed by a return" in *tai* hexagram best explains the cyclic nature of change.

Based on *I Ching*'s discourse, all contradictions in the universe should be resolved in the process of this cyclic movement. Any unresolved contradictions will bring about a negative effect. Moreover, the cyclic thinking leads the Chinese to develop a holistic view on the observation of the world (Liu, 1992; Starosta & Chen, 2003). The holistic principle unfolds the developmental feature of the cyclic movement in which individual components are interdependent and interdetermined in a network of relations. In other words, "In unity there is the infinite interfusion of diversities but in each diversity we find the total potentiality of unity" (Chang, 1963). The mutual dependency relationship reflected in the part-whole interdetermination also indicates that all individual components are equally valid outcomes of *Tai Chi* or the dialectic interaction of *yin* and *yang*.

The Forces of Change

Any movement requires a force to keep it going. In *I Ching* the eight trigrams symbolize eight different forces pushing and pulling among one another to form a multidimensional and multidirectional change which is reflected in the 64 hexagrams.

According to Wang (1983), first, *qian*, symbolizing heaven, moves straight forward on an upward direction. The upward force is moving like a "Flying dragon in the heavens" (Zhu, 1974, p. 2). It is strong and firm and represents the force of creativity.

Second, *kun*, symbolizing earth, moves in a receptive manner with a direction of square which gently forms a peaceful or calm space. The force of square movement can be described by the following: "The earth's condition is receptive devotion" (p. 8). Thus, *kun* represents the force of receptivity.

Third, *kan*, symbolizing water, moves in an undulantly curving manner which represents the revolving curve of downward water to an abyss. The force of curving movement is like "Water flows on uninterruptedly and reaches its goal" (p. 46). *Kan* is then the force of the abysmal.

Fourth, *li*, symbolizing fire, moves in an all-embracing manner with an oblique direction. The force of all-embracing fire "clings on things" (p. 47). It is the force of clinging.

Fifth, *gen*, symbolizing mountain, in a sense is a move to stop an ongoing movement.

The force of flattening or delaying movement is described thus: "*Kun* means stopping. When it is time to stop, then stop" (p. 76). *Gen* can be regarded as the force of dilatoriness.

Sixth, *sun*, symbolizing wind, moves in a pointed manner in a specific direction. The entering force is defined by "sun is going into" (p. 121). Sun is then the force of penetration.

Seventh, dui, symbolizing lake, moves in a circulating manner which resembles the function of lake as a circle. The force of circulating movement is like the nature of kun, where "The firm is in the center, the yielding on the outer edge... thus does one submit to heaven and accord with men" (p. 83). Dui is the force of circulation.

Finally, the eighth is *zhen*, symbolizing thunder, moves in a rolling manner with a direction of forwarding on a plane that arouses people. The rolling forces is described as that "Zhen comes — oh, oh!... It terrifies for a hundred miles" (p. 74). *Zhen* is then the force of arousing.

The eight forces of change, i.e., creativity, receptivity, abysmal, clinging, dilatoriness, penetration, circulation, and arousal (symbolized by the eight trigrams), systematically construct the laws of change of *I Ching*. In other words, based on the movement of the eight trigrams, the 64 hexagrams were originated. "Therefore the strong and the weak interact and the Eight Trigrams activate each other" (p. 92) explains the cyclic change that reveals the core discourse of *I Ching* dictating that "it is a rotation of phenomena, each succeeding the other until the starting point is reached again" (Wilhelm, 1990, p. 283). It is the interaction of these eight forces that forms the movement of the universe.

The Forms of Change

From the pushing and pulling of the eight forces that induces the process of the cyclic transforming movement we can identify seven forms of change: quantity change, quality change, gradual change, sudden change, equilibrium, negation, and negation of the negation.

The quantity change refers to the movement of position in each line of the hexagrams, while the overall quality of the hexagram does not change (Wang, 1970). In other words, although *yin* and *yang* lines switch their position in the hexagram, they still hold the number and ratio between them. Take the transformation from the *dun* hexagram to *da zhuang* as an example, before the change, *dun* contains two *ying* and four *yang* lines, and it remains the same after it is transformed to *da zhuang*, though the positions of *yin* and *yang* lines have been switched. It is like that a river running a thousand miles is still the river, even if the different parts of the river show that temporal and spatial contingencies are changing.

Moreover, the transformation of human beings from birth, youth, to old age shows the change of a person's physical and mental state, but no matter how it changes, a human being is still a human being.

The quality change refers to the change from *yin* to *yang*, and visa versa, in each line of the hexagrams. The transformation of *dun* hexagram into *lin* is an example. *Dun* originally contains four *yang* and two *yin* lines, but becomes two yang and four yin lines after it is changed into *lin*. It is like water being vaporized into steam or frozen into ice. By nature, water, steam, and ice are different in terms of its quality. In addition, a new management system is adopted to replace the old one to improve a company's performance also shows quality change from the perspective of leadership and management.

The gradual change referring to the coming and going of things is based on an accumulation of step by step movement. As indicated in *kun* hexagram, "Where there is hoarfrost underfoot, solid ice is not far off" and "Where a servant murders his master, where a son murders his father, the causes do not lie between the morning and evening of one day. It took a long time for things to go so far" (Zhu, 1974, p. 8). Before the stark winter or the decay of things is coming, the first sign or warning will be revealed and more appear before final dissolution arrives.

The sudden change refers to the acceleration or violence of movement when the gradual change reaches its saturation level. Thus, the sudden change is considered as the result of the gradual change in which the old system is replaced by a new one in a quick pace. The *ge* hexagram is the image of sudden change which symbolizes revolution. As the hexagram says, that *ge* is like "Water and fire subdue each other. Two daughters dwell together, but their views bar mutual understanding. This means revolution" (p. 70). The sudden change therefore provides an opportunity of renewal.

Equilibrium refers to the movement in a state of dialectic balance between the *yang* force to further and the *yin* force to preserve. This coordinating or interdetermining existence between the contradictory *yin* and *yang* forces brings forth two states of change: *bao he* (Great Union) and *tai he* (Great Harmony). As indicated in the *qian* hexagram, "The way of the Qian works through change and transformation, so that each thing receives its true nature and destiny and comes into permanent accord with the Great Union and Great Harmony" (p. 3). Great Union represents the state of balance being preserved in a stable condition; and Great Harmony is the foundation for the flowing of heaven and earth in the stable state of Great Union. In other words, Great Union provides a constant space where Great Harmony can develop its course in a symmetrical and congruent condition. Wang (1970) pointed out that the state of Great Harmony goes beyond the limitation of the law of contradiction, and which forms the cardinal thought of *zhi zhong / shou zhong* (holding the *zhongy*) in Chinese culture.

Negation refers to the movement to break-through or resolute a problem. As *guai* hexagram stipulates, "*Guai*, break-though. It is the same as resoluteness. The firm resolutely dislodges the yielding" (p. 63). According to I Ching, negation is a decision itself to move into a positive result. It represents a progressive step in the developmental process of change. In Great Treatise, the following is stated: "It is the great virtue of heaven and earth to bestow life" (p. 106). This quote reflects that the negation of death or darkness is to live or to produce.

Finally, negation of the negation refers to the resolution of a positive movement into a negative state. The Great Treatise's assertion that "Changes mean production and reproduction" (p. 96) explains the meaning of negation of the negation in which reproduction begets production. It is like "the dark begets the light and the light begets the dark in ceaseless alternation" (R. Wilhelm, 1990, p. 301). "When one change had run its course, they altered. Through alteration they achieved continuity. Through continuity they achieved duration" (p. 106) also expounds the positive sense of continuous negations that is emphasized in I Ching, in contrast to the emphasis of the negative effect of the transformation of negation of the negative which develops a vicious cycle of movement. (Wang, 1970).

The Outcome of Change

Any change will lead to an outcome. According to I Ching, from the perspective of human affairs, the outcome of change is located on a continuum woven by ji (good fortune) and xiong (misfortune). Six consequences array on the continuum between the two polarities of good fortune and misfortune: *li* (furthering), *heng* (success), *wu jiu* no blame, hui (remorse), lin (humiliation), and li (danger). The sequence is as follows:

Good Fortune ← furthering ← success ← no blame ⟷ remorse → humiliation → danger → Misfortune

As indicated in the Great Treatise, "Therefore good fortune and misfortune are the images of gain and loss" (Zhu, 1974, p. 93). Good fortune (*ji*) is a state of gaining benefits in which things are moving smoothly without difficulties. *I Ching* emphasizes that when a change is in harmony with the laws of the universe, the desired goal will be attained. This situation is said to be in the state of good fortune. In contrast, misfortune is a state of losing benefits which brings about undesirable consequences or disasters. It happens when the change is in opposition to the laws of the universe.

Depending on the volume, scope, and intensity of the change, the consequence can either move towards the direction of fortune (no blame, success, to furthering), or move towards the direction of misfortune (remorse, humiliation, to danger). The stage of no blame reflects a state of missing erroneous behaviors. The movement towards no blame is determined by the stage of remorse in which minor faults appear. If one shows repent or regret and tries to improve the problem, the change will move to the direction of no blame, or will drift into humiliation. As the Great Treatise says, "No blame means that one is in position to correct one's mistakes in the right way" (Zhu, 1974, p. 94). Both remorse and humiliation refer to minor imperfections and "are the images of sorrow and forethought" (p. 93) in which humiliation drives one into a confounding, debased, and dishonored situation.

The lack of repentance and improvement in the stages of remorse and humiliation will eventually drag one into a dangerous position. As described in *da zhuang* hexagram, "The inferior man works through power, the superior man does not act thus. To continue is dangerous. A goat butts against a hedge and gets its horns entangled" (p. 52). The movement in this situation doubtlessly mirrors the face of misfortune.

The immediate remedy of imperfection in the stage of remorse will have the trend proceed to the stage of no blame, and the successful effort will naturally lead to the stage of success in which, as indicated in tai hexagram "the small departs, the great approaches… In this way heaven and earth unite, and all beings come into union… The way of the superior man is waxing; the way of the inferior man is waning" (p. 23). In a sense, *heng* (the success) is defined by *tong* (penetration) through which "The going forward and backward without ceasing" (p. 102). The state of success provides a space where things are stimulated and set in motion so that continuity can be reached.

Therefore, nature must be furthered in order to make up for deficiencies and be abundant. The *Tai* hexagram says, "He furthers and regulates the gifts of heaven and earth, and so aids the people." According to R. Wilhelm (1990), "aids" in Chinese word means literally being "at the left and the right," which denotes the penetration between yin and *yang* at the right time and right place provided in the stage of success. The continuous penetration of the two opposite forces leading to the time of flowering pictures the stage of furthering. Thus, furthering is a stage of appropriateness and having gains. When it reaches the fullness of possession and at the height of change, as indicated in *da you* hexagram, "He is blessed by heaven. Good fortune. Nothing that does not further" (p. 28). Therefore, to stay in which stage of the outcome of change is based on the ability to regulate change.

Conclusion

This essay, based on the discourse of *I Ching* or the *Book of Changes*, attempts to explicate the key concept of change (bian). The concept of change is approached from five perspectives, including the attributes, the principle, the forces, the forms, and the outcome of change. It is clear that the discourse in this essay is limited on the philosophical level, although the explication helps to better understand the concept. For future study, it is important to apply the concept to explain the real life situation such as human interaction in a society. As mentioned in the Great Treatise, "What is above the form is called the Way (*tao*); what is within form is called tool (*qi*)" (p. 104). The philosophical tao transcends the spatial world which is the field of living symbolized by tool, but as well acts upon it by providing rules and guidelines of movement in the visible world. Thus, how to regulate change based on *I Ching*'s philosophical guidelines deserves scholars' attention.

The secret of appropriately regulating change is in the ability of holding the *zhong* (centrality) mentioned previously. According to Chen (2001, 2005, 2007) and Wu (1976), *I Ching* points out three possible abilities embedded in *shi* (temporal contingencies), *wei* (spatial contingencies), and *ji* (the first imperceptible beginning of movement) to achieve the goal of holding the *zhong*. The authors' efforts shed a valuable light on future research. In other words, how to foster the knowledge and skills that originated from the three concepts in order to know and act in the right time at the right place based on the trace of the movement reveals a potential of fusing the *tao* and the tool and also opens up a direction of inquiry in this area. The translation of *I Ching* adopted in this essay is based on the work of three scholars: W-T. Chan, R. Wilhelm, and J. Legge, and the version of *I Ching* used in this essay is X. Zhu's "A collected interpretations of I Ching."

References

Chai, C, & Chai, W. (1969). Introduction. In J. Legge (trans.). *I Ching: Book of changes* (pp. xxvii-xcii). New York NY: Bantam.

Chan, W-T (1963). *A source book in Chinese philosophy*. Princeton NJ: Princeton University.

Chang, C-y (1963). *Creativity and Taoism: A study of Chinese philosophy, art, and poetry*. New York NY: Harper & Row.

Chen, G. M. (2001). Towards transcultural understanding: A harmony theory of Chinese communication. In V. H. Milhouse, M. K. Asante, and P. O. Nwosu, (Eds.), *Transculture: Interdisciplinary perspectives on cross-cultural relations* (pp. 55-70). Thousand Oaks, CA: Sage.

Chen, G. M. (2002). The impact of harmony on Chinese conflict management. In G. M. Chen & R. Ma, (Eds.), *Chinese conflict management and resolution* (pp. 3-19). Westport, CT: Ablex.

Chen. G. M. (2005). A model of global communication competence. *China Media Research*, *1*, 3-11.

Chen, G. M. (2006). Asian communication studies: What and where to now. *The Review of Communication*, 6 (4), 295-311.

Chen, G. M. (2007, November). *A Chinese model of global communication competence*. Paper presented at the annual convention of the National Communication Association, Chicago, Illinois.

Chen, V., & Chen, G. M. (2002, November). *He xie* (harmony): *The axis of Chinese communication wheel*. Paper presented at the annual convention of the National Communication Association, New Orleans, Louisiana.

Cheng, C-Y. (1987). Chinese philosophy and contemporary human communication theory. In D. L. Kincaid, (Ed.), *Communication theory: Eastern and Western perspectives* (pp. 23-43). New York NY: Academic.

Huang, S. (1999-2000). Ten thousand businesses world thrive in a harmonious family: Chinese conflict resolution styles in cross-cultural families. *Intercultural Communication Studies*, *9* (2), 129-144.

Legge, J. (1955) (Trans). *The doctrine of the Mean*. Taipei, Taiwan: Wen Yo.

Li, K. I. (1987). *I Ching jie shi (An interpretation of I Ching)*. Taipei, Taiwan: Shi Jie.

Liu, C. L. (1990). Zhou I's cyclic views and Chinese thinking patterns. *Zhong Hua I Xue, 11* (3), 14-16 and *11* (4), 13-18.

Liu, C. L. (1992). *Chinese wisdom and systematic thinking*. Taipei, Taiwan: Shang Wu.

Starosta, W. J., & Chen, G. M. (2003). "Ferment," an ethic of caring, and the corrective power of dialogue. *International and Intercultural Communication Annual*, *26*, 3-23.

Wang, H. S. (1957). *Tai Chi Tu*. Taipei, Taiwan: Min Zhu Xian Zheng.

Wang, H. S. (1970). *An annotation of I Ching*. Taipei, Taiwan: Xin Shi Ming.

Wang, H. S. (1982). *A new view on mind law*. Taipei, Taiwan: Longhua.

Wang, H. S. (1983). *The study of movement*. Taipei, Taiwan: Long Hua.

Wilhelm, H. (1960). *Eight lectures on the I Ching*. Princeton, NJ: Princeton University Press.

Wilhelm, R. (Trans.) (1990). *The I Ching*. Princeton, NY: Princeton University Press.

Wu, Y. (1976). *The concept of change in I Ching*. Chuon Kuo Yi Chou, 754, 19-21.

Xiao, X. (2003). Zhong (Centrality): An everlasting subject of Chinese discourse. *Intercultural Communication Studies*, 12 (4), 127-149.

Xu, Z. R. (1994). *An interpretation of yin yang and trigrams in the Book of Changes*. Taipei: Li Ren.

Yang, H. J. (1989). *On the relationship between heaven and man*. Taipei, Taiwan: Shui Niu.

Zhu, X. (1974). *A collected interpretations of I Ching*. Taipei, Taiwan: Wen Hua Tu Shu.

Zhu, X. (1978). *A collected interpretations of Si Shu*. Taipei, Taiwan: Zhong Guo Zi Xue Ming Zhu Ji Cheng Foundation.

Persuasion in Chinese culture:
A glimpse of the ancient practice in contrast to the West[1]

Ling Chen   Hong Kong Baptist University, China

Abstract

Throughout Chinese history, scholars had devoted extensive and intensive study to the practice of persuasion, which was regarded as a means to understanding of humanities, people, and politics. Persuasion and argumentation were indispensable tools for important practical purposes and had remained an integral part of scholarly inquiries. This paper discusses rhetorical or persuasive strategies used in ancient times and compares similarities and differences between China and the West at earlier times. Cultural influences on persuasion practices and studies were also discussed. It is shown that Western classical rhetoric developed earlier as a systematic subject of scholarly inquiry of persuasion, while Chinese of the same period practiced persuasion with high sophistication in different pursuits and not treating it as a subject in its own right.

Documented Study and Practice in Chinese History

Throughout Chinese history, there are ample records on persuasive communication practices at different times, especially those in the Pre-Chin Autumn-Spring and Warring States period (770-250BCD). According to the history, this was a time where persuaders (shuike meishi) traveled from state to state, recommending themselves to the ruler or the lord of the land. Aided by eloquent talks and persuasive speeches, they presented to the rulers their ideas on political strategization. Youshui (traveling around to persuade) and jinjian (offering opinions to the ruler to do the right) have since become part of the long tradition in Chinese politics. In spite of the prevalence of such practice, there is no available

---

[1] A revision of a speech at University of Texas-Austin, 2002. Part of an earlier version was incorporated into a chapter in a book, Chen, L. (2004), *Persuasive Communication: Process and Practice*, Taipei: Wunan. The current version was reprinted, with minor revision, from Chen, L. (2005). Persuasion in Chinese Culture: A Glimpse of the ancient practice in contrast to the West. Intercultural Communication Studies, 14, 29-41.

documentation on the study of this practice as a scholarly subject. It defies the common sense that in the over two thousand years of Chinese civilization, no scholars had paid attention to this most basic of all communication practice. In fact, ancient scholars (up to 280AD) had devoted extensive and intensive study to the practice of persuasion, although it was not a direct subject of inquiry, but exclusively studied as part of some other subjects, such as politics and government, or philosophy.

Indeed, one of the ancient schools of Chinese philosophy, known as mingbian (name argument) scholars, stands to testimony of the academic interest in persuasion by ancient scholars (Hou, et. al. 1957). Mingbian scholars specialized in various pure philosophical topics and were interested in the logic of various arguments. Thus, persuasion and argumentation were indispensable tools for their inquiries. Similarly, in studies of government and politics, persuasion skills were regarded as essential tools to present and argue for a political positioning. Studies of persuasion served the purpose of these other, main subjects. Persuasion, thus, was regarded as a means to understanding of humanities, people, and politics. For all schools of thought, approach to persuasion started from and was inseparable from their approach to politics and government.

Traditional study of persuasion or rhetoric was carried out as an auxiliary part of other scholarly pursuits, as a way to understand human nature, government of people and corresponding cosmic order. Persuasion or rhetoric was a product of philosophical and political studies. Although never the main focus of those studies, it had remained an integral part, as all scholarly exchange of ideas involved clear presentation of ideas and arguments for a particular point of view. In academic discussions, one must communicate and persuade fellow scholars to see things one's own way. In politics, one must persuade a ruler or a people to accept a certain political proposition before moving them to action. The close attention ancient people had paid to persuasion is seen in a rich vocabulary related to persuasive activities.

Related vocabulary

Chinese language has a rich vocabulary to describe persuasion of various types. According to Lu (1998), classical Chinese had at least 6 terms used for reference to persuasion in practice or in conceptualizing persuasion, in addition to other meanings.

yan (言) referred to use of sleek languages to deceive a ruler or arguments about politics that would have certain effects, or language that reflect political ambition or cultural training, or particularly evocative languages that stirred up discontent of the authority. All these verbal communication involved direct or indirect attempt at persuasion.

ci (辞) similar in meaning to yan, but specifically referred to written or oral language use that was elegant and refined to have certain artistic effect. The art and beauty of such language added to the credibility of language user so they became more persuasive with more success in persuasion. On the other hand, ci might also refer to people using fine language to cover their lacking in substance. Thus the term might bring to the individual fame or bad names accordingly.

jian (柬) was a particular kind of persuasion done by hired or appointed officials toward a ruler. The purpose was to persuade the latter to retract or reconsider a previous order/policy or to correct a wrong or to mend behavior, for the good of the state and people. The practice of jian was by nature directed upward between individuals of unequal status. Its success to a large extent hinged upon the openness of the ruler to advice from councilors. In practice, jian might be carried out by an individual or a group of individuals. The latter was sometimes considered to be more effective, being reflective of a common viewpoint.

shui (说) was persuasion between peers or to a ruler, usually on political and military matters in policy or action. It was done by individuals of wisdom or of great learning.

ming (名) meant to name as a verb or name as a noun. This word did not directly referring to persuasion but stipulated the moral rules for persuasion activities to be proper and acceptable.

bian (辩) meant to distinguish and to tease out differences with description. The ability to do this was essential in debate of the vice and virtue of something and making an argument for or against. It involved separating ideas by listing of pros and cons of each and comparing the advantages and disadvantages in political matters. In scholarship, where definition was a necessity, it was to be done by clear a distinction between related or similar concepts and ideas. The term means to debate in modern Chinese.

The 6 terms represent ancient Chinese understanding of verbal persuasion with nuances for situational differences. Each term expresses one or more aspect of persuasion with some overlapping but never interchangeable. The full meaning of each term is revealed only when it is put in a context and in contrast to other terms. All combine to present a relative comprehensive picture of traditional Chinese conception of verbal persuasion.

Persuasion practice

In ancient China, formal persuasion mostly took place in three types of situations: government, moral education, and scholarship, where persuasion was carried out by professional persuaders, such as ceshi, shushi and xueshi. shi is a generic term for well-educated individual. shi invariably gained social status of a nobility because of their learning. shi usually went on to be an appointed government official and, thus, became part of the social elite. Three main categories existed to distinguish shi of different expertise and specialties. There were those known as ceshi (策士) who specialized in government including diplomacy and wars for external affairs and administration and public policy for internal affairs. Some had knowledge on divinity and related matters such as climate pattern for agricultural, magic medicine for longevity, etc. These are called shushi (术士)。 Last category of shi referred to those that devoted themselves to studies of cosmology, philosophy, ethics, governments and social order. These were scholars and were called xueshi (学士). There were many subcategories with finer distinction of specialties. E.g., bianshi (辩士) specialized in argumentation; moushi (谋士) in strategizing; cashi (察士) in investigation; wenshi (文士 in good writing; shuishi 说士 in general persuaion; jianshi 柬士 in righteous persuasion; youshi (游士 in traveling-pursuasion、言谈之士 in talks on various topics, etc. (Lu, 1998, pp.64)。

Persuaders were of three types in ancient China, so were persuadees in terms of status between the communicators. From the discussion on terms earlier, we can see that, most often the target of persuasion was the ruler, which was the case for jian (柬), shui (说), yan (言) and ci (辞) types of situation. Besides, the target of persuasion might also be peers when it was shui (说), ci (辞), yan (言) and bian (辩). In a few situations when shui (说) and yan (言) were used, the target of persuasion might also be an individual of lower status. ming (名) was applicable to all persuasion situations as it dealt with general principle of form and content. Regardless of the status differences, in most situations, all parties in the persuasion communication were individuals of social status with good education. Rhetoric in ancient China, thus, was a game for the social elite. The terms for various types of persuasion indicate that Chinese of ancient times had noted factors such as social status and background of the audience that must be taken into account for persuasion to occur in proper manner and for it to be effective.

Rhetorical method

Many rhetorical methods or strategies used in ancient times are still very common today. First, classical Chinese rhetoric put great emphasis on the force of morality, which was considered of paramount importance in making appeals to others. An important component of morality was maintenance of social order in compliance to the role expectations of the society. Thus, an effective rhetorical method was to point out the extent to which a conduct was consistent to social role expectation. This may be illustrated in a story about yanzi (see yanzi chunqiu), a Confucian scholar of Pre-Chin period. A king of the kingdom of Qi was once very angry with a commoner that had committed some petty crimes. The king wanted to execute him with a cruel punishment of severing his limbs. When the criminal was brought before the Court, yanzi stepped forward with a knife in hand. He grabbed the arm of the person and asked, "At which part of a person's body would one begin severance according to the sage kings of the past?" On hearing this, the King changed his mind and said, "Release him." Here, yanzi managed to dissuade the King from cruelty. He skillfully used the indirect tactic to point out that the punishment did not fit the crime and was not consistent to the moral standards set up by sage kings in the past. Moral appeals were the strongest when applied to the persuader's character. This is seen in the case of Zhang Yi, a prime minister of the kingdom of Qin who had made great contribution to Qin's eventual integration of China. No sooner than the Qin King whom Zhang had served died, many officials long jealous of Zhang's achievement and status approached the new king and started slandering Zhang. They accused that he was a person of no loyalty, for he was from the kingdom of Wei and yet had served Qin for his own gain. In other words, he was not a person of good moral character that could be trusted and should not be given a position of importance; whatever he said about government could not be believed either.

Another common persuasion tactic is quoting real-life examples from history or present time, to make a case or prove a point. China was a society of precedence where history was important and so were the historical lessons. Events from the past could not be changed, neither could they be erased, and had thus gained strength as an effective persuasive tool. A story from "zhanguoce (A history of warring states)" serves as an example. A gentleman by the name of Lu Jun (鲁君) once made a toast and presented a persuasive talk at a celebration banquet held by a king of the kingdom of Liang. Lu recounted four events some from the past and some were contemporary. He said, in the past, the daughter of Emporer Shun, one of the first Chinese emperors, had a master made some very fine wine and presented to a later emperor, Dayu, who found the wine extremely good. Since then Dayu kept a distance from that maser and stopped drinking. He said, one day someone in later generations would lose the kingdom because of drinking. A King of Qi, one night had stomach discomfort, and an official, named Yiya, cooked meat with delicious spices for him. The King ate the meat and slept well until day broke. Since then, the King refused meat and said, someday in later generations, someone would lose a kingdom because of fine foods. A king of Jing was once presented a beautiful woman, Nan, and did not attend to his kingly duties for three days. Since then, the king kept away from Nan and said, someday in later generations, someone would lose a kingdom for being fond of beautiful women. A king of Chu once climbed up to a pavilion on a mountaintop. There was a river on the left, a lake on the right, and another river right below, all surrounded by green ridges of mountains stretching far. The scenery was so breathtaking and beautify that one could forget about even death there. Since then the Chu king vowed to never climb again, saying, someday in later generations, someone would lose a kingdom for being attracted by the beauty of sceneries. Now, your majesty the king had the drink of the master, fine food of yiya, accompanied by beautiful women like Nan, while standing in front of beautiful sceneries. Any one of these fine things was enough to corrupt a king and cause him to lose a kingdom. Now you had all four, wasn't it time for you to become alarmed and forego the enjoyment? The Liang king was persuaded by the four historical examples given by Lu Jun and adopted his suggestions.

Using historical stories as analogy for today is one particular way of comparison. Ancient Chinese persuasion also used fabricated stories or things that happen in nature as another way of comparison to the case in question. In modern Chinese, there are a lot of set phrases or sayings that have originated from such stories. A common one such as "a mantis going after cicada unaware of the bird behind him" (螳螂捕蝉，黄雀在後) came from persuasive remarks by Zhuanxin to a king of the kingdom of Chu. Zhuan used the case of mantis to compare the situation of the Chu king, admonishing him from being enjoying a good life while totally unaware of the grave danger lurking nearby. The point was to get the king be diligent and be always on an alert for the possible disasters and foreign invasion. The saying of "a snipe fighting a clam to the benefit of the fisherman"(鹬蚌相争，渔翁得利) came from Sudai in persuasion of the Zhao king who was contemplating attacks on the kingdom of Yan. The situation was compared to when a snipe trying to pick into a clam and was pinched by the shells. As neither would give up, both were stuck on the spot only to be picked up by a passing fisherman who was pleased at this windfall. Thus, if the kingdoms of Zhao and Yan fought each other, neither was strong enough to win but would hurt each other, while the stronger kingdom of Qin was certain to take advantage of the situation and take both without any effort. One more set phrase, "heading toward north to go south" (南辕北辙), came from Jiliang dissuading a king of Wei not to attack Zhao. At the news of Wei king's intent, Ji went to see the king and told him the following story. Ji said he ran into a person driving a carriage toward north who wanted to go to the kingdom of Chu in the south. When told he was heading in the wrong direction and would never make it, the person claimed to have strong horses, ample funds and skillful driver. All these advantages would only accelerate his mistake and take him further away from where he wanted to go. Ji was likening Wei king's wish to be the leader of all lords as the gentleman's goal to visit Chu in the south. Attacking Zhao by Wei was wrong as was the direction of north was to the traveling gentleman, because such would be an act of bullying the weak and would reflect badly on Wei and its trustworthiness. Thus, the stronger Wei might be the more severe its attacks on Zhao would be, the more other states would distrust Wei, and the further away Wei would be from being recognized as the leader by other lords. This kind of comparison put things of different type together and allows people to see the similarity in an unexpected way, who are thus more willing to accept the argument and be convinced.

There is another type of comparison that does not involve stories but lay out all related facts for a comparison of strengths and weaknesses of different scenarios, leading to a decision for the most advantageous option. This is demonstrated in a large-scale persuasive venture by a disciple of Confucius, Zigong, known for his oral skills. He once at the request of his mentor went traveling from state to state persuading the respective lords and advocating for certain actions. Zigong managed to thaw the plan of a powerful official of the kingdom of Qi, Tianchang, who was going to attack Lu, the native land of Confucius and many of his students. Zigong first went to see Tianchang and told him that attacking Lu was a wrong move, because Lu was smaller and weaker than Qi that had a people who did not like war and a king with generals who were incompetent. Attacking Lu would bring difficulties and problems. In comparison, he should turn to attack Wu instead, which was large, rich and well equipped, with good generals. When Tian was angered by this absurd counterintuitive argument, Zigong continued to point out that Tian did not have a very strong position in his own state and was vulnerable. Lu might be easy to win, which would strengthen the king of Qi and the generals who fought the battles, leaving Tian without awards being merely the strategist with no substantial contribution. Thus a victory over Lu would bring difficulties and problems for Tian in his quest for power. In contrast, attacking Wu was difficult and defeat was more likely, which would root out generals who fought in the war, or at least weaken their powers. Then there would be fewer competitors in the court, so the king would have to rely more on him as a main counsel. This way, Tian could easily control the king and virtually rule the state. Zigong's presentation and comparison brought the point home to Tian, who was persuaded to attack Wu in stead. Zigong then moved on to the kingdoms of Wu, Yue and Jing, talking to each king in the similar fashion. Zigong's peruasive expedition spared people of Wu the misery of a war, and much changed the inter-state situation of that time.

Lastly, Ancient Chinese routinely used emotional appeal as an effective persuasion method. As mentioned before, the moral appeal most important to Chinese culture is ultimately an emotional appeal. The traditional beliefs in such virtues as "ren--kindness, yi--righteousness, zhong--loyalty, xin--faith, cheng--sincerity" were the source of moral appeals, which were all built on the foundation of emotions and were reflected in conducts and actions. A belief in these virtues and morality is a belief in feelings and emotions. Good persuasion is such because it is able to stir up feelings that people trust, which induces conviction. Two cases serve as illustrations of this common method. In Tan dynasty, a General Xin serving the emperor then was a good soldier and a good general. He once killed someone for private vengeance and was put on a death roll for capital punishment. One official, Li, spoke to the Emperor that Xin was due to die for a long time. The Emperor was curious and asked the reason for this remark. Li said, Xin's father and brothers all fought for the country and died in battles. Xin was the only one that had survived and should have joined his family in death; his death was long overdue. At this, the Emperor felt sympathy and gratitude for Xin and his family, then ordered Xin's sentence be reduced to demotion. Li was begging for clemency on behalf of Xin, by appealing to the tender emotions of the Emperor toward the accused and persuaded the latter to spare his life.

Emotions the persuasion may appeal to also include other types, e.g., the well-known scare tactics. Here is a story that created another set phrase for the Chinese, weiruleinuan (more dangerous than stacking eggs). In Spring-Autumn period, a king of the kingdom of

Jin intended to build a pavilion of 9 stories, which would demand huge labor and other resources and would deplete the treasury. Against opposing voices from below, the king declared to kill anyone who dared to dissuade him of this plan. Then an official, Sunjin asked to see the king, claiming he could perform a very difficult trick of stacking up 9 chess pieces with 9 eggs on top of them. The king was intrigued and ordered to have all materials ready for Sun to perform. Sun carefully put chess pieces one on top of another to stack them up, and then, very gingerly put one egg on top, then another and another ... Sweats ran out of Sun's face as he went on with utmost care. The stack grew higher and higher, and became less and less stable, and the atmosphere in the house grew more and more tense. Every official watching was holding the breath in case air vibration would shake the stack. The king was very nervous and murmured, "so dangerous, so scary." Sun immediately put in, "This is not dangerous. There are things more dangerous than this." The king was surprised and asked for an explanation. Holding a last egg in one hand, Sun said, "Building the 9-story pavilion is more dangerous, which would take at least 3 years. In the 3 years, many strong labors are needed to do this, so is a huge sum of money. By the time it is done, people would be exhausted and disgruntled. The treasury would be empty and the state very weak. Neighboring states would take advantage of the situation to attack us, when we are at our weakest. Then we would not be able to defend ourselves. The kingdom of Jin would be conquered. And your majesty would be no more. Is that not more dangerous than stacking eggs?" The Jin king was so shaken by the scenario and ordered the immediate halt to the building plan. Here, Sun in his persuasion appealed to the worse fear of every ruler, the loss of his throne and his kingdom, which had proved to be very effective.

Views and talks on persuasion

Chinese cultural tradition, especially from the Confucius school, had held morality as a key element for human conduct including communication. Early thinkers, such as Confucius, Mencius, and Xunzi, had all discussed the relationship between verbal activity and morality in this way. Such that "Persons of virtue would speak," "Virtue expressed in words are to be expressed in deeds" (Confucius); "One with no virtue would not be listened to by others;" and being persons of virtue, "Gentleman would speak of virtue;" "The gentleman has virtues, practices virtues, and enjoys speaking virtues."(Xunzi) Regarding talk and virtues, there were many discussions from the opposite aspect: "Quick talk disrupts virtue" and "sharp tongues confuse morality;"(Confucius) "ineptitude in talk rather than speech of no virtues"(Mencius). Talks and remarks that were against moral criteria must be sanctioned and not allowed to spread. Thus one's duty was to retort such speech, which was different than just idle arguing. As Mencious remarked "one did not enjoy arguing but could not help it when provoked by talk of no virtue". Or as Xunzi put it, "with virtue one would not give way but to argue one's best". Even practitioners of Zongheng School (vertical and horizontal coalition strategies), who were known for their utilitarianism in approach, recognized the importance of virtue and morality. Zongheng practitioners regularly cited virtue to support their points and used morality as criteria of assessment of persuasion by others (e.g., Peng, 1996).

In association with virtue was the emphasis on names and naming. Naming was a verbal activity that concretized the notion of morality and was closely related to persuasion. Name as opposed to content, represented a relationship with many implications. Name as label was external form, as opposed to substance that was internal quality. Where morality was concerned was the consistency between name and content. A name inappropriate to the content was a rhetorical problem but a form inconsistent to substance was an ethical issue. Then what does name appropriateness have to do with morality? Listen to Confucius, "when names are not correct, what is said will not sound reasonable; when what is said does not sound reasonable, affairs will not culminate in success; when affairs do not culminate in success, rites and music will not flourish; when rites and music do not flourish, punishments will not fit the crime; when punishments do not fit the crime, the common people will not know where to put hand and foot. Thus when the gentleman names something, the name is sure to be usable in speech, and when he says something, this is sure to be practicable. The thing about the gentleman is that he is anything but casual where speech is concerned". Thus was established the connection between the rhetorical practice of naming and morality. On this, Xunzi held a similar view: "Name is not such by nature but by convention. When a name fits the convention, it is appropriate; when it does not fit the convention, it is not appropriate." Not being appropriate was not (socially) reasonable and thus went against morality. The moral connection of naming is presented here from a different angle.

Naming is one of the few areas where ancient scholars made inquiries that involved pure logic, all at the same time of its practical implications for law enforcement and government. More in character is ancient scholars' view and many discussions on talks and deeds in relation to naming. Confucius contributed much to this discussion. One finds many related references in Analects, "The gentleman should be reluctant to talk but ready to act;" "The gentleman would be ashamed to speak but not to do;" "apt at action and cautious at talk". In comparison to talk, action was infinitely preferable and worthier of trust. Deeds were yardstick that speech must measure up to, thus action was primary and talk secondary. This principle of action over word applied to persuasive communication as well. When something could be said and done, then doing comes first, although talk must be done if necessary. A natural question then is what to say, or what is worthy of speaking or necessary to talk about? One criterion was relevance to virtue. Xunzi said, "Speak no virtue, then keep silent rather than speak, then speak badly rather than argue well". In other words, when speaking, what was said must be consistent with the moral standard. Otherwise, one should not speak — because it was not worthy. Only what was consistent to morality was worthy of speaking. He also pointed out, "Argue and not avail is wasteful and useless"; "argument that cannot be applied is fruitless effort and must not be done in government and moral cultivation." In other words, only things that could be done or carried out in practice should be said. Specifically, "knowledge of the past must be of use to today; knowledge of divinity must be of use to earthly matters. Talks of value can stand the test of reality and practice." Similar remarks are found from other scholars. For example, "Speaking often without the ability to act or do is empty talk" (Mozi). "Talk can be broad and deep but useless" (Hanfeizi). This kind of contrast rendered talk completely inadequate and useless unless it served some practical purpose of doing something or helped in moral cultivation. Following this thinking, communication or rhetoric was nothing until it accomplished some moral or practical deeds. This view on speaking and talk applied to other means of persuasion as well.

Ancient Chinese had long recognized the role of action and conduct as a means for persuasion, and held it as more effective than verbal persuasion. It was said, "No attendance, no doing, no one believing" (Sijing). Without being there doing that, no one would trust what you were saying. Also, "Act in righteous manner, others follow without order; act not in righteous manner, others will not follow even ordered" (Anelects). The persuasive power of example was self-evident. In comparison to acts, "fine talks do not go deep into heart as do fine deeds" (Mencius). Good conducts moved people more than good words and were thus more persuasive. "Talk with acts and no words, tell without saying; tell without saying, not no talking "(Zhuanzi). One could talk with acts and not words and talk better that way. Such action-talks "far surpass any actual talk"(Laozi). This kind of faith in action as persuasion was extended to talks about action as persuasion. It can be seen in the discussion earlier on rhetorical methods, where persuaders cited other's action in the past or present as examples for people to follow and to be moved. Besides being a direct example, one's own action and experience were commonly quoted as analogy in talks to persuade, known as "self-example persuasion"(现身说法). One well-known example is an official, Zouji, of a Qi king, who used his own experience to persuade the king as follows. Zou said, he had thought of himself as good looking and asked respectively his wife, his concubine, and a visiting guest, how he himself compared to a known handsome man Master Xu. All said Zou looked better. Then one day, Zou had a chance to meet the said Master and realized Xu was indeed more handsome than himself. He explained to the king, that the three people that had praised him to be better looking, did so because, his wife favored her own husband and would not tell the truth; his concubine feared him and would not tell the truth; while his guest had asked something of him and would not tell the truth to jeopardize the chance. Thus, he was unable to get the truth from all of them. This might be compared to the situation of the king, who was surrounded by people who either favored him, or feared him, or wanted something from him, therefore, none would tell the truth about his weakness. The king was persuaded and ordered to reward anyone that would point out his shortcomings or mistakes.

Self-example persuasion, just like examples, was also employed in action. Here is a case in point. Han Gaozhu, an emperor of Han Dynasty had a wet nurse when he was an infant. This nurse once committed a crime. The emperor did not have the heart to punish her and just sent her to remote regions away from the capital. The woman did not want to go that far and sought advice from a favorite actor of the emperor. Taken the latter's advice, she went to say good-bye to the emperor, then turned immediately to walk out of the palace. On her way out, she turned her head around to look at the emperor at every step, appearing difficult to just tear her herself away. The actor standing nearby shouted to her, "Woman, just go. The majesty is a grown man and does not need you any more." The emperor on the other hand was deeply touched by the behavior of the wet nurse and ordered to allow her to stay. With her acts as an example of what she had wanted to say, the woman was successful in her persuasion.

Ancient Chinese Persuasion and Western Classical Rhetoric

Based on the available documents, in both China and the West, there were active persuasive communication activities as early as the 8th Century BC. The study of persuasion followed shortly afterwards. The discussion above has set grounds for some similarities and differences between Ancient China and the West at about the same period. Here we turn to examination of cultural influences on persuasion practices and studies.

Research approaches

The classical rhetoric in the West (500BC – 500 AD) had long been a subject of study in its own right, complete with systematic theorization (Ehninger, 1968). While the three main schools of moral philosophy, scientific approach and education philosophy (Golden, Berquist, & Coleman, 1976) each had different emphasis, their approach to rhetoric and theorization were quite compatible. All main elements were defined and analyzed, whereas all relevant aspects specified and classified. The study was comprehensive to cover most of the elements and aspects that are still applicable today, from topic to form, to different participants, to organization, to style.

Chinese social tradition had generally placed function and content before forms, and was suspicious of any emphasis on form, regarding interests in form as placing the cart before the horse. In relation, scholarship of any type held essential the practical relevance of any knowledge, whereas pure knowledge of any kind was deemed useless and irrelevant to the society, hence ignored if not considered outright unacceptable. Knowledge of persuasion and rhetoric were by classification tools and form that served other purposes than mere persuasion. It was not an independent, substantive subject of study, hence of no importance on its own. Ancient Chinese scholars studied persuasion as part of other subjects, such as philosophy and government, and would follow the need for development of these other subjects. Study of persuasion was never systematic, nor independent of other subjects. However, in some particular aspects, especially when persuasion was related to government and humanities, the scholar had put forth some unique and rather comprehensive discussion and conceptualization. Their works touched upon such important topic as effectiveness of persuasion (Xunzi) (Lin, 1994) and audience adaptation (Han Feizi)(Lu, 1998). In terms of approach to persuasion, different schools of thought all had their own conceptualization in service to the social moral view each espoused (Zhao, 1994; Garrett, 1993b; Lu, 1998).

Cultural aspects of persuasion

Ethics and morality is an aspect important to both Ancient Chinese persuasion and classical Western rhetoric. For the latter, ethic and moral standards apply to the persuading communicator, or at least the perception of such, and the method used in persuasion. Thus, untruthful or misleading methods were not acceptable. For Ancient Chinese, morality was the main motivation and purpose for persuasion. Where these were lacking, either in the persuader or in the content of persuasion, there should not be persuasion. Standards of moral conduct overlapped but were not identical to those used in the West.

For the Western classical rhetoric, the speaker and the audience were citizens, who were social equals. A basic assumption of rhetoric was rationality of the audience who would assess and interpret the persuasive messages in rational manner. Thus, the main objective of a speaker was to evoke rational thinking on part of the audience, so they would follow the line of argument presented to them and made judgment of soundness and validity. The areas of topic cover everything of interest to the public in terms of public policies, legal issues as well as ceremonial occasions. Speech was part of citizen education, an essential skill for every freeman. In comparison, ancient Chinese persuaders were learned scholars of high social status, often addressing a ruler or a king as their sole audience. The communicators were not only in an unequal relationship, but the superior was one that held the power of life and death, and could wield it at whims. A main assumption of persuasion was the listeners' wisdom as human beings that was reasonable and based on their social experience. A main objective of a persuader was to touch the heart of the listener, by encouraging the latter to judge on the basis of social rules and associated social feelings about the matter. That the society had a view that should be complied to was deemed necessary and taken as an effective persuasive point. The view on the relationship between persuasion and morality put great constraints on the topic of persuasion, which was limited to social norms and governments, divinities and humanities. The ability to speak well and to argue was of use only to social elites, who needed it for their own ambition or simply as an accomplishment or a game.

Classical rhetoric of the West developed from public speaking and put a great deal of emphasis on the speaker. The speaker was considered the dominant party who, with skills, could bring out expected reaction from the audience. The speaker, thus, had been the center of scholarly attention, while the role of the audience was passive and to be influenced by the speaker. Audience analysis was needed so that the speaker could adapt the message and make the speech more effective. Human rationality was assumed and the same was assumed of the study of rhetoric in terms of arguments being sound and valid for effectiveness. Emotional appeals were less trusted as they preyed on the irrational side of the audience. It is in this aspect that Ancient Chinese had a different approach. In persuasion as in other aspects of life, Chinese tradition held a holistic view of emotion and reason. Heart and mind were one and the same, while reason referred to a sense of the way things work from experience rather than mental faculty capable of abstraction that stripped away feelings and emotions. Traditional cultural values of "ren--kindness, yi--righteousness, zhong--loyalty, xin--faith, cheng--sincerity" were each one of them affectively based. The moral appeals of these values also paved the way for emotional appeals as a legitimate means of persuasion. The moral stipulation of persuasion, on the other hand, probably had also diminished the concern over the ethics of persuasive methods in this regard. As a matter of fact, the ability to provoke emotions was considered a prized skill in persuasion and a sign of professional maturity.

Considering the fact that most persuasive communication in ancient China were carried out toward a ruler, a king, it was of paramount importance to know and understand the emotional inclinations of this superior audience, so that even if persuasion was not successful, the persuader would not end up bringing harm to himself. In this sense, persuasion in ancient China had its own unique understanding of audience analysis and adaptation. Many scholars, e.g., Confucius, Mozi, Gost Vally Master (guiguzi), Mencius, Zhuanzi, had elaborated on this aspect. According to Gong (Gong, 1994) Chinese audience analysis had generalized two points: weighing of power (liangquan 量灌 — measure power) and assessing the person (chuaiqing 揣情 — assess feeling). Power weighing involves a complete understanding of some essential external factors that may have affect the survival of the target, including his power status, strength in resources, popularity among people and diplomatic relations. Feeling assessement involves knowing internal factors of the persuasion target, including personality, emotions, moods, likes and dislikes. Both type of audience information could be had, besides research in advance, through observation of the target and his self-disclosure or self-revelation in interaction. The audience, in this sense, was much more part of the persuasion activity.

Lastly, use of nonverbal cues was emphasized in the Western classical rhetoric in delivery. By body languages and facial expressions, the speaker reinforced what he had to say verbally, so as to better influence the audience. In ancient Chinese persuasion, nonverbal elements were taken as an integral part of persuasion, from action as message and model, to nonverbal behaviors as information about the audience. Action in particular occupied a very prominent place, much more so than the Western tradition, which took great stock in the nonverbals associated with speaking.

Commonly used persuasive strategies

Many strategies and devices can be found in both Western rhetorical and Chinese persuasive practices, with differences in preference or frequency of usage.

Traditionally, Chinese culture stressed the importance of societal order represented in social hierarchy, set great stock on morality and virtue, and believed in the emotional appeals. This tradition has influenced the preferred rhetorical approach in persuasion. A most common mode of proof in ancient times and today is argument by authority.

Second, arguments often appear in what is known as Chinese sorites, where a chain of syllogisms are presented in such a way that the conclusion of one is the premise of the other that follows immediately (Garrett, 1993a). The set of arguments are not necessarily deductively linked but rather set out the conditional parallels for the final conclusion (e.g., Confucius on naming).

Another common mode of proof is argument by consequences. In Shiji, there is a story about Warring States period, when a person by the name of Cai had the idea of himself to become prime minister of the kingdom of Qin, and set out to persuade the then Qin Prime Minister Fan to step down. Cai made his point by citing cases of three other important officials of other states, who had made great contributions to their respective states and were all once very powerful statesmen. Yet, each had met a very tragic fate in the end, being prosecuted or tortured to death. Using these predecessors' miserable ending as proof, Cai was making the argument that similar consequences was waiting for Fan, if he did not resign at the prime of his career to preserve himself from being prosecuted later by other ambitious new comers. He was making the point that being loyal to the lord and being good for the state was no guarantee for a peaceful old age. Although Cai did not succeed in this particular case, the method was a well-tested one.

Yet another mode of proof is argument by comparison, which we have discussed earlier on examples and comparison of strengths and weaknesses. Even in argument by consequences above, comparison was explicit.

Lastly, arguments in Chinese persuasion almost all involve some kind of narrative, which may be one of the unique aspects of Chinese persuasion. It is unique not because it is exclusive to the Chinese but due to its prevalence and its importance to the line of reasoning. All of the examples mentioned above have used one narrative or another to indirectly prove or bring out a moral. In a sense, narratives are an integral part of Chinese persuasion, which is consistent to characterization of Chinese culture as one dominated by mythical structure of consciousness (Chen, 1993; Gebser, 1984). Given the tradition of upward persuasion, mostly of a ruler that held the power of life and death, the indirectness of a story was crucial to keep a distance between the points made and the person making the point. So when things did not go as planned, at least the persuader had the recourse of arguing for a different interpretation or outcome.

In comparison, the classical rhetoric of the West put much more emphasis on the rational reasoning as a basic mode of argument and had generalized a large set of argument lines. Syllogism often presented in enthymeme was a most common form of argument presentation, including logical and rhetorical. For that aim, efforts were also made to identify fallacious arguments, which were also classified as a category on its own. Of all arguments, the more rigorous in logic the more likely arguments were considered to be sound and effective. Rhetorical arguments being resting often on probability were considered less forceful although acceptable. With regard to evidence, physical or factual evidence, including statistics, held much weight as support in the argument, while hearsay and other secondary evidence were treated with caution or even distrust. Lastly, rhetoric and narrative were two different subjects, although not mutually exclusive.

The brief comparison here shows that, whereas there is much similarity in Chinese and Western persuasion in ancient times, there are also culturally influenced aspects of difference. Most differences, however, are a matter of emphasis or priority rather than a matter of compatibility. Western classical rhetoric developed earlier as a systematic subject of scholarly inquiry of persuasion, while Chinese of the same period simply practiced persuasion with high sophistication yet without treating it as a worthy subject in its own right. The study in the West was also more comprehensive and analytical in nature, while the Chinese study was much less systematic with narrower focus. An understanding of where Chinese persuasion stands vis-à-vis the West provides a basis for intercultural understanding for societies following the two traditions.

References

Chen, L. (1993). Chinese and Americans: An epistemological exploration of intercultural communication. *Howard Journal of Communications, 4*, 342-357.

Dong, Y. (1994). *Tongue battle skills: Ancient Chinese argumentation tactics*. Beijing: Beijing Press. (In Chinese)

Ehninger, D. (1968). On systems of rhetoric. *Philosophy and Rhetoric*, *1* (Summer), 131-144.

Garrett, M. M. (1993a). "Pathos" reconsidered from the perspective of classical Chinese rhetorics. *Quarterly Journal of Speech*, *79*, 19-39.

Garrett, M. M. (1993b). Wit, power, and oppositional groups: A case study of "pure talk". *Quarterly Journal of Speech*, *79*, 303-318.

Garrett, M. M. (1991). Asian challenge. In S. K. Foss, K. A. Foss, & R. Trapp, (Eds.), *Contemporary perspectives on rhetoric* (pp. 295-314). Prospect Heights, IL: Waveland.

Gebser, J. (1984). *The ever-present origin*. Athens, OH: Ohio University Press.

Golden, J. L., Berquist, G. F., & Coleman, W. E. (1976). *The rhetoric of Western thought*. Dubuque, IA: Kendall/Hunt.

Gong, W. (1994). *Persuasion: Studies on appealing to the heart*. Beijing: Dongfang Press. (In Chinese)

Hou, W., Zhao, J., Du, G., Qiu, H., & Lu, et al (1957). *A complete history of Chinese thoughts, Vol.1: Ancient thoughts*. Beijing: People's Press. (In Chinese)

Lin, J. (1994). Is China a nation with no rhetoric? A first exploration of Xunzi's view on persuasion. *Chinese Communication Studies Forum*, 79-93. (In Chinese)

Lu, X. (1998). *Rhetoric in ancient China: Fifth to third century B.C. E.* Columbia, SC.: University of South Carolina Press.

Peng,Y. (1996). *Chinese vertical and horizontal scholars*. Beijing: Religion & Culture Press. (In Chinese)

Yao, Y. (1996). *Contemporary Chinese rhetoric*. Guangzhou: Guangdong Educational Press. (In Chinese)

Zhao, Y. (1994). Confucius and Aristotle. Chinese Communication Studies Forum, 54-77. (In Chinese)

MULTICULTURALISM AND MULTILINGUALISM

English across cultures and intercultural awareness

Nobuyuki Honna Aoyama Gakuin University, Japan

Abstract

In order to enrich English as a language of multicultural communication and to ensure intercultural communicability among speakers of its different varieties, it is important that we develop internationally collaborated and coordinated educational programs. Most effective is the introduction of language awareness into school curriculums. Teaching awareness of language aims at our clear understanding of how language is designed and how people use language. Thus, it can be useful for students to become conscious of the function of language in multilingual and multicultural settings. In this presentation, the study of metaphor will be emphasized as a means of enhancing intercultural literacy, which is needed for improved mutual communicability among different varieties of English.

In order to enrich English as a language of multicultural communication and to ensure intercultural communicability among speakers of its different varieties, it is important that we develop internationally collaborated and coordinated educational programs. This paper addresses some of the important issues involved in intercultural awareness as a pedagogical response to actual and potential inconveniences of incommunicability caused or to be caused by the spread of English as a multicultural and multinational language.

Intercultural awareness is explored in terms of intercultural literacy in which teaching awareness of language plays an important role. Teaching awareness of language aims at our clear understanding of how language is designed and how people use language. Thus, it can be useful for students to become conscious of the function of language in multilingual and multicultural settings, thereby enhancing intercultural literacy, which is needed for improved mutual communicability among different varieties of English. In this connection, the study of metaphor will be emphasized, accompanied by reports from training sessions intended for metaphorical analysis of everyday language.

Intervarietal Incommunicability

The world-wide spread of English has not ended up with the global acceptance of

American English or British English as the norm of usage. Rather, the global spread of English has prompted the multicultural diversification of English (Route 2, in Diagram 1). One of the implications, or rather complications, of these multicultural enrichments continuously added to the English language concerns mutual communicability among world Englishes. This is an actual and immediate problem as well as a potential concern. Cases of zero communication/miscommunication in intervarietal interactions are abundant.

In fear of a new Babel, people often cry for a return to American English or British English as the standardized norm (Route 3, in Diagram 1). However, it is important to recognize here that standardization or eventually re-standardization of the de-standardized standards is not a plausible way of dealing with the current multiculturalism and multi-formalism of world Englishes.

People tend to believe that a common language is a uniform language. But this is not true. English can be a common language on a multinational basis only when its cultural diversity is accepted. A common language has to be a multicultural language (Honna, 2000, 2003). A lot of allowances have to be made, and differences accepted. If the American English standard, for example, was imposed upon all users of English, English would never become an international common language. Thus, if we are to establish English as a multicultural language and use it as an international language, we have to address the issue of diversity management by means of intercultural awareness (Route 4).

Diagram 1: Global Spread of English

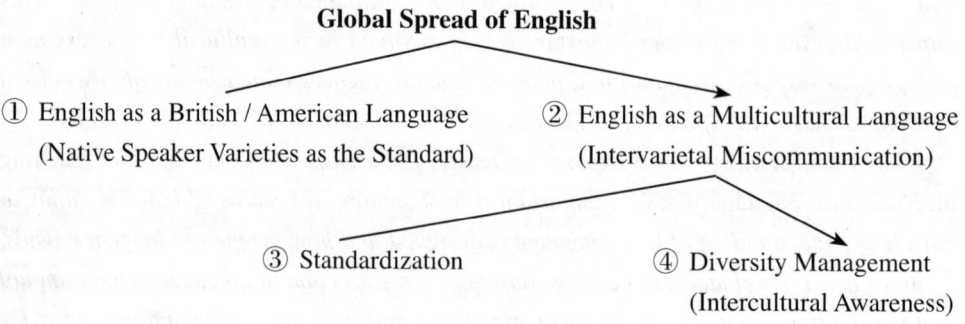

Before we go any further, it is important to be reminded of the implausibility of possible standardization measures. Firstly, standardization (or re-standardization) was essentially a measure meant to have prevented the multiculturalization of English and has evidently failed to perform its job. American English or British English per se did not become a global language. English has spread as a multicultural language across the world. It would be illogical to expect the measure that did not stop the new trend to work as a new role of reversing it.

Secondly, it is natural that diffusion should cause adaptation or mutation. Where the apple is not a local product and apple polishing is not practiced, it is often more difficult for local people to internalize the idiom than normally imagined. Instead, local people recall a semantically similar set-phrase in their vernacular and put it into their usage of English such as "shoe shining" (Malaysia) and "sesame grinding" (Japan). Likewise, things and ideas that are not codified in American English or British English have to be referred to in new coinages by local people. Thus, Japanese speakers cannot help but saying "paper driver" (driver who has a driver's license but has not driven a car), "hot carpet" (electrically warmed carpet) or "washlet" (wash + toilet: electrically warmed stool equipped with two bidets intended for the two different private parts). These and many others, including such greetings as "Where are you going?" and "Have you eaten?", cannot be inhibited.

Furthermore, the mythology behind the appeal to uniformity is baseless in view of world Englishes and should be rectified. A frightening source of many don'ts for nonnative speakers, the mythology states that if you deviate from native speakers' patterns, you will not be understood. Japanese bookstores are full of titles written by native speakers, whose theme is common: Japanese English is unintelligible to them. The fear is reinforced by self-righteous Japanese teachers of English.

A scant analysis indicates, however, that unintelligibility is not the matter. It is unbelievable native speakers find it difficult to understand the meaning of "this restaurant is delicious" (Japanese English?). Some may protest, "The restaurant is a building and a building cannot be delicious. It simply does not make sense!" But when native speakers say "he is sharp," no one insists, "he is a person and a person cannot be a cutting tool". The hidden agenda is differences, not intelligibility. Japanese speakers let a restaurant refer to the food served there, which native speakers do not, while both natives and non-natives see a person as a sharp instrument that the person has as part of his or her characteristics. These differences can be ironed out through educational programs (see below).

At the same time, the fear of rejection is so strong that Chinese students often "surmise" the difficulty native speakers may have in understanding Chinese-based sentences, such as:

(1) I will go look-look. (To a knock on the door of an apartment room: Singaporean English)
(2) We should give him some face. (Chinese English)

However, as syntactic reduplication is a widely witnessed phenomenon in Asian and African Englishes, native speakers coming to these parts of the world are expected to inform themselves of this linguistic dynamism. So is the case with face expressions which are important local burgeons born to grow to be internationally appreciated in the region. In view of an increasing number of users of English as an additional language, native speakers and non-native speakers alike are required to prepare themselves to understand those elements of another variety that they need to know if any meaningful intervarietal communication is to be established and maintained.

Intercultural Awareness

Diversity management by raising intercultural awareness can be approached in two ways. I would like to call the one as accommodation and the other as intercultural literacy through educated awareness of language. A typical example of the accommodation approach is found in Harris and Moran (1991). As international trade expanded in the late 20th century, American business people became increasingly aware of differences between English as an American language and English as an international language.

In an effort to motivate American business people to adjust themselves to the reality of English as an international language, Harris and Moran (1991) listed 20 measures, which covered lexical, idiomatic, syntactic, semantic, and pragmatic dimensions of language use. Their two pragmatic suggestions are reproduced here (Harris & Moran, 1991, p. 47):

If possible, one should determine and reflect the cultural values of the reader on such dimensions as … emphasizing individual versus collective accomplishments…When in doubt, a variety of value orientations should be included: "I want to thank you [individual] and your department [collective]…"

Whenever possible, either adopt the cultural reasoning style of your reader or present information in more than one format: "Trust among business partners is essential [deductive]; and our data show that our most successful joint ventures are those in which we invested initial time building a personal trusting relationship [inductive].

Works have been accumulated in phonology and syntax done along these lines including Jenkins (2000). Granted that these approaches will be useful for managing the increasing diversification of English, I am inclined to see some flaws in them: (a) although they are not conformist, they are restrictive and prohibitive; (b) although they are not mono-cultural and mono-central, they often smack of intercultural neutralization; and (c) they are particularistic rather than general. They are simply different sides of the same coin.

Restrictive and Prohibitive

For example, Harris and Moran (1991, p. 46) suggest American business people refrain from using "'word pictures', constructions that depend for their meaning on invoking a particular mental image (e.g. 'run that by me', 'wade through these figures', 'slice of the free world pie'...)". There is no doubt that these suggestions are well intended. It is a good lesson to Americans, letting them know that they cannot always have their own way because American English cannot be an international language. Interlocutors are expected to be linguistically and culturally considerate of their counterpart in intervarietal communication. Yet, if an extended list of don'ts restricts and prohibits speakers' free exchange of expressions, it backfires. Non-native speakers deprived of their metaphorical expressions would find themselves linguistically handicapped and source-less.

Culturally Neutral

These approaches could be successful only if people were disposed to say the same thing to a similar set of events. Actually, however, people are made to see the set differently. Human beings grow up to be able to choose one form from a set, with the choice governed by a sociolinguistic rule of "who says what to whom when/where". In any language, a mere parting event is referred to by many different expressions: Goodbye, Bye, See you again, See you soon, See you around, Take care, Take it easy, I will see you when I see you, See you on the ice, See you alligator, etc. If people were told to always use Goodbye to anyone, anytime, anywhere, they would neither welcome nor follow the decree. Similar attitudes should develop among speakers of world Englishes mostly because they tend to express themselves in a variety full of unique characteristics transferred from their national language and culture. Consequently, any attempt to deculturalize intervarietal interaction is bound to get nowhere, as much as Anglo-Americanization in the name of standardization is doomed to failure.

Particularistic

Accommodation approaches basically are case-by-case studies. Business people, travelers, students, or scholars are supposed to look up references to study how people of the country they are scheduled to visit think, behave and speak, thus mapping out communication strategies to adjust themselves to local contacts. The benefits of these approaches can be best obtained at workshops specialized in some cultural aspects of a certain country and designed to help persons planning a trip there. With episodes and cases being their main features, it is difficult to prepare a general course.

Intercultural Literacy and Language Awareness

Instead of accommodation approaches, I have explored issues of diversity management in terms of a pedagogical concept of intercultural literacy. Here is my definition of intercultural literacy (Honna, 2003, p. 165-170):

1. Intercultural literacy is an attitude, preparedness, and competence to transmit one's message and understand others' appropriately in a cross-cultural encounter;
2. It involves an ability to adjust intercultural differences in a mutually beneficial manner;
3. Intercultural literacy is the literacy of the fourth kind after basic literacy (reading and writing plus mathematics), media literacy, and information literacy; and
4. It is expected to be introduced to the school curriculums across disciplines from primary, through secondary, to tertiary education.

At the same time, I have placed teaching awareness of language as a fundamental component in intercultural literacy. The role of language awareness in intercultural literacy is based on the assumption that part of language awareness is to improve sensitivity to, and tolerance of linguistic diversity, as is witnessed in Hawkins (1987, 1992), Donmall (1985), and James & Garrett (1991).

For example, Hawkins (1987) has this to say:

We are seeking to light fires of curiosity about the central human characteristic of language which will blaze throughout our pupils' lives. While combating linguistic complacency, we are seeking to arm our pupils against fear of the unknown which breeds prejudice and antagonism. Above all we want to make our pupils' contacts with language, both their own and that of their neighbors, richer and more interesting, simply more fun. (p. 6)

Furthermore, Hawkins (1987) continues to say:

Linguistic tolerance does not come naturally; it has to be learned and to be worked at. The first reaction to language that cannot be understood (as to other forms of social behavior that are different) is suspicion, frustration, even anger. It is hard to believe that people who can behave so mysteriously (linguistically) can be all like us. (p. 17)

Prior to Hawkins' comments, Halliday (1971) attempted to explore the issue and linked awareness of language to competence of diversity management, declaring that "… the development of awareness [of language] in the pupil will have a positive effect on his competence, though this effect is likely to be indirect and may not show up immediately" (p. 10).

To recapitulate, here is how I see awareness of language contributing to overcoming of inconveniences of incommunicability of English across cultures. The key here is the improved sensitivity to, and tolerance of linguistic diversity intralingual and/or interlingual.

>   Diversity Management
>   (Intercultural Literacy)
>   ↓
>   Teaching Awareness of Language
>   (Understanding How Language is Designed
>   And How People Use Language)
>   ↓
>   Improving Sensitivity to, and Tolerance of
>   Linguistic Diversity
>   (Overcoming Inconveniences of Incommunicability
>   of English as a Multicultural Language)

While I mention awareness of language as an indispensable constituent of language teaching at all levels of formal education, I suggest that we should selectively incorporate some basic elements of cognitive linguistics and sociolinguistics into teaching English as an international language (TEIL), aiming to overcome the major inconvenience (that is, intervarietal incommunicability) caused or to be caused by the spread of English as a multicultural language across the world. All the topics such as listed in Hawkins (1987) or Van Lier (1995) are not necessary for our purposes.

Metaphorical Competence

One thing that I would like to see included in these programs is the study of metaphor (metonymy and synecdoche included). In many countries, the fact remains that metaphor, a cognitive and expressive device human beings are universally equipped with, is considered as a technical term limited for literary analysis, appreciation, and criticism, not as an operation ordinary people employ in all domains of their daily lives.

As a result, Japanese schools from primary to tertiary levels do not offer systematic studies of the structure and function of metaphor in the Japanese Language courses. Similar situations are witnessed in other East Asian countries.

Metaphor has relevance to English across cultures, or world Englishes, to a great extent. If sentence 1 below is a correct sentence, so is sentence 2 and, of course, so is sentence 3, all enjoying the equal correctness and legitimacy status. These sentences are all formed in accordance with the metaphorical understanding that THE WHOLE IS THE PART.

1. Yoko is sharp.

As a human being, Yoko literally cannot be sharp. This sentence makes sense only when Yoko is referred to as her head, which is further referred to as an instrument for cutting because the head's main function is to think and thinking is understood as analysis (cutting). This is why the example sentence is homonymous with "Yoko has a sharp head." This relation does not hold between "An elephant is long" and "An elephant has a long trunk."

2. "The Arab street is angry, but the street is honest and sincere and we should listen to it", Qatari Foreign Minister Hamed bin Jassin said in support of the popular guerrilla movement (The Japan Times, July 17, 2006, p. 5).

Similarly, the street here is understood as people who come out there for a protest and a demonstration.

3. That restaurant is very delicious. (Japanese English)

Similarly, too, the restaurant stands for the food served there.

Although these three sentences are constructed on the basis of the same metaphorical understanding of different phenomena, sentence 3 is generally unpopular. A Hong Kong respondent said, "…native English speaker may have difficulties to understand it and I personally can not accept it as proper English," while another stated, "I'd see it as a kind of lazy form of ellipsis (deleting information that's already known) rather than as being ungrammatical (Whether deleting known information is a lazy act or not is another question to be seriously asked). Prominent here is the apparent lack of metaphorical awareness. It is to be hoped that tolerance of differences will be heightened by intercultural literacy.

Moreover, with the spread of English as an additional language, people are creating a variety of new expressions locally based on their first-language experiences. With the nature of world Englishes being what it is, it would be hard to accept the presupposition that sentences 1, 2, 3 below are incorrect and illegitimate because these are non-native while sentences 4, 5, 6 are correct and legitimate simply because they are native-based. A culturally equal treatment is in order.

1. He has long legs. (African English: is well known, influential)
2. He has hard ears. (Caribbean English: stubborn)
3. He has a thin face. (Philippine English: is shy)
4. He has a bitter tongue.
5. He has a sweet tooth.

6. He has green fingers.

Actually, speakers of English as an additional language are positioned to produce a variety of unique expressions. Firstly, they are learners of the language and are hardly expected to master its full lexicon. Yet, they often find themselves pressed to use the language in intercultural communication. The name of the game is "speak English now however limited your proficiency may be." Under these circumstances, Japanese speakers might resort to expressions such as:

8. He has a wide face. (is well known, influential)
9. He has a tall nose. (is boastful)
10. He has a black belly. (is roguish)

These utterances may occur anywhere in the world first as spontaneous and sporadic expressions when speakers are pushed to speak but are not well versed in idiomatic phrases from American English or British English. They are often considered as mistakes because they are not part of the standard phrase book. Erring speakers have allegedly committed two sins: they did not know correct expressions, and they did not speak the way native speakers would have done.

At the same time, these utterances can be established as local expressions because they are not included in the lexicon of native varieties and because local speakers insist upon their unique phraseologies. These utterances are what and how they wish to say as a response to what they see and feel. It is natural that we should be hearing these novel expressions more and more in the near future around the world. Japanese speakers rarely use these expressions currently because they are under the social pressure that proclaims, "Do not speak English until you can speak it like Americans". With the idea of world Englishes pedagogically taught and socially accepted, the situation should change in due course.

The crux of the matter is that it is not fair if non-native expressions are invariably turned down while native expressions are upheld. These expressions cannot be banned or stigmatized. Rather, meanings have to be negotiated. We need to be ready to deal with the situation positively and creatively. It is hoped that language awareness programs to be offered in TEIL will be geared to help resolve these potential problems of Non-native Speaker Englishes.

Furthermore, if people of the world are aware of the structure and function of metaphorical extension, they should not be confounded to hear some Japanese say in English: I can't read his belly. If people saw what metaphor is involved here, they would not have difficulty making sense of this sentence: I can't understand what he really wants. Japanese extend the head, chest (or heart), and belly as containers, each intended for a different type of content. Thus the head is a container of knowledge ("He crammed everything into the head"), the chest of romantic thoughts ("He has his love for her hidden in the chest") and the belly of emotions ("He decided to contain this conversation in his belly"). This applies substantially to all varieties of English, native and non-native alike.

Reports from Experimental Awareness Training Sessions

In my exploratory survey based on experimental awareness training sessions, I found that a short introduction of metaphorical analysis to Japanese college students could improve their willingness to enjoy and their ability (although limited) to interpret unfamiliar phrases from world Englishes. In a junior-senior course in English as an International Language that I teach in my university, students had an period (90 minutes) of basic awareness training in cognitive and expressive aspects of metaphor based on examples mostly from the Japanese language. Then, they were led to analyze Japanese expressions from a metaphorical point of view. Finally, they were given English sentences and asked to interpret them.

Discussing Metaphor

In this project, my introduction was actually very brief (60 minutes). The emphasis was that metaphor is a concept formation and understanding device, which is applied to everyday language, not to mention creative language, as is well delineated in Lakoff and Johnson (1980). Here is what we discussed, with examples drawn mainly from Japanese.

What is Metaphor?

1. Metaphor is a mental device human beings are universally equipped with.
2. Its function is both cognitive and linguistic.
3. It enables us to use familiar, fundamental, and concrete concepts to understand unfamiliar, profound, and abstract concepts.
4. It is based on our perception of similarities between the two things, phenomena, or concepts.
5. Examples are TIME'S PASSING IS A RIVER'S FLOWING and LIFE IS A JOURNEY. (The former is illustrated by "Let's go upstream and see what happened in Edo Era (Japanese)," where UP IS THE PAST, too, because it is known experientially that a river runs typically from the mountain to the sea. The latter allows the formation of "restarting one's life as a soba maker" or "the final terminal of one's life."

6. Finally, in scientific fiction, the most logical and efficient language would seem to be one where one word has only one meaning. There would be no need for contextual interpretation. But if we had this kind of language in our brain, we could not have achieved our civilizations. We could not even have stood up. In order to store trillions of words invented for every single aspect of our life, our heads would have been horribly huge and heavy. Fortunately, our language is characterized by metaphor, a creative system that makes it possible for one word to have multiple meanings. Our language is made to be stored in our head.

We also discussed metonymy and synecdoche, because they are easier to comprehend and their examples are ubiquitous.

What is Metonymy?

1. Metonymy is a kind of metaphor that makes it possible for us to employ something's characteristics to represent something itself: THE GOLDEN BADGE FOR THE DIET PERSON in Japan.

2. Similarly, the part can be seen as the whole, or vice versa---the process often referred to as synecdoche: THE FACE FOR THE HEAD, as is in "Please do not put your face out of the window," a public-speaker notice by a conductor in a railway train in Japan.

Since metaphor is a cognitive and expressive device, it is important that we understand the apparatus in terms of thought and action on an everyday basis, too. Thus, our predisposition to use a few instances to lead to a conclusion was illustrated with some examples. Students were also made aware of our daily acts induced by our metaphorical conceptualization by discussing acts of substitution as representatives of metaphors in action, such as using a sake (rice wine) cup as a pencil stand.

Figure 1: A Sake Cup for a Pencil Stand (photographed by the author)

Metaphors in Thought and Action

1. Although people have a few Thai acquaintances or had a few visits in Bangkok, they tend to talk about the Thais or Thailand in general.
2. Japanese old sayings such as "One instance shows the rest" (One who steals a pin will steal anything) express these characteristics of human cognition.
3. Acts of substitution are examples of metaphors in action: a sake cup as a pencil stand.

Analyzing Japanese Metaphorical Expressions

After a brief lecture, students were invited to analyze the metaphorical foundations of everyday expressions. Here I chose body-part expressions because they are more familiar than others with reference to metaphors in Japanese.

Exercise in Analyzing Metaphors: Some Examples:

Why is it that the following sentences are all normal in Japanese? Explain each one's metaphorical background:

1. Someone's mouth spins well, is heavy, is light, etc.

Because the mouth is understood as a tool (production machine). As the machine produces things, so does the mouth word. If a person's mouth is heavy, it is slow in producing words, and if it is light, it is fast in doing so, since SLOW IS HEAVY and FAST IS LIGHT.

2. To ride someone's mouth (and lose a lot of money)

Because the mouth is perceived as a tool (vehicle, possibly a cart). While a cart carries goods, the mouth carries a message.

3. To beat the never-diminishing mouth

Because the mouth is thought as a drum or a bell. As a drum or a bell, when beaten, makes a sound, so does the mouth, when prompted, speech.

4. To put into your head

Because one's head is understood as a container to store information and knowledge for memorization and further exploitation. The head is hard when the imaginary container is not plastic enough to let in something extraordinary. The head is soft when otherwise.

5. Someone's head is sharp, dull, weak, etc.

Because the head is taken as a tool for cutting such as a knife or a razor. The association stems from the understanding that the head functions as the thinking organ and thinking is cutting (analyzing). A sharp (dull) knife is referred to as a sharp (dull) head.

6. He has a fat belly. His tolerance to all sorts of men is remarkable.

Because Japanese people assume the belly as a container to contain emotional matters, usually said of men, not women. The fatter the belly, the more in volume and kind it holds (reference to its size). As an influential person rarely shows his belly, people around him cannot read his belly (reference to its content). In a touch-and-go situation, he may break his belly. How he hides or displays his belly is referred to as the belly art.

7. Suginami Ward is the navel (belly button) of Tokyo.

Because the navel is at the center of a human body, it is extended to anything that is at the center of something.

English Metaphors Interpreted

After a 90-minute, one-session lecture on metaphor and workout in Japanese metaphorical expressions, students were led to decipher metaphors from world-wide varieties of English. The assumption was that if we understood the structure and the function of metaphor, or those of language on a larger scale, in Japanese, we would be able to apply the experience more successfully than otherwise to other languages being learned. And as we will see below, students actually proved that this is really the case. I gave these four sentences in a 2006 survey:

1. At a news conference in the White House.
   A Reporter: Mr. President, I have a question.
   President: OK. Shoot. (American English)
2. The government in that country is toothless against the international terrorist group. (General English)
3. Our boss is away today, so we can shake legs all day. (Singaporean and Malaysian English)
4. My friend in China does not come from a privileged family. He joined the city's police department, the country's iron rice bowl, immediately after high school. (Adapted from TIME 3/21/05) (Chinese English)

In a 2007 survey, these four sentences were used after a similar metaphorical awareness training:

1. How about this blouse?
   I'm afraid this is too loud for me. (General English)
2. If he doesn't agree to this proposal, I will ask his boss to lean on him. (American English)
3. She is so thin-faced and dislikes speaking in public. (Philippine English)

4. It's useless talking to him any more. He has hard ears. (Caribbean English)

In addition to these metaphorical interpretation drills, information was elicited from students as to (a) their knowledge of metaphor prior to these training sessions, (b) their evaluation of the sessions, and (c) their familiarity with the metaphors in question. The information was needed in order to prepare a realistic and an effective introduction of metaphorical awareness to TEIL.

Results and Observations

Few Knew Metaphor in Ordinary Language. In my two-year surveys done in 2006 and 2007, it was immediately clear that a sizable number of Japanese students did not have the experience of studying metaphor before they entered college (30/66=45%, 2006; 22/60=37%, 2007). Moreover, most of my students who knew something about metaphor (36/66=55%, 2006; 38/60=63%, 2007) said that they had first learned it in cognitive and other linguistics courses they had taken before my course. Since these courses unfortunately are not offered to general students on many campuses, it is very likely that a huge number of students in Japan exit from college without metaphorical awareness.

Many Thought Awareness Exercise Useful. At the same time, my students who participated in the surveys rated high the short sessions on the importance of metaphor in terms of intervarietal communication, and considered them as effective and heuristic in trying to understand the unfamiliar expressions given them from world Englishes (Completely Effective 20%, Very Effective 61%, N=65 [2006]; Completely Effective 27%, Very Effective 54%, N=60 [2007]). Actually, the test sentences contained such semantic extensions that contemporary Japanese does not share and students were expected to deal with them intellectually. And they obviously took advantage of the knowledge they acquired or reinforced immediately prior to the exercises (see Table 1).

Unknown Metaphors Correctly Decoded. In the interpretation exercises, I wanted to know how many students were acquainted with the given metaphors so that I could see how well those students with no prior knowledge tackled with the problems. Thus, when it comes to the shoot expression, very few (51 out of 66) knew the WORDS ARE BULLETS (or LANGUAGE IS A WEAPON) metaphor (see Table 1). Nevertheless, all students who did not know this metaphorical expression were able to decode it correctly. Actually, quite a few students were able to zero in on the targets fairly well, as is demonstrated in the figure below.

Yet, there was an exception to the generally high correct answer rate. Most students (87%) were at a loss and didn't know how to make sense of iron rice bowl. Further studies are required to reveal the nature of metaphors that turn out to be difficult for people from different cultural backgrounds to uncover. In fact, there should be many others enormously difficult to crack. Those that are heavily culturally loaded may look undecipherable and invincible and those that appear similarly phrased interlingually can be confusing and puzzling. (Consider, for example, differences of English and Japanese "bite one's tongue" or "pull one's legs.")

Table 1: Understanding Phrases

	Phrase	Don't know			Correct Answer		
		#	N	%	#	N	%
	Survey2006						
1	shoot	51	66	77%	51	51	100%
2	toothless	55	66	83%	50	55	91%
3	shake legs	62	66	94%	49	62	79%
4	iron rice bowl	64	66	97%	8	64	13%
	Survey2007						
5	loud for me	47	60	78%	38	47	81%
6	lean on him	56	60	93%	40	56	71%
7	thin-faced	59	60	98%	36	59	61%
8	hard ears	57	60	95%	52	57	91%

Nevertheless, this does not diminish the desirability of introducing language awareness and metaphorical awareness to TEIL. It only means that a well-prepared curriculum is imperative and it needs to be based on solid research findings. Work on metaphorical competence by Azuma (2005, p. 156) shows how Japanese students of English activate a Japanese schema in an attempt to decipher metaphorical expressions of English.

Her findings imply that it would be productive to introduce the basics of metaphor into formal mother tongue education in Japan and reinforce the awareness nurtured there in TEIL from intercultural points of view. If it takes a long time to introduce language awareness to our National Language syllabuses, then it is our urgent business to do so in TEIL.

Conclusion

This chapter dealt with issues in intervarietal incommunicability among speakers of different varieties of English. As an educational response to these actual and potential inconveniences caused and to be caused by the diffusion of English as a multicultural language, teaching awareness of language was explored as an indispensable component in intercultural awareness/literacy. Reports from training sessions indicated that metaphorical awareness could enhance improved communicability in the use of English across cultures.

While current English has a centrifugal tendency for intracultural and intranational purposes, it also has a centripetal force for intercultural and international engagements. When speakers of English converge for information exchange and mutual understanding, they are strongly motivated to adjust their respective speech manners. They are prepared to learn how they can make it. This is where language awareness training comes in, to help them help themselves in this endeavor.

References

Azuma, M. (2005). *Metaphorical competence in an EFL context*. Tokyo: Toshindo.

Donmall, B. G. (Ed.). (1985). *Language awareness*. London: Centre for Information on Language and Research (CILT).

Halliday, M. A. K. (1971). In P. Doughty, J. Pearce and G. Thornton, (Eds.), *Language in use* (pp. 10). London: Edward Arnold.

Harris, P. R., & Moran, R. T. (1991). *Managing cultural differences: Leadership strategies for a new world of business* (5th ed.). Houston, TX: Gulf Publishing Company.

Hawkins, E. (1987). *Awareness of language: An introduction*. Cambridge: Cambridge University Press.

Hawkins, E. (1992). Awareness of language/knowledge about language in the curriculum in England and Wales: An historical note on twenty years of curriculum debate. *Language Awareness, 1* (1), 5-17.

Honna, N. (2000). Some remarks on the multiculturalism of Asian Englishes. *International Communication Studies, 10* (1), 9-16.

Honna, N. (2003). *Sekaino eigowo aruku* [Exploring World Englishes]. Tokyo: Shueisha.

James, C., & Garrett, P. (Eds.). (1991). *Language awareness in the classroom*. London: Longman.

Jenkins, J. (2000). *The phonology of English as an international language*. Oxford: Oxford University Press.

Lakoff, G., & Johnson, M. (1980). *Metaphors we live by*. Chicago, IL: Chicago University Press.

Van Lier, L. (1995). *Introducing language awareness*. London: Penguin Books.

Disadvantages of global English for English-speaking nations

Svetlana Ter-Minasova   Moscow State University, Russia

Our future — as well as our present and past — is directly connected to the capacity for COMMUNICATION. Natural human communication. Ponder the words: hu-man, na-tu-ral! These words refer to something that has been given to us, humans, initially, by nature and God. It is thanks to COMMUNICATION that the development of rational man, Homo sapiens, became possible. Communication rules the world and people's lives, and determines our future. And man's most important means of communication is, as before, language.

The modern age, with its direction and development, is conditioned by the sudden, rapidly accelerating and multiplying, unheard-of, and unprecedented achievements of scientific-technological progress, of which even fantasts could not dream. All of these great discoveries of the human genius are directed toward one thing: the facilitation, improvement — optimization — of human communication.

Television, mobile telephones, and the Internet give people the opportunity to communicate, overcoming both time and space.

And once again at once the Tower of Babel looms ahead: the ability together, as a whole planet, to build, grow crops, buy and sell, educate, and so on and so forth.

And new signs have begun to flicker: Global Village, the United States of the Earth, Globalization …

In the Global Village, the entire population of the planet lives together, peacefully, and amicably. Since the invention of high-speed means of transportation and communication strongly decreased the earth's parameters, everyone has realized that there are no longer any far away kingdoms; we have one common — and not so large — planet and it is necessary for all of us together to look after it.

We live together, work together, and unite our achievements, talents, and minds. Together we struggle for the life and security of both the planet itself and the people populating it.

Gigantic multinational organizations, factories, and corporations serve all of mankind, and do so quickly, skilfully, and profitably.

And globalization is the mutual action and mutual dependency of all people and all countries. If I may express myself through our good old lexicon, this is peace and friendship among peoples. Who then can object to this? Where did the anti-globalizationists come from?

Alas! Globalization is a contradictory phenomenon. In other words, a dialectic one. And dialectics, the battle and oneness of antitheses, is the condition for progress. It is a pity, of course, that progress, the development of mankind, are impossible without conflicts, without strife; it is a pity that this progress is bought through blood, misfortunes, and the lives of millions of people.

Now, very briefly, the pros and cons of globalization.

Pros — these are the main ideas of globalization: peace, friendship, cooperation, the union of all peoples' efforts. International industry, trade, scientific activity, agriculture, education, healthcare, environmental protection, the fight against crime, international tourism, sports, and so on and so forth.

Much is happening already.

The cons are the human factor: languages, cultures, civilizations. National identity, national language, and national culture are under the threat of absorption, leveling, and annihilation.

The cons include, to be sure, the unsuccessful, distorted, and perverted pros. Evil is always more active and organized than Good. Using technological achievements, terrorists from around the world, criminal groups, and drug traffickers have united. Their united efforts are much more effective than the united efforts of the police, Interpol, and fighters against terrorism, narcotics, and so forth. The growth of the economy provoked by globalization only increased the gulf between the handful of the planet's wealthiest people and the billions (yes, yes!) of poor people. (I was shaken by the figures of 2002: the fortune of the 200 wealthiest people on earth is higher than the aggregate income of 40%, or 2.4 billion, of the planet's inhabitants. This means that right now the gap is even bigger …)

And again, much is already happening.

Gigantic international corporations have conquered the world, everyone drinks the same beverages (Coca Cola, Pepsi, vodka, and so on), eats the same food — sometimes fast (pizza, hamburgers), sometimes not — wears popular, widely available clothing, all children play with toys made in China…

Global organizations — the UN, UNESCO, WHO, World Bank, WTO, and Greenpeace — play an important role in the life of all mankind.

Discussion are underway on worldwide citizenship (and on the worldwide risk connected to it), and global rights. There is even a project for Worldwide University.

However, it is languages and cultures that hinder the unification of all people. Without a global language and (since language is inseparable from culture) a global culture, there can be no global community and there is no possibility of building a new Tower of Babel, that is, a Peaceful Global Community.

The absence of a global language puts the brakes on the union of mankind for the resolution of universal problems.

The establishment of a single global language is appealing in the opportunity it offers to solve many problems as, for instance: facilitate international communication, cut the enormous financial expenditure of international organizations, companies, and corporations on written and oral translation, to stimulate the exchange of information, and thus the acceleration and improvement of scientific-technological progress, trade, and business.

Surmounting the linguistic and cultural barrier could be a commercial goal and without a doubt is the cherished dream of traders, businessmen, and politicians.

Right now the English language confidently pretends to — and in actuality carries out — the role of a global language. English in particular is the language of international communication. The achievement of this status was facilitated by an entire row of fully concrete socio-historical reasons, so evident that it's not worth it to pause on them especially. (All that's necessary is to slip right away and say that of course the matter by no means lies in the quantity of speakers (who can compare here to the Chinese?!), nor in the myth of the special easiness, flexibility, convenience, and similar qualities of the English language).

It's just that, first of all, the sun, which never set in the British Empire, now never sets in the empire of the English language.

Secondly, this is the language of the main – and now only – remaining superpower, which rules the world. No wonder that in France and many other countries globalization is called Americanization.

Thirdly, it is the language of the "electronic village."

The French and German ambassadors to Great Britain, Daniel Bernard and Hans-Friedrich von Ploetz, wrote in the journal Spectator (17 Feb. 2001), "a global free market, labour mobility, as well as the emergence of the Internet and the e-economy seem to have endorsed the role of English as the new lingua franca. English is not only the language of science and the great superpower, but also that of the electronic village."

The triumphal march of the English language across the planet is so well-known that it hardly requires extensive substantiation.

The problems of English as the global language have been widely discussed all over the globe but mostly – in terms of a threat that the universal domination of English may pose to non-English speakers' languages and culture.

In this paper, however, I would like to dwell upon a different issue: what negative consequences may await English and English-speaking peoples, what harm can be inflicted on them in the situation of globalization with English as the global language.

Their advantages are obvious.

But is there harm, and, if there is, what kind?

Here is what I managed to find as possible answers to this question after many years of studying English, teaching it to Moscow University students, and interacting with colleagues from different countries — interacting both directly and indirectly, by reading books.

First of all, what everyone knows and what representatives of English-speaking nations talk about with sadness: the unwillingness to study other languages.

Indeed, the study of foreign languages in the English-speaking world is not very popular for understandable reasons: "the entire world studies our language, all even slightly educated people study English, so we don't need to worry." As a familiar example, English hinders the business of English-speaking nations: their companies and enterprises abroad lose much because their representatives do not know (and do not study) local languages and cultures. They study — on a scale incomparable with the rest of the world — the language of the closest neighbors: the British study French, Americans — Spanish, Australians — Chinese and Japanese. According to the data of 2001, 90% of Britons stop studying foreign languages at the age of 16.

This, of course, is a minus, since the knowledge of other languages and, through them, cultures, spiritually enriches one, broadens horizons, and gives a new outlook on the world. Moreover, the great Goethe was absolutely right when he said that one must also study foreign languages so as to get a better grip on one's own. R. Phillipson gives an example from the experience of student exchanges in the context of EU programs. British students who came to study at a university in Denmark were inferior in their knowledge of written English to Dutch students, for whom the language was foreign.

And the sadly well-known dislike of the British for foreign languages and all things foreign is connected to this as well. You cannot remain indifferent to the people whose language you study.

Thus the first is the unwillingness to study foreign languages.

Secondly, in the opinion of D. Crystal, in this situation there arises a linguistic elite consisting of native speakers that can use English for sordid motives and manipulation in various spheres.

Thirdly, and very importantly, having become a language of international communication, English has, as it were, crossed over into general use; it has become universal, international, and global property.

Two consequences are connected to this.

First, since language is not only a barrier separating nations, but also a shield protecting national identity, English-speaking peoples, have given over (sacrificed?) their native language into foreign "international" hands, and are losing their shield and facing the threat of losing their national identity.

It seems that right now the English language, the culture imbedded in it, and thus

English national identity are on display, as it were, in a certain global shop window with the commercial slogan, "use it, our language is your best means of communication." And everyone uses it, and the number of those who want to grows every day.

This impression became formulated after a certain episode in my academic life. I was in Italy at a linguistic conference on the problems of teaching English at universities. After the lectures, many conference participants went to have dinner at the nearest café. There we found both local dwellers and delegations from different countries. Our Russian gang discussed with pleasure in the native language the conference lectures, Italy, and the Italians. We felt good because Russian was our defense and we spoke on all kinds of topics easily and freely. Our neighbors were two young men who were talking in English on very intimate subjects. We unwillingly began to eavesdrop, and I saw that the Italians, French, and Finns sitting at neighboring tables were doing the same. The entire small café understood them and was listening with interest to their private conversation. They were put out for show, as it were; their language did not protect them, was not a shield to them, because everyone knew it.

As you know, language carries out two basic functions in relation to the ethnic group formed and "served" by it: it serves, first of all, as a means of communication, and, secondly, as a means of identification. Because of its global nature, English is highly weakened in terms of performing the function of identification. Of course, it is the language of communication among English – speaking peoples, but as a language of identification, as a shield, it is already very thin and in fact transparent. It is a fragile glass shield: the entire world observes, studies, criticizes, and borrows all that the English language mirror reflects, that is, the life, everyday reality, and culture of English-speaking peoples. This calls to mind the nightmarish TV reality show Behind the glass. It is the high price paid by speakers of the great and mighty English language for its status as the means of international communication.

And secondly, since English is given over to the use and power of the entire world, all nations, especially large ones, tamper with it to fit their culture, mentality, and language, that is, they create their own versions of English. In other words, along with the American, Australian, and Canadian versions of "archetypal" British English, there exist, develop, and multiply versions created in "other countries": Indian English, Chinese, Japanese, Russian, and so on.

When millions of multilingual people use one language, it shows in the level and quality of the language. And since the number of foreign users greatly exceeds that of native speakers and grows much quicker, the future of natural or original English inspires some apprehensions. I heard a story from foreign colleagues about how an international digest rejected a native speaker's article and asked him to rewrite it because his English was "not like everyone else's." To me, this story seems improbable, but the very fact of its appearance in the world — even as an anecdote, myth, or joke — is telling.

The term "World Englishes" has become very popular right now and an academic journal under this name is published by Blackwell Publishing in Oxford, UK, and Boston, U.S.

The ex-president of TESOL, David Nunan, discusses the same topic:

In becoming the medium for global communication, English has detached itself from its historical roots. In the course of doing so, it has also become increasingly diversified to the point where it is possible to question the term English. World Englishes has been used for quite a few years now, and it is conceivable that the plural form Englishes will soon replace the singular English…

Fourth, the problem is that such a massive expansion of English as a global language has led to the creation of a certain variety in the "English as a foreign language" taught at schools and universities, a certain form neutralized and simplified for "poor foreigners," a standard, unified, "distilled" language. The author of Basic English, Charles K. Ogden, wrote in 1930 that the question of global communication (he called it "debabelization") must be resolved not with the help of a false language, but rather through a simplified form of English. (Basic English, a dictionary that was shortened by Ogden to 850 words, was designed as an auxiliary international language).

In Russian academic literature, the "educational" variant of English received the name pragmalinguistic. This style occupies a special place since in it neither the function of message nor that of impact dominates in its pure form. Its main purpose is to serve as a basis for creating linguistically irreproachable educational aids, to give students examples of lexis, grammar, phonetics, and so on. Accordingly, its basic characteristic feature is a strict normativeness on all levels: from phonetics (RP, Received Pronunciation) to lexis (no slang, dialectisms, or jargon).

I would like to remind the reader that what is being discussed here is not the quality of educational materials from the outlook of foreigners; this is a separate problem that is now being widely investigated. In fact, I believe that from the foreigners' point of view, everything is all right: give to Caesar what is Caesar's, give to foreigners what is the foreigners'; we must know our — foreign — place in using a foreign language. For deviation from the norm, games, defacement, and creativity, we have our own native languages. This is like behaving as if you were at home when you are a guest. The topic at hand is the problems of natural English that appear in connection with such a wide distribution of its pragmalinguistic international variant. This is the fourth problem. The gap between foreign and authentic English is growing and deepening.

Fifth, this "authentic, real English" does not exist at all as such. There are several variants of "authentic" English among which the two basic ones, used as material for studying English as a foreign language, are British and American. And the gap between them also grows all the time. The British variant is more prestigious (history, great literature, a vividly expressed national character, traditions), American is more practical and profitable for a career. In "other countries," the older generation is, as a rule, in favor of the British variant, while the youth prefers the American one.

Both variants, by the way, stumble upon big problems.

America is a country of immigrants and the "American" language is represented by a big collection of variants, beginning with the most primitive. This is problem #1.

Since it was in America that the idea of fighting for human rights was born, it is not surprising that it was there that the question of recognizing linguistic rights as human rights arose. This is problem #2, directly connected to problem #1.

The difficulty of this question is well illustrated by an incident that T. Lobachev describes in the academic collective monograph "The Resolution of National-Linguistic Questions in the Modern World."

The gist of this incident is that a certain Mexican woman named Marta Sandoval sued the Alabama state government for denying her a driver's license "because of poor knowledge of English." In this state, there is a law on the monopoly of English in everything not related to speakers' private lives. The plaintiff, on the other hand, appeals to a foundational law — a 1964 act on civil rights that prohibits any kind of discrimination on the basis of nationality. Since such discrimination is prohibited in the 1964 law in all institutions that receive state funds in one form or another (the relationship in the private sector is regulated differently), the Department of Mobile Vehicles of Alabama must submit to this law since it falls under this category.

The British variant has its own problems, connected directly or indirectly with the global status of English.

Modern British English shows a tendency toward the erosion and loosening of linguistic norms, toward a departure from RP (Received Pronunciation) and the Queen's English. This is expressed in the fact that jargon, slang, dialectisms, a lower vocabulary, and vulgar expressions are now used in literary, standard English, in the language of the mass media. This is what MSU professor V. S. Elistratov, following a well-known Soviet philologist B.A. Larin, calls "barbarization," which accompanies the end of any stable epoch. According to Elistratov, "the historical evolution of any literary language can be presented as a row of subsequent 'reductions,' barbarizations."

In the early 90s, The Times commented on the soon-to-be-published dictionary BBC English in the following way: "The BBC is to publish the first comprehensive guide to 'BBC English' in its history in an attempt to rid programmes of Americanisms, cliché's, jargon, inaccuracies and bad taste" (The Times, 5 July, 1993).

Nonetheless, despite the publication of dictionaries and society's concern, the violation and thus transformation of norms can no longer be stopped. In his lecture on the theme, "The

Changing English Language 2000-2010," given at the MSU Faculty of Foreign Languages and Regional Studies, a British linguist Ron Carter said, "What is being said right now on British television, 20 years ago would have caused the immediate dismissal of the entire editorial staff, 10 years ago — a torrent of indignant viewer responses, but now it does not provoke any kind of reaction."

A serious blow in this same direction was struck by the use of English as a global language for electronic communication. Here is what the ambassadors of France and Germany to the UK say about this: "You should protect yourselves from Electronic English. Electronic communication is a good thing. But it is equally important to maintain the quality of spoken and written English" (The Spectator, 17 Feb 2001, op. cit.).

Yes, this is important, but impossible and impractical.

Presumably, one of the reasons — in my opinion, the main one — for the "barbarization" of modern British English is the ever growing globalization of English. This loosening of norms can be seen as an attempt to depart from normative language, which has been given for communication to the "global village," and thus enter into a substandard, "reduced" variant, inaccessible for "those foreigners." It can become a new shield, a language of identification. The question is precisely this: what will it identify? What kind of a nation will this be?! The British, who speak (and write!) in jargon, vulgarisms, and so on?! It turns out that they give away their exquisite, elegant costumes, the models of which were created by great tailors (Shakespeare, Swift, Wordsworth, Byron, Austin, Dickens, Thackery, Shaw, and many, many others), and put on rags or modern youth clothes.

Hence, British English has its own problems in connection with its global status. This problem is seen especially clearly in the example of the British literary language, a paragon for all variants that followed or were born in its womb. But in reality, this problem concerns all the existing Englishes of all English-speaking peoples, and thus the sixth tendency is a threat of barbarization of all "authentic" Englishes.

Finally, the seventh: as a global language, English acquires a certain negative tinge, and this can provoke a negative attitude to those who use English as a means of communication — first and foremost to English-speaking nations.

English's negative connotations are determined by a whole host of reasons.

A dominant position always provokes discontent. English has the mark of prestige, elitism, prospect, and the promise of material prosperity. This irritates other nations, especially those that have lost their high international status (French for many years was the exclusive language of diplomacy and correspondence; Russian ruled over the huge Soviet space and its neighbors; German was the language of science, etc.), as well as those that never had it. Each has its own language, the language of its homeland, its mother tongue, beloved and dear.

The growing negative attitude toward English is provoked also by the fact that the opinion held by people of many countries about the international policy of the U.S. has taken a turn for the worse. Just as in the SAR Afrikaans lost its dominant position after being labeled the "language of aggressors," English faces the threat of getting the same label with corresponding consequences. In our country, after WWII interest in German (and thus the amount of those studying it), drastically fell: one of the main reasons was the association with violence and aggression.

Negative feelings toward a language can be — unfairly, but logically — transferred to its speakers. In Russia we experienced this in both directions: from language to people and from people to language. Indeed, in many of our republics and countries of the "socialist camp" dissatisfaction with the political regime took on the form of the rejection of Russian. And neither Pushkin, nor Tolstoy, nor Dostoevsky, nor Chekhov, nor Sholokhov saved it.

In connection with all the "negative consequences" of the global status of English the role and mission of its faithful and devoted servants, i.e. teachers of English, looks contradictory.

The traditional view of foreign language teachers and translators: these are people who bring nations together, allow them to find a common language (in the direct and figurative sense), missionaries and peacemakers who selflessly and fearlessly go out into the jungle of an alien language and culture in order to lay in them the roads of peace and friendship. This is all true, and my whole life I have lived with a feeling of pride in my profession, in my choice, in my colleagues.

But now the problems of globalization have arrived and the language that I serve along with millions of my fellows at work turns out to be at the center of attention, or rather at the center of the fight for and against that attention. For all the millions of non-native English teachers suddenly a very important question arose: who are we? Whose side are we on? Whom do we serve? All of us have a native, beloved language and culture. And then it turns out that the language we study and teach, to which we have dedicated our talents and life, threatens our own language and culture. And after all, while teaching English, we realize that we are simultaneously promoting the ideology, views, lifestyle, and value system of the English-speaking world, which is not always friendly to us, sometimes foreign spiritually, always foreign literally, sometimes hostile.

Who are we then — courageous and selfless fighters for peace and friendship among nations, or the so-called fifth column (that is, traitors) in our own country, conductors of foreign ideas and values?

Cutting the long answers short, there are a few things we know for sure.
1. English is the main language of international communication. It has received its status for certain socio-historical reasons. This has been determined by the course of human history.
2. Of course, teaching a language means advancing the culture placed therein — the

culture of the language's speakers. There is nothing bad about getting to know another culture; it is only beneficial. It widens the horizons and enriches the native culture, all the more so because behind English there stands a great culture. It is bad if this is forcedly imposed or leads to obsequious imitation. But these are extremes.

3. A remarkable and unexpected paradox: the prospect of globalization and of the invasion of a global language forced all nations to shudder, wake up, and become conscious of their national identity, to value their culture and language more deeply, and to start taking care of them.

4. Another significant and unexpected result of global processes is the recognition of the need to study foreign languages. In the wonderful, often-cited article written by Daniel Bernard and Hans-Frienrich Von Ploetz, the ambassadors of France and Germany to the UK, it states, "Learning one or more foreign languages is the true way of becoming 'global.'"

On this musically major note we will stop.

East-Asian cultures through a looking-glass of the English language thesaurus

Zoya Proshina   Moscow State University, Far-Eastern National University, Russia

Abstract

The cognitive paradigm, which is very popular nowadays in Russia, suggests looking on a language thesaurus as a worldview that reflects concepts actualized in words. Language imposes this or that worldview on a person and reflects a person understands of the world. English as an intermediary language in communication between speakers of different cultures helps in creating a new worldview that is specific of an interlocutor's culture and at the same time carries some traces of the intermediary language. The aim of this article is to show which words of East Asian origin have become indicative of new concepts reflected in the English-language thesaurus and through this to reveal the domains that have become of paramount importance for Eastern and Western culture contacts and can be cognized by representatives of a third culture. East Asian loan words in the English-language thesaurus also help us find the difference between generally common spheres of life in China, Japan, and Korea. Besides, the English language thesaurus reveals words coined by English speakers and reflecting their relationships with the Chinese, Japanese and Koreans. Thus language proves to be one of the tools to study intercultural interactions.

The cognitive paradigm, which is very popular nowadays in Russia, suggests looking on a language thesaurus as a worldview that reflects concepts actualized in words. Language imposes this or that worldview on a person. A native language reflects a primary worldview formed in the natural setting from one's childhood. A secondary worldview is created by acquiring or learning a second or foreign language at an educational institution (Ter-Minasova 2004: 58), and a tertiary, or an intermediary worldview is characteristic of a lingua franca used by non-native speakers – for example, in English-language communication between a Chinese and a Russian interlocutors, people form their worldviews of their interlocutor's culture through the intermediary language, i.e. English (Proshina 2001). This worldview mirrors new culture concepts indirectly, with three languages participating in the process. Since English is the most popular lingua franca nowadays, its thesaurus can facilitate a cognitive process of acquiring new concepts for English-speaking bilinguals. The aim of this article is to show which words of East Asian origin have become indicative of new concepts reflected in the English-language thesaurus and through this to reveal the domains that have become of paramount importance for Eastern and Western culture contacts and can be cognized by representatives of a third culture.

The four-century contacts of the English-speaking people and the Chinese, Japanese and Koreans can be traced in the English vocabulary. This is the result of English functioning as a link world language in various cultures and as such including various ethnic culture-loaded words into its stock. However, as Braj Kachru truly noted, "the aspect that has been least studied is the acculturation of English in various non-Western contexts" (Kachru 1985: 282). Kachru enlisted a number of devices used to achieve the acculturation: lexical borrowings, extension of the semantic range of English words, and translation (calquing) of native formations into English. These new formations are gradually assimilated in English. East-Asian culture-bound words, or code words, are of various degrees of assimilation in English. The best integrated words are included in English language dictionaries, such as Cannon (1996); Evans (1997); less assimilated words occur in reference books related to ethnic cultures (De Mente 1994, 1996, 1997, 1998; Honna & Hoffer 1986). While comparing these loans, we can state what kind of East Asian heritage is most essential to the Western world.

Method and material

The methods employed for this research are comparative and quantifying analyses of thematic groups of culture-loaded loans related to Chinese, Japanese, and Korean cultures, as well as to words of English origin referring to American-Asian culture contacts. The words, collected in the English-Russian dictionary of East Asian cultures (Proshina 2004) were picked up from over 80 English dictionaries and about 200 texts, including those from reference books, such as encyclopedias and guidebooks, as well as from fiction, newspapers and magazines, literature for children, popular literature about sports, medicine, etc. We have distributed all culture-loaded words into 44 thematic fields: administration, aesthetics, architecture, arts, botany, business, calligraphy, chemistry, cuisine, customs and traditions, dance, education, ethics, everyday life, finance, geography, geology, history, information, law, leisure, linguistics, literature, mathematics and physics, measurements, medicine, military, music, mythology, nature, philosophy, policy, population, psychology, relatives, religion, sex, social and economic relations, sport, technology, textile, theater and movies, transportation, and zoology, The next step was to single out the ten fields containing the greatest number of terms and compare them in reference to Chinese, Japanese and Korean cultures,.

Chinese culture-loaded loans

In the 19th century, what mostly interested Europeans in China was tea, fabric, fruit, and porcelain (china) (Zhou and Feng 1987). These were the domains that contributed the majority of loans from Chinese to English, at that time primarily to British English. In the 20th century, the thesaurus made up from American sources reveals a different picture.

Over 12% of 2000 Chinese culture-loaded words refer to the sphere of cuisine, testifying to the popularity of Chinese restaurants all over the world. Chinese cuisine terms include names of dishes, most famous of which are dimsum, small pastries filled with shrimp, fish, pork, chicken or vegetables, Peking duck, chow fan, or fried rice, wonton, stuffed piece of dough, jiao-zi, steamed dough stuffed with meat or vegetables and symbolizing luck, chow mein, fried noodles. Among the most popular Chinese dishes is one, unknown to the Chinese. This is chop suey, hot meat mixed with vegetables. This dish is said to have been invented by a Chinese chef in America.5 Nowadays in Hawaii, one can find a number of Chinese restaurants called chop suey houses. Since the English-speaking people dealt mostly with the South Chinese migrants, most words referring to the Chinese cuisine are of Cantonese origin (cf. Cantonese tea and Mandarine cha).

A more detailed analysis of Chinese cuisine terms testifies to the popularity of dishes made of flour (steamed baozi, shaomai, mantou, noodles like bai fun, chow fun, tantzu, etc.). Since in Asian cuisine rice is a staple, it is only natural that dishes made of rice came to be known to the Westerners – congee, mooncake, tzungtzu, etc. Soy sauce and other soy products also became very popular – hong shao pork (beef, fish, duck, eggplant), doufu, and sang chow. Meat dishes are made mostly from pork (laap cheong, a smoked sausage, chahr siu, grilled pork, mooshu pork, fried in dough with vegetables, etc).

Among Chinese beverages, the Westerners single out mainly two – tea (congou, Oolong, pekoe, etc.) and strong alcohol (mao-tai, rice alcohol, samshu, yuan jiu, etc.)

For Westerners the unusual products, used in Chinese cuisine, include mah tai, edible chestnut, lien gee, lotus seed, lien ngow, lotus root, suehn, bamboo shoots, ahp sun, dried duck stomach, bird's nest, soup made from the mucilaginous lining of the swifts' nests;

pidan, an egg preserved in lime; and seaweeds – gee choy, dried violet-black seaweed, faht choy, hairy seaweed, etc.

Another big thematic group of Chinese loans (over 7%) includes sport terms, especially those referring to kung fu, or Chinese martial arts (the original Chinese meaning of the word was "hard and diligent training, both physical and mental"). The Chinese sport terms used by Westerners name types of martial arts (wu-shu, chinna, hsing-i, tai chi chuan, Bagua); styles (ho, or 'crane', jeet kune do, the kung fu style of Bruce Lee, nei-gong, soft qigong); movements (jin, moving a foot forward, lie, or spreading; dim muk, a mortal touch resulting in the opponent's death in some time); names of exercises (changquan, or long punch, Ni-Chan, a spiral movement); methods and principles of fight (Man, slow movement in tai-chi; Ting-Chin, ability to feel the opponent's energy; chan nien chin, adhering and sticking energy); names of postures and stances (hsu bu, or cat stance, Tan Pan, posture for sitting meditation in tai-chi), and titles of sportsmen and instructors differentiated by their experience and gender (si bok, a kung-fu instructor of high rank, si poo, a female instructor in kung-fu, si-di, a novice in kung-fu; sifu, a kung-fu instructor).

Chinese martial arts are closely related to Chinese medicine. Many soft styles of kung-fu are breathing exercises, controlling qi, or vital energy. Therefore, many medical terms (about 5%) are used when describing qi circulation along body meridians and canals, through certain points of the body, and accounting for the mechanism of this or that kind of martial art (qigong, hsing-ch'i). Names of organs in Chinese medicine are categorized somewhat differently from those in Western anatomy. There are six Yin/Chang organs (usually capitalized) including Heart, Lungs (meaning the whole breathing system), Liver, Spleen, Kidney, and the so-called Pericardium responsible for blood circulation, breath and sexual functions. Yin/Chang organs store energy, while the six Yang/Fu-organs – Stomach, Large and Small Intestines, Bladder, as well as an unusual (for a Westerner) organ called Triple Burner – are considered to be "shops" for producing, directing and assimilating energy.

Philosophy and religion infiltrate the Chinese way of life; therefore, many words absorbed by English from the Chinese culture denote rites, customs, and traditions related to specific Chinese religions and philosophy. This can be exemplified by harong, the ceremony of ancestors' memory; Festival of Pure Brightness, Qing Ming, a memorial day when the relatives take care of the graves, offer food to their ancestors, and light fire to drive away evil ghosts. Sometimes it is very difficult to differentiate between philosophical and religious terms related to the Chinese culture. Semantically very close to them are mythological terms rooted in Dao (e.g., xian, an immortal saint, Eight Immortals, the symbol of luck, representing eight states of life – youth, old age, poverty, wealth, nobility, common life, masculine and feminine gender; qilin, a unicorn symbolizing welfare and happiness; feng-huang, a two-gender phoenix, also a symbol of well-being, a.o.)

Western cultures and the English language also borrowed Chinese ethic terms that make part and parcel of Chinese philosophy and religion. To describe Chinese Confucian and Daoist ethics code words like de (virtue), jen/ren (humanity), qian (modesty), hsin (honesty), and others are used. A great many of these terms have the semantic component of "respect": zuxian (respect for the ancestors), xiao di (respect for the elder brother), shiao (filial debt to parents), ko(w)tow (ceremony of reverent greeting of the senior people). Special features of ethnic psychology are also revealed in borrowed code words emphasizing the Chinese collectivism and close ties with community (gangqing, a friendly feeling; chaoyin, a person dealing with policy but feeling oneself outside the society), Chinese self-reflection, drive to realize oneself as a part of the macrocosm (hong, looking at things in depths; ming yi, self-control; yuing chi, mind balance, karma), desire to have energy (ganjin, power; gung ho, ardent, devoted, faithful; lin, readiness as a tai-chi principle).

In general, terms from philosophy, religion, mythology, ethics, sport and medicine make up over a quarter (29%) of the Chinese culture-loaded vocabulary used by English-speaking people.

It is very common that a great number of culture-loaded words are related to everyday life. Among these are the terms naming Chinese traditional clothes and their details (qipao, cheongsam, nankeens, mandarin collar, Mao jacket, Sun Yat Sen jacket), kitchen ware and equipment (nimble brothers, chopsticks, kang, wok, hot pot), types of rooms (shu fang, a kind of office; ce suo, a toilet; fan ting, a dining room; tang, the main room in the house), construction and architecture (sihe yuan, a court-yard house consisting of four parts; zou lang, a roofed passage between the wings of the building; ying bi, a wall in front of the entrance to the court-house), everyday actions and processes (chi fan, to eat; foot-binding). It is quite natural that traditional units of measurement have been borrowed into English to speak about life in China: words denoting measures of weight (fen, dan, jin), length (chang, cun, li), square measures (mou, mu, p'ing), volume (dou, sheng), and time units (ke, shi, double-hour).

Geographical terms indicate the names of provinces, cities. They are used mostly in the attributive function (Shanghai food, Harbin festival) or sometimes as calqued nicknames of the places (Garden City, or National Hygienic City, a nickname of Nanning; Sandalwood Mountains, a Chinese name for Hawaii, etc.).

One of the top ten thematic groups is the group of words from social and economic sphere (about 4%). These words denote social ranks, mostly historical (Son of Heaven, the Chinese Emperor; Wang, a governor, prince; shi, a minor aristocrat, a learned official; tanka, people dwelling in boats); societies and associations (tong, a political party or a fraternal and secret society; renmin gongshe, people's commune; hui-kuan, an association of people coming from the same region); people's relations (guanxi, personal connections; mui jai, a debtor's daughter given to the creditor as a payment for the debt); economy concepts (juntian, or equal-field system; Forced Job Placement; iron ricebowl, the guaranteed job-for-life system).

Difference between Chinese and Western painting is the reason for a great number of borrowed art terms in English (about 4%). They denote art styles (gongbi, painting characterized by minor details; guohua, traditional Chinese painting; hsieh-sheng, naturalistic style of painting); techniques (cunfa, brushes showing the texture of trees, rocks and mountains; dian(fa), point painting; meigu, or "boneless" method of painting without a black ink contoir); objects of painting (shanshui, "mountain and water" landscape; t'ao t'eh, the head of a mythical animal; wu fu, five red bats, symbol of family hapiness); painted porcelain and china (anhua, a 'secret decoration', visible only when held up to the light; nankeen, a sort of white china with blue painting; sancai, a three-colored painting used on porcelain); colors and paints (ch'ing, bright blue; lokao, Chinese green; yang bong, a transparent red color).

On the whole, the first top ten thematic fields of Chinese culture-loaded words occurring in English texts refer to the following spheres:

1. cuisine (12.16%)
2. sport (7.43%)
3. philosophy (6.76%)
4. everyday life (5.51%)
5. geography (4.89%)
6. population (4.78%)
7. religion (4.73%)
8. medicine (4.57%)
9. social and economic sphere (3.79%)
10. art, policy, ethics (3.74%)

Japanese culture-loaded loans

The Japanese contributed to the global English thesaurus most of all in the sphere of sport (about 16% of 3000 words). These terms include names of sports, general (budo, bujutsu, kempo) and specific (aikido, iaido, judo, karate, jujitsu, kendo, kyudo, sumo); names of styles (butokan, Shotokan, jodo-ryu); methods and techniques (age uke, ashi-guruma, geri); exercises (kata, dandori, empi); postures (aguar, hira, ichimonji); tools (bo, tonfa, bokuti); form and equipment (gi, hakima, fundoshi); sportsmen (aikidoka, ozeki, rikishi); degrees (black belt, hachidan, kyu); competitions and matches (basho, chui, ippon, kumite); sport facilities (beya, or a stable; heya, a place where sumoists live and train before their marriage; dojo, training hall); interjections (hajime! Begin!; kiai! a cry before the attack; matte, stop!). A great number of these terms have been borrowed from English into Russian, which is evident in their pronunciation. The list of Japanese sport terms is much wider than that of Chinese terms, as it includes a greater variety of details (names of uniform, equipment, degrees, facilities, interjections), which might hint at a great popularity of Japanese martial arts in the USA and Europe. Besides kempo terms, the Japanese have verbalized their achievements in gymnastics (Tsukahara vault, Tsukahara dismount; Yamashita vault) and even invented a new game similar to croquet (a geito boru < gate-ball).

Another big field of Japanese loans in English (about 10%) is cuisine. The popularity of Asian food is increasing every year. While Chinese restaurants are considered to be very democratic and unexpensive, Japanese restaurants are among the most exquisite and expensive. English-speaking people use Japanese words denoting dishes cooked in specific ways (agemono, a dish fried in deep oil; karaage, a dish fried in batter; teriyaki, a dish of grilled slices of meat, fish, or chicken that have been marinated in soy sauce; mushimono, a steamed dish; nimono, a boiled dish; suboshi, unsaulted dried sea product.)

Borrowed Japanese cookery terms reveal a great number of fish dishes (dashi, fish broth; suimono, a clear fish broth with seaweed; surimi, minced fish specially prepared; sashimi, a dish from thin slices of raw fish; sushi, etc.); dishes from sea products (ika-meshi, a dish from squid stuffed with rice; noshi, a long piece of dry abalone); seaweed (chakobu, a seaweed cut into small pieces; aonori, dried green seaweed; wakame, brown seaweed).

Like the Chinese, the Japanese value rice. Therefore their cuisine is characterized by a great number of rice dishes: shake-nori (a rice puff stuffed with salmon and rolled in the seaweed leaf); sekihan (rice with azuki beans, traditional New Year dish); gyudon (rice with beef and onions), onigiri (rice rolls with plum), and others. The thesaurus has a great number of words naming dishes made of beans, especially soy and azuki beans. The most famous product, which is also used in Chinese cuisine, is tofu, soy cheese, fried or used in soups.

Like with Chinese cuisine, the Westerners have paid attention to Japanese alcoholic drinks (sake, shochu, toso; dry beer) and tea (koicha, gyokuro, amacha), though for the Japanese it is the tea ceremony that seems much more valued than the drink itself. In the United States people came to know one more drink with the Japanese name, kombucha tea, which is said to have come from Mongolia and Russia and is still very popular in Russia.

Everyday life also provides a great many culture-loaded words related to Japan (7%). Americans and Europeans pay attention to traditional Japanese clothes (kimono, obi, a sash tied about the waist; hakama, loose male pants with a great number of folds in front; tabi, a sock with a separate stall for the large toe); footgear (geta, a traditional wooden clog; zori, a sandal with a thong passing between the first and second toes); hair styles (momoware, a young geisha's hair dress; katsura, a type of female wig; shimada, a hair dress typical of the 17th century); ceramics and porcelain (Arita ware, satsuma, chawan); coverings and boxes (bento, a box for food; furoshiki, a wrapping napkin); equipment and utilities (kama, seiro, rice boilers; hashi, chopsticks; chasen, a tea stirrer); fans (ogi, folding fan; jinsen, a flat fan from bird feathers on the iron support; kyo sensu, a small folded paper fan); lanterns (chochin, a paper lantern; toro, a stone lantern, etc.); furniture and room equipment (tatami; kotatsu, a table-heater, covered with a blanket; tokonoma, a wall niche with a shelf for art and religious objects; futon, a matress; furo, a bath for all the family members); places to eat (ryotei, a Japanese-style restaurant; sobaya, a place specializing in soba, buckweet noodles; sushi bar); and dwellings (okiya, geisha's dwelling; ryokan, a hotel in the traditional Japanese style; capsule hotel with very small rooms).

A great number (6%) of Japanese loans referring to the field of arts testifies to the Japanese contribution to the world art. These words denote genres of painting (shunga, erotic art; ukiyo-e, a picture of everyday life depicting courtesans, kabuki actors; bijin-ga, a portrait of a beauty, etc.); painting styles (kanga, Chinese style; nanga, Japanese painting); technique (suiboku; white-and-black ink painting; tarashikomi, putting a paint layer over a wet one); prints (beni-e, a two-colored print; kakemono-ye, a big hanging print; surimono, a small colored print used for greeting and congratulating); ceramics (nishikide ware, bekkoware; kiyomizu-yaki); lacqued things (japan; maki-e, negoro); applied arts (byobu, paper or silk screen; hakata doll; netsuke); paper things (chigiri-e; origami, kiri-e); and structures imitating nature (bonsai; ikebana; tsukiyama). Scholars believe that special attitude to nature is what differs people from Asian and Western cultures – in Western cultures a person dominates nature; whereas in Asian cultures a person venerates nature, trying to become part of macrocosm (Mikhailov 1995).

The Japanese society has always been vertically structured, which makes it different from Western societies (Gudykunst and Tsukasa 1994; Kornilov 1991). Therefore, words to show social hierarchy, both historical and current, have also entered the English language thesaurus (mikado, shogun, samurai, daimyo, ronin; honcho, boss, urakata, a back-side person of special knowledge, kuromaku, a shadow person with great influence and power.) Hierarchy is also typical of family relations, which is seen from the loan vocabulary: koshu, head of the house; soryo, a system of heritage making one of the relatives the head of the clan, etc.

One of the social features concerning the Japanese is their collectivism, groupism (Goldstein, Tamura 1975). In Japanese culture a person is assessed by the company s/he belongs to, the bonds s/he is keeping (Locke 1992). The Japanese make a clear distinction between those who belong to the group and those who do not. This classification into 'ingroup' and 'outgroup' is also reflected in the culture-loaded thesaurus borrowed by English: uchi, belonging to the group, soto, an outsider; batsu, a group of people from the same university, family, location, etc.; gakubatsu, graduates from the same school supporting other students and graduates from the same school.

Economy terms borrowed into English also have the component of groupism and unification: zaibatsu, a big family industrial and trade clan, conglomeration, after World War II transformed into keiretsu; shoshu, a transnational company of Japanese origin.

Semantically very close to social and economy terms are business words. Japanese economic miracle raised keen interest from people of other countries, the USA in particular. The Japanese business experience and management became a topical theme to discuss, and the discussions brought a great many calques and loans into the English language. New words denote ranks and positions (bucho, director; hancho, head of the department; kacho, head of the section; office lady, a secretary). From the Japanese loans in the English thesaurus we come to know that many Japanese are moretsu shain, workaholics, who are not afraid of dekasegi, working far away from their home, or of baribari, routine monotonous work, or of three K's [from Japanese kitanai, kitsui, kiken], dangerous, dirty and difficult job. One of their main working principles is kaizen, continuous perfection of working skills. Akirame ga warui, inability to stop, may result in karoshi, death because of their being overtired. The working day in many companies starts with chorei, morning meeting. Decisions are developed not only by the executives, but also by the rank and file employees, for which quality circles, or Creativity Circles, or goningumi are organized to make proposals and analyze complaints. Due to ringi seido, a consultative system of making a decision, when proposals in written form go from the bottom to all those concerned, the Japanese have a special form of management, informated factory, to carry out the business philosophy principle of involving all the employees to management, control and planning. To nourish the collectivist spirit, the practice of personnel rotation, jinji ido, is employed. Before taking a final decision, managers discuss them in kondai kai, after-hours informal chats, holding nemawashi, informal, behind-the-scene discussions, often on a one-on-one basis, among all the key people who would be concerned with or involved in implementing any decision made.

The Japanese community, famous for politeness and ceremoniousness, scrupulously observes etiquette norms. The Japanese etiquette reflects social relations. Culture-loaded words from the ethics and etiquette sphere refer to people's relationships (amae, dependence on somebody's favor; en, personal connections; tsukiai, social debt, social obligation);

moral principles and values (wa, harmony; enryo, personal reserve, subordinating personal interests to those of community; giri, social debt; giri-ninjo, conflict between personal feelings and debt; haji, shame); behavior (aizuchi, nodding as a sign of agreement; low profile, modesty; omiage, a gift to colleagues after returning froim business leave).

Religion in Japan also inspires interest in Western people. Peaceful coexistence of different types and schools of religion (Shintoism, Butsudo, Zen Buddhism, Amidism, Nichiren, Rinzai, Soto, etc.) and their synthesis, shinbutsu-shugo and honji-suijaki, have become known to Westerners in their Japanese verbal form. Borrowed are also names of religious followers (bonze, so, sennin, kannushi, Miko), ritual and sacred objects (kei, ofuda, Daibutsu, manji), rites (norito, Butsuji, chanoyu), religious methods (zazen, mondo, koan), philosophical categories (mu-shin, relieving from ego; Satori, sudden brightness; ai, cosmic harmony); beliefs and superstitions (yakudoshi, unlucky age; taian, the most favorable day of the week); and ritual places (tera, Buddhist temple or monastery; bonxery, Buddhist monastery, mikoshi, movable Shinto shrine; kamidana, home Shinto altar).

A great number of loans are made in the field of botany. G. Cannon who studied Japanese borrowings into English, philosophically remarked, "The West has artistically benefited from the lovely flora of Japan, where botany is viewed more as an art rather than a science" (Cannon 1996: 39). It is absolutely true. Plants brought from Japan are known in America to be used in the decorative function (flowers: ebine, an orchid, Kurume, an azalea, kiku, chrysanthemum, the national symbol of Japan; trees and bushes: aogiri, Nikko fir, sakura; vines: fuji a.o.). A lot of plants are edible: wasabi, Japanese green horse radish; daikon, white radish; winter cherry; adzuki beans; tanenashi persimmon, satsuma orange; nashi, Japanese pear; etc. Very popular in the U.S.A. are Japanese mushrooms: maitake, shiitake, nameko. There are plants with Japanese names used in medicine – aburachan that gives medicinal oil; gingko tree; hijiki, a seeaweed. Americans build up constructions using hinoki, a cypress, matsu, a pine-tree, sugi, a Japanese cedar. Japanese plants are also used for technical purposes: to extract oil (akebi, kuro-moji); or to produce paper (kozo, mitsumata) and lacquer (urushi).

Many Japanese words are used in leisure. These are names of traditional Japanese games, such as karuta, a card game, its main objective is to collect a poem, parts of which are written on cards; go, a game resembling chess; janken, a hand game ("scissors, paper, and stone"), pachinko, a kind of Chinese billiards. Currently, video and electronic games have become popular all over the world: Nintendo, Pacman; Sega video system; tamagotchi, Pikachu, Transformer. Invented in Japan karaoke has become a favorite pastime in almost all countries.

To sum up, Japanese loans have mostly contributed to the English language in the following top ten spheres:

    1. sport (15.84%)

2. cuisine (9.79%)
3. everyday life (7.01%)
4. arts (5.96%)
5. social and economic relations (5.43%)
6. religion (4.72%)
7. botany (4.63%)
8. leisure (3.74%)
9. business (3.64%)
10. ethics (3.21%)

Korean culture-loaded words

Korean loans, though scarcely reflected in dictionaries, are used in English texts (about 1500 in our material) when describing every day life of the Koreans. Loans of this thematic field dominate over others. Direct loans are used when mentioning traditional clothes (hanbok, Korean traditional costume; poson, traditional white socks; paji, loose baggy pants tied around the waist, a part of man's traditional costume, etc.); headgear (kat, man's black hat made of horse hair; samo, a round black hat made of silk); decorations (maedup, Korean weaving; pinyo, a decorative pin); fans and umbrellas (hapchukson, hwa-kae, tanson); furniture (ch'aekchang, a bookcase; ch'antok, a kitchen shelf; chang, a chest of drawers, soban, a low dining table); house equipment (ondol, heated floor; pangsok, a thick mat for sitting; tok, a clay pot); ceramics (paekcha, Korean porcelain; pisaek sogu, small bluish-green cups made of celadon); lanterns (hyondung, a big hanging lantern, oedung, a street lantern, ildung, sun-shaped lantern); cloth produce (chogakpo, napkin; hotpo, kind of quilt; sangbo, a tablecloth; ppallaepo, a bag for linen; pokjumoni, a traditional purse).

Since Korean culinary terms represent popular exotic dishes, they are also borrowed plentifully, naming general things (anju, snacks; changkuksang, main dish; Hanshik, Korean meals), and meals cooked in various ways (chon, fried dish; chorim, a dish with soy sauce cooked on slow fire; kui, grilled dish; much'im-ch'ae, preserving vegetables without using salt).

Judging by the names of Korean dishes, Westerners are most interested in the following: sea food (chotkal, sea food sauce; haemuljungol, vegetable broth with seaweed; kimbap, vegetables and rice rolled in seaweed, Korean sushi; ojing-o, dried squid), fish (bahn-chahn, fish with vegetables; maeuntang, hot fish soup); meat dishes (posintang, stewed dog meat; samgyet'ang, a chicken stewed with ginseng; shinsollo, a hot-pot dish; bulgogi, fried slices of marinated beef; bulkalbi, ribs fried in teriyaki sauce); vegetable dishes, the main one being kimch'i, and a number of soy sauces; soups (kuk), noodles (chapchae, kuksu, naengmyon), rice (bibimbab, rice with meat and vegetables; ttok, rice cake; pap, unsalted steamed rice); desserts (kangjong, fried rice dough covered with honey; tot'orimuk, acorn jelly). The Korean cuisine is famous for a great variety of tea (boli cha, barley tea; hodo cha, wallnut tea; insam cha, ginseng tea, etc.). Alkoholic drinks are not unknown to the Koreans (makkoli, popchu, soju, etc.).

Korean music proves to raise interest, and the terms denoting musical genres and forms, as well as musical instruments have become known to English-speaking people: aak, ritual court music; sogak, Korean folk music, p'ansori, kind of singing; nagak, a spiral shell used a wind instrument; sogum, a bamboo flute; haegum, a two-stringed violin, kayagum, a 12-stringed zither; changgo, a drum; p'yon-gyong, stone bells, a.o.

Korean sports, in particular fighting and self-defense, are as popular as those in Japan and China. Among the most popular are taekwondo, and ssirum, traditional wrestling. Many sport terms borrowed into English are related to these two types of sports: dojang, taekwondo training hall; dobuk, a uniform; chung, a chest-covering; hoshinsul, defense and attack technique; ahp cha-gi, a kick; negong, inner power and energy control.

Leisure activities in Korea are very much competitive. Therefore, quite a number of loans are in-between leisure and sport fields: kossaum, kind of tug-of-war game; tongch'aessaum, a "battle"; or ku-ne, a swinging game.

Mass popular customs and traditions, rites and rituals are typical of Korean traditional culture and are fixed in the English vocabulary as well. Among them are rites of passage, such as dol, first birthday celebration; paekil, 100th day from birthday; hwangap, a 60-year-old celebration; jingap, a 70-year-old jubilee; kyerye, girl's coming-of age ceremony, ch'inyong, a wedding ceremony, chesa, a memorial ceremony, a.o.

Many of the rites are of religious origin, particularly coming from musokchi, Korean shamanism. The English language thesaurus reflects the most significant cultural things, like kut, a rite, kosa, appeasing home gods; mudang, a shaman; sanshin, a mountain god, etc. Besides shamaism, Buddhism, or Korean Pulgyo, with all its schools and divisions (Chogye, Kyo, Son, Won) can also be traced in the English vocabulary stock.

The sphere of art has yielded a lot of Korean loans. Some of them name ornamental patterns: pidanmuni, a pattern of elegant geometrical design; tanch'ong, a pattern of five cardinal colors on wooden frames. Some of the words go deep into the details of designs: chongcha-mun, the Chinese-character grids; kobung-mun, a repetitive tortoise shell pattern; posanghwa, a flower pattern, etc. Korean art terms denote traditional Asian motifs: ch'aekkori, depiction of scholarly implements; hwajo-hwa, a bird and flower painting; sansuhwa, Korean landscape painting that depicts mountains and river. Since Korea is famous for its crafts, a lot of loan words name artefacts: e.g., maebyong vase, reminding of a plum; punch'ong, celadon vase; nakjuk, a fan drawing made with heated iron rod; sudo, wall embroidery. The Korean art is bright and multicolored, with the red shade domineering over others, which is revealed through the loan word componential analysis: sokkanju, dark-red; chut'o, reddish-brown.

Korean loans from the sphere of social and economic relations are similar to Japanese and Chinese ones. They stress Korean collectivism as the main principle of relationship in the Korean community (chaegim, collective responsibility; chebol, collective punishment; day lamp, a person not interesting for a company; tongchang hoe, graduates of the same school); types of organization (chaebol, a gigantic industrial complex; hwarang, an ancient voluntary organization trained as a group in the arts of war, literary taste and community life; kye, a public supporting organization); social ranks (kolpum, a system of aristocratic ranks; yangban, an aristocrat, ch'onmin, common people); family relationship (chib, home, family; yang chop, a concubine; minmyonuri/ an ancient marriage system when a 6-11 year-old girl was sent to live with the her future husband's family); and social relations (ujong, friendship; tongnip, independence; pujong, a second-rate attitude to a woman; yeon, personal connections).

Business terms reveal the specifics of Korean management: shin sang pil bol, carrot and stick policy of personnel management, insa idong, workplace rotation; kyojesul, business drinking. From the terms we know that in Korea's business, komun, or consultants are very important, as well as experienced go-betweens, chungjaein, and shadow heads of the companies, makhu shil yokwa, "curtain" people. To arrive at a decision on a number of problems one needs anun saram, personal connections.

To sum up, the top ten spheres of Korean life that provide loans in the English language are as follows:
1. everyday life (14.61%)
2. cuisine (12.36%)
3. music (8.19 %)
4. sport (7.41%)
5. customs and traditions (6.49%)
6. religion (5.36%)
7. art (5.01%)
8. social and economic relations (4.80%)
9. leisure (4.38%)
10. business (2.68%)

Contrastive analysis of the East Asian cultures through the thesaurus

The thesaurus of East-Asian culture-loaded words allows us to make conclusions about the intensity of culture and language contacts and about the most significant life spheres of the Chinese, Japanese and Korean people, from the Western point of view. The largest group of culture-loaded Asian words is made up by Japanese loans (over 3000 in the selected material). Some of the Japanese loans are of Chinese origin and are associated with Asian culture as such (shiatsu, tofu, kabuki, judo). The second large group is composed of Chinese words (about 2000 units). As compared with these two groups, the Korean culture has provided the global English with the least number of loans (about 1500), which justifies, to some degree, Korea's former status of a closed country for the Westerners who called her by the nickname of the Hermit Kingdom.

The specific feature of all East Asian cultures and, consequently, language thematic fields is the interlink of all life spheres, their deep interpenetration, which is known as the philosophical "principle of nonduality," (Snitko 1999: 97) or "one in other" (for example, philosophical and religion concepts lie in the basis of the Oriental medicine, sport, martial arts in particular, arts, etc.); so linguacultural fields, vaguely bordered, tend to cross and overlap.

The greatest number of words borrowed into English have come from the spheres of Asian cuisine, sport, everyday life, art, and religion. These are the main domains of vital activity and ethnic consciousness, and their serving as loan sources proves their significance for other nations using English as a lingua franca.

Through the English-language thesaurus we are able to find the difference between generally common spheres of East Asian life. Thus, the comparison of Chinese, Japanese, and Koream culinary terms reveals the Chinese preference to steamed dishes (baozi, steamed puffs; mantou, steamed bread; qingzheng yu, steamed fish, etc.); the Japanese preference to fried dishes (sukiyaki, fired slices of beef; tempura, fish, prawn or vegetables in batter, etc.), whereas the Koreans are fond of both steamed and fried dishes. The Chinese culinary terms name much more pork dishes, the Japanese words denote mostly fish dishes and seafood; the Koreans appear to prefer beef and seafood. The three cultures widely employ soy and rice. Rice is the main source for producing alcoholic beverages. Tea, whose origin is in ancient China, is cooked not only from the tea bush but also from other plants, a great variety of teas is mostly typical of Korea.

Sport terms also differ from culture to culture. What is common to the three linguacultures is the dominance of words referring to wrestling, fighting and self-defense (Chinese wu-shu, tai-chi chuan; Korean taekwondo, ssirum; Japanese aikido, judo, karate, sumo). The difference lies in the principles of movement. Since the Chinese martial arts are based on the philosophy of slow perpetual endless motion resulting from the yin and yang opposition and the energy spread in concentric waves, most of the Chinese sport terms denote rather soft, smooth, flowing movements (Man, slow tempo of movements as the main principle of tai-chi; ts'uan, a movement symbolizing water in hsing-i; Yuan, circular movement). Great attention is paid to breathing and controlling energy qi (qigong, a system of controlling qi; tao-yie, movements aimed at providing every body organ with breath; gin like, development of inner energy). While the Chinese exercises are group-centered, the Japanese tend to develop individual defense skills, so they perfect their skills in a one-to-one combat (tai-jutsu, hand-to-hand fight; kumite, a free sparring; randori, free-fighting.) Japanese sport terms indicate low-centered kicks and blows (dojime, leg scissors; gedan zuki, lower punch; otoshi uke, dropping block; ukemi, breakfall). Sparrings are usually conducted on tatami (newaza, groundwork) or in the special site (dohyo, a circular sumo site). Special or subsidiary tools may be used (bo, a stick; bokken, a wooden sword; chikaraishi, a one-foot stick with a ten-pound round stick on its end). Korean sport terms demonstrate the synthesis of the Chinese arts and the Japanese do, "way" (tae-bo, a blend of ancient arts of self-defense, dance and boxing). Since history taught the Koreans to defend themselves against both mounted and unmounted enemies, their fight includes jumps and leaps (pandalch'agi, a kick upward; kisa, mounted bowing). Another specific feature of Korean sport terms is that they mirror a great number of mass folk games (kosam-nori; tongch'aessaum; ke-chuldarigi).

In the sphere of religion the Far Eastern cultures are unified by Three Teachings – Buddhism, Daoism, and Confucianism. Many religious concepts are named by parallel terms, such as Ch. yin / yang, Kor. um / yang, Jap. in / yo. Venerable attitude towards the ancestors is characteristic of the three cultures, which can also be seen in the thesaurus. Traces of unique native religions, however, differentiate the cultures and are mirrored in the English thesaurus – Korean shamanism, Japanese Shinto, with the cult of kami considered to be the essence of the being. Culture-loaded words prove the main difference between the Eastern and Western cultures, with the former being nature-centered, the latter – human-centered.

Thus the thesaurus of East Asian culture loaded words used in the English-speaking communication familiarizes us with the life of Chinese, Japanese and Korean people. By emphasizing the common features of Asian cultures and their differences, the thesaurus includes the words essential to the crosscultural communication from the perspective of Westerners, Americans in particular. By creating an intermediary view of the East Asian world, the English language becomes a lingua franca in crosscultural communication.

English words relating to cross-cultural contacts with East Asians

Besides Asian loans, the English thesaurus also contains words coined by the English-speaking people, yet reflecting their relationships with the Chinese, Japanese and Koreans. To prove that these English words are related to Asian cultures or cross-cultural relations, we take into consideration the following factors:
- word attribute (Japanese allspice, Korean conflict);
- Asian root in a derivative (japannery, mandarin duck);
- word definition (Jesuit ware, Chinese porcelain of the early 18th century, decorated with Christian motifs, usually in black and gold on a white background);

- semantic component of the word (peke-faced, having a small wrinkled face like that of a Pekingese);
- word etymology (golden oak mushroom, from English golden + half-calque from Japanese shiitake, name of a mushroom)

The number of English-Asian cross-cultural words depends on the length and intensity of cross-cultural contacts. The earliest Asian immigration to the USA was a Chinese one; so the longest language and culture contact in America was English-Chinese. The number of English words related to the English-Chinese relations is the greatest (54%). The second group is made up of words reflecting English-Japanese contacts (40%). English-Korean cross-cultural contacts yield only 4% of words, whereas the remaining 2% of words characterize English-Asian contacts in general (dragon, one of the fast-developing high-tech Asian countries; Oriental spruce).

Thematically classified into the same domains as the East-Asian loans, English words with the East Asian semantic component refer to the following top fields: biology (bamboo fern, Japan Judas-tree), everyday life (honey-bucket, a container for excrement, an ironic word used by American soldiers during the Korean conflict; Chinese balance, a weigh with four suspensions), history (Tumulus period, picture bride, Pacific War, Assembly Center), population (shanghai-lander, resident of Shanghai; One-Point-Five generation, Korean Americans brought to America in their childhood; banana, a nickname for an Asian American).

Biological terms (in the sphere of botany, zoology, ornithology, ethnology) often denote things brought to America and Europe from Asia, mostly from Japan. Everyday words mostly refer to the life of Chinese immigrants (whereas loans from this domain are related mostly to the Korean culture). Historical words reflect landmarks in Western and Asian contacts. Political and military terms are very close to history terms (Chinese revolution, Korean conflict). Quite a number of words belonging to the ethnic domain mirror sharp ethnic conflicts caused by Asian immigration to America (chink, Jap, F.O.B.).

Many other English words referring to Asians are negatively connoted (Chinese ace, banana, Jap, Gook), which also demonstrates the complicated attitude of the Westerners to Asians that has existed until recently.

In general, English words with East Asian component reflect Asian things as they are seen by Westerners, as well as essential moments of interethnic and international contacts that took place in various spheres in different periods of history.

Conclusion

As a lingua franca the English language has a culture-transmission function. When in contact with East Asian people, speakers of English borrow Asian culture-bound words as loans and calques, thus enriching the English language, turning it into global English.

Through the thesaurus of global English as an intermediary language it is possible to state the most essential moments of cultural contacts, to single out the most interesting items in ethnic Asian cultures as seen by Westerners, and to trace the interethnic attitudes and relationships. The complicated history of American-Asian relations is also mirrored in the English thesaurus. Thus language proves to be one of the tools to study intercultural relations. This is of great significance today since, as Andy Kirkpatrick truly marked, "many non-Anglo or non-Western ways of thinking have received international attention through English" (Kirkpatrick 2007: 36).

Growing with the spread of Asian cultures, Chinese, Japanese, and Korean English loan words will become known to other people and this leads us to a certain ELT inference: if our students have to communicate successfully with their neighbors, we have to raise their awareness in localized English words they are sure to encounter in their intercultural communication as well as in the appropriate communicative strategies for effective negotiation.

References

Cannon, G. (1996). *The Japanese contributions to the English language: A historical dictionary*. Wiesbaden: Harrassowitz.

De Mente, B. L. (1994). *NTC's dictionary of Japan's cultural code words*. Lincolnwood, Illinois: NTC Publishing Group.

De Mente, B. L. (1996). *NTC's dictionary of Japan's cultural code words*. Lincolnwood, Illinois: NTC Publishing Group.

De Mente, B. L. (1997). *NTC's dictionary of Japan's cultural code words*. Lincolnwood, Illinois: NTC Publishing Group.

De Mente, B. L. (1998). *NTC's dictionary of Korea's business and cultural code words*. Lincolnwood, Illinois: NTC Publishing Group,.

Evans, T. M. (1997). *A dictionary of Japanese loanwords*. Westport, Connecticut, London: Greenwood Press.

Goldstein, B. Z. & Tamura' K. (1975). *Japan & America: Contrastive study in language and culture*. Rutland, Vermont: Tokyo, Japan: Charles E. Tuttle Company.

Gudykunst, W. & Nishida, T. (1994). *Bridging Japanese / North American differences*. Thousand Oaks, London, New Delhi: SAGE Publications.

Honna, N. & Hoffer, B. (1986). *An English dictionary of Japanese culture*. Tokyo: Yuhikaku Publ. Co.

Kachru, B. (1985). *American English and other Englishes*. In D. Byrd, N. Bailey, M. Gillermon, (Ed), *Landmarks of American language and linguistics*. Vol. 2. Washington, D.C.: Office of Language Programs, Bureua of Educational and Cultural Affairs, US Department of State.

Kirkpatrick, A. (2007). *World Englishes. Implications for international communication and English language teaching*. Cambridge: Cambridge University Press.

Kornilov, M. N. (1991). Yaponiya, Vostok I Zapad (problema "obschego" I "osobennogo" v zarubezhnykh kul'turologicheskikh issledovaniyakh (Japan, East, and West — problems of "the general" and "the specific" in culture studies abroad). In: Kul'turnoe nasledie: preemstvennost' I peremeny (Cultural legacy: continuity and changes), *Reviews*. INION. Issue (2). Moscow: Russian Academy of Sciences.

Locke, C. D. (1992). *Increasing multicultural understanding: A comprehensive model*. Newbury Park, London, New Delhi: SAGE Publications,

Mikhailov, M. I. (1995). "Chelovek i mir" v kul'turakh Vostoka — Zapada — Rossii (Person and World in the cultures of East — West — Russia). In Kul'tura I Mir, (Ed.), *Vostok — Zapad* (Culture and World: East — West). International conference abstracts. Nizhny Novgorod.

Proshina, Z. G. (2001). *Angliiskii yazyk i kul'tura narodov Vostochnoi Azii* (The English Language and Culture of East Asian People). Vladivostok: Far Eastern University Press.

Proshina, Z. G. (2004). *Perekryostok* (Crossroads). *English-Russian contact dictionary of east asian cultures*. Vladivostok: Far Eastern University Press.

Snitko, T. N. (1999). *Predel'nye ponyatiya v zapadnoi I vostochnoi lingvokul'turakh* (The ultimate concepts in Western and Eastern linguacultures). Piatigorsk: PGLU Press.

Ter-Minasova, S. G. (2004). *Yazyk i mezhkul'turnaya kommunikatsiya* (Language and Intercultural Communication). Moscow: Moscow State University Press.

Zhou, Z. P. & Feng, W. C. (1987). The two faces of English in China: Englishization of Chinese and Nativization of English. *World Englishes* 6, (2), 111-125.

INTERCULTURAL MEDIA STUDIES

Intercultural mass communication:
A new frontier for intercultural communication research

Sun Youzhong   Beijing Foreign Studies University, China

Abstract

Communication takes place at various levels of social organization, i.e. intrapersonal, interpersonal, intragroup, institutional/organizational and society-wide (mass communication). Traditionally, intercultural communication research focuses on the interpersonal communication between individuals of different cultures. With the rapid expansion of mass media within national boundaries and across sovereign borders, mass communication has become a more and more important channel of interaction between different cultures. The author argues that intercultural communication research, which literally means the study of communication between cultures, should readily accept intercultural mass communication as its legitimate domain. The author defines intercultural mass communication research as the study of mass-mediated communication between two or more cultures and proposes numerous potential research topics and approaches for this promising academic new frontier.

The author believes that the study of intercultural mass communication will not only extend the sphere of traditional intercultural communication research, but also reinforce the study of intercultural interpersonal communication per se.

How should we define "intercultural communication"? This seems to be an anachronistic question now that intercultural communication research has witnessed a half-century glorious history of booming growth worldwide ever since the publication of *The Silent Language* by Edward T. Hall (1959). Numerous undergraduate, M.A. and Ph.D. programs in intercultural communication have been established in universities throughout the world; countless academic institutions, national and international, have emerged for the study of intercultural communication; and journals and books dealing with intercultural communication are simply too many to list. Yet, this discipline still sees the need to redraw its boundaries, which can, of course, be regarded as evidence of its vital potential and prospect.

One of the most popular definitions of intercultural communication is probably the one given by William B. Gudycunst (2002) in his latest edition of *Handbook of International and Intercultural Communication*. According to him, "[i]ntercultural communication generally involves face-to-face communication between people from different national cultures" (p. ix). In line of this conceptualization, Gudykunst made a careful distinction between intercultural communication and international communication as "separate areas of research." He wrote, "Intercultural communication researchers tend to focus on the individual as the unit of analysis. International communication researchers, in contrast, tend to work at the macro level using units of analysis such as the nation, firm, world systems, groups, and movements"(p. x). In the first chapter of the book, Rogers and Hart echoed this differentiation. They defined international communication as "the study of heterophilous mass-mediated communication between two or more countries with different backgrounds," stressing that "INC takes place at the societal level, as opposed to the interpersonal level, which distinguishes it from ICC" (p. 5).

Yet in the same book, Barnett and Lee offered a different definition: "Intercultural communication is the exchange of cultural information between two groups of people with significantly different cultures." They put the stress on the exchange of cultural information, which makes it possible for them to envisage intercultural communication occurring "on many levels," among which "mediated" intercultural communication, they pointed out, is worth special notice. They agreed with Gudykunst and others that face-to-face exchange of information among different cultural systems would result in "the reduction of uncertainty about the future behavior of the other system," but they went further to maintain that mass media artifacts, such as films, videos and recordings about other groups or produced by members of other groups, could just as well reduce "individuals' uncertainty about other cultures." They argued that "with the developments in communication technologies and the globalization of the economy, most intercultural experiences are mediated rather than face-to-face" (Gudykunst and Mody, p. 276). Obviously, there is disagreement among Western scholars as to whether mediated communication should be incorporated into intercultural communication.

In China, intercultural communication research was first introduced by Professor Hu Wenzhong and other scholars into the English departments of universities in the early 1980s. Since the central concern of teachers of English was how to enhance students' ability to communicate with foreigners, their primary interest in intercultural communication, understandably, was first oriented to "the problems that arise in communication between people of different cultural backgrounds and how to solve these problems" (Hu, p. 24). This interest shared by teachers of English directly resulted in the establishment of the China Association for Intercultural Communication. Up until today, this organization has remained to be the only one in China entirely devoted to intercultural communication research.

However, not all Chinese scholars agree that intercultural communication should only deal with interpersonal face-to-face communication between people from different cultural groups. The fact that scholars disagree on the Chinese version of the term "intercultural communication" betrays the controversy over the boundaries of this discipline. Those who translate the term into "跨文化交际", mostly researchers from the discipline of foreign languages and literature, understand intercultural communication as essentially face-to-face communication while those who translate it into "跨文化传播", mostly researchers from the discipline of journalism and communication, tend to equate intercultural communication with mediated communication between two or more cultures or nation-states (Tong, 2005, p. 237).

Among the latter group of researchers, some would simply embrace any kind of communication between individuals, organizations and nations of different cultural backgrounds as belonging to intercultural communication regardless of the channels used for communication (Liu, 2000, p. 45; Tong, 2004). In his book entitled *Intercultural Communication Studies*, Guan Shijie (1995) took this inclusive position, maintaining that intercultural communication occurs at three levels, namely interpersonal, inter-organizational and international (pp. 51-52). Interestingly, however, in his more recent book *International Communication Studies* Guan (2004) made a special effort to distinguish international communication from intercultural communication. He pointed out two major differences between these two areas of study: 1) The agent of intercultural communication is the individual while that of international communication is national media or international organizations; and 2) Intercultural communication research is concerned about the verbal or nonverbal exchange of information between individuals of different cultural groups while the latter about national sovereignty and international relations. Yet at the same time, Guan admitted that there is a trend of mutual incorporation between these two areas of study, with the focus of international communication studies moving from mass media communication or "macro analysis" toward interpersonal communication or "micro analysis" while that of intercultural communication going in the opposite direction (pp. 3-4).

In general, Chinese researchers have preferred three major parallel definitions of intercultural communication. The first definition limits it to the realm of interpersonal face-to-face communication between individuals of different cultures; the second definition, by contrast, equates intercultural communication with international communication or communication between cultures via mass media; the third definition intends to marry intercultural communication with international communication. These three approaches contending against each other marks the current state of intercultural communication studies in China. As Luo Yicheng and Si Jingxin (2005) pointed out after reviewing the existing scholarship of Chinese mainland academic circles from 1990 to 2003, "a clear definition of 'intercultural communication' is still lacking, no consensus has been reached yet, and the boundaries of the research field are blurred".

As a tentative solution to this triangular impasse, I propose to redefine intercultural communication as the information exchange between different cultures through interpersonal interaction and mediated communication. This definition is based on the following line of reasoning: Intercultural communication literally means the communication between different cultures; since communication basically means "the giving and taking of meaning, the transmission and reception of messages" (McQuail, p. 13) or, in plainer language, the exchange of information; and the exchange of information across cultures is made possible today, most importantly, through either interpersonal or mediated interaction, intercultural communication, therefore, can logically be understood as the information exchange between different cultures through interpersonal interaction and mediated communication.

Here a look at Barnett and Lee's "structural model of intercultural communication" would help clarify the implications of my definition (Gudykunst and Mody, p. 278).

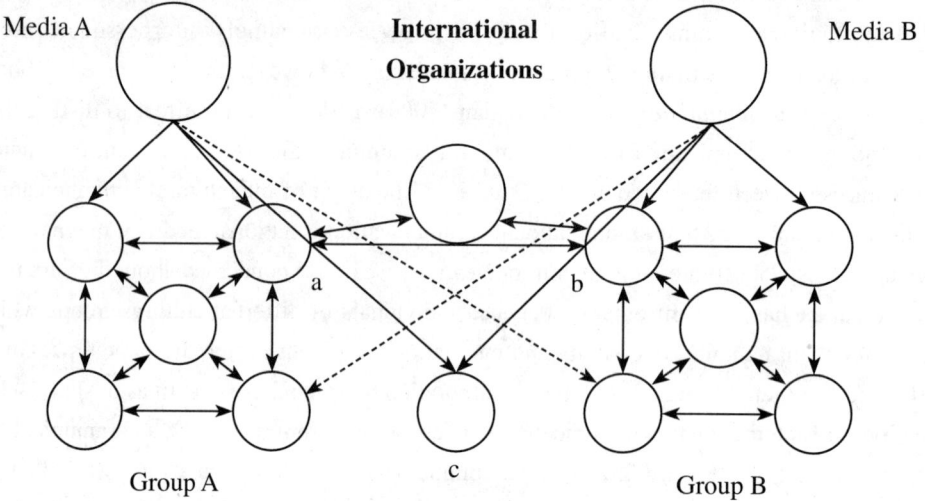

Structural Model of Intercultural Communication

This figure is intended to illustrate the process of intercultural communication between two interacting groups, A and B, each with its own distinct culture. Individuals or other information sources are represented as circles and the communication flows as lines. Arrows indicate the direction of information flows. The communication between the two culturally distinct groups occurs at three levels. At the individual level, members of Group A and Group B interact directly or by way of individual c, a "multicultural man [woman]" (Adler). At the level of mass communication, Media A and Media B expressing the culture of Group A and Group B respectively serve as connections between the two cultural groups. At yet another level, international organizations also play a role in linking the individuals of different cultural groups.

According to my definition, intercultural communication deals with not only the interaction between individuals a and b (or via individual c) of the two cultural groups, but also the communication between the two cultural groups via Media A and Media B.

Then is there any difference between intercultural communication and international communication now that mass communication across cultural boundaries is annexed by the former? Yes.

First, intercultural communication deals with communication between cultures while international communication that between nations. As geographical parameters, culture and nation may overlap, but more often they diverge. And as functional or structural parameters, they are fundamentally different.

Second, intercultural communication is concerned with the relations between culture and communication while international communication the relations between nation-state and communication. For example, the impact of culture on communication, whether interpersonal or mediated, is a primary concern of intercultural communication (Hall) while propaganda, the use of mass communication to promote national interests worldwide, has been an enduring topic of international communication (Lasswell).

Third, the agent of intercultural communication is the individual or a medium representing and expressing a distinct culture while that of international communication is the government representing and expressing national power or interests. In this sense, intercultural communication researchers might be interested in revealing the American values or way of life demonstrated in Hollywood movies that are popular around the world while international communication researchers would critique the vast out-flow of American pop culture as evidence of American "cultural domination" (Schiller).

In spite of the distinctions that can be drawn between intercultural communication and international communication, these two areas are interrelated in many respects. What I want to stress is that it is possible to incorporate intercultural mass communication into intercultural communication without losing the identity of the latter. Just as Hu Wenzhong, former president of the China Association for Intercultural Communication, has proposed on several academic occasions, intercultural communication should remain open to new perspectives and interdisciplinary approaches to broaden its horizons. And so we are faced with a new frontier.

If intercultural mass communication can be accepted into intercultural communication, then what novel topics can be added to the existing research agenda of intercultural interpersonal communication? The following are some potential approaches to the study of intercultural mass communication.

Analyzing Intercultural Media Texts

Media texts can simply be defined as print, sound or pictorial artifacts produced by mass media. They are "the vast body of 'messages' and 'meanings' which are continuously being transmitted and received from all kinds of different media" (McQuail, p. 304). In the context of intercultural mass communication, two general approaches are especially promising: 1) the representation of exogenous cultures in domestic/foreign media texts; and 2) comparison of media texts across cultures.

The Representation of Exogenous Cultures in Domestic/Foreign Media Texts

This approach is based on the assumption that individuals of a certain cultural group largely depend on domestic/foreign media for information about exogenous cultures. There is no doubt that people also acquire knowledge about other cultural groups through face-to-face encounter, and opportunities for interpersonal communication across cultures certainly have been on the rise with the rapid expansion of international tourism, trade and cultural exchanges. However, the advent of information age has put the mass media in a strategic position in the social structure of a nation, "constitut[ing] a primary source of definitions and images of social reality and the most ubiquitous expression of shared identity", and serving as "the largest focus of leisure time interest, providing the shared 'cultural environment' for most people and more so than any other single institution" (McQuail, p. 4). It can be argued that most people today learn about foreign cultures by reading the international news columns of domestic newspapers or the foreign culture sections of domestic magazines, by watching documentaries, cartoons, soap operas, advertisements directly or indirectly representing foreign cultures on domestic or foreign TV, by watching imported movies, by listening to exotic music, or logging onto millions of websites where national boundaries simply disappear. If that is the case, examining the components, quantity and quality of the textual content about exogenous cultures as transmitted by intercultural mass media, domestic or foreign, to the native people would indeed greatly contribute to our understanding of the process of intercultural communication in general and intercultural mass communication in particular.

Numerous case studies of national image fall into this category. For example, in his book *The Social Construction of International News: We Are Talking About Them, They're Talking About Us*, Wasburn (2002) investigated how U.S. media portrayed other nations and how media of other nations such as Russia, Indonesia, Japan, Britain, Canada and France, by contrast, constructed American image. Another impressive example is *Image of China in World Mainstream Media* by Liu Jinan et al. (2006). The authors conducted comprehensive content analysis of 8 major newspapers from the United States, Britain, France, Japan and Spain respectively in order to describe the international image of China and to reveal prejudices or stereotypes imbedded in the coverage of China by foreign media.

Comparison of Domestic and Foreign Media Texts

The content of mass media is regarded by historians, anthropologists and sociologists as evidence of values and beliefs of a particular time and place or social group. The underlying assumption is that media content generally responds to the prevailing hopes, fears or beliefs of the people and reflects common values (McQuail, p. 305). This theory can be adopted to guide the comparative study of domestic and foreign media texts. It is believed that such comparative study could help reveal the differences or similarities in values and beliefs between two or more cultural groups.

A typical example taking this cross-cultural approach is "The Construction of Beauty: A Cross-Cultural Analysis of Women's Magazine Advertising" by Katherine Frith, Ping Shaw, and Hong Cheng (2005). According to the authors, advertising offers a unique opportunity to study how the beauty ideal is constructed across cultures. They analyzed the content of advertisements from women's fashion and beauty magazines in Singapore, China, and the U.S. to compare how beauty was encoded in different cultural environments. They found that there was a noticeable difference between the portrayals of women from the U.S. and from the two East Asian societies in terms of sexual portrayal, and that Asian ads contained a large proportion of cosmetics and facial beauty products whereas the U.S. ads were dominated by clothing. Their findings suggest that beauty in the U.S. may be constructed more in terms of "the body," whereas in Singapore and China the defining factor is more related to a pretty face.

Analyzing Intercultural Media Audience and Effects

In mass communication theory, an audience can be defined in different and overlapping ways. They can be defined by place according to where they are; by people in terms of their age, gender, political belief or income category; by the particular type of medium, or channel involved; by the content of its messages in terms of genres, subject matter or styles; by time in the sense of the "daytime" or "primetime" audience (McQuail, p. 360).

These different approaches to audience analysis can shed light on our understanding of the constitution and nature of intercultural media audience. Who are they? Where are they in the structure of the society? What are their general characteristics in terms of age, gender, political belief or income category? What intercultural media or channels do they habitually use? What kinds of intercultural content mostly interest them? Why do they choose to use or get exposed to intercultural media? All these fundamental questions concerning intercultural mass communication, unfortunately, have not yet been systematically investigated.

From the perspective of the relationship between source and receiver, an audience can be defined as "target", "participants" and "spectators" respectively. In the case of audience as target, the communication process is considered primarily as the sending of signals or messages over time for the purpose of controlling or influencing the target audience. In the case of audience as participants, communication is understood as a process of sharing and participation in order to increase the commonality between sender and receiver. In the case of audience as spectators, communication is conducted simply to capture the attention of an audience, regardless of communicative effect (McQuail, p. 377).

These mass communication perspectives are also relevant to our study of the relationship between the intercultural media and their audience. Are the latter passive target of the former? Or active participants? Or indifferent spectators? Or can we view the audience as self-centered users of intercultural media products or as meaning constructors or self-reliant decoders of intercultural media texts? These are questions still awaiting exploration.

One of the most praise-worthy efforts ever made in this respect is a book entitled *The Export of Meaning: Cross-Cultural Readings of Dallas* by Tamar Liebes and Elihu Katz (1993). *Dallas* was a popular, long-running American primetime television soap opera about the Ewings, a very wealthy Texas oil family. Having been broadcast in over 90 countries, it is considered to be one of TV's most successful drama series ever, and is one of its longest running. In order to find out whether it is possible for native people to actively "read" imported American pop culture, Liebes and Katz conducted a systematic focus group study of different cultural groups of viewers of *Dallas* selected from Israel, Japan and the United States. The authors concluded that decoding by overseas audiences of the American hit program, *Dallas*, shows that viewers use the program as a "forum" to reflect on their identities. They become involved morally (comparing "them" and "us"), playfully (trying on unfamiliar roles), ideologically (searching for manipulative messages), and aesthetically (discerning the formulae from which the program is constructed). In other words, active construction of meaning by the local audience is possible in intercultural mass communication.

Liebes' and Katz' qualitative study of the reception of *Dallas* is typical of the cultural studies tradition that investigates foreign media influence. This approach is based on Stuart Hall's theory of encoding/decoding that draws a distinction between the sender's message and what the audience gets out of it in terms of the encoder's "preferred" meaning and the meaning that viewers negotiate for themselves at the time of decoding (Hall, 1980). The primary concern of researchers in this tradition is how viewers interpret media and programs within particular time-and-place cultural contexts. It is generally agreed that how the media are received varies, depending on the local situation in terms of ethnicity, gender and class.

Another productive approach seeks to quantify intercultural media effects. Some of the major findings include: 1) Audience influences are selective due to the fact that choice and discrimination are exercised in relation to media and content within media; 2) Audience interest and social categories such as gender, socioeconomic status, religion, rural-urban residence tend to qualify media power, uses, and gratifications; 3) The effects of television on individuals are not uniform, depending on interaction between the characteristics and goals of the viewer, the content of what is watched, and the media. Briefly speaking, as Yaple and Korzenny pointed out, media effects on individuals across national and cultural groups were small, detectable, and varied according to audience selectivity, context, and culture (Gudycunst and Mody, pp. 390-392).

Compared with media effects studies in the domestic context, research in intercultural media effects is sporadic and unsystematic. There are still many academic gaps to be filled. In addition, researchers of intercultural interpersonal communication may find numerous topics of interest relevant to their traditional concerns. For example, how does exposure to intercultural mass media affect one's identity? How does exposure to intercultural mass media affect one's behavior in interpersonal communication across cultures? Is there a causal relationship or correlation between exposure to intercultural mass media and intercultural communication competence? In what ways can exposure to intercultural mass media reduce uncertainty about the future behavior of the other system through an increase in understanding of the other social group? How do we evaluate the quality of the pop culture transmitted by intercultural mass media? How do we assess the short-term and long-term impact of mediated foreign cultures on local individuals in particular and local culture in general? How do people make use of new communications technologies to facilitate their interpersonal communication across cultures? Exploring these and other questions would certainly contribute to our understanding of the ramifications of accelerated intercultural encountering in the age of globalization.

More Questions for Further Exploration

One of the most exciting research areas of intercultural interpersonal communication is intercultural communication competence, an area that is significant both theoretically and practically. It is the same case with intercultural mass communication research. With the constant extension of international media networks into every corner of the world leading to increased interactions between various cultures, media organizations of every kind committed to intercultural communication thirst for knowledge and know-how about how to mass-communicate successfully across cultures. Meanwhile, the booming intercultural media industries have created millions of rosy career opportunities looking for talented individuals who are both bilingually and interculturally competent.

To meet the urgent needs of intercultural media organizations and individuals, researchers should be ready to address the following questions: What are the typical cultural obstacles that block or affect effective intercultural mass communication? What strategies can media organizations take to strengthen their intercultural presence? Particularly, with regard to the use of language, sound and imagery in intercultural mass communication, what concrete feasible solutions can we develop to arm intercultural professionals for the challenges they face in the workplace? Is it possible to develop a set of criteria to evaluate the intercultural communicative competence of mass media or media professionals? What factors are most likely to determine the intercultural communication competence of mass media (Think about the model of knowledge, motivation and skills formulated by Spitzberg and Cupach [1984])? What role can educators play in this respect?

There is also a theoretical dimension of intercultural mass communication. As a relatively new field, intercultural mass communication can borrow theoretical tools from neighboring fields and adapt them to the new needs of the field. One of the most relevant neighboring fields is cultural studies, whose conceptual constructions such as gender, ethnicity, cultural identity, hegemony, cultural commodification, globalization and so on can all be applied to critique the performance and influence of intercultural mass communication.

Finally, intercultural mass communication involves ethical issues. Fundamentally, how can people from diverse cultures live together without destroying themselves and the planet? What sort of intercultural ethic must we develop if we are to improve the art and science of intercultural communication (Samovar & Porter, p. 430)? Specifically, how do we balance cultural diversity with universal human values? How do we balance loyalty to one's own cultural identity with tolerance of others? How do we distinguish international propaganda from intercultural mass communication? Given the cultural relativity of ethics, under what conditions is it permissible for people of one culture to attempt to persuade people of other cultures to accept their values (Samovar & Porter, p. 471)? In a word, how can intercultural mass communication contribute to world development and harmony?

References

Adler, P. S. (1982). Beyond cultural identity: Reflections on culture and multicultural man. In L. Samovar & R. Porter, (Eds.), *Intercultural communication: A reader* (3rd ed.). Belmont, CA: Wadsworth.

Frith, K., Shaw P. & Cheng, H. (2005). The construction of beauty: A cross-cultural analysis of women's magazine advertising. *Journal of Communication, 3*, 56-70.

Gudykunst, William B. & Mody, Bella. (Eds.) (2002). *Handbook of international and intercultural communication.* Thousand Oaks, London, New Delhi: Sage Publications.

Hall, E. T. (1959). *The silent language.* New York: Doubleday.

Hall, S. (1980). Encoding / decoding. In S. Hall, D. Hobson, A. Lowe, & P. Willis, (Eds.), *Culture, media, language: working papers in cultural studies*, 1972-1979.

London: Hutchinson.

Lasswell, H. D. (1971). *Propaganda technique in the world war*. Boston: Knopf.

Liebes, Tamer and Katz, Elihu. (1993). *The Export of Meaning: Cross-Cultural Readings of Dallas*. Oxford: Polity Press in association with Blackwell Publishers.

MacQuail, Denis. (2000). *McQuail's communication theory*. London, Thousand Oaks, New Delhi: Sage Publications.

Samovar, L. A. & Porter, R. E. (Eds.) (2003). *Intercultural communication: A reader*. Australia: Thomson Wadsworth.

Schiller, H. I. (1976). *Communication and cultural domination*. White Plains, NY: International Arts and Science Press.

Spitzberg, B. H., & Cupach, W.R. (1984). *Interpersonal communication competence*. Beverly Hills, VA: Sage.

Wasburn, Philo C. (2002). *The Social Construction of International News: We Are Talking about Them, They're Talking about Us*. Westport, CT: Praeger Publishers.

关世杰,(1995),《跨文化交流学》,北京: 北京大学出版社。
　　[Guan, S.J. (1995). *Intercultural Communication*. Beijing: Peking University Press.]

关世杰,(2004),《国际传播学》,北京: 北京大学出版社。
　　[Guan, S.J. (2004). *International Communication*. Beijing: Peking University Press.]

胡文仲,(1993),试论跨文化交际研究,《语言与文化多学科研究》,陈建民、谭志明主编,北京: 北京语言学院出版社。
　　[Hu, W.Z. (1993). On intercultural communication research. In Chen, Jianmin & Tan, Zhiming (Eds.). *Language and culture: An interdisciplinary approach*. Beijing: Beijing Language and Culture University Press.

刘继南等,(2006),《镜像中国: 世界主流媒体中的中国形象》,北京: 中国传媒大学出版社。
　　[Liu, J.N. (2006). *Image of China in World Mainstream Media*. Beijing: China Communication University Press.]

刘双,(2006),《跨文化传播》,哈尔滨: 黑龙江人民出版社。
　　[Liu, S. (2006) *Intercultural communication*. Harbin: Heilongjiang People's Publishing House.]

罗以澄、司景新,(2005),中国大陆跨文化交际研究1990-2003,《跨文化传播新论》,单波、石义兵主编,武汉: 武汉大学出版社。
　　[Luo, Y.C. & Si, J.X. (2005). Intercultural communication research in Chinese Mainland 1990~2003. In Shan Bo & Shi Yibin, (Eds.), *Intercultural communication: A new perspective*. Wuhan: Wuhan University Press.]

童兵,(2004),试析跨文化传播中的认识误区,《新闻大学》第3期。
　　[Tong Bing (2004). Misunderstandings of intercultural communication. *Journalistic University*, Vol. 3.]

童之侠,(2005),《国际传播语言学》,北京: 中国传媒大学出版社。
　　[Tong, Z.X. (2005). *International communication and language studies*. Beijing: China Communication University Press.]

INTERCULTURAL COMPETENCE AND FOREIGN LANGUAGE EDUCATION

Teaching English as intercultural education: Challenges of intercultural communication[1]

Song Li   Harbin Institute of Technology, China

Abstract

The development of globalization has turned intercultural communication into reality for more and more people around the world. In this process, English has taken on the role of an international language and thus brought into question the traditional paradigms of teaching English as a second or foreign language. A high proficiency in English and even a good command of native-speaker cultural knowledge alone cannot empower the learners to transcend cultural boundaries or build up understanding with their cultural others through (re)construction of meanings and identities in the lingua franca of English. To meet the new challenges in the era of globalization, ELT should be oriented towards the promotion of intercultural competency education in and through English. Based on a discussion of the conceptualization of intercultural education and intercultural communication competence, the author argues for the privileges of English in intercultural education and calls for a paradigm shift towards teaching English as intercultural communication. Some general pedagogical principles are also proposed.

Introduction

Frequent communication between different nations and peoples for economic, political, cultural and educational needs at national as well as individual levels has now turned intercultural communication into reality for all nations and people in this age of globalization and multiculturalization. The coexistence of interdependence and cultural conflicts demands all cultures and nations to go beyond their own cultural bondage and learn to appreciate different ideas and different ways of life, to share with others limited world resources, and to celebrate diversity. Consequently, intercultural education

---

[1] This article is based on the author's presentation at the 14th NATE @ 7th FEELTA Conference — "Building Bridges with Languages and Cultures", June 26 - 28, 2008, Far Eastern National University, Vladivostok, Russia.

for effective intercultural communication has become imperative for all, which also demands that English teachers rethink of the mission ELT undertakes in the promotion of intercultural understanding. As English has become an international language for intercultural communication between speakers from both English speaking cultures and non-English speaking cultures, or to use Kachru's terms, from speakers of English in the Inner Circle, Outer Circle and Expanding Circle (Kachru, 1992), the traditional ideology as well as practice of English language teaching has been challenged. As an international language, English has spread, diversified and developed to embody diverse cultures and ways of life. In this sense, English language teaching is intercultural teaching by nature. This suggests that English language education has become intercultural education in which interculturasl literacy through and in English gives new meaning to ELT to speakers of other languages. In this paper, the author wishes to address four questions regarding teaching English as intercultural education: 1) What is intercultural education? 2) What privileges does ELT have in intercultural education? 3) What constitutes intercultural communication competence? 4) How can ELT be shifted towards intercultural education? The author will conclude that ELT as intercultural education should be set for intercultural communication, and be practiced as intercultural communication and of intercultural communication.

Understanding Intercultural Communication

The concept of intercultural education can be understood in relation to the understanding of intercultural literacy. Heyward conceptualizes intercultural literacy as "the understandings, competencies, attitudes, language proficiencies, participation and identities which enable effective participation in a cross-cultural setting" (2004, p.19). An interculturally literate person, according to Heyward, "possesses the understandings, competencies, attitudes and identities necessary for successful living and working in a cross-cultural or pluralist setting. This person has the background required to effectively "read" a second culture, to interpret its symbols and negotiate its meanings in a practical day-to-day context" (2004, p. 51).

The United Nations has been trying to promote intercultural understanding and intercultural competences of all peoples on earth through implementing the frameworks, principles and guidelines initiated from many of its international conferences and researches on intercultural education. It is stated clearly in *the UNESCO Guidelines on Intercultural Education* that the aim of intercultural education is "to go beyond passive coexistence, to achieve a developing and sustainable way of living together in multicultural societies through the creation of understanding of, respect for and dialogue between the different cultural groups" (UNESCO, 2006, p.18). Three Principles are laid down to guide the intercultural approach to education around the world:

Principle I Intercultural Education respects the cultural identity of the learner through the provision of culturally appropriate and responsive quality education for all.

Principle II Intercultural Education provides every learner with the cultural knowledge, sattitudes and skills necessary to achieve active and full participation in society.

Principle III Intercultural Education provides all learners with cultural knowledge, attitudes and skills that enable them to contribute to respect, understanding and solidarity among individuals, ethnic, social, cultural and religious groups and nations.

(UNESCO, 2006, p.33)

These principles well reflect the nature and the mission of intercultural education. The term "intercultural literacy education" is also used in literature. To the understanding of the present author, the two terms, intercultural education and intercultural literacy education are synonymous. The difference between them is that with literacy in the phrase, more emphasis is placed to the fact that being intercultural is the very basic qualification that everyone needs to have in order to function in a globalized world, just as what being literate or culturally literate has been to an individual in a modern society. Intercultural literacy also implies that it is for all and to be learned by all who cannot but to confront intercultural situations in their everyday life.

Privileges of English Language Education in Intercultural Education

The present author believes that English language education is the most effective and also the most relevant way to gain intercultural literacy. This can be justified by the significant role of language, and foreign language in particular, in intercultural literacy education as well as by the special features of English and English language teaching.

Language Education and Intercultural Education

Firstly, the nature of and the relationships between language and culture determines the importance of language education as means for intercultural literacy education. This is written clearly in *the UNESCO Guidelines for Intercultural Education*:

Language is one of the most universal and diverse forms of expression of human culture, and perhaps even the most essential one. It is at the heart of issues of identity, memory and transmission of knowledge.

Linguistic diversity is likewise a reflection of cultural diversity and cannot be precisely quantified or categorized. Bilingualism and multilingualism are a consequence of linguistic diversity on an individual or collective level, and refer to the use of more than one language in daily life.

Language issues are central to culture. Languages result from a historical and collective experience and express culturally specific world views and value systems.

Language issues are also central to concepts of education. Linguistic competencies are fundamental for the empowerment of the individual in democratic and plural societies, as they condition school achievement, promote access to other cultures and encourage openness to cultural exchange.

(UNESCO, 2006, p.13)

Given the intrinsic relationship between language and culture, language education has much to contribute towards the understanding of cultural diversities in perception of reality and solutions to worldly problems as represented in the linguistic forms and patterns of discourse. In language teaching and learning, language necessarily becomes both the means and content of intercultural literacy education. Therefore, UNESCO "supports language as an essential component of inter-cultural education in order to encourage understanding between different population groups and ensure respect for fundamental rights"(UNESCO, 2006).

Secondly, the fact that literacy operates through language gives special prominence to language teaching in intercultural education. In calling upon Americans to acquire cultural literacy for survival in the modern world, Hirsch points out that the complex undertakings of modern life "depend on the cooperation of many people with different specialties in different places. Where communications fail, so do the undertakings. ... The function of national literacy is to foster effective nationwide communications" and "Our chief instrument of communication over time and space is the standard national language□ which is sustained by national literacy. Mature literacy alone enables the tower to be built, the business to be well managed, and the airplane to fly without crashing. All nationwide communications, whether by telephone, radio, TV, or writing are fundamentally dependent upon literacy, for the essence of literacy is not simply reading and writing abut also the effective use of the standard literate language" (1987, p.2). The national cultural literacy works through the effective use of a national language in communication. What Hirsch has said about how modern life operates within USA as a country also applies to the global society where cooperation and interdependence between nations is realized through communication as well. In place of a national cultural literacy, what is needed for surviving the global village, and for effective international and intercultural communication in particular, is intercultural literacy. Since English has undertaken the role of an international language in world wide communication, the teaching and learning of English is of crucial importance in intercultural literacy development.

English Language Education and Intercultural Education

Of all the means of intercultural literacy education, school education is the most basic and formal channel. Within the school contexts, formal teaching and learning is done through the execution of a curriculum (Lu Weiqun, 2003). And in the school curriculum, foreign language is the most intercultural and therefore has the biggest potential for intercultural literacy education. As Sercu has stated, in her discussions on teaching foreign languages in an intercultural world, foreign language education is intercultural by definition. To bring a foreign language to the classroom "means connecting learners to a world that is culturally different from their own. Therefore, all foreign language educators are now expected to exploit this potential and promote the acquisition of intercultural competence in their learners" (Sercu, 2005, pp.1-2). Lu Weiqun (2003) also believes that foreign language teaching itself is the practice of intercultural education as the teaching of a foreign language unavoidably involves the teaching of the foreign cultures.

Foreign language teachers are, therefore, by profession intercultural educators. And within the field of foreign language teaching, ELT has particular privileges in intercultural literacy education.

1) ELT presents multiculturalism and cultural diversity to the learners. English as an international language is the embodiment of multicultural identities and therefore offers ready access to cultural diversities. As an international language, English is a language of multiculturalism; it is used by people of different cultural and linguistic backgrounds to voice their ideas and attitudes. Since language use is socioculturally defined, when teaching how English is used by culturally diverse people, the diverse values, beliefs, world views, ways of thinking, and patterns of life embedded in the linguistic forms and the manner by which the selected linguistic forms are put into speech or text, can also be brought to the awareness of the learner.

2) ELT offers unique chances for intercultural experience. On the one hand, the target international cultures are brought to the knowledge of the learner through various teaching materials, class activities and personal interaction with international teachers and students. On the other hand, the process of English language teaching and learning is a process of intercultural communication between LC1 and LC2[2], between the self and the cultural Other (Song, 2007). In English, the Other takes up the plural form as the language itself has become plural in its process of globalization and diversification. Throughout the process,

---

2 LC1 stands for Linguaculture 1 or the learer's first linguaculture and LC2 stands for Linguaculture 2 or the learner's second linguaculture.

teachers and learners are engaged in negotiation of meanings, construction or reconstruction of identities in between their own lingualculture and that of others. English language learning is an experience of personal growth into an intercultural person.

3) ELT is the most effective means of intercultural education for students. English is the most learned foreign language and most widely used medium for intercultural communication all over the world. No other language can replace English in the number of learners it can influence and the diversity of cultures it can represent. English is a compulsory course for most countries; intercultural literacy education through English can benefit the largest number of learners than any other training programs.

In general, ELT has a unique role to play in intercultural literacy education. It provides students opportunities to come into contact with other cultures and people without going abroad. In the intercultural encounters through English teaching and learning, alternative ways of communication and ways of living are unfolded and thus the ideology of cultural relativity will be gradually built up in the learner with the enhancement of his/her cross-cultural awareness. Moreover, by learning to use English in socioculturally appropriate manners, the learner will acquire the skills for effective communication and successful undertakings in the global intercultural world.

Understanding Intercultural Communication Competence in ELT

With the above discussion of intercultural education and the unique roles that English plays in intercultural education, it is clear that intercultural communication competence serves as the ultimate goal as well as the central link between intercultural education and English language teaching. Most studies view intercultural education as consist of four aspects: knowledge, attitudes, skills and behaviors (e.g. Lu Weiqun, 2003; Heyward, 2003). By definition, linguistic competence and the ability to participate effectively in cross-cultural communication constitute an important part of intercultural literacy. This demand on intercultural communicative competence falls in line with the goal of English language education. In Sercu's words, the objective of language learning "is no longer defined in terms of the acquisition of communicative competence in a foreign language. Teachers are now required to teach intercultural communicative competence" (L. Sercu, 2005, pp.1-2). To orient ELT towards intercultural education basically depends on how ELT professionals can turn the learners into intercultural speakers of English. In other words, the teaching of intercultural communication competence is at the core of teaching English as intercultural education. Thus, understanding of what constitutes intercultural communication competence (ICC) becomes crucial in intercultural education in and through ELT.

Defining Intercultural Communication Competence

An understanding of what characterizes and constitutes communicative competence will certainly throw light on our exploration into intercultural communicative competence. Competence, and intercultural communication competence in particular, is perceived as internal to the person in the present study. The author shares Kim's view that intercultural communicative competence is "located within a person as his or her overall capacity or capability to facilitate the communication process between people from differing cultural backgrounds and to contribute to successful interaction outcomes" (Kim,1991, p.263).

In the field of foreign or second language teaching, the idea of communicative competence is associated with the advocates of the communicative approach under the influence of Dell Hymes (1971), the essence of whose original concept of communicative competence is that speakers of a language have to have more than grammatical competence in order to be able to communicate effectively in a language; they also need to know how language is used by members of a speech community to accomplish their purposes. It is about knowing what to speak, when, with whom, how and why, etc. This notion of developing learners' ability to use language appropriately in socio-cultural contexts has been reformulated by later scholars like Canale and Swain (Canale & Swain 1980; Canale 1983) and van Ek (1986) at both sides of the Atlantic Ocean. Their interpretations of communicative competence generally cover two aspects: linguistic competence and pragmatic competence (for details, see Orwig 1999). Underlying the ideology of communicative language teaching is the assumption that the question of communicative competence in EFL/ESL is mainly addressed to communication between native speakers and non-native speakers, where the non-native speakers of the language are expected to abide by the rules of the native speakers.

The competence for effective intercultural communication, therefore, is complicated by the interculturality of the interaction. What makes the interaction intercultural is that the interactants are from different cultural backgrounds and they carry all those cultural bearings that make up their identities: the qualities that make who they are and what they are, though often beyond their own awareness. The intercultural interaction is, first of all, challenged by the meeting of diverse cultures mediated through the communicative behaviors of the interactants. Since intercultural communication is sharing and understanding between interlocutors of diverse cultural backgrounds, a shared set of linguistic code, e.g. proficiency in English, may not lead to intercultural understanding because the sharing of linguistic code does not mean a sharing of world views, sociocultural norms and values that prescribe and proscribe how people perform their roles of social actors through their choice of expressions, their manners of speaking or writing and ways of relating to others. Another challenge the intercultural interactants face is their ability to handle the interpersonal conflicts in intercultural settings. Byram points out that intercultural competence is "more complex than communicative competence, precisely because it focuses on 'establishing and maintaining relationships' instead of merely communicating messages or exchanging information" (2000, p.298). Relationship building and maintenance involves not only interactive skills in using the language, but more importantly flexible personalities and positive attitudes towards others, particularly in cases of sociocultural confrontation. The cultural Other in the global context can be people from any cultures, not necessarily from the culture of the target language. In the case of intercultural communication in English, the interlocutors can be just anyone from any culture. Therefore, a readiness to embrace global diversity is necessary for successful English learning and teaching.

With the above said, intercultural communication competence entails not only communicative competence in linguistic and pragmatic terms of the language used in the intercultural encounter, more importantly it demands awareness of different sets of cultural scripts and the ability to mediate between different cultural identities. Intercultural communication competence can be thus defined as a person's ability to engage in productive intercultural dialogues of meanings and relationships with people from different cultural backgrounds. To make the intercultural interaction productive, one needs to have the ability to construct meaning and rapport with people from different cultural backgrounds through appropriate and effective use of verbal and nonverbal language.

Construction of Intercultural Communication Competence

With regards to the foreign language learner, to learn and to use the target language for intercultural communication means to learn alternative ways of constructing and negotiating meanings and relationships through that language. At this point, an intercultural dialogue is seen to be taking place within the foreign language learner's own self: a negotiation of ways of meaning making and relating to others in between two cultural scripts: that of LC1 and that of LC2. Whether or not one can find the meeting point where he/she can enjoy meaningful interaction and pleasant relationships depends on how aware he/she is of the two scripts, and how willing or ready he/she is to go beyond his/her own linguacultural bound and embrace the differences and open to negotiation and change. Productive intercultural dialogue, therefore, involves three aspects: cognitive — knowledge of LC1 and LC2, behavioral — verbal and nonverbal participation and interpersonal — relating to others.

Based on the above understanding of intercultural communication competence (ICC) and earlier studies (Byram 1997; Byram. & Zarate 1997; Song L., 2003; Song L. & Fu L., 2004), Song L. (2008) proposes that three competence dimensions build up ICC:

1) communicative competence in one's first lingualculture (LC1), 2) communicative competence in the foreign or second lingualcutlure (LC2), and 3) transcultural competence (see Figure 1). Linguacutlure is a borrowed term from Agar (1994) used here to emphasize thse fact that when people learn a foreign or second language, they also learn a new way of social practice, particularly alternative ways of approaching people and the world around them in and through the target language. To teach language is to not just to teach language in culture or culture in language; it is to teach language as culture and culture as represented and (re)formed through language (Song L., 2008).

Figure 1 is a graphic descritption of the basic components of intercultural communication competence (Song L., 2008), In this ICC model Communicative Competence in LC1 refers to the speaker or language learner's ability in communicating effectively in his/her first language and native cultural context on cognitive, behaviorial and interpersonal dimensions. With such competence the speaker should be able to acquire knowledge and information of the world, conduct everyday activities through use of verbal and non-verbal codes and cope with interpersonal relationships in a manner acceptable in the native cultural environment. Communicative Competence in LC2 is the speaker or language learner's ability in communicating effectively in his/her second or foreign language with native as well as non-native speakers of the target language. This ability is also demonstrated on three dimensions: cognitive, behaviorial and interpersonal. But it differs from Communicative Competence in LC1 not only in the language used and the cultural context involved, but more importantly, it requires that the speaker or learner of the second or foreign language develop a critical cultural awareness and be able to transcend linguacultural boundaries and interact with people from own culture and other culture(s) in a manner that is conducive to effective communication. Transcultural Competence refers to the learner or speaker's ability to cross linguacultural boundaries in coordinating between differences, and negotiating meanings and identities with people from other cultural groups on the basis of mutual respect and understanding.

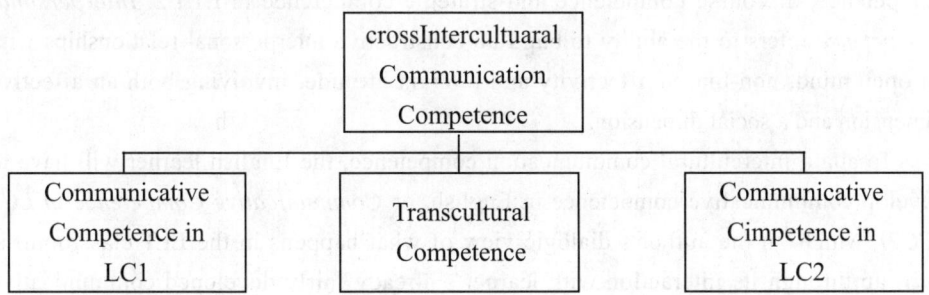

Figure 1 Constructs of Intercultural Communication Competence (Song Li, 2008)

Figure 2 illustrates in more detail the primary constructs and the interactive relationships between all identified elements in ICC.

An Interactive Model of Intercultural Communicative Competence and Its Components

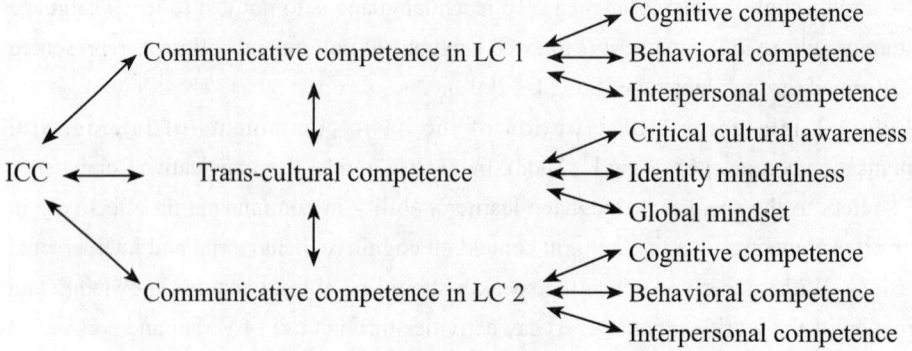

Figure 2 An Integrated Interactive Model of ICC, adapted from Song L. (2003), Song L. & Fu L. (2004), Song Li (2006))

Some explanations of terminology will help to clarify the above construction of intercultural communication competence.

Drawing on previous sociolinguistic conceptualizations, the present author regards communicative competence as consisting of three aspects: cognitive, behavioral and interpersonal. *Cognitive Competence* is used to mean one's knowledge of his/her native culture (C1) and the foreign culture (s) (C2), including encyclopedic knowledge, belief and value systems, norms and rules, and his/her knowledge of the first language (L1) and the foreign or second language (L2). *Behaviorial Competence* is the ability to do things with language, both verbal and non-verbal. This includes: linguistic competence, sociolinguistic competence, discourse competence and strategic competence in L1/L2. *Interpersonal Competence* refers to the ability to build up constructive interpersonal relationships with an open mind, non-biased affectivity and tolerant attitude, involving both an affective dimension and a social dimension.

To attain intercultural communication competence, the English learner will have to develop communicative competence in English, or *Communicative Competence in LC2 (CC2)*, which, in the author's dialogic view of what happens in the ELT classroom, is built up through its interaction with learner's already fairly developed communicative competence in his/her first language and culture, *Communicative Competence in LC1 (CC1)*. The two communicative competences influence each other, with CC1 as the basis and frame of reference for CC2, which in turn counteracts upon the learner's established ways of using his/her first language. Researches have shown that the more competent a learner is in his/her first language, the more competent he/she is likely to be in his/her second language (e.g. Hu Wenzhong & Gao Yihong, 1999).

Transcultural Competence entails three qualifications. *Critical Cultural Awareness* is the term borrowed from Byram, meaning the "ability to evaluate critically and on the basis of explicit criteria perspectives, practices and products in one's own and other cultures and countries" (1997, p.53). This involves both a high degree of sensitivity to linguacultural diversity and the ability to make unbiased evaluation of both one's own and other cultural groups. *Identity Mindfulness* emphasizes one's awareness of and attentiveness to multiple social and cultural identities that each participant may have and the sociocultural values and norms associated with these identities in communication scenarios, in particular the sensitivity to the role of language in identity construction and negotiation. Mindset is a fixed mental attitude or disposition that predetermines a person's responses to and interpretations of situations. And *Global Mindset* means the development in an individual an unbiased, ethnorelative attitude and a readiness to embrace diversity from a global perspective. This term is taken from G. M. Chen, who asserts that global mindset "equips individuals with a mental ability to scan the world in a broad perspective and always consciously expect new trends and opportunities, so that personal, social, and organizational objectives can be achieved in a harmonious way. Built on the foundation of openness, global mindset represents the decrease or absence of ethnocentrism and parochialism" (2005, p.4). Critical cultural awareness, identity mindfulness and global mindset are necessary conditions for an individual to willingly go beyond the boundary and the limitations of a specific culture, either C1 or C2, and negotiate meanings and identities in between both cultures.

As can been seen from Figure 2, a person's intercultural communication competence in a foreign language is a co-construction of his/her communicative ability in both his/her native and the foreign linguacultures in cognitive, behavioral and interpersonal terms and his/her ability to transcend cultural boundaries to engage in effective communication with people of diverse social and cultural identities. Intercultural education is fundamentally the education for intercultural communication competence and to this end, English language teaching should be geared.

Shifting ELT towards Intercultural Education

Reorientation of ELT towards intercultural communication competence teaching suggests a renewed understanding of the nature as well as the practice of English language teaching.

Reconceptualizing ELT as Intercultural Education

By shifting the goal of ELT from communicative competence to intercultural communication competence, ELT is changed from the pure practice of foreign or second language teaching to intercultural education with the products of ELT to be changed from proficient English learners to competent intercultural learners/speakers. The intercultural communicative approach proposed by Song Li (2008) gives an explicit description of how ELT qualifies as a process of intercultural education.

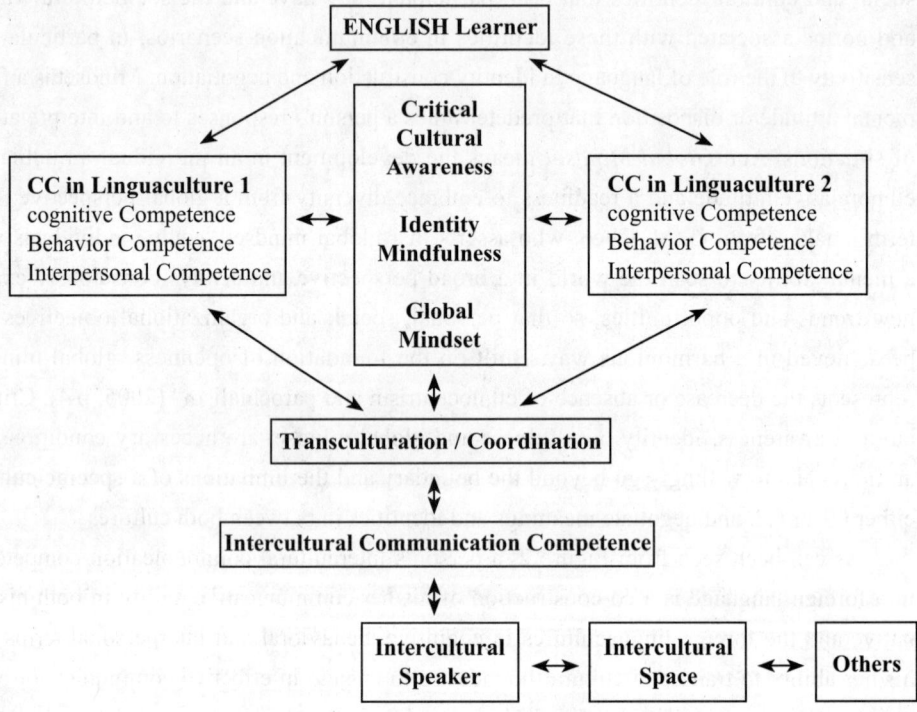

Figure 3 Framework for an intercultural communicative approach to ELT (Song Li, 2008)

As is shown in Figure 3, the goal of ELT as a foreign or second or rather an international language is shifted to the production of competent intercultural speakers in the intercultural communicative approach. The process of gaining ICC is understood as the process of learning to become intercultural speakers, who not only possess communicative competence in both native and target languages but have developed a high degree of cross-cultural awareness and are able to make critical judgment as well as appropriate choices of behavior as demanded by the specific contexts of communication through coordination and negotiation with other people, native and non-native alike, and between other choices.

ENGLISH is written in the upper case to emphasis the lingua franca nature of English as an international language, implying the global function and the plurality of its variation. With the acquired intercultural communication competence, the English learners will be able to enter the "third place" (Lo Bianco, et al, 1999; Kramsch, 1993) or "intercultural space" (Byram, 1997) where they can enjoy the pleasure of transcending the barriers of language and culture into a world of unity within diversity. The intercultural communicative approach proposed by Song (2008) is concerned with the teaching of English in China backgrounded against a global multicultural and international context and it is also applicable to ELT to speakers of other languages in general.

Implications of Teaching English as Intercultural Education

In recognizing the importance and privileges of English teaching as intercultural education and humanistic education in general, learning English is perceived as a process of personal growth on the part of the learner in terms of his/her learning to relate his/her own self to others in an intercultural space and as an intercultural speaker. This personal growth is realized through the development of intercultural communication competence. As is illustrated in Figure1, Figure 2 and Figure 3, intercultural communication competence is developed from the process of transculturation where the learner gradually acquires the ability to use the target language for the negotiation and interpretation of meanings, identities and relationships facilitated and enhanced by a critical cultural awareness of the diversities between LC1 and LC2, identity mindfulness and global mindset. To learn English is to learn to become an intercultural speaker who is able to position himself/herself in relation to others in the intercultural space and engage in productive intercultural dialogues with the cultural others in and through English.

Teaching English as intercultural education suggests that English be learned and taught for intercultural communication, of intercultural communication and as intercultural communication.

Teaching English for intercultural communication requires that the goal of ELT be set for the development of learners' intercultural communication competence. Any ideas and practices that are against this goal should be rejected. Proximity to native speaker norms advocated in the traditional communicative approach will no longer be held as the sole criteria for good teaching and learning. What is emphasized in the ELT classroom is not just the grammatical usage and sociolinguistically appropriate use of English, but how English as an international language can be used by people from different cultural backgrounds as an instrument for constructing meanings, relationships and identities. Learners are expected to become intercultural speakers through English education rather than mere proficient speakers of the target language.

Teaching English of intercultural communication means all teaching activities should pertain to intercultural communication, from goals to content, to methods, and to assessment. The content for teaching should be conducive to cross-cultural awareness building, the fostering of ethno-relative view of Self and Other, and to a realistic representation of English around the world and in the learner's own locality. To bring out the full value of the selected resources for intercultual communicative teaching and learning, class activities that engage learners in intercultural communication are encouraged. And the evaluation should be made on progress of intercultural learning instead of exclusively on linguistic knowledge and skills. All that helps to build up ICC and the constituent competencies are potential resources for organizing classroom teaching and learning.

Teaching English as intercultural communication is to view the teaching and learning process as a process of intercultural communication. Intercultural dialogicality saturates every stage of teaching and learning on intrapersonal, interpersonal and intercultural levels. Intercultural interaction characterizes the ELT classroom and at the same time effectuates productive learning and teaching. Recognizing the ongoing intercultural interactions at different levels and between different subjects will help the teacher to understand the nature of ELT and find out the most effective way to ensure intercultural teaching and learning.

Implimentation of Teaching English as Intercultural Education

In her proposal for an intercultural communication approach for English language teaching, Song L. outlines four fundamental principles for curriculum development, claiming that "Of all principles in the organization of teaching activities, the principle of interculturality, the principle of interactivity, the principle of unity of language and culture and the principle of integration of the global and the local are the four most fundamental ones and should be used as the guiding lines in every dimension of the curriculum development and implementation" (2008, p.121-123). These principles are further explained below as to provide the general principles for teaching English as intercultural education.

The Principle of Interculturality requires the recognition of the presence of interculturality in the ELT classroom. Since the learner is exposed to all kinds of opportunities to experience the different cultures represented in English and different people from those cultures, ELT naturally involves the meeting of two or more cultures. The Other comes alive to meet the learner in the English they intake with their eyes and ears. And the learner as well as the teacher brings their own cultural bearings and identities with them to meet the Other when they are engaged in the constructions of meaning, relationships and identities in their English teaching/learning experience. Without going elsewhere and even without a foreigner in sight, the teacher and learner can always expect to be involved in an intercultural encounter in and through English. With the Principle of Interculturality the teacher should take the advantage of the intercultural environment in the ELT classroom and find every opportunity possible to build up the learners' intercultural sensitivity and critical awareness across languages and cultures.

The Principle of Interactivity asks for the recognition of the dialogic nature of what happens between the participants in the teaching/learning process. These participants could be the teacher and the learner, learner and learner, teacher/learner and the speaker/writer of a text. It is the dialogic interactions between participants that make a teaching/learning activity meaningful and productive. Teachers, therefore, are expected to make the teaching activities as interactive as possible.

The Principle of Unity of Language and Culture demands language be taught/learned as culture. The teaching of language should at no time be separated from its cultural dimension. That language is culture and culture is language must not be overlooked in the classroom pedagogy. The cultural dimension of language is present at all levels, phonological, lexical, syntactical and discoursal. It is both in the linguistic structures and forms, and in the pragmatic use of these structures and forms. In other words, language is culture in linguistic forms. The cultural markedness is of special significance in constructing and unfolding a speaker's identity. This is true with both L1 and L2. Awareness of the cultural dimension of the linguistic structures and forms will enhance the learner's linguistic competence.

The Principle of Integration of the Global and the Local calls for the internationalization and localization of ELT. Internationalization of ELT involves the teaching of English as an international language, which entails the inclusion of elements of world Englishes, in addition to "native speaker" varieties. Localization of English involves the teaching of the local variety of English as representation of the learner's own culture and as an alternative medium for constructing meanings, relationships and identities. Integration of the global and the local is also an important means for intercultural teaching and learning.

The four principles mentioned above suffice to distinguish the intercultural communicative approach from all other approaches to ELT, and distinguish ELT as intercultural education from ELT as foreign/second language educaiton. In deciding on the objectives, content, methods and evaluation of the curriculum and carrying them out in the teaching/learning activities, adherence to these four principles will significantly determine to what extent English teaching is practised as intercultural education.

Concluding Remarks

To conceive English language teaching as intercultural education has great signicance for the profession. Such a view breaks the confinement of traditional ELT to the language teaching industry, or the field of applied linguistics and second or foreign language acquisition; it broadens the visions of English teachers and learners into the multiplicity, plurality and interculturality as manifested through language and language use. More importantly it places ELT into the framework of generic education, and thus rightfully connects ELT to the goals of education in other school subjects to form part of the big picture and make it beneficial for the learners' life long engagement in personal development as intercultural speakers and global citizens.

References

Agar, M. (1994). *Language shock: Understanding the culture of conversation.* New York: William Morrow.

Byram, M. & Zarate, G. (Eds.). (1997). *The sociocultural and intercultural dimension of language learning and teaching.* Strasbourg: Council of Europe.

Byram, M. (1997). *Teaching and assessing intercultural communicative competence.* Clevedon: Multilingual Matters.

Canale, M. & Swain, M. (1980). The theoretical bases of communicative approaches to second language teaching and testing. *Applied Linguistics, 1* (1), 1-47.

Canale, M. (1983). From communicative competence to communicative language pedagogy. In Richards, J. C. & Schimdt, R. W., (Eds.), *Language and Communication.* Harlow: Longman.

Canale, M. (1983). From communicative competence to communicative language pedagogy. In J. C. Richards & R. W. Schmidt, (Eds.), *Language and Communication* (pp. 2-27). London: Longman.

Chen, G. M. (2005). A model of global communication competence. *China Media Research, 1* (1), 1-9.

Heyward, M . (2004). *Intercultural literacy and the international school -* Doctorate dissertation, University of Tasmania.

Hirsch, E. D., Jr. (1987). *Cultural literacy: What every American needs to know.* New York: Vintage Books.

Hu, W. & Gao, Y. (1999) Foreign language teaching and culture. Changsha: Hunan Education Press. (In Chinese)

Hymes, D. (1971). On communicative competence. Philadelphia: University of Pennsylvania Press. Extracts available in Brumfit, C. J. & Johnson, K., (Eds.), (1979). *The communicative approach to language teaching* (pp.5-26). Oxford: Oxford University Press.

Kachru, B. B. (Ed.). (1992). *The other tongue: English across cultures.* Urbana and Chicago: University of Illinois Press.

Kim, Y. Y. (1991). Intercultural communication competence. In S. Ting-Toomey & F. Korzenny (Eds.), *Cross-cultural interpersonal communication* (pp. 259-275). Nsewbury Park, CA: Sage.

Kramsch, C. (1993). *Context and culture in language teaching*. Oxford, England: Oxford University Press.

Lo Bianco, J., Liddicoat, A. J. & Crozet, C. (Eds.). (1999). *Striving for the third place: Intercultural competence through language education*. Canberra: Language Australia.

Lu, Weiqun. (2003) *A prologue to intercultural education* Doctorate dissertation, Central China Normal University. (In Chinese)

Orwig, C. J. (1999). Aspects of communicative competence. In *Guidelines for a language and culture learning program*. SIL International: LinguaLinks Library, Web Edition. Retrieved Feb.18, 2002 from http://www.sil.org/lingualinks.

Sercu, L. (2005). Teaching foreign languages in an intercultural world. In L. Sercu, et al. (Eds.). *Foreign language teachers and intercultural competence: An international investigation*. Clevedon: Maltilingual Matters.

Song, L. (2008). *Intercultural communicative English language teaching in China* Doctorate dsissertation, Shanghai International Studies University, China.

Song, L. (2007). *Intercultural dialogicality between LC1 and LC2 in the EFL /ESL classroom*, Paper presented at The 12th International Conference Russia and the West: The Dialogue of Cultures, Moscow, Nov. 28-30.

Sercu, L. (2006). The foreign language and intercultural competence teacher: the acquisition of a new professional identity. *Intercultural Education, 17* (1), 55-72.

Song, L. (2003). *An intercultural approach to teaching English as communication*. Paper presented at the Annual Conference of International Association of Intercultural Communication Studies, California State University, Fullerton.

Song, L. & Fu, L., (2004). Intercultural communicative language teaching: Rethinking the communicative approach to ELT in China. *English Australia Journa, 22* (1), 20-42.

van Ek, J.A. (1986). *Objectives for foreign language learning, Vol. 1: Scope*. Strasbourg: Council of Europe.

Intercultural training for foreign language teachers

外语教师跨文化能力培训研究

张红玲
上海外国语大学

Abstract

Intercultural foreign language teaching has become the tide of today. But Chinese foreign language teachers are not yet capable of implementing this new teaching philosophy in their classroom teaching, which makes teacher training imperative. After examining the rich contents of the concept of intercultural competence of foreign language teachers, this paper proposes a framework for intercultural training for Chinese English teachers, expounding its objectives, contents and methods. To illustrate how the training can be conducted, the last section of the paper offers an example of a two-day training program.

1 引言

跨文化交际能力培养作为外语教学一个重要内容已经得到广大中国外语教育工作者的广泛认可。近年来，有关如何将外语教学与跨文化交际能力培养有机结合的研究和探讨层出不穷。本文作者最近出版的《跨文化外语教学》一书更是系统阐述了跨文化外语教学的重要意义和内涵。[1]

然而，目前的中国外语教学实践表明外语教学中的跨文化交际能力培养仍然是一句口号，只停留在比较肤浅或边缘的层面，与笔者提出的外语教学的最终目标还相差甚远。导致这一现状的原因很多，其中教师缺乏进行跨文化交际能力培养的素质和技能是一个主要原因。

针对这一问题，本文将在对中国英语教师进行需求分析的基础上，尝试提出一个英语教师跨文化能力培训框架，以弥补学校英语教学的不足，促进他们跨文化外语教学能力的提高。

---

1 张红玲:《跨文化外语教学》，上海外语教育出版社，2007年.

2 跨文化外语教学的基本思想和重要意义

当人类进入21世纪以后,全球化、国际化和多元化的时代特征愈加明显。这些特征一方面促使人们不得不进行广泛的跨文化交际,另一方面又导致各种冲突和误解频频发生。在这种情况下,培养具有跨文化交际能力的新时代的人才非常迫切,跨文化外语教学思想就是在这样的背景下提出的。

2.1 跨文化外语教学的基本思想

跨文化外语教学与传统外语教学思想的主要差别在于后者是以一个具体的语言群体为目标,从语音、语调、语法等语言本身的学习到语用、文化等语言使用的训练都是以这个目标群体为参照,其目的是掌握目标语言,与该语言群体的人们进行有效交际。跨文化外语教学则是通过某一语言的学习,在掌握使用这门语言技能的同时,培养跨文化交际能力,不仅与该语言群体的人们进行交际,而且能够与来自世界各个不同文化群体的人们进行恰当、有效的交际。

跨文化外语教学思想认为外语教学应该包括两级目标:语言文学的初级目标和社会人文的高级目标。前者以掌握目的语言的知识结构和使用技能为标志,后者则是以具有跨文化意识和跨文化交际能力为目标。外语交际能力作为外语教学的初级目标一直是我们追求和关注的重点。但是,长期以来我们却忽视了外语教学另一个更具意义的目标,即培养善良、宽容、独立、具有洞察力和跨文化交际能力的人。跨文化外语教学兼顾两级目标,以培养跨文化交际能力作为最终目标。

跨文化外语教学的本质在于将语言教学与文化教学有机结合,这个结合体现在外语教学的各个环节,包括教学目标和目的、教学原则、教学内容、教学方法、教材、测试等。

2.2 跨文化外语教学的意义

跨文化外语教学首先体现了外语教学服务社会政治和经济发展的宗旨,是新时代人才培养的需要。随着全球化、国际化和多元化成为时代特征,培养能够应对这些挑战的新时代的人才成为教育界的中心任务之一。虽然跨文化交际能力的培养有待于整个教育界共同努力,通过各门课程配套实施,但是外语教学在这个方面具有无可替代的巨大优势,应该成为跨文化交际能力培养的重要阵地。这是由外语教学的本质特点决定的。

其次,跨文化外语教学符合外语学习规律,能够促进外语教学的有效进行。外语教学不可能,也不应该与文化教学分割开来,否则学习者学到的就只是僵化的躯壳,而不是血肉相连的、鲜活的语言。跨文化外语教学将文化教学融入到语言教学中符合外语教学规律。对学习者而言,这样的外语教学方法更加有趣,与他们的生活经历更加相关,因此更能激发他们的外语学习积极性。

最后,跨文化外语教学思想有利于更正人们对外语学习的错误认识,提升外语教学的社会地位，唤起社会和人们对外语教学的重视和信心。如果将跨文化交际能力培养作为外语教学的一项重要任务，那么外语学习的意义就更加重要，这有利于纠正很多人的外语工具论的错误认识。实际上，具有跨文化交际能力的人不仅应该具有很强的外语表达能力，而且对文化差异比较敏感，善于根据不同的交际对象调整自己的文化参考框架，与来自不同文化的人们进行恰当、有效的交际。因此，我们培养学生的跨文化交际能力，也有利于培养他们多视角、多纬度的立体思维能力，同时也培养他们宽容、理解、善良等品质。这不正是我们教书育人的最终目的吗？如果外语教学能取得上述效果，那么外语教学的重要性和社会地位自然能够得到重视，同时还能纠正人们对外语教学的一些错误认识。

3 中国英语教师现状分析

中国英语学习者达3亿之多，需要大量的英语教师，而师范院校英语专业的毕业生人数远远不够，即使加上其他非师范院校英语专业毕业、愿意从事英语教学的大学毕业生，也不能满足如此庞大的英语学习队伍的需要。数量尚且如此，质量就更无从谈起。根据笔者的调查，目前大多数英语教师并没有接受必要的岗前和在岗培训，很多教师甚至今天还是学生，明天就站在讲台上给学生授课，其结果往往是新的教学思想得不到贯彻和落实。

就跨文化外语教学而言，教师问题更是非常严峻。具体说来，中国英语教师存在以下问题：

1. 较好地掌握了外语语言知识，但是语用知识和文化能力相对较弱。我国的外语教学受应试教育的影响，长期以来采用传统的语法翻译法，关注语法规则和词汇句型的学习，却忽视了语用规则的学习和文化对于语言使用的作用，从而培养出来的学生往往语言知识比较丰富，但语用失误和文化性问题严重。我们今天的英语教师大都接受的是这样的英语教育，因此他们也不可避免地存在类似问题。一个很多人都熟悉的、由于不知道"freeze"一词的语用意义而被误杀的日本留学生的故事充分说明这一点。

由于目前我国英语学习者真正运用英语进行跨文化交际的机会比较有限，他们学英语基本上是为了应付各种考试，而传统的教学方法满足了他们这个方面的需要，对于忽视语用文化规则的学习可能带来的严重后果，他们无法感受，也就不可能重视。

2. 普遍缺少教学培训。近年来，由于英语专业教学受到重视，英语教师的语言基本功基本能够得到保证，但是英语教师的业务培训相对不足。来自师范院校英语专业的毕业生在教学技能方面的培训虽然比较系统，但是大都停留在抽象的理论层面，教学实践的培训又受实习学校教学体制、学生人数和传统教学方法的限制，很难体现新的教学理念。而大批从非师范大学毕业的英语教师在教学技能和教学理念方面更是不足。目前虽然各个学校也要求新上岗的教师接受培训，取得教师资格证，但是这些培训以教育学理论为主要内容，真正的课堂教学培训非常有限。其结果就是自己当初怎么学,今天就怎么教,新的教学思想根本无法贯彻。

我国英语教师培训滞后一方面是因为社会对英语教师的需求一直很旺,相关机构来不及对教师进行培训;另一方面,英语教学培训本身缺乏科学研究和规划,培训效果欠佳,不能满足实际教学的需要。

3. 英语教师自身运用英语进行跨文化交际的机会不多,其跨文化敏感性不强,跨文化交际能力较弱。出国进修对于大多数中国英语教师而言只是一个不可能实现的梦想,虽然近年来有机会出国进修的英语老师人数有所上升,但是总体说来,我国英语教师的语言文化知识基本上来源于在本国的学习。正因为如此很多英语教师对英语国家的文化和世界其他国家的文化的了解非常肤浅,大都是一些零碎的二手信息,不仅不成系统,而且有可能是一些错误的认识或偏见。因此,指望他们对学生进行文化教学是不现实的。我们应该对他们进行全面、系统的培训,帮助他们完善自己的文化知识结构,培养他们跨文化意识和跨文化交际能力。

4. 就跨文化教学本身而言,中国教师大都理解和支持在外语教学中进行文化教学和跨文化交际能力培养,但是他们对跨文化外语教学思想理解不够透彻,担心会因此增加学生和自己的负担,同时也不知道如何开展跨文化外语教学。

上述问题的存在是我国英语教学发展的瓶颈,不予以解决,我们就不可能跳出语言知识扎实、语用能力薄弱的怪圈,培养出来的学生往往成为流利的傻瓜(fluent fool),即语言表达流畅,但语用失误不断的外语"人才"。

4 外语教师跨文化能力的内涵

4.1 外语教师跨文化能力的内涵

外语教师的跨文化能力包括两个方面,即他们自身的跨文化交际能力和他们跨文化外语教学的能力。

(1)跨文化交际能力。一般来说,跨文化交际能力包括态度/情感、知识和技能三个层面。一个跨文化能力强的人应该对异族文化持宽容、尊重、理解的态度,应该对不同的文化表现出兴趣,愿意甚至喜欢与来自不同文化背景的人们进行交际。其次,他具有丰富的文化知识,既熟悉本族文化的历史现状,也了解目的语文化的价值观念和社会习俗,同时对于世界其他地区的文化也有较多的了解。行为技能是跨文化交际能力的最高表现层次,因为态度和知识只有转化成具体的行为,才能保证跨文化交际的有效性和恰当性。跨文化交际的行为技能指的是能够运用跨文化交际的普遍规律,根据不同的文化语境,灵活调整自己的文化参考框架,使自己的语言和非语言行为恰当、有效。具有跨文化交际能力的人通常能够立体地、多维地看待、分析和解决问题。

除了以上态度/情感、知识和技能三个层面之外,跨文化交际能力还应该包括一个敏感性或意识层面。跨文化意识和敏感性培养对于缺乏跨文化交际体验的人们来说非常重要。这是因为人们经过多年的熏陶,在自己熟悉的文化环境中大都自觉地、无意识地遵循其文化习俗和规范,对于文化对我们言行的制约作用往往熟视无睹,毫无察觉。只有当他们离开本族文化语境,与陌生的文化习俗和规范亲密接触,经历文化冲撞时,才可能意识和认识到文化的作用以及文化差异的存在。因此跨文化意识和敏感性培养非常重要,它是跨文化交际能力的重要层面,是态度/情感、知识和技能培养的前提条件。

综上所述,跨文化交际能力可以归纳为下图所示:

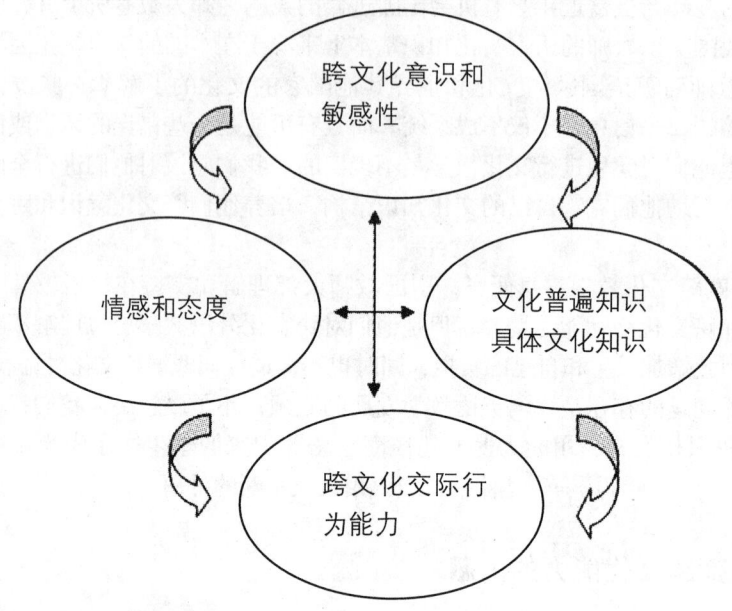

图1:跨文化交际能力

(2)跨文化外语教学能力。具备了跨文化交际能力只是教师进行跨文化外语教学的一个必要条件,教师还必须在教学观念和教学技能上与时俱进,不仅要充分认识跨文化外语教学思想的重要意义和基本内涵,还要掌握如何通过大纲制定、教学活动设计、教学方法运用、教学材料选编以及评价与测试等各个教学环节,去具体实施跨文化外语教学的技能。跨文化外语教学能力也可以从态度、知识和技能三个层面进行考量。所谓态度就是对跨文化外语教学新理念的认可和热情,这同时意味着摆脱一些传统、过时的外语教学观念,如将文化教学看作是外语教学的副产品,可有可无。所谓知识就是对跨文化外语教学基本思想的了解,包括其原则和方法等。所谓能力就是能够在实际教学中根据跨文化外语教学的原则,制定教学大纲,选择教学方法,设计教学活动,选编教学材料,并进行恰当的教学评价。

跨文化交际能力和跨文化外语教学能力构成外语教师的跨文化能力,它是有效实施跨文化外语教学的重要保障,是目前外语教师培训的目标。

4.2 外语教师跨文化能力的具体表现

外语教学是一个特殊的教学活动，与其他科目的教学相比，它更多地涉及教师和学生的主观世界，触及他们的人生观和价值观。这一特点对于外语教学是一把双刃箭，一方面它可能使教师和学生因为彼此之间或者他们与教学材料反映的观念冲突而感到不解、彷徨、恼怒、甚至痛苦；另一方面，如果合理利用这个特点进行社会人文教育，教师和学生都有可能从中获取语言教学和学习以外的、个人体验上的丰富和素质上的进步。从这个角度来看，外语教师应该具备以下几个方面的能力：[1]

(1) 跨越不同思维方式的能力

一名合格的外语教师应该了解东西方思维方式的差异。思维方式是指人们的思维习惯或思维的程序。思维方式是社会文化的产物，它受历史传统、价值观、哲学思想、语言文字等方式的综合影响，不同社会文化背景下人们的思维方式不同，所以东西方的思维模式的比较和转换应当成为外语教学的重要内容。[2]西方人是线性思维，在语言表达上开门见山，实话实说，直抒胸意，将重点放在最前面，以期引起读者或听众的注意；东方人的思维模式则是螺旋式，表达上比较含蓄、委婉，喜欢绕弯子，将重点放在最后，即迂回曲折地表达自己的思想意图。在跨文化交际时，有必要了解东西方思维方式的差异，避免交际的障碍。Stuart Chase[3]通过汉语和英语比较指出，汉语是一种较为特殊的多价语言，而不是像英语等西方语言那样为两价的语言。西方人对事物的评价必定为非对即错，非黑即白，事物的细微差别往往可以忽略不计。与西方人相反，中国人很留心事物的细微差别，奉行中庸之道，认为黑白之间有无数的灰，而非非黑即白。外语教师只有在了解了东西方思维差异时，才能更好地帮助学生培养跨文化交际能力。

(2) 跨越不同世界观和价值观的能力

一名合格的英语教师需要具备跨越不同世界观和价值观的能力。世界观和价值观决定了人们的处世方式和价值取向。以中国人和西方人为例。在人与自然的关系上，中国人是主张天人合一，而西方人是主张天人相分。在人际关系上，中国人采取的是群体取向，而西方人采取的是个人主义。在对变化的态度上，中国人在儒家学说影响下，认为万物不变或万变不离其宗，而西方人则认为万物皆变，在变中不断创新。在静与动的问题上，中国人追求求稳不求变，好静不好动，而西方人求变、喜功、冒险，在个人奋斗中克服常规，追求效率，讲求创造。在时间观念上，从时间的取向来看，中国人采取过去的取向，凡事，其行为

---

1 王咪研究生为此节提供了部分资料，在此致谢。
2 侯瑞君：高校外语教师跨文化交际能力的培养，《黑龙江高教研究》2003年第6期，第74-75页。
3 Chase, Stuart. 1954. Power of Words. New York: Harcourt, Brace.

往往以过去为标准，做事循规蹈矩。从时间的使用来看，中国人比较随意，灵活性强，而西方人则很大程度上受制于时间，追求精确，凡事准确无误。[4]

东方和西方有不同的世界观和价值观。中国人崇尚集体主义，认为国家利益、集体利益高于一切，个人利益应该服从集体利益，倡导团结友爱，互帮互助，重视集体的作用，强调社会和人际关系的和谐，即和为贵，集体至上。个人主义在中文中常常带有贬义的色彩，因为它被认为是不服从大局，贪图个人利益。而在西方，人们崇尚个人主义，认为个人是最重要的，个人独立是美德，倡导个性张扬和实现自我，认为依赖他人是软弱的表现。西方人比较注重自立，重视突出个人，注重隐私，张扬个性。这或许能从一个方面解释为什么英语中的"我"（I）必须大写。

(3) 跨越不同社会体制的能力

一名合格的外语教师需要具备了解不同社会体制的能力。社会体制是社会的组织方式和组织结构，包括经济体制、政治体制、文化体制和家庭体制等，是文化体系的表层。不同的文化有不同的政治、经济、文化和家庭体制。反过来，各种社会体制又影响着文化，从而对人们的交际行为也产生影响。外语教师必须了解不同社会体制的存在，才能在跨文化交际和外语教学中，考虑到这些差异对个人的作用，才能更深入、全面地理解跨文化交际的特点和规律。

(4) 跨越不同社会规范的能力

一名合格的英语教师需要了解不同社会规范的异同。社会规范（conventions）包括社会习俗、道德规范、宗教规范、历史传统、社会契约等，它是影响交际是否成功的一个主要方面。因此，外语教师在教学过程中必须通晓这方面的知识。东西方社会规范有很大的不同，分别从属于各自的文化传统，主要表现在日常生活的各个方面。例如，在中国"送钟"是非常不吉利的，因为"送钟"和"送终"是谐音。在表示颜色的词汇中，如红色，东西方人语义联想大有不同。中国人以红色为吉祥，西方人为暴力、血腥和活力；白色，西方视其为喜服，新郎新娘在婚礼上着白色婚纱，象征纯洁；中国人只有在葬礼上才身着白服，而西方人在葬礼上往往穿黑色衣服。在中国文化中，不赡养老人是不道德的；而在美国文化中，人们对赡养老人的观念相对比较淡薄，核心家庭的生活方式占主导地位。外语教师应该了解这些社会规范和道德规范上的文化差异，以避免交际失误。

(5) 跨越历史的能力

历史与文化水乳交融，是无法割裂开来区别对待的。历史有如一条奔流不息

4　贾玉新:《跨文化交际学》，上海外语教育出版社，1997年，p133-135.
5　章方:论外语教师的跨文化性角色特征，《石油化工管理干部学院学报》，2006年第1期，第12-16页.

的长河，沟通了过去和未来。外语教学活动是一个跨越历史的时间活动，教师首先要做的就是从自己的时代深入他者的历史。[5]外语教育传播可以是与同时代的人的交流，即文化的共时性。也可以是跨越不同时代的，与古人的交流，即文化的历时性。无论是处理共时性的文化内容还是处理异时性的文化内容，外语教师作为文化的传播者都不能回避历史。

(6) 跨越不同宗教的能力

宗教是文化的一个重要组成部分。宗教形成了文化习俗，并巩固了文化秩序。[6]欧美的基督教、阿拉伯国家的穆斯林教和东亚的佛教作为世界的三大文化圈充分体现了宗教对文化的巨大影响力。宗教一方面维系着社会道德秩序，推动着社会进步。另一方面宗教也被统治者利用来为其统治服务。作为外语教师，无论是否信仰宗教，无论信仰何种宗教，都需要具有跨越不同宗教信仰的能力。美国的很多节日和宗教有关，例如复活节、情人节、万圣节、感恩节和圣诞节，现在这些宗教节日日益世俗化，其中象圣诞节和情人节还越来越受到我国年轻人，特别是英语学习者的追捧。外语教师借此机会向学生介绍这些节日的宗教背景和意义，帮助他们认识不同信仰的存在及其对人们日常生活和交际的影响，并培养他们尊重他人宗教信仰的意识。

(7) 跨越不同交际风格的能力

交际风格上的差异是导致跨文化交际误解和冲突的主要原因之一。东亚国家，如中国、日本、韩国等，受儒家思想的影响，特别关注交际过程的和谐，尽可能避免正面冲突，这样既为了保住自己的面子，也可以给他人面子。不仅如此，在交际过程中，交际双方的社会背景及他们之间的关系也在很大程度上决定交际活动的内容和形式。强势的一方通常主导交际过程，而弱势的一方则往往多听少说，谦虚谨慎。如果双方关系密切，彼此熟悉，那么他们之间的交际一般比较随意、亲热，而且直接。如果是互不认识的两个人进行交际，就比较正式、客气、委婉，有时显得冷漠。这种语境因素起着重要作用的交际风格被Hall称为高语境交际风格（High-context communication style）。[7]

美国等一些西方国家属于低语境交际风格（Low-context Communication Style），他们注重语言的表达，喜欢讨论和辩论，关注交际的目的，不太在意交际双方的背景和关系，因此他们的交际往往表现出直接、民主、平等的特点。在我们看来，这种交际风格不重感情，有咄咄逼人之势，而我们的交际风格却给他们一种不够真诚、缺乏效率的印象。

值得注意的是，交际风格既受文化的影响，也具有个性，同一文化群体的人们，不同的性格和经历也会使他们的交际风格不同。而且，交际风格并不是一成

---

6 Hall, E.T. 1976. Beyond Culture. Garden City, NY: Doubleday. P74.
7 Ting-Toomey, S. & Chung, L.C. 2005. Understanding Intercultural Communication. Los Angeles: Roxbury Publishing Company.

不变的，它可以培养和拓展。外语教师应该了解交际风格的这些特点在教学中有意识地进行这方面的介绍和训练。

(8) 具有应对和解决跨文化交际冲突的能力

跨文化冲突是指来自不同文化背景的人们在交际过程中由于彼此价值观念、习俗规范、面子取向和身份认同等方面的差异，而产生的理解上的偏差和情感上的痛苦。一般来说，跨文化交际的目的是为了达成理解，增强关系，但是在此过程中冲突不可避免。一名从事跨文化外语教学的教师必须首先了解冲突产生的原因及其在不同文化中的不同表现形式，以培养对跨文化冲突的敏感性和认识。此外，外语教师还应该掌握如何应对和解决跨文化冲突的能力，如面子管理能力、留意倾听能力、换位思考能力和积极调整能力。目前跨文化冲突已经成为研究热点，丰富的研究成果可以成为教师自学和教师培训的内容。

外语教师跨文化能力主要体现在以上八个方面，外语教师培训应该以此为依据。

5 我国英语教师跨文化能力培训

培养一名具有跨文化能力的英语教师是一个复杂、长期的过程，不可能通过一次短期的培训就能完成。教师自己接受的英语教育，特别是课程设置、教学方法等，对他们的跨文化交际能力具有重要的作用。换句话说，为了保证我国英语教师的跨文化素质，我们应该在各个阶段的外语教学中，既关注外语教学的语言文学的初级目标，也要重视其社会人文的高级目标；既要帮助学生掌握目的语言的知识结构和使用，又要培养他们的跨文化意识和跨文化交际能力。这是英语教师跨文化能力培训的基础。没有了这个基础，再好的培训项目也只能在一定程度和层面上帮助教师进行跨文化外语教学。

当然，一个好的培训项目也是外语教师培养的必要条件。本节以大学英语教师为对象，提出一个能有效培养他们跨文化交际能力和跨文化外语教学能力的培训框架。

5.1 我国大学英语教师的跨文化培训需求分析

目前我国大学英语教师大都年纪较轻，思维活跃，教学热情高，但是由于工作任务重，进修学位和科研压力大，他们用来阅读思考、更新观念、进行教学改革探索的时间相当有限，所以对他们进行培训是非常必要的。

为了促进跨文化外语教学思想在大学英语教学中得到贯彻落实，我国英语教师需要三方面的培训：自身跨文化素养的培养、教学观念的更新和实际教学能力的提高。首先，跨文化素养是一个内涵极为丰富的概念，它包括跨文化敏感性、跨文化知识、跨文化交际能力等。大学英语教师具有丰富的知识，对不同文化的差异也都有所了解，而且他们好奇心强，也善于学习，因此跨文化知识不应该成为本项培训的重点。但是，由于他们普遍缺乏真实的跨文化交际的体验，他们的跨文化敏感性和交际能力相对较弱，所以我们的培训应该弥补他们跨文化交际的缺失，以增强敏感性和提高跨文化交际能力为主要目标。其次，跨文化外语教学是一个与时俱进的、新的教学思想，对教师提出了新的要求。如果教师不能理解这个新的教学思想的重要意义和基本特点，就不可能在教学实践中积极予以实施。最后，教师也需要掌握跨文化外语教学的具体方法和技能，了解如何在教学实践中将外语教学与跨文化交际能力培养有机结合。

这三方面的需求也就构成了本项培训的内容。

5.2 培训时间、目的和方法

鉴于外语教师工作繁忙，空余时间少，笔者建议培训时间为两天，第一天以增强英语教师的跨文化敏感性和交际能力为主要内容；第二天的重点是关于跨文化外语教学思想的学习、讨论和实践。

根据培训需求和内容，可以确定本项培训的目的：

● 丰富文化知识，增强对文化差异的敏感性，培养跨文化意识和跨文化交际能力；

● 全面、透彻理解跨文化外语教学思想，正确认识外语教学与跨文化交际能力培养之间的关系；

● 掌握跨文化外语教学的方法和技能。

就培训方法而言，由于整个培训涉及教师的情感、态度、认知、行为等各个层面，而且不同教师具有不同的认知和学习风格，所以两天的培训采用多种不同的方法，既有以认知理解和知识学习为主要目的的短小讲座（mini-lecture）、案例分析（case studies），又有以培养情感态度和敏感性为目的的模拟游戏（simulation games），角色扮演（role plays），还有促进反思和交流的小组讨论（panel discussion）、故事分享（story telling）等方法。总之，培训采用说教式和体验式相结合的培训方法，促进受训者在认知、情感、态度、行为等各个层面的转变和提高。

5.3 培训计划举例

为了更好地说明如何利用两天的时间对大学英语教师进行跨文化能力培训，笔者设计了一个培训计划如下：

第一天日程安排：

上午（8：30–12：00）：跨文化意识和敏感性培养

8:30　培训项目简介（10分钟）：介绍整个培训项目，包括目的、内容、方法及时间安排等

8:40　　自我认识（30分钟）：认识自己的文化身份、性格特点、学习风格

9:10　　短小讲座（20分钟）：了解民族中心主义（ethnocentrism）、感知

和归因（perception and attribution）、刻板印象（stereotypes）、文化冲撞（culture shock）等核心概念和现象

9:30　分享个人观点和体验（10分钟）：通过理论联系实际，巩固对上述概念和现象的理解

9:40　看录象并讨论（30分钟）：通过《刮痧》和《喜宴》片段，分析文化差异及其对跨文化交际的作用

10:10　茶歇（20分钟）

10:30　短小讲座（25分钟）：介绍跨文化敏感性发展模式（DMIS），让学员了解敏感性培养的过程

10:55　问答与讨论（5分钟）：进一步理解跨文化敏感性发展模式

11:00　模拟游戏（60分钟）：通过Bafa Bafa这个模拟游戏，让学员感受跨文化交际，感受心理和情感的冲击，了解其艰难和痛苦

12:00　午休

下午（1:30-5:30）：跨文化交际能力培养

1:30　热身游戏（20分钟）：通过"为被蒙上眼睛的伙伴带路"这个游戏，让学员体会交际的重要性

1:50　短小讲座（30分钟）：让学员了解各种不同交际风格的存在以及中国式的交际风格与美国等西方文化群体交际风格的差异

2:20　小组讨论及故事分享（20分钟）：以上述理论为基础，联系个人的经历和理解，进一步巩固对交际风格的认识

2:40　案例分析（20分钟）：通过两个经典案例（Are you mad at me? A motivational speech）的研究和讨论，让学员进一步了解不同交际风格可能产生的误解和冲突

3:00　茶歇（20分钟）

3:20　视觉象游戏（Visual Imagery）（30分钟）：通过"沉船"游戏（"Shipwrecked" group work），让学员体会团队交流与合作以及跨文化冲突

3:50　短小讲座（30分钟）：让学员了解跨文化冲突的本质以及如何面对和解决跨文化冲突

4:35　看录象并讨论（20分钟）：通过观看中英商务人员之间的一段冲突录象，让学员进一步认识跨文化冲突，并通过交流与讨论进行反思

4:55　短小讲座（25分钟）：通过介绍几个跨文化交际能力框架，让学员全面了解构成跨文化交际能力的各个要素

5:20　小组交流讨论（10分钟）：巩固对跨文化交际能力的认识，并反思自己的不足

5:30　结束第一天的培训

第二天日程安排：

上午（8：30-12：00）：跨文化外语教学思想的理解与研讨

8:30	热身讨论（20分钟）：我对外语教学的认识和感受	
8:50	专家讲座（60分钟）：跨文化外语教学的基本思想	
9:50	小组交流与讨论（15分钟）	
10:05	茶歇（20分钟）	
10:25	专家讲座（60分钟）：跨文化外语教学在中国实施的建议	
11:25	小组交流与讨论（20分钟）	
11:45	实施跨文化外语教学的困难和障碍讨论	
12:00	午休	

下午（1：30-5：00）：跨文化外语教学实践方法

1:30	专家讲座（40分钟）：跨文化外语教学的原则和方法	
2:10	课堂教学演示（1）（30分钟）：跨文化英语听力教学	
2:40	课堂教学演示（2）（30分钟）：跨文化英语口语教学	
3:10	茶歇（20分钟）	
3:30	课堂教学演示（3）（30分钟）：跨文化英语阅读教学	
4:00	课堂教学演示（4）（30分钟）：跨文化英语写作教学	
4:30	交流与讨论（20分钟）	
4:50	即兴课堂教学演示（30分钟）	
5:20	培训总结（5分钟）	
5:25	学员反馈与评价	
5:30	培训结束	

6 结语

在新时代呼唤新的外语教学理念的今天，跨文化外语教学思想当仁不让地成为当今外语教学的潮流和发展趋势。然而，教师素质决定教学效果，我国外语教师的跨文化能力还远远不能胜任跨文化外语教学新理念的要求。科学、有效的教师培训是惟一出路。

本文着重对外语教师跨文化能力的内涵进行了阐释，认为一名合格的外语教师不仅具有较强跨文化意识和敏感性，对不同文化持宽容、理解和积极的态度，能够灵活应对不同文化环境，调整自己的文化参考框架，进行有效和恰当的跨文化交际，而且充分认识跨文化外语教学的重要意义，在各个教学环节中能够积极践行跨文化外语教学思想原则。为了培养具有这些素质的外语教师，本文还对外语教师跨文化能力培训的目的、内容和方法进行了阐述，并设计了一个两天的培训计划予以举例说明。

跨文化外语教学在我国还是一个较新的思想，有待进一步研究和推广，而与之密切相关的教师跨文化能力培训研究更是一个全新的课题。本文的研究只停留在思辨和设计层面，有待实践的检验。

参考文献

Chase, Stuart. (1954). *Power of Words*. New York: Harcourt, Brace.

Hall, E. T. (1976). *Beyond culture*. Garden City, NY: Doubleday.

Ting-Toomey, S. & Chung, L.C. (2005). *Understanding intercultural communication*. Los Angeles: Roxbury Publishing Company.

张红玲, (2007),《跨文化外语教学》, 上海: 上海外语教育出版社。

[Zhang, H. L. (2007). *Intercultural approach to foreign language teaching*. Shanghai: Shanghai Foreign Language and Education Press.]

侯瑞君, (2003), 高校外语教师跨文化交际能力的培养,《黑龙江高教研究》第6期, 第74-75页。

[Hou, R. J. (2003). On the development of college foreign language teachers' intercultural communication competence. *Heilongjiang Researches on Higher Education*. 6, 74-75.]

贾玉新, (1997),《跨文化交际学》, 上海:上海外语教育出版社。

[Jia, Y. X. (1997). *Intercultural communication*. Shanghai: Shanghai Foreign Language and Education Press.]

章方, (2006), 论外语教师的跨文化性角色特征,《石油化工管理干部学院学报》第1期, 第12-16页。

[Zhang, F. (2006). On cross-cultural role characteristics of foreign language teacher. *Journal of SINOPEC Management Institute*. 1, 12-16.]

CROSS-CULTURAL TRANSLATION

Intra-discourse translation and inter-discourse translation: A new approach to translation and culture

话语内翻译与跨话语翻译：翻译与文化的新视角

许力生
浙江大学

Abstract

This paper attempts to offer a new perspective for viewing translation and its relationship with culture. It proposes that translation should be further divided into two types: intra-discourse translation and inter-discourse translation. They are fundamentally different: inter-discourse translation is cross-cultural whereas intra-discourse translation is not. The two types of translation will present the translator with different problems. Therefore, different strategies and techniques have to be employed and different standards should be applied to evaluating translation.

1 引言

雅各布森（Jakobson,1959:233）以及后来斯坦纳（Steiner,1975:7）都把翻译分为三类，即语内翻译（intralingual translation）、语际翻译（interlingual translation）和符际翻译（intersemiotic translation）。在这广义的翻译范畴内，翻译研究所关注的主要还是语际翻译，即不同语言之间的翻译。因此，翻译研究的重点在相当长时间里都放在了不同语言系统之间的异同上，语言学理论与方法也自然成了许多翻译研究的基础。然而，面对困扰翻译工作者和研究者的一系列问题，语言学似乎又难以给出令人满意的解答。在这种情况下，有人认为，语言学不能解决翻译的问题（Nord,1997:26）；也有人断言，语言学已经将翻译研究引进了死胡同（郭建中 Guo, 2000:107）。

可是，应当看到，包括语言学在内的一些相关学科已有了很大的变化。近年来，以话语为中心的语言研究发展迅速。与以语言（结构）为中心的语言学不同，以话语为中心的语言学主要研究社会语境中实际发生的语言使用，也就是曾被语言学研究长期忽视的"言语"。而且，"言语"不再被看作是杂乱无序、毫无规律，而是被视为与特定社会领域及社会活动紧密相关，自成体系，并有其规则。可以说，对话语的研究正在更高层次上将语言学及其相关研究过去几十年中发展出来的一些分支逐步整合起来，有可能形成规模更大、视野更宽、包容性更强、研究面更广的超学科。与此同时，从一开始就是跨学科研究的跨文化交际学也取得了很大进展，从不同方面拓展和深化了人们对交际与文化以及一系列相关问题的了解和认识。这些都为翻译研究提供了新的思想和思路。

在这样的背景下，我们可以试图从一个新的视角来探讨和分析翻译及其有关问题，以求得到更加全面而深刻的认识。

2 作为系统的话语

在话语研究中，一些学者曾提出过"话语社团"（discourse community）的概念。

比泽尔（Bizzell,1982:214）指出，"话语社团"是指遵循共同语言使用惯例的一个群体。这些惯例包括两方面：一是文体惯例，规定群体内部及其与外界的社会交往方式；二是规范化的知识，以调整和统一社团成员的世界观，决定其对各种现象的解释。赫斯伯格（Herzeberg,1986:1）认为，"话语社团"意味着话语是维持和扩展该群体的知识和吸引新成员加入该群体的手段，而话语是知识性的或者说构成该群体的知识。斯威尔斯（Swales,1993:29）强调，一个群体只有在形成自己的言语交流方式和文体惯例之后，才能被称为话语社团。舒密得（Schmidt,1993:3）则补充说，话语社团就是采用共同的表达、组织、传递及评价意义方式的一个群体，其成员关注同样的事物或问题，并具有共同的思维模式、交流模式、评价模式。

与语言社团（speech community）不同，话语社团被认为可能具有广泛的地域性，其成员可以来自不同的国家，属于不同的民族，甚至说不同的语言。因此，说同一语言的人则不一定都属于相同的话语社团，他们之间的言语交流不可避免地会在话语层面遇到障碍。而同一话语社团的成员有可能说不同的语言，但他们之间的沟通常常并不十分困难，困难仅在语言表层，因为他们不仅共享相同的话语方式，而且对事物或现象具有基本相同的背景知识和阐释框架。

后来，斯考仑等（Scollon & Scollon,1995）进一步提出了"话语系统"（discourse systems）的理论，深化了对话语的认识。他们提出，话语系统由四个部分构成：1. 意识形态（ideology），即群体成员共有的特定观念，类似于比泽尔所说的规范化知识；2. 社会化（socialization），即个人通过对特定话语的认同而成为其群体成员的过程；3. 话语形式（forms of discourse），即作为群体成员身份标志的一套独特话语方式，近似于比泽尔所说的文体惯例；4. 面子系统（face system），即群体成员之间话语互动时所受制于的人际关系。

斯考仑等（Scollon & Scollon,1995:14）认为，在话语系统中，意识形态观念决定了人际交往中礼貌（面子）策略的选择，而这又导致采用特定的话语形式。特定的话语形式意味着特定的社会化方式，也正是这些方式决定了人们会习得什么样的意识形态。这一切之间存在着一个循环制约的关系。他们提出，从话语和交际研究的角度来看，最好是把"话语形式"这一基本元素放在首位，因为正是话语的常规模式导致话语系统的形成。

斯考仑等（Scollon & Scollon,1995）比较细致地分析了当代西方占主导地位的话语系统，即他们所称的"实用主义话语系统"（utilitarian discourse system）。按照他们的分析，这个话语系统在上述各方面与其它话语系统有明显的根本性不同。例如，在话语形式方面，实用主义话语系统有六个主要特征：1、反修辞的（尽量避免明显的修辞手法）；2、实证主义–经验主义的（强调科学思想、弱化人与人际关系因素）；3、演绎的（话题先行，降低人际关系作用）；4、个人主义的（强调陈述的新颖、独到之处）；5、平等主义的（话语系统成员之间被设想为平等的）；6、公共的（体制认可的，即个人只能在公共话语认可的范围内自由表达）。这些都被认为是承载着其相关意识形态的理想话语形式特征，它们在绝大多数的实用主义话语中都能不同程度地显现出来。

斯考仑等（Scollon & Scollon,1995:162-163）还认为，话语系统是社会文化的基本构成部分，一个社会中往往会存在多个不同的话语系统，尽管其中之一可能占有主导或统治地位。人们通常所说的文化（如中国文化，美国文化，日本文化等等）往往都是由多个不同话语系统所构成。相比之下，话语系统比文化更具有内部的同质性（homogeneous）。这意味着，同一话语系统内部的交流比跨越不同话语系统之间的交流更容易做到精确的理解与沟通。话语系统可以以较为清晰明确的方式来讨论与分析，而要这样来讨论包罗万象的整个文化则几乎不可能。

3 翻译的话语分析

长期以来，翻译活动一直被看作是从一种语言系统向另一种语言系统的转换活动。然而，一个语言系统通常会包括多个话语系统，而一个话语系统则有可能跨越不同的语言系统，即不同的语言系统中可能包含有相同或相似的话语系统。这样，使用某一语言的某些人可能会与使用另一语言的某些人属于同一个话语系统。尽管语言不同，这些人之间的交流却是同一话语内的交流，比较容易做到相互理解，障碍主要产生于语言上的表层差异。而对于那些既不属于同一语言系统、又不属于同一话语系统的人们来说，他们之间的交流不但会有语言上的障碍，而且还会因话语系统各方面的不同而遭遇更大困难。所以，同一话语系统内的交流与不同话语系统间的交流是很不一样的。

因此，语际翻译应该进一步区分为"话语内翻译"（intra-discourse translation）与"跨话语翻译"（inter-discourse translation）。所谓话语内翻译，指的是跨越语言系统但并不跨越话语系统的翻译，也就是说，是在不同的语言之间、但却是相同或相似的话语内进行的翻译活动。而所谓跨话语翻译，是指同时跨越不同的语言与不同的话语系统的翻译活动。二者之间存在着根本性的差异，揭示这种差异对于更好地认识翻译活动及其有关问题非常重要。

3.1 话语内翻译

在当今世界上，人们使用不同语言但却属于同一话语系统的情况并不鲜见。科技界就是一个典型例子。全世界的科技界可以说是共有一个超越不同语言、相对同质的话语系统，也就是上面提到过的"实用主义话语系统"。我们知道，中国近现代科学的产生和发展主要依靠于对西方科技的引进和吸收。中国科技工作者通常说的语言虽然与他们的西方同事不一样，但他们都属于这同一个话语系统。在这个范围内，他们的意识形态观念、知识结构（社会化的结果）、话语方式（语用习惯）及对相互关系的认识上基本相同，对科技文本有着相同的话语期待。尽管他们使用的语言之间会有许多差异，但这些差异基本上是语言表层的，在他们之间进行翻译实际上比较容易。

请看下面这段科技论文摘要：

1981–1986年，用脊柱支撑器治疗78例胸腰骨折脱位并截瘫的病人。其中41例不完全瘫痪者，功能得到了恢复；37例完全性瘫痪者中，18例感觉和运动有了部分恢复。作者认为脊柱支撑器是这类截瘫病人康复的比较有效的治疗手段。

(Seventy-eight cases of thoracico-lumbar fracture-dislocation with paraplegia were treated with Harrington Instrument during the period of 1981 to 1986. Of 78 cases, 41 with incomplete paraplegia recovered their functions, while only 18 out of 37 patients with complete paraplegics partly regained sensation and motion. It is suggested that Harrington Instrument is a better way to rehabilitate this kind of patients.)

这则摘要包含三个句子，分别陈述了研究的过程，结果和结论。中文摘要和它的英译在话语方式上基本相同，在不同程度上都体现了承载着其相关意识形态的理想科技话语形式的主要特征，如避免明显的修辞用法，强调科学思想，话题先行，弱化人与人际关系因素，等等。

由于同一话语系统在意识形态、社会化过程、话语方式及面子（人际关系）系统方面的一致性，其成员往往会有相同的话语期盼，通常还拥有一定数量的共同（专业）词汇。因此，这样的话语内翻译易于做到严复提出的翻译标准中的"信"与"达"，译文与原文有可能在多方面达到较高程度的对等。

3.2 跨话语翻译

跨话语翻译的情形就比较复杂了，因为不同语言中并不都存在对应等同的话语系统。有些话语系统看上去相似，实际上却截然不同。这在中西医话语的对照中可以清楚地看出。虽然都是医学，都以人体为研究对象，其最终的目的都是为了保健与治病，但中医与西医却对人体的机能与病理有着各自不同的认识，形成不同的医学理论体系并采用不同的治疗方法，其话语方式也大不一样。

以夜盲症（night-blindness）为例。西医认为夜盲症是视网膜逐渐硬化的起始症状，由视网膜色素沉淀和视网膜萎缩引起，而《金针王乐亭》却有另一种描述和解释：

> 所谓夜盲，即日落入夜之后，视物模糊不清，至天明又复正常，多因肝肾阴亏、精气不能上输于目所致。患者系因精血不足、肝窍失荣所致。肾藏精，肝藏血，精血同源，目得血而能视；肾精亏损，水不涵木，肝目失养，精血不足，故傍晚视物不清；精血不足，髓海亏虚，以致血虚头痛。

毫无疑问，这样的中医话语是很难转换成西医那种实用主义话语并被西方人所理解的。中医的理论基础是古代朴素的辨证法与阴阳五行学说，体现了一种整体平衡观，认为人和自然界息息相关，人如果能做到内与外、天与人、阴与阳互相协调，邪气就不能侵害，就能保持身体健康。否则，与自然环境不协调，就会生病，所以将夜盲症归根于"阴亏"，认为是由于人体被邪气入侵所致。

而西医的理论基础则是唯物主义，将各种病理现象看作个别的、具体存在的客观对象，以对其进行具体、细致的描绘。疾病的产生被认为是由于人体本身机能受损所致。夜盲症就被认为是视网膜本身发生的一种病变，而不是某种看不见、摸不着，只能靠感觉来判断的症状。

在话语方式上，中医由于"天人合一"思想的影响，认定"一物之理即万物之理"，其论说往往充满假设、猜想的成分，用语并不求精确、严密，文体形式多种多样，传统典籍中有歌咏，有诗赋，语言陈述常带有浓厚的文学味。在上例中就可见到很多四字结构，追求对仗工整。而西医作为现代科学的一支，其表述追求客观、准确，不带任何感情色彩，用语以明晰、严密见长，避免明显的修辞用法，体现了实用主义话语的特征。

这样，中医文献的西译必然是一种跨话语的活动，因为在西方语言中还没有完全形成与汉语中的中医话语相同的话语系统。意识形态观念上的不同使西方读者一般很难理解诸如"气"、"精"之类的概念以及它们与夜盲症的关联，而话语方式上的不同又会使他们的话语期盼受挫，不可避免地会造成更大的理解障碍。这意味着，跨话语翻译要更多地考虑到目的语读者所属的话语系统，并根据其具体状况，在翻译中做出适当的调整和改变，以达到不仅跨越语言系统也能跨越话语系统的交流目的。

另一个比较典型的情况是法律文本的翻译。世界各国都有法律，但往往分属于不同法系。众所周知，作为英国法律基础的普通法（common law，又称"习惯法"或"判例法"case law）和作为多数欧洲大陆国家法律基础的民法典（the civil code）就属于不同的法系，二者之间有诸多差异。民法典倾向于概括性和普遍性，而普通法则注重特殊与细节，其同样内容的条文后者比前者要长很多；大陆法系的法律起草者追求法律能被一般民众所理解，用词较为普通，而英国的法律起草者则似乎更关心法律条文不要被专业人士所误读，用词非常专业化，要理解一个条文往往会涉及许多其它的相关法律条文和背景知识（Batia,1993:137）。

法系的不同造就了不同的话语系统，它们各自都有其不同的法律文本构建方式。因此，法律文本的翻译也是各不相同的。可以说，属于同一法系的法律文本在不同语言之间的互译是话语内的翻译,因为它们的法律文化与规约基本相同。而把某一法系的文本转译成归属于另一法系的另一种语言,就是跨话语的翻译,如将英美法系的英语法律文本转译为大陆法系的另一种语言的法律文本。在两种法系之间进行翻译,涉及的就远远不止是文字符号上的差异,而是一系列相关的意识形态观念,与同一法系内的翻译可以说有许多本质上的不同。

3.3 从跨话语翻译到话语内翻译

可以想象,因其社会、文化状况不同,不同语言中的话语状况和话语资源会有许多不同,这自然使翻译活动变得十分复杂、有时候甚至极其困难。然而,随着两种语言之间的交流不断扩大和加深,与源语中特定话语系统相似或相同的新话语系统可能会在目的语中逐渐形成。这意味着某些跨话语翻译会随着时间的推移逐渐转化为话语内翻译。

我们知道,近代中国科技主要是从西方引入的,科技翻译在中国就经历了一个由跨话语翻译到话语内翻译的过程。如西医在最初被译介到中国时就是一种跨话语的翻译活动,因为当时的汉语中还没有类似的话语系统。但随着西医文献的大量翻译,越来越多的人了解并从事这一领域的工作,一个西医话语系统就逐渐在中国形成并最后占据了医学界的主导地位。发展到今天,西医文献的中译早已是一种话语内的翻译活动了。

所以,进行翻译需要考虑两种语言中的话语状况,看两种语言中是否存在相同的话语系统,目的语中有哪些可供翻译借用的话语系统资源,翻译的主要读者对象属于目的语中的哪种话语系统,等等,并根据不同的情况来确定与之相适应的翻译原则与标准,选择较为恰当的翻译策略。换句话说,语言之间话语格局上的异同对翻译有着决定性的影响。

需要指出的是,人们常常说翻译是创造性的劳动,其实这种创造性主要体现在跨话语的翻译中,译者为在目的语中构建新的话语与话语系统做出了贡献。创造的结果是改变了目的语文化的话语格局,触发或推动了目的语文化的变化与发展,使之不与世隔绝,失去生机。通常所说的某种文化(如中国文化,美国文化,日本文化,等等),其面貌如何主要取决于它由一些什么样的话语系统构成,话语系统之间有着什么样的相互关系。话语状况与格局发生了变化,文化必定会有实质性的变化。跨话语的翻译从源语文化向目的语文化注入新的话语,这种来自外部的异质的东西,有可能使目的语中产生新的话语系统(如中国文学界新诗话语的产生),对原有的文化权力结构产生强大的"颠覆"作用。19世纪末到20世纪上半叶,中国社会与文化格局发生巨大变化,应该说是跨话语的翻译做出了不可磨灭的贡献。

4 从话语视角看翻译中的一些问题

4.1 国外不少学者(如朗贝尔 Jose Lambert 等)认为翻译不仅是语言转换,

更是文化之间的转换，翻译都具有跨文化性质，差别只是程度上的不同（Gentzler,1993:186）。国内学者也认为，翻译从本质上看，是跨文化的信息传播，文学翻译是美学信息的跨文化传播，科技翻译是科技信息的跨文化传播，应用文体的翻译是实用信息的跨文化传播，等等（吕俊、候向群 Lv & Hou,2001:2）。

然而，这样的认识过于笼统，因为情况并非都是如此。事实上，当今世界有相当数量的翻译并不具有明显的跨文化性质，应该把它们与真正的跨文化翻译区分开来，而不要混为一谈。对翻译研究来说，我们不能笼统地把一切翻译都视为跨文化翻译。从话语内翻译与跨话语翻译的区别可以看出，只有跨话语翻译才真正具有跨文化的性质。所以，西医文献的中译现在已经不再具有跨文化性质，而中医文献的英译在很大程度上还是跨文化的。

纽马克（Newmark,1991:33）认为"翻译意味着填补语言之间的空白"。准确地说，跨文化翻译所填补的是不同语言之间在话语上的空白。也正是从这个意义上说，翻译不仅仅是技术上的事情，它本来就是一种思想资源。瞿秋白当年就曾指出：翻译"有一个很重要作用，就是帮助我们创造出新的中国的现代言语"（沈苏儒 Shen,1998:101）只有通过翻译在本国语言文字中构建起新的话语系统，外来文化才会成为本国文化的一部分，同时又不是传统的。

4.2 严复提出的"信，达，雅"翻译标准，在翻译界影响很大，争论也很大。不少人认为，严复翻译思想中最成问题的就是"雅"这个标准。译介西方近代哲学与社会科学的学说，严复偏偏采用桐城派的古文笔法，他的理由是："精理微言，用汉以前字法句法，则为达易；用近世利俗文字，则为达难。"（《天演论》译例言）

应当看到，严复当年的翻译是有明确的中国读者对象的，是为了让士大夫们能够吸收外国思想，以促使中国社会与文化的转变。那时候的中国社会基本不存在与西方知识界相同或相似的话语系统。当时的知识分子只崇尚古文，他们所读的书主要是先秦及隋唐诸子之说，已习惯于这种以"汉以前字法句法"写的精理微言。不管从哪方面说，他们所属的话语系统与西方知识分子的话语系统相去甚远。因此，如果用"近世利俗文字"来翻译西方著作，士大夫们对话语形式本身首先就会抵触，哪里还谈得上接受其中包含的新思想了。为了减少翻译可能遇到的抵抗与阻力，严复选择了当时认为比较高雅的先秦文体来转译西方的思想，以求至少在话语方式上尽可能接近士大夫们。

用有关话语理论来分析，严复所采取的"雅"的做法就是用目的语文化读者所归属的话语形式来包裹源语文本所属话语的意识形态，以形式上的迁就、妥协来求得内容上一定程度的被接受，并随着接受程度与广度的增加，逐步在目的语中构建起新的话语系统。当然，如纽马克（Newmark,1981:64）曾经指出的，"一旦改变了形式，就歪曲了思想"。严复用先秦文体对西方思想的"包装"，不可避免地在某种程度上改变了原有内容，已经不再是"原装"的"西学"了，多多少少溶入了"中学"成分。但这也是不得已而为之。否则，士大夫们一点不接受,再好的"原装"也白搭。换句话说,跨话语(也就是跨文化)翻译应该追求的不是译文与原文的绝对一致或者完全对等,而是要使属于某一个话语系统的读者接收到来自另一话语系统的信息,这种信息常常是读者原来那个话语系统中所没有的或者所排斥的。

4.3 关于翻译中的"对等"(equivalence)问题,这些年来有过不少争论,主要围绕奈达(Nida)提出的"对等原则"展开。奈达反对只追求表面上的形式对等,提出"最近似的自然对等",即"动态对等"(dynamic equivalence)(Nide & Taber,1969:12);后来改称"功能对等"(functional equivalence)(Waard & Nida,1986:7)。对此,译界的学者们意见分歧,支持者和反对者都不在少数。

实际上,翻译要做到(无论哪种)对等都非常困难,而且多数情况下只有在话语内翻译中才有可能,因为属于同一话语系统意味着有共同的话语方式。奈达从事的大多是跨话语的翻译(圣经翻译),他之所以要坚持用"对等"这样颇具争议的概念,无非是要为其翻译实践中一些偏离传统翻译规范的做法寻求"合法性"。

在不少人看来,对等是翻译得以成立的基础,是翻译区别于改写、重述的关键所在。可是,所谓译文与原文的一致,译文与原文的等值、等效,译文绝对忠实于原文,等等,只是在话语内翻译时才有可能做到。在跨话语翻译中,两个话语系统在意识形态、社会化、话语方式及面子体系上可能都有相当大的差异,何以能求得对等?从某种意义上说,跨话语翻译只能促使不同话语系统及其成员之间的接触与接近,对等是只能在文本层面讨论的问题,而文本又只是翻译过程中的一个部分。翻译完成的是文本的转换,但翻译要考虑的却还有文本之外的许多因素。

跨话语的翻译实际上是谋求差异之间的互通。能够通多少、通到什么程度,起决定性作用的往往不是翻译本身,而是不同话语系统之间的差异状况。因此,评判译文的优劣,绝不能只是看其与原文是否一致、等值,而是要看它是否充分考虑了不同话语系统之间的差异并促进它们之间的互通。严复的翻译之所以有意义、有价值,不是因为其译文与原文达到了高度的一致,而是因为他成功地使西方话语系统在当时中国社会知识分子使用的语言中得以(至少是部分的)重构,并在一定程度上开始改变汉语中的话语格局。

将源语中某一文本译入目的语,选择用什么样的话语来进行翻译,往往是一个很重要、但又很费斟酌的问题。针对目的语中不同话语系统成员的翻译,译法可能会大相径庭。同理,什么才是好的翻译、恰当的翻译,也不大可能有完全统一的标准。直译也好,意译也好,归化也好,异化也好,强调"信"也好,强调"达"也好,其实都有其道理,但又都不是放之四海而皆准的真理。一切都取决于具体的情况,取决于各方面因素的综合考虑。在这当中,相关话语系统的状况恐怕是最重要的因素之一。

5 结语

区分跨话语翻译与话语内翻译，这给我们提供一个考察与分析翻译问题的新视角。当然，一个话语系统的形成往往要经历相当长的时间，翻译由跨话语向话语内的转化也是一个渐变过程，很难绝对地划分跨话语翻译与话语内翻译。但是，这一视角无疑有助于建立辩证的、历史的翻译批评观，也有助于更全面地看待翻译界长期争论的一些问题。

翻译被认为是语言之间的转换过程，翻译研究也一直以语言系统和文本的分析对比为其主要任务之一。现在，翻译界越来越多的人都感到纯粹语言结构的分析过于狭隘，对翻译实践中的许多问题拿不出解决办法，因此认为翻译要更多地注重文化分析。斯内尔-霍恩比（Mary Snell-Hornby,1988:31）就提出把文化而不是文本做为翻译的单位来研究，而这一观点被有的人视为具有"划时代"的意识，标志了翻译研究领域的"文化转向"（cultural turn）（Gentzler,1993:188）。但是，若将翻译的一切和一切的翻译都置于文化的大伞之下，过分强调文化的无所不在，把所有问题都归结到文化上，容易导致泛泛而论，反而不利于翻译研究的深入。在翻译研究中，更为需要的是对话语的细致分析，因为任何具体的翻译所涉及的都不会是整个文化，而主要只是相关的话语系统。

我们认为，比较合适的是介于两者之间的中间层次，那就是语言与文化的结合点——话语。如前所述，相对于通常说的文化而言，话语系统更具有内部的同质性，话语系统是社会文化的基本构成部分，易于以较为清晰明确的方式来讨论与分析，而要这样讨论整个文化则非常困难。话语研究的一些理论与方法，也为我们进一步深入认识文化问题和研究跨文化交际提供了比较好的分析工具与思路，有助于克服研究中过于笼统和概括的倾向，为其开拓出新的研究路径。

参考文献

Batia, V. K. (1993). *Analysing genre: Language use in professional settings*. London: Longman.

Bizzell, P. (1982). *Cognition, convention, and certainty: What we need to know about writing*. PRE/TEXT 3: 213-41.

Gentzler, E. (1993). *Contemporary translation theories*. London: Routledge.

Herzberg, B. (1986). *The politics of discourse communities*. Paper presented at the CCC Convention, New Orleans, La, March, 1986.

Jakobson, R. (1959). *On linguistic aspects of translation*. In Reuben A. B., (Ed.), *On translation*. Cambridge, MA: Harvard University Press.

Newmark, P. (1991). *About translation*. Clevedon: Multilingual Matters Ltd.

Newmark, P. (1981). *Approaches to translation*. Oxford: Pergamon Press.

Nida, E. A. & Taber, C. R. (1969). *The theories and practice of translation*. Leiden: E.J.Brill.

Nord, Christiane (1997). *Translation as a purposeful activity: Functionalist approaches explained*. Manchester, UK: St Jerome.

Schmidt, G. D. (1993). *Communities of discourse*. London: Prentice Hall.

Scollon R. & Scollon S. (1995). *Intercultural communication: A discourse approach*. Oxford, UK: Blackwell Publishers

Snell-Hornby, M. (1988). *Translation studies: An integrated approach*. Amsterdam: John Benjamins Publishing Company.

Steiner, G. (1975). *After babel: Aspects of language and translation*. London: Oxford University Press.

Swales, J. M. (1993). *Genre analysis*. Cambridge: Cambridge University Press.

Waard, J. de & Nida, E. A. (1986). *From one language to another: Functional equivalence in Bible translating*. Nashville/Camden/New York: Thomas Nelson Publishers.

郭建中,(2000),《当代美国翻译理论》,武汉:湖北教育出版社。

[Guo, J. Z. (2000). *Contemporary Translation Studies in USA*. Wuhan: Hubei Education Press.]

吕俊、候向群,(2001),《英汉翻译教程》,上海:上海外语教育出版社。

[Lv, J. & Hou, X. Q. (2001). *Translating from English into Chinese: A Course Book*. Shanghai: Shanghai Foreign Language and Education Press.]

沈苏儒,(1998),《论信达雅——严复翻译理论研究》,北京:商务印书馆。

[Shen, S. R. (1998). On Fidelity, *Accuracy, and Elegance: Yan Fu's Theory of Translation*. Beijing: The Commercial Press.]

NON-VERBAL COMMUNICATION ACROSS CULTURES

Smiling in the People's Republic of China and the United States: Status and situational influences on the social appropriateness of smiling

Richard L. Wiseman California State University, Fullerton, USA
Xiaohui Pan City University of Hong Kong, China

Abstract

Facial displays, especially smiling, serve not only to express internal emotional states but also to present appropriate and competent social behavior by the expresser. Appropriate social behavior is governed by cultural display rules that inform the expresser how much, to whom, when, and where to express one's internal emotional state. Cultures are the socializing agents for these display rules. This study examined the cultural effects on the levels of the facial display of smiling and individuals' attributions for their smiling behavior. Extrapolating from Hofstede's (1980) cultural dimensions of individualism-collectivism and power distance, the study investigated cultural (US and China) and situational influences on respondents' intentions to and attributions for smiling behavior in nine different situations. A total of 160 US and 134 Chinese college students were presented nine situations that operationalized differences in relational status, familiarity, and group identity. For each of the nine situations, respondents indicated whether they would smile and what the rationale for their behavioral choice would be (i.e., attributions based on emotion, social appropriateness, modesty, other person's status, and the other person's face or esteem). Multiple and univariate analyses of variance revealed significant cultural and situational differences in respondents' likelihood for smiling and attributions for smiling behavior. While not as potent predictors of behavior and attribution as cultural origin, significant correlations were found between the cultural variables of individualism, collectivism, and power distance and the smiling measures (i.e., likelihood and attributions). The implications of this study should enhance our understanding of cross-cultural similarities and differences between the United States and China, and, in turn, improve Sino-American communication.

Review of Literature

As Frijda (1986) stated, "people not only have emotions, they also handle them" (p. 401). People regulate how they feel about certain emotional events (control of feeling) and how they behave or respond to emotional events (control of emotional expression). People control their emotional expressions in order to act appropriately according to cultural norms, i.e., a sense of propriety and obligations toward the feelings of others (Frijda, 1986). These cultural norms have been referred to as "display rules" by Ekman and Friesen (1969) and they govern which emotions may be displayed in various social circumstances.

This study will investigate the cultural effects on display rules and emotional expressions. To increase the generalizability of the study, it will utilize Hofstede's theoretical analysis by focusing on two of his cultural dimensions, namely, individualism-collectivism and power distance. The cultural dimension of individualism-collectivism explains how the role of the group differs in each culture (e.g., group harmony is more emphasized in collectivistic cultures than in individualistic cultures). It also explains the attitudinal differences of people toward groups in each culture (e.g., people in collectivistic cultures draw a clearer line between an ingroup and an outgroup than in individualistic cultures). The cultural dimension of power distance examines members' sensitivity to social status and authority. In low power-distance cultures, people tend to minimize power and status differences, and they tend to communicate more positive emotions to lower-status others and more negative emotions to high-status others. People in low power-distance cultures are freer to display negative emotions to social superiors without fear of repercussion. For the purposes of this study, China was chosen to exemplify collectivistic, high power-distance cultures, while the United States was chosen to exemplify individualistic, low power-distance cultures.

Cultural Variations in Emotional Expressions: Individualism-Collectivism

There is evidence that culture influences how we express and control our emotions. For example, Ekman (1972) provided a neuro-cultural theory of facial expressions of emotion utilizing display rules. The model explains cultural differences as well as universal determinants of facial expressions. When comparing several cultures and their influences, a concept or framework that is common to each culture is needed to increase the generalizability of the findings on how cultures influence emotional expression. Individualism-collectivism is one cultural dimension that helps explain emotional expressions.

Individualistic cultures emphasize the independence of each individual, and in such cultures personal needs and interests are valued more than group goals. In individualistic cultures people have more ingroups, making the ties between a person and her/his ingroups unstable. People in individualistic cultures are better at meeting and getting along with outsiders and forming new ingroups. On the other hand, in collectivistic cultures "individuals may be induced to subordinate their personal goals to the goals of some collective, which is usually a stable ingroup" (Triandis, Bontempo, Villareal, Asai, & Lucca, 1988, p. 324). In collectivistic cultures, there are fewer ingroups and they tend to be more stable than in individualistic cultures. Members of collectivistic cultures make a clear distinction between an ingroup and an outgroup, so "cooperation is high in an ingroup but is unlikely when the other person belongs to an outgroup" (Triandis et al., 1988, p. 325). Thus, the behavior of members of collectivistic cultures can be highly individualistic toward outgroup members.

People in all cultures manipulate their behavior, including emotional behavior, depending on with whom they are communicating (ingroup or outgroup) (Triandis et al., 1988). However, the difference between one's behavior toward ingroup and outgroup members is more differentiated in collectivistic than in individualistic cultures. Thus, there should be a cultural difference in emotional behavior between individualistic cultures and collectivistic cultures when we take into account the concept of self-ingroup and self-outgroup communication. In other words, in collectivistic cultures there should be greater difference between self-ingroup communication and self-outgroup communication than in individualistic cultures.

Ingroup and Outgroup Communication

An ingroup in collectivistic cultures is illustrated by one's family, friends, and other people concerned with one's welfare (Triandis, 1972). Wheeler, Reis, and Bond (1989) stated that ingroups in collectivistic society are few in number. Triandis et al. (1988) described that ingroups in collectivistic cultures are mainly "family and friends." However, Triandis et al. (1988) suggested that the definition of an ingroup can depend on the situation. For example, employees of Nissan refer to themselves as "we" (ingroup) while Toyota is referred to as "they" (outgroup).

In individualistic cultures the ingroup is defined as people who are similar to oneself in social class, race, beliefs, attitudes, and values (Triandis, 1972). Ingroups in individualistic cultures cover a much broader spectrum than in collectivistic cultures. Wheeler et al. (1989) explained that people in individualistic cultures might consider their work group, the neighbors, and clubs as ingroups in addition to family and friends. According to the results of Triandis et al.'s (1988) study, Japanese (collectivistic culture) have an "inner ingroup" (parent, close friends), "outer ingroup" (close relative, coworker, neighbor), and an outgroup (person hardly known, person from another country). Whereas Americans (individualistic culture) have a wider "inner ingroup" (parent, close friend, close relative, coworker), a small "outer ingroup" (neighbors), and an "outgroup" that is treated basically the same as "outer ingroup."

Because there seems to be variability in the conceptualization of ingroups in different cultures it is necessary for us to take this into consideration when we conceptualize ingroups and outgroups. In this paper, ingroup is conceptualized as the common groups that are considered to be inner ingroups in both collectivistic and individualistic cultures, namely, family and close friends. Outgroup members will be operationalized as mere acquaintances or strangers.

Power-Distance Cultures

As noted by Triandis (1994), power distance reflects "the tendency to see a large distance between those in the upper part of a social structure and those in the lower part of that structure" (p. 153). Members of high power-distance cultures tend to display emotions that emphasize or maintain status differences, whereas members of low power-distance cultures tend to display emotions that minimize power and status differences (Matsumoto, 1991). People who live in low power-distance cultures are freer to display emotions to individuals with different social status, because status differences are small, however, people who live in high power-distance cultures are more constrained in their emotional expressions with individuals with different social status.

Cultural Differences in Emotion

Theoretical frameworks to explain cultural differences in emotion have been provided by Gudykunst and Ting-Toomey (1988a). They utilized Hofstede's (1980) dimensions to compare cultural variability and several aspects of emotion to the results provided by previous research. They focused on attitudes toward emotion, antecedents of emotion, and reactions to emotion. In analyzing attitudes toward emotion, they found some cultural differences could be explained with the individualism-collectivism construct. Originally, the respondents in Izard's (1971) study were asked several questions concerning attitudes toward emotion: "which emotion do you understand best?" which emotion do you prefer to experience? etc. Although the data in Izard's (1971) study indicated an interaction between culture and emotion in all the questions, he did not provide a theoretical interpretation.

According to Gudykunst and Ting-Toomey (1988a), Izard's (1971) findings are consistent with the characteristics of individualistic and collectivistic cultures. They stated that emotional independence is expected in individualistic cultures, while in collectivistic cultures, emotional dependence is expected. Gudykunst and Ting-Toomey

(1988a) found that nonvocal reactions (i.e., face, body parts, and whole body) and verbalization were correlated positively with individualism. Thus, the more individualistic the culture, the greater people's nonvocal reactions and verbalizations of the emotion are. According to Gudykunst and Ting-Toomey (1988b), those findings are consistent with characteristics of the individualism-collectivism dimension. Verbal communication is stressed in individualistic cultures, while in collectivistic cultures verbal communication is not emphasized and is often indirect. In addition, in collectivistic cultures, a receiver's ability to decode subtle nonverbal cues is emphasized. People in individualistic cultures value a sender's ability to convey messages explicitly (Okabe, 1983). In other words, in individualistic cultures, more explicit nonvocal reactions sent by an encoder are expected than in collectivistic cultures. Gudykunst and Ting-Toomey (1988a) stated that most comparisons of nonverbal communication between individualistic and collectivistic cultures suggest that people in individualistic cultures use nonverbal displays in reaction to emotional experiences more than people in collectivistic cultures. Based upon the Gudykunst and Ting-Toomey's (1988a) analysis, it can be concluded that the individualism-collectivism constructs explain cultural differences in attitudes toward emotion, antecedents of emotion, nonvocal reactions, and verbalizations of emotion.

There have been some inroads in the analysis of the interaction between individualism-collectivism, power distance, and ingroup / outgroup communication in explaining emotional expressions. Matsumoto (1989) tested whether the perception of emotion and the dimensions of individualism-collectivism, power distance, and uncertainty avoidance were correlated. Perception of emotion was operationalized with three types of data: the percentage of members of each culture correctly identifying the emotional expression, the mean intensity level attributed to each of the expressions, and the amount of variability associated with the intensity ratings of each expression. There were no significant correlations between the cultural dimensions and the correct judgments of emotions or the cultural dimensions and the variability index of perception. On the other hand, there was a positive correlation between individualism and judgments of the intensity of negative emotions, i.e., people from individualistic cultures tended to make more intense ratings on negative emotions than people from collectivistic cultures. The dimension of individualism-collectivism seems to explain the cultural differences in the perception of emotion, namely, the intensity of emotions.

Matsumoto (1991) provided a theoretical framework to better understand the cultural differences in emotional expressions. He applied the cultural dimensions of individualism-collectivism and power distance to the social distinctions of ingroup-outgroup and status. His argument was that in collectivistic cultures emotional displays of the members who maintain and facilitate group cohesion, harmony, or cooperation are fostered to a greater degree than in individualistic cultures.

Emotional display is influenced more by the context and the target of the emotion in collectivistic cultures than in individualistic cultures (Matsumoto, 1991). For example, when negative emotion is a reaction to persons in the ingroup it would be inappropriate to show the negative emotion in the ingroup. To do so would jeopardize the group harmony valued in collectivistic cultures. When the same emotion occurs in public, it is also inappropriate to display the emotion because of the negative ramifications to the group or individuals. To display such emotion in public makes the group or individuals lose face. However, when negative emotion is a reaction to persons in a rival group (i.e., outgroup), it would be appropriate to show the emotion in the ingroup because it should foster ingroup cohesion.

Matsumoto (1991) also noted that people in individualistic cultures are more likely to express positive emotions (and not display negative emotions) to members of the outgroup than people in collectivistic cultures. When a member of an individualistic culture communicates with an outgroup member, it is viewed more as one-to-one relationship than self-outgroup relationship. Individualistic cultures foster expression of cohesion-producing emotions among outgroup members, while collectivistic cultures foster less cohesion-producing emotions with outgroup members. The difference in the amount of emotional behavior displayed between ingroups and outgroups in individualistic cultures should be larger than in collectivistic cultures, because individualistic cultures encourage greater variance in emotional expressions. There is a wider range of emotional display in individualistic cultures than in collectivistic cultures.

Gudykunst and Kim (2003) agreed with Matsumoto's (1991) conclusion that people in individualistic cultures express more positive emotions to members of outgroups than do the people in collectivistic cultures. However, Gudykunst and Kim (2003) differed with Matsumoto's conclusion regarding negative emotions, they noted that members of collectivistic cultures are more likely to express negative emotions with members of outgroups than are members of individualistic cultures. Collectivistic cultures' orientation of "do whatever you can get away with" (Triandis et al., 1988, p. 325) applies to the negative emotional expression towards members of the outgroup. Members of outgroups in collectivistic cultures often are treated as "nonpersons." In other words, people in collectivistic cultures can be highly individualistic when it comes to members of outgroups (Triandis et al., 1988).

In sum, the important issues that should be considered when comparing cultural influence on emotional expressions are: individualism-collectivism, status, and ingroup / outgroup communication. The elicitor of the emotion (ingroup or outgroup) should be regarded as well as the target of the emotional expression (ingroup or outgroup). In the present study, the targets of the emotional expression will include friends / strangers, high / low status others, and ingroup/outgroup members. The following examination of the research on emotion in

China and the US should further our understanding of these dynamics.

Research Hypotheses

Hypothesis 1: Due to differences in status, social appropriateness, and relational obligations, different situations will lead to variances in smiling preferences for both Chinese and US respondents.

Hypothesis 2: Due to the constraints of modesty, social restraint, and concern for face, Chinese respondents will smile less than United States respondents who tend to be more direct, emotionally expressive, and individualistic.

Hypothesis 3: Chinese and US respondents will differ in terms of their attributions for their smiling behavior, namely, the two cohorts will differ in terms of their use of attributions based on emotions, social appropriateness, modesty, other person's status, and concern for other's face when explaining their choices of smiling behavior.

Hypothesis 4: Cultural variables of individualism, collectivism, and power distance will be correlated with smiling likelihood and attributions for respondents' choices in smiling behavior.

Method

Sample

The study intends to employ survey methodology in ascertaining the nature and reasons for respondents' smiling behavior. A total of 253 Chinese college students and 160 U.S. college students participated as respondents. In terms of the demographics for the two subsamples, the average age of the Chinese respondents was 25.1 (sd =5.4), 58.1% were male, and all were students at a major university in southeast China. For the US respondents, the average age was 22.8 (sd = 7.2), 32.5% were male, and all were students at a major university in southern California.

Questionnaire

The questionnaire consisted of three parts: First, nine situations manipulating relationship type (friend/stranger), status (high/equal status), and ingroup/outgroup context were presented (see Table 1) and respondents were asked whether they would engage in smiling behavior and to attribute reasons for their behavioral choice. Five possible attributions for their behavioral choice were provided for their ratings: their emotional state, the social appropriateness of the situation, their modesty, the status of the other person(s) in the situation, and the respect for or face of the other person(s). The influence of these five possible attributions were rated on a four-point scale from 1 (= not an influence) to 4 (= great influence on my decision to smile or not smile in the situation).

Table 1: Situations

1. You are a student in an upper-division class in your major. You are with about 30 of your classmates sitting in the classroom at the time. Then, your esteemed professor walks into the classroom and says hello to the class. Would you smile at the professor as the professor greets the class?
2. You are at a party with some of your friends and their acquaintances. There are about 20 people at the party and they seem to be having a good time. You notice a person who you do not like standing near you. All of a sudden this person drops his or her food and drink and is embarrassed. Would you smile in this situation?
3. You are having an informal conversation with one of your friends. The friend then tells a joke that you really do not think is very funny. Would you smile in this situation?
4. You are looking for a local restaurant and are not sure of the directions to the restaurant. You approach a stranger who is walking nearby and ask for directions. While you are asking for directions from the stranger, would you smile at the stranger?
5. You and your friend are students in the same course. Recently, you both took a major test that you put a lot of time studying for. You received a very high grade on the test, but your friend received a lower grade. Even though your friend did not receive a high grade, would you smile when talking with your friend about the high grade you received?
6. You are having a difficult time understanding a class assignment and you decide to go to your professor's office to ask about the assignment. The conversation with the professor is business-like (task-oriented) and helps you understand the assignment. During the conversation with the professor, would you smile at the professor?
7. You are having a difficult time understanding a class assignment. Your friend is in the same class and has been very good at doing past assignments in the class. You decide to talk to your friend about the assignment. The conversation with your friend is business-like (task-oriented) and very helpful in your understanding the assignment. During the conversation with your friend, would you smile at your friend?
8. You are attending an art exhibit at a local museum. To encourage people to come to the museum, the museum staff has decided to give a prize (worth about $30) to one of the people at the museum. The person receiving the prize is chosen at random. Beside yourself, there are about 100 people attending the art exhibit, but you do not know any of them. When they have to draw for the prize, your name is chosen!

When you go on the stage to receive your prize, would you smile at the museum staff and the 100 audience members?
9. You are walking on the street. A complete stranger approaches you and asks directions to a local landmark. During the conversation with the stranger while giving directions, would you smile at the stranger?

Second, three scales will be presented operationalizing individualism, collectivism, and power distance. The individualism and collectivism scales were extracted from Gudykunst et al.'s (1996) individualism and collectivism scales. The power distance items were extracted from Hofstede's (1980) power-distance scale. Third, two demographic questions were asked to ascertain the characteristics of the respondents (namely, their gender and age). After the questionnaire was constructed in English, a Chinese version of the questionnaire was translated by the second author.

Results

Smiling Preferences Table 2 on the next page presents the results on preferences for smiling behavior across the nine situations. Overall, the respondents indicated greater likelihood for smiling in three situations: winning a prize among strangers, greeting a professor in a classroom situation, and asking a stranger for directions. Each of these situations involves different emotions, status, and familiarity (i.e., in-group/out-group). Further, respondents indicated lesser likelihood for smiling in two situations: one where the respondent earned a high grade on a test that a friend had failed and another where a person the respondent dislikes had embarrassed oneself. To provide a more rigorous test of these impressions, a univariate analysis of variance (ANOVA) was computed to determine whether there were significant differences among the situations on the likelihood of smiling. The ANOVA indicated a significant effect for situation (F [8/3696] = 118.2, p < .0001, eta2 = .21). A conservative Tukey multiple comparisons test was then performed to determine which situations different from each other. The results are presented in Table 3. Four homogeneous subsets emerged (in order of most likely to least likely to smile): (1) winning a prize, (2) greeting professor / asking stranger for directions / getting help from friend, (3) getting help from professor / stranger asking for directions / friend tells unfunny joke, and (4) disliked person embarrassing self / receiving a high grade while friend failing. These results provide support for the first hypothesis, that situational differences will emerge in the likelihood for smiling behavior.

A multiple analysis of variance (MANOVA) test was computed to determine whether there were significant cultural differences in smiling preferences across the nine situations. The MANOVA revealed that there was a significant effect for culture (F [9/399] = 10.8,

Pillai's Trace = .20, p < .001). Given a significant MANOVA effect, individual analyses of variance (ANOVAs) were computed to determine which situations yielded significant cultural differences in the preferences for smiling behavior (see Table 3). Of the nine situations, there were statistically significant differences for culture (U.S./China) on four of them. For all four of these, the U.S. respondents indicated a greater likelihood for smiling behavior. The greatest differences were in the situations where a disliked person embarrasses self (US mean = 4.50, China mean = 2.83, F [1/407] = 75.3, p < .0001, eta2 = .16) and a stranger asks for directions (US mean = 5.08, China mean = 4.44, F [1/407] = 40.5, p < .001, eta2 = .03). In these situations, differences in the social norms governing loss of other's face, communicating with higher status individuals, and dealing with out-group members seem to vary between China and the United States.

Table 2

Situational Differences in the Likelihood for Smiling

	Homogeneous Subsets			
	1	2	3	4
5. Received High Grade on Test, but Friend Failed Test	3.16			
2. Disliked Person Embarrasses Self	3.48			
3. Friend Tells Unfunny Joke		4.42		
9. Stranger Asking for Directions		4.69		
6. Getting Help from Professor		4.74		
7. Getting Help from Friend			5.16	
4. Asking Stranger for Directions			5.25	
1. Greeting Professor in Class			5.37	
8. Winning Prize Among Strangers				6.16

Tukey Multiple Comparisons Test, Alpha =.05.

Table 3

Cultural Differences in Smiling Behavior Across Situations

	Mean	Means	Overall F	p	eta2
Greeting Professor in Class	5.38	5.40* 5.37*	.0	n.s.	.00

Situation	U.S. Mean / Chinese Mean		F	p	
Disliked Person Embarrasses Self	3.48	4.50 / 2.83	75.3	.0001	.16
Friend Tells Unfunny Joke	4.43	4.43 / 4.42	.0	n.s.	.00
Asking Stranger for Directions	5.24	5.50 / 5.08	.2	.02	.02
Receiving High Grade on Test, But Friend Failed Test	3.15	3.15 / 3.16	.0	n.s.	.00
Getting Help from Professor	4.85	4.85 / 4.69	2.5	n.s.	.00
Getting Help from Friend	5.16	5.30 / 5.07	4.9	n.s.	.00
Winning a Prize Among Strangers	6.17	6.38 / 6.04	11.7	.009	.02
Stranger Asking for Directions	4.69	5.08 / 4.44	40.5	.001	.03

*Upper mean represents U.S. sample; lower mean represents Chinese sample.

Attributions for Smiling Behavior Another motivation for this study was to examine whether there were cultural differences in the attributions or explanations for smiling behavior. It was posited that cultural differences should be reflected in attributions such as one's emotional state, the social appropriateness of the smiling behavior, one's modesty, the status of the other person in the social episode, and the other person's face or social esteem. Table 4 presents a summary of the cultural differences in these five attributions across the nine situations.

Table 4
Cultural Differences on the Situational Attributes

	Emotional State			Socially Approp.			My Modesty			Other's Status			Face of Other		
	Mean	F	p	Mean	F	p	Mean	F	p	Mean	F	p	Mean	F	p
1. Greeting Professor in Class	2.94*	10.0	.001	3.03	.1	n.s.	2.33	5.8	.02	2.61	5.3	.02	3.02	2.1	n.s.
	2.64*			3.06			2.54			2.38			3.16		
2. Disliked Person Embarrasses Self	2.88	26.1	.001	2.74	2.6	n.s.	2.32	.7	n.s.	2.13	9.7	.003	2.70	7.0	.008
	2.34			2.91			2.24			1.84			2.98		
3. Friend Tells Unfunny Joke	2.50	4.1	.05	2.99	.2	n.s.	2.28	.4	n.s.	2.41	21.6	.001	3.01	2.7	n.s.
	2.29			3.03			2.34			1.96			3.05		

Situation	US/CN	Mean	F	p	Mean	F	p	Mean	F	p	Mean	F	p	Mean	F	p
4. Asking Stranger for Directions	US	2.52	24.3	.001	3.34	.0	n.s.	2.54	.9	n.s.	2.43	24.5	.001	2.99	.3	n.s.
	CN	2.03			3.38			2.64			1.92			3.05		
5. Receiving High Grade, but Friend Failed	US	2.57	3.9	.05	3.26	11.7	.004	2.90	.6	n.s.	2.47	18.0	.001	3.50	10.4	.001
	CN	2.36			2.94			2.98			2.02			3.22		
6. Getting Help from Professor	US	2.59	38.2	.001	3.33	8.5	.004	2.45	26.0	.001	3.35	20.3	.001	3.27	2.5	n.s.
	CN	1.96			3.09			2.94			2.91			3.12		
7. Getting Help from Friend	US	2.69	15.8	.001	2.92	.0	n.s.	2.36	35.1	.001	2.56	18.3	.001	3.00	.3	n.s.
	CN	2.26			2.91			2.92			2.12			3.05		
8. Winning a Prize Among Strangers	US	3.54	6.0	.01	3.42	18.6	.001	2.69	5.9	.02	2.64	32.4	.001	2.85	.0	n.s.
	CN	3.32			3.04			2.44			2.00			2.84		
9. Stranger Asks for Directions	US	2.60	6.2	.00	3.07	1.3	n.s.	2.33	.0	n.s.	2.33	8.0	.005	2.84	.1	n.s.
	CN	2.34			2.97			2.34			2.03			2.86		

*Upper mean represents U.S. sample; lower mean represents Chinese sample.

Emotional State. A MANOVA indicated a significant effect for culture on respondents' attributions of their smiling to the emotional state they may be feeling (F [9/399] = 7.4, p < .0001, Pillai's Trace = .14). Univariate ANOVAs revealed significant statistical differences for culture on emotional attributions in all nine situations. For all nine situations, U.S. respondents made greater attributions to their emotional states for their smiling behavior than did Chinese respondents. The three situations revealing the greatest attributional differences involved the respondent getting help from a professor (US mean = 2.70, China mean = 1.96, F = 15.8, p < .001, eta2 = .09), seeing a disliked person in an embarrassing situation (US mean = 2.88, China mean = 2.34, F = 26.1, p < .001, eta2 = .06), and asking a stranger for directions (US mean = 2.52, China mean = 2.03, F = 24.3, p < .001, eta2 = .06). Two of these situations involved receiving help from another (namely, higher status other or stranger), while one of the situations involved an embarrassing situation threatening the face of another.

Social Appropriateness. A MANOVA computed on the social appropriateness attributions revealed a significant cultural difference (F [9/400] = 5.1, p < .001, eta2 = .11). Univariate ANOVAs found significant cultural differences in social appropriateness attributions on three of the nine situations: winning a prize in front of strangers (US mean = 3.42, China mean = 3.04, F = 18.6, p < .001, eta2 = .04), receiving a high grade on a test which a friend had failed (US mean = 3.26, China mean = 2.94, F = 11.7, p < .004, eta2 = .03), and getting help on a class assignment from a professor (US mean = 3.33, China mean = 3.09, F = 8.5, p < .004, eta2 = .02). In all three of these situations, the US respondents felt that it was more socially appropriate to engage in smiling behavior in these three situations. In two of the situations, US respondents felt it appropriate to express smiling even when others in their presence may not be feeling happy or content.

Modesty. A MANOVA found a significant effect for culture on the attributions for smiling behavior due to the modesty of the respondent (F [9/399] = 9.0, $p < .001$, eta2 = .19). As can be seen in Table 4, univariate ANOVAs indicated significant cultural differences on four of the situations. US respondents noted a greater likelihood of making attributions to their modesty for their smiling behavior in one situation: smiling after winning a prize among strangers (US mean = 2.69, China mean = 2.44, F = 5.9, $p < .02$, eta2 = .02). Chinese respondents noted a greater likelihood of making attributions to their modesty for getting help from a friend (US mean = 2.36, China mean = 2.92, F = 35.1, $p < .001$, eta2 = .06), getting help on a class assignment from a professor (US mean = 2.45, China mean = 2.94, F = 26.0, $p < .001$, eta2 = .06), and greeting a professor in class (US mean = 2.33, China mean = 2.54, F = 5.8, $p < .02$, eta2 = .02). In these latter situations, it would seem that modesty plays a greater role in deciding whether or not to smile in situations where the Chinese respondents receive help (either from a friend or higher status other) than it does for US respondents.

Other Person's Status. It was conjectured that since the Chinese tends to be more status conscious than the Americans, the other person's status would influence the attributions for Chinese respondents' decisions on smiling more so than for US respondents. A MANOVA indicated that there was a significant effect for culture on the attributions due to other person's status (F [9/399] = 5.6, $p < .001$, Pillai's Trace = .11). As presented in Table 4, univariate ANOVAs found significant differences for culture on attributions due to other's status on all nine situations. However, contrary to our expectations, US respondents indicated a greater likelihood for making these attributions than did the Chinese respondents. The three situations reflecting the greatest cultural differences were: winning a prize among strangers (US mean = 2.64, China mean = 2.00, F = 32.4, $p < .001$, eta2 = .07), asking a stranger for directions (US mean = 2.43, China mean = 1.92, F = 24.5, $p < .001$, eta2 = .06), listening to a friend's unfunny joke (US mean = 2.41, China mean = 1.96, F = 21.6, $p < .001$, eta2 = .05), and getting help from a professor (US mean = 3.35, China mean = 2.91, F = 20.3, $p < .001$, eta2 = .13). From these results, it would appear that US respondents are more influenced by other's status when making attributions than are Chinese respondents.

Other's Face or Esteem. A MANOVA of these data found that there was a significant effect of culture on respondents' attributions based on other's face when making decisions about smiling behavior (F [9/371] = 3.9, $p < .01$, Pillai's Trace = .09). Univariate ANOVAs found significant cultural differences in only two of the situations: receiving a high grade on a test that a friend had failed (US mean = 3.50, China mean = 3.22, F = 10.4, $p < .001$, eta2 = .04) and smiling when a disliked person embarrasses self (US mean = 2.70, China mean = 2.98, F = 7.0, p < .008, eta2 = .02). In the former situation, US respondents reported a greater likelihood for making attributions on the basis of other's face, while in the latter situation, Chinese respondents reported a greater likelihood for making attributions on the basis of other's face. The former situation involves possible loss of face for a friend, while the latter involves loss of face for a disliked acquaintance.

Cultural Variables and Smiling Behavior Another purpose of the present research was to determine the relevance of the cultural variables of individualism, collectivism, and power distance in predicting smiling likelihood and attributions. Reliability analyses determined that adequate levels of inter-item reliability were attained for the three measures of cultural variability (individualism α = .73, collectivism α = .77, and power distance α = .75). Given satisfactory levels of inter-item reliability, mean summed scores were computed for the three measures, such that the larger the value of the measure, the more the trait purported to be measured. These three measures were then correlated with the respondents' likelihood for smiling and their attributions for smiling across the nine situations.

The correlational analyses found that the three cultural variables were significantly and negatively correlated to culture (as measured US = 1 and China = 2), suggesting US respondents reported greater individualism (r = -.51), collectivism (r = -.17), and power distance (r = -.37). While the correlation with individualism was expected, the latter two correlations were not. One explanation for the unexpected results may lie in the nature of the two samples, namely, the US sample was disproportionately female and tended to be liberal arts majors, while the Chinese sample was disproportionately male and tended to be engineering majors.

In terms of the respondents' likelihood for smiling, only collectivism was significantly correlated (r = .15), suggesting that higher levels of collectivism were associated with a greater likelihood to smile. Further, collectivism was significantly and positively correlated with all five attributions for smiling, suggesting that greater collectivism seems to be associated with greater concern for both internal and social motivations for smiling behavior. The individualism measure was significantly and positively correlated with two types of attributions: emotional attributions and attributions based on other's status. Finally, the power distance measure was significantly and positively correlated with only one type of attribution, namely, other's status.

Correlations were also calculated across the nine situations between the likelihood of smiling and the respondents' attributions for smiling behavior. Three significant and positive correlations were found: emotional attributions (r = .26), social appropriateness attributions (r = .19), and other's status attributions (r = .14). These results suggest that one's emotional state, the social appropriateness of the situation, and the status differential among communicators is most salient in predicting one's decision to smile or not.

DISCUSSION

The present study contributed to our knowledge of smiling behavior in the United States and China. The results suggest that both cultural and situational factors influence the likelihood of smiling behavior and the attributions individuals make regarding their decisions whether to smile or not. Some support was found for each of the four motivating hypotheses for this study.

First, evidence was discerned regarding the situational variability of individuals' likelihood for smiling behavior. For both Chinese and U.S. cultures, it was deemed more appropriate for individuals to engage in smiling when winning a prize, requesting or providing help, and greeting a higher status individual. Further, it was deemed less appropriate for individuals to engage in smiling when someone is embarrassed (even if the embarrassed other is disliked) or when the other person may be unhappy or saddened by the expression of smiling. It would appear that display rules exist such that if the expression of smiling or happiness occurs at the cost of the other, it would be socially inappropriate to engage in such expression. This is consistent with research on display rules (Ekman, 1972) and facework (Ting-Toomey et al., 1991).

Second, the results of this study found that cultural differences in the likelihood for the expression of smiling both across situations and in most of the nine individual situations. Across all the situations, there was a tendency for Chinese respondents to report that they would engage in less smiling than their U.S. counterparts. This result is consistent with considerable scholarship that suggests Chinese culture is more collectivistic (Hofstede, 1980), indirect (Gudykunst & Ting-Toomey, 1988b), and restrained in social situations (Buck, Losow, Murphy, & Costanzo, 1992). The differences between Chinese and U.S. respondents' likelihood for smiling was accentuated in certain situations, especially when those situations involved the loss of face for the other person, an out-group stranger, or a higher status person. These greater differences reflect more collectivistic and power distant orientations.

Third, the findings of this study supported our hypothesis that cultural differences would also be found in the attributions respondents made for their decisions regarding the expression of smiling. The reported attributions were fairly consistent with the cultural orientations reflected in Chinese and U.S. cultures. More specifically, there was a strong tendency for U.S. respondents to emphasize attributions based on internal emotions for their reasons for smiling, with culture accounting for 24% of the variance in emotional attributions. This finding is consistent with the individualistic orientation of U.S. culture. Also, there was a tendency for Chinese respondents to emphasize attributions based on the modesty and the face of the other person when explaining their decisions for their smiling behavior. These findings reflect the more collectivistic orientation of Chinese culture. The unexpected results from the attributional analyses were in regards to social appropriateness and other person's status. It was originally believed that Chinese respondents would utilize these attributions more; the results disconfirmed this expectation. A number of explanations could be offered for the unexpected findings. One of the most plausible of the explanations may lie in the contextual nature of social appropriateness and relational status. It is possible that the Chinese and U.S. respondents perceived these two attributions differently. Further research needs to utilize more precise operationalizations of these constructs.

Fourth, only tentative support was found in regards to our last hypothesis that predicted associations between the cultural variables of individualism, collectivism, and power distance, and the measures of smiling likelihood and attributions. Most troublesome are the findings that our U.S. respondents were more collectivistic and had higher levels of power distance than our Chinese respondents. These results were inconsistent with our initial expectations. Two possible explanations could be forwarded for these unexpected results: flaws in the measures or biases in the sample. In terms of the former, it could be that trait-like measures for cultural variables are inappropriate for explaining individual behavior in specific situations. Certainly the theoretical research on self-construals (e.g., Markus & Kitayama, 1991; Kim, Hunter, Miyahara, Horvath, Bresnahan, & Yoon, 1996) lends support to this explanation. In terms of the latter explanation, there are a number of differences in the two samples that could confound cultural differences, e.g., the Chinese sample was disproportionately male, engineering students, and more urban than the U.S. sample. These demographic characteristics would facilitate less of a collectivistic and more of an individualistic orientation. Future research needs to attempt to exert greater control in sampling in order to attain sample cohorts that are more comparable on relevant demographic characteristics.

It is hoped that this research and future research that this study may stimulate will increase our cross-cultural understanding of the communication patterns in China and the United States. To the extent that we have greater understanding, we can minimize potential misunderstandings due to differences in verbal and nonverbal communication rules. With fewer misunderstandings between communicators, we will enhance the perceived communication competence of both communicators and build the bonds that tie us together.

References

Buck, R., Losow, J. I., Murphy, M. M., & Costanzo, P. (1992). Social facilitation and inhibition of emotional expression and communication. *Journal of Personality and*

Social Psychology, 63, 962-968.

Ekman, P. (1972). Universal and cultural differences in facial expression of emotion. In J. R. Cole, (Ed.), *Nebraska symposium on motivation* (pp. 207-283). Lincoln: University of Nebraska Press.

Ekman, P., & Friesen, W. V. (1969). Nonverbal leakage and cues to deception. *Psychiatry, 32*, 88-106.

Ericsson, K. A., & Simmon, H. A. (1980). Verbal reports as data. *Psychological Review, 87*, 215-251.

Friesen, W. V. (1972). *Cultural differences in facial expressions in a social situation: An experimental test of the concept of display rules*. Unpublished doctoral dissertation, University of California, San Francisco.

Frijda, N. H. (1986). *The emotions*. New York: University of Cambridge Press.

Gudykunst, W. B. (1991). *Bridging differences*. Newbury Park, CA: Sage.

Gudykunst, W. B., & Kim, Y. Y. (2003). *Communicating with strangers: An approach to intercultural communication* (4th ed.). New York: McGraw-Hill.

Gudykunst, W. B., Matsumoto, Y., Ting-Toomey, S. Nishida, T., Kim, K. S., & Heyman, S. (1996). The influence of cultural individualism-collectivism, self construals, and individual values on communication styles across cultures. *Human Communication Research, 22*, 510-543.

Gudykunst, W. B., & Ting-Toomey, S. (1988a). Culture and affective communication. *American Behavioral Scientist, 31*, 384-400.

Gudykunst, W. B., & Ting-Toomey, S. (1988b). *Culture and interpersonal communication*. Newbury Park, CA: Sage.

Hample, D. (1984). On the use of self-reports. *Journal of the American Forensic Association, 20*, 140-153.

Hofstede, G. (1980). *Culture's consequences*. Beverly Hills, CA: Sage.

Izard, C. E. (1971). *The face of emotion*. New York: Appleton-Century-Crofts.

Kim, M. S., Hunter, J. E., Miyahara, A., Horvath, A., Bresnahan, M., & Yoon, H. (1996). Individual- vs. cultural-level dimensions of individualism and collectivism: Effects on preferred conversational styles. *Communication Monographs, 63*, 28-49.

Langer, E. (1978). Rethinking the role of thought in social interaction. In H. Harvey, W. Ickes, & R. Kidd, (Eds.), *New directions in attribution research* (pp. 35-58). Hillsdale, NJ: Erlbaum.

Markus, H., & Kitayama, S. (1991). Culture and the self: Implications for cognition, emotion, and motivation. *Psychological Review, 2*, 224-253.

Matsumoto, D. (1989). Cultural influences on the perception of emotion. *Journal of Cross-Cultural Psychology, 20*, 92-105.

Matsumoto, D. (1991). Cultural influences on facial expressions of emotion.

Southern Communication Journal, 56, 128-137.

Matsumoto, D., Kudoh, T., Scherer, K. R., & Wallbott, H. G. (1988). Antecedents of and reactions to emotions in the U.S. and Japan. *Journal of Cross-Cultural Psychology, 19,* 267-286.

Nisbett, R. E., & Wilson, T. D. (1977). The halo effect: Evidence for unconscious alteration of judgments. *Journal of Personality and Social Psychology, 35,* 250-256.

Okabe, R. (1983). Cultural assumptions of east and west. In W. B. Gudykunst, (Ed.), *Intercultural communication theory* (pp. 21-44). Newbury Park, CA: Sage.

Scherer, K. R., Wallbott, H. G., Matsumoto, D., & Kudoh, T. (1988). Emotional experience in cultural context: A comparison between Europe, Japan, and the United States. In K. R. Scherer, (Ed.), *Facets of emotion.* Hillsdale, NJ: Lawrence Erlbaum.

Ting-Toomey, S., Gao, G., Trubisky, P., Yang, Z., Kim, H. S., Lin, S. L., & Nishida, T. (1991). Culture, face maintenance, and styles of handling interpersonal conflict: A study in five cultures. *International Journal of Conflict Management, 2,* 275-296.

Triandis, H. C. (1972). *The analysis of subjective culture.* New York: Wiley.

Triandis, H. C. (1994). *Culture and social behavior.* New York: McGraw-Hill.

Triandis, H. C., Bontempo, R., Villareal, M. J., Asai, M., & Lucca, N. (1988). Individualism and collectivism: Cross-cultural perspectives on self-ingroup relationships. *Journal of Personality and Social Psychology, 54,* 323-338.

Wheeler, L., Reis, H. T., & Bond, M. H. (1989). Collectivism-individualism in everyday social life: The middle kingdom and the melting pot. *Journal of Personality and Social Psychology, 57,* 79-86.

Wallbott, H. G., & Scherer, K. R. (1986). How universal and specific is emotional experience? Evidence from 27 countries on five continents. *Social Science Information, 25,* 763-795.

Aspects of intercultural nonverbal communicative competence

Bates L. Hoffer   Trinity University, USA

Abstract

Intercultural communication competence includes language competence in a shared language and competence in the nonverbal system (NVS) that accompanies the verbal language. Native speakers of a language have some difficulty in understanding the NVC of people from other areas of their own country and nonnative speakers often have little understanding of the other language's NVC. Three areas of study within NVS that are included below are facial expressions and gestures, socializers, and nonverbal expressions in prose. Facial expressions are often misread across cultures and the communication is thereby less complete. Gestures across cultures may not be interpreted as meaningful at all or be interpreted incompletely or wrongly, resulting in faulty or erroneous communication. Socializers are those movement and sounds that accompany a verbal interaction and signal such things as "I'm paying attention," "It's your turn to speak," and so on. Communication becomes quite difficult when the other person uses his own socializers instead of those that make conversation flow. Nonverbal actions reported in prose may have little or no meaning, even to one fluent in the other's language. In these cases the reader becomes confused or does not even realize the author is subtly communicating something to the reader.

The Fairbanks[1] Rule: If you do not know a language well and you make an offensive gesture or other behavior, the other person will assume that you do not know any better and will tend to ignore the potentially offensive action.

If you know a language well and you make an offensive gesture or other behavior, the other person will assume that you did it on purpose and will most likely never forgive the offensive action.

---

1   Gordon Fairbanks, a long-time linguistics professor at Cornell University, was fluent in several languages.

Introduction

As suggested by the Fairbanks Rule, when dealing with the field of communication, a useful distinction is that between linguistic competence and communicative competence. In general, linguistic competence refers to the level of acquisition of a language in terms of its phonological system, its word formation system, its syntax, and its vocabulary. Communicative competence usually includes a wide range of other topics that accompany interpersonal communication such as paralanguage and the various topics listed under nonverbal communication. The study of communicative competence has progressed greatly in the last many decades. In addition, the study of communicative competence in the intercultural situation has made some progress, in some of the topics to be discussed later.

Three general topics in intercultural nonverbal communicative competence are outlined below. The first major section deals with some of the basics of **nonverbal communication and behavior**.[2] The second section deals with **socializers**, a term for the verbal / vocal / nonverbal behaviors that influence the channels of interpersonal communication across cultures. The third section deals with **nonverbal phrases** that are encountered in prose. Those interested in increasing their intercultural communicative competence need to learn at least the more frequent patterns of nonverbal behavior in the other culture.

Nonverbal Communication

The field of nonverbal communication is often divided for convenience into the areas of **facial expressions**, **gestures**, **gaze behavior**, **proxemics**, and **haptics**. Other areas than these exist, but the material in this section is limited to the first three of these topics.

Facial Expressions

Facial expressions are a vital part of intercultural communicative competence because the face is usually the first thing noticed when conversing with another person. Although people tend to think that interpreting someone else's facial expression is easy and natural, they need to learn of the various differences across cultures — even in the facial expressions exhibiting basic emotions. Research has shown that the interpretation of even the basic facial expressions in a different culture is often wrong. These misinterpretations may have a significant impact and lead to miscommunication or partial communication.

---

2   Several basic studies in nonverbal communication are listed in the References section.

Emotional expressions have received the most attention of all nonverbal behaviors. (Ekman 1982, Ekman & Friesen 1975; Hoffer 1991) One area of research deals with the basic number of expressions that carry emotion and another area deals with those expressions that may be universal across cultures. There is some agreement that the basic set of expressions that carry emotional meaning consists of: happiness, sadness, anger, fear, surprise, and disgust. Research in many cultures around the world has found these emotions expressed. Posed pictures of these expressions have been tested on people of the same culture as the one pictured. The accuracy rates vary somewhat, but the chart below which gives the percentages of accuracy indicates a general awareness of the emotion. Also on the chart is the set of statistics for the same posed expressions being tested on people of a much different culture.

	Same Culture	Different Culture
Happiness	100%	73%
Sadness	84	68
Anger	92	51
Fear	93	18
Surprise	86	27
Disgust	91	46

The second column represents the percentages of correct answers by college students in the U.S. who were viewing pictures of emotions being produced by people from New Guinea. The accuracy rate indicates that the expression is conveying information, but at a much lower accuracy rate than for pictures from the same culture. Posed pictures are used as one step in the research because they should be easier to recognize. If they prove difficult, spontaneous expressions that last only a short time would prove much more difficult. There is some evidence that training in awareness of facial expressions can increase the accuracy rate. Some early research reported an increase in accuracy of between 5 and 50 per cent or so. The current use of videos, CDs and other instructional media has improved this situation.

Similar research was done by using posed expressions which were first pre-tested for accuracy within one group and then tested on people from various cultures. The accuracy percentages on the Ekman & Friesen (1969) study are given on the chart below.

Group	Happiness	Sadness	Anger	Fear	Surprise	Disgust
U.S.	97%	73%	69%	88%	91%	82%
Argentinean	94	85	72	68	93	79
Brazilian	97	82	82	77	82	86
Chilean	90	90	76	78	88	85
Japanese	87	74	63	71	87	82

The low accuracy for Japanese — and the lower accuracy for Africans who were tested later — may be a result of less awareness of the emotions when viewing another culture or they may be a result of translation difficulties in constructing the test.

There is another important aspect to inaccurate awareness of expressions. The viewer may mistake Surprise for Disgust and misinterpret the other person's reaction to, for example, a new food or other item in the viewer's culture. The nonverbal communication may be taken as accurate and the miscommunication may cause difficulties in interpersonal interaction. This type of misreading or non-reading needs more research on specific pairs of cultures.

The study of cross-cultural recognition of basic facial expressions has been receiving much attention over the past few decades as interest in intercultural studies — especially intercultural communication — has grown. General attention has been drawn to the similarities and differences between cultures, including their nonverbal communication. The percentage of people with experience in other cultural settings has grown rapidly in the past 50 years. Jet travel, global TV coverage, and foreign films and TV programs are among the many ways people have "encountered" other cultures. They have seen both similar and dissimilar facial expressions and have reported a wide range of reactions. On the one hand, in some cases viewers report that they can see little difference in facial expressions. On the other hand, in some cases the viewers report bewilderment at their inability to understand the expressions. The research into the universals in facial expressions of emotion has been focussing on the defining characteristics of each expression. The following paragraph outlines some of the arguments and evidence for one such universals.

The "smile" may be used as an example to show how much we have learned over the past few decades about facial behavior and emotion. For many decades writers reported that "smiles" could be signs of joy, but they could also be used in situations where they mean contempt or incredulity or affection or so on. The word "smile," unfortunately, covers too many different facial expressions to be useful as a technical term. Ekman and Friesen (1975) distinguished many such smiling expressions which involve various different sets of muscles. If attention is only on the lip corners moving upwards, the research can go no further. By using close descriptions of facial muscle movements other than those that control the upward movement of the corners of the mouth, important distinctions can be made. Thus, there can be both muscle movements that are universal and other similar muscle movements that are used in different ways in various situations in different cultures.

Dual and Masked Expressions

Several researchers (e.g. Leathers 1986) have reported that facial expressions may show more than one emotion at a given moment. The facial muscles are sufficiently complex and independent for the discrete muscle patterns in different parts of the face to move in a pattern which presents the elements of two or more emotions. Some of these blended or **Dual Expressions** are observable even in still photographs. In the research, the combination of "Anger and Determination" seems to be the most recognizable of the dual expressions. Others that are less recognizable are "Anger and Surprise" and "Sadness and Determination." The level of complexity of the research into dual expressions dictates caution in drawing more than general conclusions.

The study of **Masked expressions** is to some extent related to the study of deceptive expressions. When a person attempts to mask a spontaneous expression such as Disgust so that an observer does not notice the basic expression, that person may use a smile or attempt to produce a different expression such as Interest. Native speakers seem to be much more accurate in interpreting the presence of masked expressions. Nonnative speakers are seldom accurate at such interpretation. For one example, some years ago there was a picture in many papers of an American diplomat talking with an Asian diplomat. The American had a slight smile on his face, but the rest of his face led 100% of a test group of my American students to interpret the smile as a mask for very strong anger. When the same picture was shown to an Asian test group, 0% perceived the underlying expression of anger.

Display Rules

The basic facial expressions of emotion listed above are universal to the human species, but each culture develops "display rules" which govern the acceptable facial expressions that may be used ("**displayed**") on particular occasions. For example, in some cultures the Happiness facial expression would be considered rude and offensive at a wake or a funeral, but in other cultures a wake or a funeral is treated as a less solemn time. For another example, an expression of Disgust is considered highly offensive when offered a particular food by your host. Thus, the display rules suggest a smile and a statement such as "Thank you. I'm not very hungry." Often some of these display rules are learned as part of the general etiquette of a group.

Gestures

The study of gestures ranges from body movements which intentionally convey precise information to other gestures which convey general information — intentionally or not — to body movements which can be interpreted by a trained observer such as a psychologist. These gestures carry their own communication or add information to the verbal communication. The study of gestures in the other culture should be an integral part of the study of the other language. This section is primarily concerned with two categories of gestures which have been studied for many but not all of the major cultural groups of the world: emblems and illustrators.

Emblems

Emblems are gestures that carry their own meaning. The use of body movement to convey information occurs in any situation where communication might be necessary. In a crowded and noisy room, a person on the far side of the room may use a hand signal that means "come here." An observer who is unsure of the intended meaning of the signal may point to his chest (or nose or whatever body part means "I" in that culture). The signaler may then use a signal such as pointing up with the index finger and quickly pointing it at the observer to mean "you got it!" ("Correct"). Here emblematic body movements have replaced a verbal exchange with precisely the same meaning. ("Come here." "Do you mean me?" "Yes.") Other examples include tapping the side of the forehead with the extended index finger to signal "smart" and a gesture with the thumb and forefinger forming an "O", meaning "OK." "OK" is an emblem which has become so widely used around the world that it is part of English as an International Language.

The emblems presented below which are used in American English vary in their understandability. Many are perceived correctly by close to 100 per cent of the observers, others by less. None of the examples here was misunderstood by more than 10 per cent of those tested. When people from a different culture are asked to interpret these gestures, the success ratio is lower to much lower. Of more importance are those that a person from the other culture is sure that his interpretation is right but in reality it is wrong.

Emblem Meaning	*Description of Gesture*
Sit down beside me	Patting the seat beside self
Be silent, hush	Upright index finger placed before lips
Come here	Upright fingers or index finger alone, palm toward self, moved back and forth toward self
Wait; hold it	Open palm toward observer
I warn you	Fist with extended index finger moved slowly up and down with palm toward side
Get lost	Extended fingers pointing downward, back of hand toward observer, flipped up a few times
Be calm	Open palms with back of hand up, hands upward at 45 degrees toward observer, moved forward and back slowly a few times

Follow me	Extended hand, palm forward, arm downward and behind hip, moved forward and backward a few times
Stop	Flat hand, palm outward and upright, moved toward observer and stopped abruptly.
Go the other way	Hand out, palm to side desired, moved in semicircle outward a few times
Hurry; quickly!	Flat palms upwards and extended, moved up and down rapidly
Crazy	Index finger pointed at forehead and moved in a circle
I don't know	Flat palms upward, held near shoulders with fingers pointing to the left and right
I promise	Index finger makes a cross over heart

As a different kind of example, there is a set of emblems used in English which deal with numbers. These emblems are those which may be used for numbers above ten. For example, 37 would have three emblems for ten and one for seven, all done in rapid sequence. Ten is indicated by palms toward observer, fingers upward and slightly separated, near shoulder level. The hands are then closed to a fist and reopened immediately for the next ten. The final seven is usually signaled by one hand open and the other with only the index and middle finger extended. Generally the thumb is the last digit to be extended to indicate either five, if one hand, or ten if both. When this gestural behavior has been tested on non-native speakers of English without special training in emblems, those tested have no idea what the gestures mean.

Incidentally, the American pattern of signaling "one" with the index finger is a strong one. In most cases even if the thumb is not curled into the palm, the index finger still means "one." For an example, some people may signal "seven" with the fingers of one hand extended and the index, middle, and thumb of the other hand extended. In Europe and other places where the thumb is the first digit to be counted, this variation of the American gesture is understood as "8." In the reverse situation, the European may interpret the gesture with only the American's index finger extended as "2." In restaurants, such misinterpretations have led to many miscommunications on drink or food orders.

The full set of emblems for each culture is still under investigation by several researchers. The examples above are in general use. Often small groups, such as those at a college, will create their own emblems known only to that group. Emblems may then be borrowed in the same dialect forms spread from one group to another. Some may eventually enter the general emblem vocabulary of the language group. An example might be the emblem from Hawaii which means something like "everything's OK." In this emblem, only the thumb and the little finger are extended and the hand is rotated clockwise and back a few times. This emblem spread to California and then was used in television shows set in Hawaii and California. It seems to have spread via television to the whole U.S.

Emblems in Other Languages

Some of the emblems used in other languages are similar enough to those used in American English to be misunderstood by Americans as if the emblem were an American one. One of the emblems for "hello" in parts of Italy has the palm up, fingers extended, and the fingers moved up and down. Americans tend to interpret the gesture as their "come here" and some report that the Italians are very friendly since they always want the Americans to come over and talk. In parts of Greece, the movements of the head which are emblems for "yes" and "no" are the opposite to American ones. In this case, the possible misunderstanding is that of completely opposite meaning.

The material on emblems across cultures contains an example which fits this category. An emblem for "come back" in Japan has the hand near the side of the head, palm down, and fingers and hand moved up and down. To an American, that gesture is part of the greeting / parting ritual, either "hello" or "goodbye." There are elaborate misunderstandings caused by this similarity. Foreign tourists may be signaled by a tour bus driver that the bus is about to leave. The tourist interprets the emblem as a "hello," as a friendly gesture of social contact. He may then use the "hello" signal which is also used for "goodbye." The bus driver thinks the tourist wants to remain at the location. When the bus leaves, the tourist thinks that he has been abandoned. Both people think total communication was achieved and that the other person is behaving strangely. In actuality, both completely misunderstood the other because of the similarity of the emblems used.

The misunderstanding of emblems can have even more serious consequences. In one reported case near an American **military** base in South **Korea**, two young adults began playing one evening too close to the fortified fence. The area near the fence was totally off-limits to any unauthorized person. The American sentries, who knew no **Korean**, tried to signal the two to leave by using the "Get lost / go away" emblem as noted above. They did not know that the gesture was essentially identical to the **Korean** emblem for "come here." When the two approached the fence and would not stop after repeated gestures, they were shot.

The more important emblems for a language should always be part of any language education program. While the nonverbal system of a foreign language was rather poorly represented in the language textbooks of several decades ago, the current language textbooks usually contain at least the most basic parts of the nonverbal communication system.

Display Rules

The first step in learning about emblems in a language is that of being acquainted with the meaning of the most frequently used ones. Later in the process, the learner must learn the conditions under which an emblem is used. Those conditions define the display rules for the emblems in the language. Emblems and their use may vary with age, sex, ethnic background, social class, and so on. Some will be appropriate only in certain situations, such as in Church, and only if used by those in certain roles, such as the priest or preacher. One of the recurring problems in language learning is applicable to both emblems and illustrators. Learners whose language teachers are of the opposite sex may unconsciously — or consciously — imitate the gestures of the teacher when using the language later. In some cases the gestures are only appropriate to one sex and the native speaker's reaction to the inappropriate behavior may range from polite ignoring through humor to suspicions of the speaker's sexual orientation.

For an example of the restriction on the use of emblems, the "shame on you" gesture may be used. In this case the signaler extends one index finger toward the other person, extends the other index finger and brushes it a few times from the base of the opposite index finger toward the other person, Ordinarily it is used to a youngster, although it may be used elsewhere in a humorous manner. It is inappropriate in any situation which is formal. For another example, there is an American emblem which seems limited to younger women: "heartthrob" or "he's a heartthrob." The fist is placed over the heart and lightly thumped against the chest as if the heart were beating faster. In this case "heartthrob" means that the young man or rock star or so on is attractive. A final example is the gesture above labeled "no, no" that should only be used by someone in authority, such as a parent, teacher, moderator, or so on. The extended index finger, pointed up, is moved slowly from side to side.

The display rules for emblems in a culture are still under investigation. For the language learner, there are further and often important restrictions which may apply to nonnatives communicating in a language. For example, in the US very close friends or group members can use nasty language and crude gestures with each other, but no outsider would be allowed to do the same. Friends may put their hands on the other person's arm or shoulder or put their arm around the other person's shoulder, but non-group members should completely avoid such behaviors.

Illustrators

The use of the hands during conversation is so frequent in some cultures that there is a saying that Sicilians, for example, cannot talk if their hands are tied. Not all the hand movements are substitutes for words or phrases. Those body movements which are not emblems and which accompany speech are defined as **Illustrators**. Different cultures may have different types of illustrators, but those which seem well established in American English are presented below.

Types of Illustrators

Illustrators are movements which are intimately tied to the content and / or flow of speech. Observation of speakers from various backgrounds usually shows that the speakers move their hands and heads at some points in their conversation. Closer study shows that some of those movements may relate directly to what is being said or correlate with the flow or rhythm of the conversations. Different groups use different types of movements and with different frequencies. Listeners from a different culture are usually not familiar with the illustrators of the other culture and see only "meaningless" movements. They then may comment on the many "strange" hand motions made by the speaker. When they listen within their own culture, they do not usually take any special notice of a speaker's illustrators because the illustrators are a normal part of their spoken communication.

The inventory of types of illustrators which currently includes all those encountered in cultures of the world is the subject of this section. The list which follows included the illustrators, a brief definition, and a short example of each.

Deictics. Movements that point to referent. Deictics may have developed from reaching movements to movements which identified the object wanted or being spoken of. Most cultures use the fingers, hands, and / or arms for deictic movements, but other patterns have been found. Among some Native American groups, the chin is used to point. In America, for example, display rules may prohibit pointing with the fingers or hands in formal occasions, so that the elbow, shoulder, or head is moved toward the referent. Americans point to their chest when they mean "I" but other cultures point to their nose or face.

Batons. Movements that accent a particular word. Even as the voice can be changed in terms of loudness or pitch to call attention to a particular word, movements may provide the accent. Various movements have been observed which act as batons, such as a nod of the head or a shake of the fist or a widening of the eyes.

Spatials. Movements that depict a spatial relationship. These illustrators usually involve the hands or arms. The hands can be held apart to illustrate the distance between objects. The hands may also move to different locations in the air as if showing the observer places on a map.

Pictographs. Movements that draw the shape of the referent in the air. These illustrators usually involve the hands, which trace in the air the outline of the object under discussion. The hand or hands draw a circle in the air for "ball", for example, or draw an upright rectangle for "refrigerator."

Kinetographs. Movements that depict a bodily action or a nonhuman action. A common example of this illustrator is used by children when they use their fingers to depict a walking action. Another frequent example is the use of the hands and fingers in the depiction of the jumping of a rabbit or kangaroo.

Rhythmics. Movements that depict the rhythm or spacing of an event. The head or hands may be moved at the same time interval being discussed, as with the frequency with which a telephone busy signal occurs when that is the subject of the conversation.

Underliners. Movements that emphasize a phrase, clause, sentence or group of sentences. Batons seem to be learned at a fairly early age, whereas underliners seem to be acquired as one of the last illustrators used by a person. Movements of the body, such as the hands, may continue for as long as a verbal sequence is being produced. For example, the hands may depict a written underline by tracing a line in the air as if across a page. The fingers, usually the index and middle on both hands, may wiggle up and down to signal quotation marks around something being said.

Ideographs. Movements that sketch the path or direction of thought. An example here is one that treats past time as if physically behind the speaker and the future in front. "Yesterday" may be accompanied by a gesture pointing backward over the shoulder. Such a gesture is meaningless to those in whose culture there is no concept similar to past being "back" and future being "forward". (Hoffer & Koo 1994)

Editers. Movements that "erase" the preceding word or words so that a replacement can be used. For example, just after a person mispronounces a word he may briefly shake his head and perhaps close his eyes before pronouncing the word correctly. Another example of editer — if a rare one — occurs when the speaker lifts his hand and "wipes" it left and right as if erasing a blackboard.

Serious misunderstandings can occur when a simultaneous translator does not know the Editer illustrators. A famous example occurred years ago when Richard Nixon was President of the US. His press secretary was asked about Nixon's awareness of the cause of some event. The press secretary said, "The president was ignorant, [editer illustrator here] was unaware of that cause." The press secretary had realized that "ignorant" might be misunderstood as ""dumb, stupid" rather than the intended "unaware." Thus he "edited" the "ignorant" and replaced it with "unaware." The translator did not know the editer illustrator and translated the sequence into something like "the President was stupid and unaware of the cause." Needless to say, the international reaction was strongly negative. This example shows that even top level interpreters of the language need to know the nonverbal communication features of the other language as well.

Gaze Behavior

Only two of the possible topics under this heading will be mentioned in this section. First is the reaction to **staring**. Children in the US are taught not to stare at another person. However, the display rule differs by area of the country. That is, in some areas a person may stare toward a second person as long as the second person is further than a certain distance away. In fact, that distance may be as short as 20 feet or so. In other parts of the country, 20 feet is still considered far too close for staring.

An example will illustrate the "culture shock" that someone might have in his own culture when confronted with the varying display rules. A female sociology professor from downtown New York City took a position in a major Southwestern US city. She began complaining about the aggression, the rudeness, and so on of the local people. She could be filling her car with gasoline, look up and see one or two men inside the store or gasoline station looking at her fixedly. She got so upset at times that she raised the gasoline nozzle and shook it at them. In their Gaze Behavior pattern, she was far outside the "no staring" zone. Although she had studied these differences in behavior across the US, she was unable to overcome the cultural differences that were causing her anguish, broke her contract with the university and retreated to the streets of New York City. Display rules can be known, but living with them might prove difficult.

The second topic in Gaze Behavior is that of eye behavior in conversation. (Leathers 1986; Samovar & Porter 1991) In one major pattern in a dyadic conversation in general US English, the speaker looks away from the addressee, makes brief eye contact every few to several seconds, and at the end of his turn makes and maintains eye contact. The addressee looks toward the speaker's eyes or face, with brief looks away, until his turn. There are several variations of this scheme, up to and including the almost complete reversal of roles. For example, in one Black pattern, the speaker looks at the addressee who avoids most eye contact. In the intercultural situation, the pattern may interfere with ease of communication. The speaker of the first pattern looks toward a potential addressee of the second pattern and waits for the latter to make eye contact. That eye contact is the signal for the first speaker to begin. However, the second person is waiting for the first person to speak. If the second looks at the first person, it could signal that the second person should begin the conversation. This reversal of patterns at times causes difficulty in, for example, inner city schools in the USA where there is a large concentration of Black students. White teachers usually have only the first pattern and they tend to misread the students' gaze behavior as lack of attention — even worse–lack of respect.

The Japanese have had a somewhat different conversational gaze behavior, at least through the older generation before so much foreign — especially Western — contact.

Little eye contact is made; often the gaze is downward or, if the head is oriented away from the other, outward. Japanese children were taught to look, if at all, at the nose / mouth area of the other. The contrast here is totally different from the general US English rule. The American system seems to be based on eye contact and the former on avoiding eye contact. The implications for semi- and mis-communication are rather clear. The American may be seen by the Japanese as trying to be very aggressive, powerful, assertive, and so on, all these being viewed quite negatively by the Japanese who value harmony in human relations. The Japanese are often misread by Americans as devious, or worse, since they avoid eye contact. The situation is sometimes worse when only a part of the basic rule is learned, as when a Japanese learning English is taught eye contact, then uses it without looking away often enough or at the appropriate times. This "staring" behavior is reported by Americans to be rather uncomfortable and causes some problems in intercultural communication.

Socializers

Socializers are a less studied part of the nonverbal communication system. Socializers are verbal / vocal / nonverbal features which "ease the friction" of social interaction. (Hoffer 1998). The study of these features cuts across verbal / nonverbal and across other types of distinctions. The topic is a component of the study of intercultural communicative competence. Mistakes in using socializers in an intercultural context can cause difficulties. For example, in a situation where a person expects the listener to acknowledge what he is saying with a nod or eye contact or a vocalization, the lack of any such feedback or an incorrect feedback often makes the speaker feel uncomfortable. There have been cases where people who have experienced this lack of feedback are so uncomfortable that they prefer to avoid talking to those of the other cultural background completely.

In this section, the topics within the study of socializers that are covered are: channel markers, channel turn-takers, channel interrupters, channel changers, channel closers.

Channel Markers — nonverbal / vocal / verbal indications that the addressee is listening, is keeping the channel of communication open.

In an American English conversation the addressee usually marks the listening channel every 5-10 seconds (varying with the pace of conversation) with a verbalization such as "yes" or "I see", a vocalization such as "uh huh", and / or a movement such as a head nod. This behavior is also called "back-channeling." Often this channel marking is done when the speaker makes eye contact, as if the eye contact is the cue for the channel marker. The channel marker may be more frequent if the speaker is speaking quickly and less frequent if the speaker is speaking slowly. There is a sort of conversational rhythm that is set up in such situations. In Japanese, by contrast, a channel marker such as the vocalization "ee ... ... ee" is usually made every 2 or 3 seconds on the phone and almost as frequently in face-to-face interaction. The cue may be timing or rhythm, but another hypothesis is that the markers occur at grammatical junctures in the speaker's discourse. Again the contrast between English channel marking and Japanese channel marking is total in terms of timing. (It may be of interest to note that American scholars who have recently returned from Japan often maintain the much more frequent markers for a few days, yet upon questioning are unaware of their behavior.) The American who uses Japanese channel markers at the slower American pace may be viewed by Japanese as aloof, uninterested in the subject or speaker, unable to understand, or so on. The Japanese who uses American markers at the Japanese pace, "uh huh . uh huh . . uh huh" rather than "uh huh ... ... uh huh ... ...uh huh," is often interpreted as wanting to take a turn to speak, since that is one way Americans signal they want to take a turn in the conversation. Hearing the frequent channel markers from the Japanese, the American stops to allow the Japanese to take a turn. The subsequent silence is quite awkward and leads to the feeling of uncomfortableness in the intercultural situation. Perhaps this is an example of partial or "semi"-communication; in the sense that the content is clear yet the communication is prematurely interrupted and full communication is not achieved.

Channel Turn-Takers

When a speaker who uses the first type of gaze behavior presented above is ready for the listener to take his turn as speaker, he usually looks at the listener as he stops talking. The listener, who has been looking at the speaker, then begins talking as he turns away.

This turn-taking behavior may be mis-used in various ways in the intercultural situation. In one type of misunderstanding, the non-native speaker looks at the listener for a few seconds as he is preparing his next utterance. The time gap may be long enough that the listener assumes it is his turn to speaker and takes over the channel of communication. This behavior may be misread as a rude interruption or other negative behavior.

Another type of misunderstanding may occur when the listener's channel markers are not a word or nod but are phrases or short comments on the speaker's words. It is not unusual for a listener in the USA to mark the channel by saying "Yes, I heard about that" or "That was too bad" or so on. The speaker may or may not pause for these longer channel markers. A non-native, however, may misread these long channel markers as turn-takers and stop talking. The resulting silence is a sign of the miscommunication and can be uncomfortable for those involved.

A subheading under Channel Turn-Taker is Channel Holder. A speaker who does wish to end his turn may use a variety of methods to "hold the floor", i.e. continue his turn. He may continue to look away from the listener. He may utter a prolonged "uuuuhhhhh" or prolong a word such as "theeeeeennnnn." He may put up his hand in a "wait" gesture. He may use a combination of these three. If the listener tries to take a turn anyway, the speaker may raise the volume of his voice and continue.

Language learners should learn the simple channel markers and their timing in the target language early in the acquisition process. The more complicated situations can be described in the later textbooks and some examples of skillful use of longer channel markers can be presented on video or CD.

Channel Interrupters

In causal conversations and in friendly conversations within a group, interruptions of a speaker may be frequent and expected. In other situations, interruptions of a speaker may be read as rude and offensive. Since interruptions may be offensive, young children in the USA are often taught to avoid interrupting adult conversations. (Hoffer & St. Clair 1981) The child may be taught that if he has a question, he may stand quietly alongside the conversationalists until he is recognized and "given the floor" to speak. If the reason for interrupting is sufficiently strong, the child may approach the adult from behind or the side and whisper the message into the adult's ear.

Adults acquire strategies for interrupting that do not cause negative reactions in most cases. A strategy may be as simple as saying, "Excuse me, but I'd like to ask you something about that." A nonverbal strategy uses a raised or slightly raised hand, perhaps with the index finger pointed up. The signal lets the speaker know that the gesturer would like to speak at the first opportunity.

The various strategies for use by natives and non-natives need careful research by scholars from both the native and the target culture. One goal of the research is a specification of the strategies that a non-native can use to cause no or little trouble when an interruption is appropriate or necessary. (Hoffer & Koo 1994)

Channel Changers

Channel Changers are verbal or nonverbal strategies to change the channel of conversation in terms of topic or formality or so on. The most direct way to change a topic is the verbal one of stating that the speaker is changing the topic, for example "But on another topic, ..." or "That reminds me of another thing." A simple strategy for a listener to change the topic at his turn is with a question about the new topic, for example "... Have you considered another possibility?" It may be considered rude to change the topic of conversation when the original speaker still has something to say about it. The question allows the speaker to continue the original topic, if he wishes, or to switch to the suggested topic. Changing the channel of conversation inappropriately is not necessarily a major problem. Even so, as noted several times above, a non-native that has communicative competence in Channel Changers causes the least amount of friction in the conversational flow.

Channel Closers

The strategies for closing a conversation are rather difficult to learn, at times even within one's own native language. Often in an intercultural conversation, the signals that a speaker uses to indicate a desire for closure are not read properly by the non-native. In such situations the conversation may become disjointed and uncomfortable. Even worse, the non-native may be misread as pushy, aggressive, insensitive or so on.

In a casual, friendly or informal situation, the strategies are rather simple. A simple announcement that the speaker must leave may be sufficient. In intercultural conversations where the speakers are worried about offending the other person, the strategies probably should be more subtle or should be more elaborate. For example, the simple announcement that one must leave could be embellished with apologies or excuses, as in "Well, I'm sorry to have to go, but perhaps we can continue this conversation some other time?"

When the Channel Closer used is less direct, the listener may not recognize it as a closer. One example (Hoffer 1976) that is treated in the literature follows. The situation is that a professor is talking to a graduate student from another culture.

Professor   "Well, I have a lot of papers to grade."
Student   "Yes. Professors are very busy, aren't they?"
[Pause]
Professor   "It's getting a bit late, isn't it?"
Student   "Yes, the sun goes down early these day."
[Pause]   [and so on.]

The professor was using Channel Closers and the student misread the situation as a meandering and perhaps friendly conversation. Eventually the professor stood up, gathered up his books and papers, and walked toward the door of the office. Only at that point did the student realize that the conversation was ending.

Years later the two met and discussed that awkward situation. The ex-student, then a professor at an American University, indicated that he too had wanted to conclude that conversation but was unable to do so without offending his professor.

Observing the nonverbal behavior of a speaker of another language after learning that person's nonverbal system helps to gain competence in understanding the meanings involved. Training can make use of native speakers, film, video, laser disk technology and student participation to help students make progress in their learning. Observation and experience are major elements in the acquisition of the nonnative nonverbal communication system.

Nonverbal Phrases in Prose

Authors are not able to use pictures in their novels to help the reader understand the nonverbal communication that they wish to convey. They must use appropriate descriptions of the facial expression or gesture or so on to try to convey what is going on between their characters. Interpreting the author's intention is sometimes difficult for those of the author's cultural background and more or even much more difficult for those of another cultural background. (Poyatos 1988; Hoffer 1993)

When descriptions of nonverbal behaviors are encountered in written form, many of them might refer to ordinary movements without special meanings. For example, "he pressed the tip of his index finger against the tip of his thumb" could refer, among other things, to pinching an object between those digits or it could refer to the emblem "OK." When these phrases are encountered in print, there is no visual context that helps to disambiguate the possible meanings of the description. A native speaking reader may, of course, make errors in interpreting the description in such a case, but usually he is accurate in interpretation as long as the writer is from the same culture.

Emblems in Prose

Since emblems are independently meaningful gestures, the description of the gesture is usually easy to understand. For example, "he held up three fingers" means the number "3." However, in some cases more information is needed to interpret the gesture. If the author does not give the extra information, even a native speaker may not be able to interpret properly.

For example, a character might "cross her fingers." That gesture has more than one meaning. It may mean "good luck," "we're close friends," or "I'm joking / deceiving / lying." One important item of information is the location where the gesture is made.

The gesture behind the speaker's back indicates that she is joking or lying. The action is to be seen by third parties in the situation so that they will know that the speaker is not telling the truth. The gesturer is also signaling to any others in the group to keep the addressee from learning that he is being tricked or fooled. Children may perform this action to eliminate or weaken the force of a lie, such as when they tell their parents that they were studying when they were not. Parents may ask to see their children's hands when they are speaking to make sure the children are not performing this gesture.

In the context of talking about friends, the gesture is made in full view of the addressee and most probably means that the speaker is indicating that the two friends are close friends, "buddies."

When someone is talking about an activity that will soon be done, the gesture probably means "good luck" in the activity.

Illustrators

Illustrators are the second major category of gestures. Illustrators are movements that accompany speech. Phrases may describe a physical activity occurring while a person is speaking, as in "He thrust his jaw at the car as he spoke."

There are various ways of pointing [a deictic illustrator] other than using a finger. This is an example that might also use "chin" in place of "jaw." The gesture is a pointing gesture. Here the phrase "at the car" is important, because the act of "thrusting out the jaw" alone can refer to being belligerent, as in "he stuck his jaw in my face." Other deictics with the meaning of "pointing" include "tilting one's head toward the car," and so on.

There are social variables at work in this category which involve display rules. For example, a child may point with the index finger in public, but as he matures he will learn that pointing with the finger or hand in public is discourteous. On formal occasions, a person may indicate direction with a slight turn of the head, a slight motion of the arm or shoulder or eyes or so on. In written form, if an adult in a formal situation points with the finger or hand, it is clear that a strong emotion has just overridden the usual display rules and that something very serious has occurred.

Gaze behavior

Gaze behavior refers to the face and eye movement in conversation. In some situations, speakers look more or less constantly at the other person when speaking and in other situations that look only sporadically at the other person. In some cultures, looking someone in the eye while conversing is considered positively, while in other cultures such behavior is somewhat offensive. In an American novel, if "he refused to meet her eyes," he is being devious or is otherwise negatively valued. In another example, "He narrowed his eyes when John said he didn't have the money," the meaning is that he got suspicious that something is wrong. Alternatively, a person described as having narrowed eyes while speaking might himself be a suspicious person.

Proxemics

Proxemics is the study of the relative distance between people when conversing.

Readers who are given no information about the relative position of the characters in the prose assume that the distance between them is "normal," that is, that the distance is appropriate to the situation, the relation between the people and so on. When the proxemics are mentioned, it often is the case that the writer is calling attention to a special situation or emotional state or so on. There are several common expressions which relate to proxemics.

One example of proxemics in prose is "She was very standoffish." This phrase refers to the fact that a person who is less friendly or so on than the situation warrants will stand further away than the normal distance. Here she is considered to be aloof, perhaps proud and arrogant, or perhaps only hesitant to engage in social interaction. The phrase is almost always a negative one.

Haptics

Haptics refers to touching behavior while conversing. An example is "She patted him on the head." Here the phrase may only refer to encouraging words or noises or smiles or so on. No touching or patting needs to take place. The phrase suggests a parenting-type behavior and the person who is being patted may be uncomfortable with the behavior.

This example illustrates that the writer may be indicating the meaning of the nonverbal phrase rather than its literal meaning. A speaker may also use a nonverbal phrase for its meaning without actually performing the gesture. For example, "I come on bended knee," indicates that I am pleading for something whether I have gotten down on one knee or not.

Examples in Prose

The rest of this section covers a few of the many examples of nonverbal behaviors that are commonly found in English prose. The organization of each entry follows the general pattern of:

Entry
Example sentence tested on several native speakers
Definition as understood by the native speakers
Description suggested by the native speakers

Entry:	Flared nostrils
Examples:	"When he heard what Sam said, his nostrils flared."
Definition:	To be or become angry.
Description:	One highly visible physical movement that occurs with the emotion of anger is a widening of the nostrils.

Entry:	Turn up one's nose
Examples:	"When she saw the janitor, she turned up her nose."
Definition:	To sneer at, feel contempt for, or feel much superior to.
Description:	The facial expression of contempt includes a tilting up of the head.

Entry:	Keep a straight face
Examples:	"Although the news was terrible, he managed to keep a straight face."
Definition:	To prevent any usual facial expression from occurring.
Description:	"Straight" in this phrase refers to lack of any facial movements, so that the face remains in its previous state. Showing no emotion when under stress is usually a positive trait.

Entry:	Put one's nose out of joint [also Knock, Slap, etc.]
Examples:	"Her snide comment about his infantile behavior put his nose completely out of joint."
Definition:	To cause one to become angry, upset, and/or resentful.
Description:	A physical blow to the face can break a person's nose, giving the appearance that the nose is "out of joint" even though the nose has no joints. The phrase refers to a verbal "blow" that offends the person's pride.

Entry:	To play it by ear
Examples:	"He doesn't know all the rules, but he can play it by ear."
Definition:	To act without a preconceived plan
Description:	The phrase originally referred to a musician who could not read music but who could play anything he could hear.
Note:	"Play by ear" is a phrase that also retains the original meaning as above.

Entry:	Have eyes in the back of the head
Examples:	"To be a good mother, sometimes you have to have eyes in the back of your head."
Definition:	To be very aware; omniscient
Description:	Exaggerated image of awareness; seemingly omnilateral vision as if one could see behind oneself.

Entry:	Money where your mouth is

Examples:	"If you really think the Steelers will win the World Series, then put your money where your mouth is."
Definition:	A challenge to back up one's talk with money
Description:	Has gambling origins, gamblers were challenged to back up their predictions with a monetary bet. No money was even put in or near the mouth. Now used extensively; not limited to gambling.
Entry:	Give lip service
Examples:	"President Clinton only gave only lip service to voters with his 'No Tax on the Middle Class' promise."
Definition:	To say something without meaning
Description:	Figuratively, the lips and mouth say the words, but there is not meaning attached to them.
Entry:	Beat one's gums
Examples:	"He tried to convince Mr. Pitman, but he was just beating his gums."
Definition:	To talk without effect
Description:	A very old, perhaps senile, person may have no teeth (hence, "gums") and may not make any sense or not have any impact when talking.
Entry:	Cut one's own throat
Examples:	"He tried to explain why he stole the car, but he only cut his own throat."
Definition:	To implicate oneself completely in a wrong or in a difficult position.
Description:	This act of suicide is metaphorically extended to mean that one has convicted himself through his own words or actions.
Entry:	Ram something down someone's throat
Examples:	"He respected the woman's religious beliefs, but did not like having them rammed down his throat."
Definition:	To force an idea or concept on someone
Description:	Exaggeration of the idea of force-feeding one's ideas in an imposing, stifling manner as if forcing that person to swallow something they did not want to consume.
Entry:	Nose will grow
Examples:	"The politician's nose grew ten inches during the campaign."
Definition:	To lie.

Description: In the children's classic "Pinocchio," the puppet who becomes a real boy has a nose which grows longer each time he lies.

Entry: Catch it in the neck
Examples: "Steve thought no one knew he had ruined his shirt, but when his mother came home he caught it in the neck."
Definition: To bear the brunt of the punishment; to be punished severely.
Description: In long past centuries, the major punishment was having your head cut off.

Entry: Throw up one's hands
Examples: "After ten tries to use his new computer, Greg threw up his hands."
Definition: To surrender, give up, stop trying.
Description: Holding up one's hands indicates one has no weapon, thus the gesture means "surrendering". In general usage, "throwing" up one's hands is an emotional act of giving up, as if exasperated by failure.

Note again that in this example as in most others, Greg may not have made any physical gesture when he gave up his attempt to use the computer.

Conclusion

The research to date on **Nonverbal Communication**, **Socializers**, and **Nonverbal Phrases in Prose** has produced some interesting results and many of the results have been applied in the teaching of communicative competence. In terms of intercultural communicative competence, however, the research is more difficult, both because of the subtleties of intercultural communication and because of the numbers of pairs of languages that need to be studied. As more scholars across cultures collaborate on research and as their results enter the textbooks and the language learning process, better intercultural communication will be achieved. The new publications on intercultural communication that have appeared over the last few years provide avenues for publication of research that is directly useful for the language and culture learner. The various conferences around the world that bring together scholars of different cultures to share information and plan joint research are a good sign that great progress will be made over the next few decades in the area of intercultural communicative competence.

References

Birdwhistell, R. (1970). *Kinesics and context*. Philadelphia PA: University of Pennsylvania Press.

Ekman, P. (1982). *Emotion in the human face*. New York NY: Cambridge University Press.

Ekman, P. & Friesen, W. (1969). The Repertoire of Nonverbal Behavior: Categories, origins, usage, and coding. *Semiotica, 1*, 49- 98.

Ekman, P. & W. Friesen (1975). *Unmasking the human face*. Englewood Cliffs NJ: Prentice-Hall.

Gudykunst, W. (1993). (Ed.) *Communication in Japan and the United States*. Albany NY: State University of New York.

Gudykunst, W. & Kim, Y. (1992). *Communicating with strangers: An approach to intercultural communication*. New York NY: McGraw-Hill.

Hoffer, B. (1998). (Mis-) Communication across Cultures. In B. Hoffer & J. Koo. (Eds.) *Intercultural communication East and West in the 90's* (pp. 1-5). San Antonio TX: Institute for Cross-Cultural Research.

Hoffer, B. (1985). (Mis-) Communication in (Cross-) Cultural (Mis-) Communication. In R. Brunt & W. Enninger, (Eds.), *Interdisciplinary perspectives at cross-cultural communication* (pp. 9-30). Aachen, Germany: RaderVerlag.

Hoffer, B. (1993). Nonverbal Phrases in Prose. *Intercultural Communication Studies III*: 2.73-86.

Hoffer, B. (1981). Patterns of Kinesic Development. In B. Hoffer & R. St. Clair, (Eds.), *Developmental Kinesics: The Emerging Paradigm*. Baltimore MD: University Park Press.

Hoffer, B. (1991). Verbal and nonverbal communication: A cross-cultural project: American, Japanese, and Korean. In P. Fendos, (Ed.), *Cross-cultural communication: East and West. Volume II*. Tainan, Taiwan: T'ai Ch'eng Publishing Company. pp. 579-611.

Hoffer, B. & J. Koo. (1994) Communicative competence in Korean. *Korean Linguistics. Vol. 8*.

Hoffer, B. & R. Santos, R. (1980). Cultural clashes in Kinesics. In W. von Raffler-Engel, (Ed.), *Aspects of nonverbal communication*. Amsterdam: Swets & Zeitlinger.

Hoffer, B. & St. Clair, R. (1981). (Eds.). *Developmental kinesics: The emerging paradigm*. Baltimore: University Park Press.

Kim, K.-O. (1992). What causes communication problems between English speakers and Korean speakers? *Intercultural Communication Studies I*. (2) 103-16.

Knapp, M. (1972). *Nonverbal communication in human interaction*. New York NY: MacMillan.

Koo, J. & St. Clair, R., (1986). (Eds.). *Cross-cultural communication: East and West*. Seoul, Korea. Samji Publishing Company.

Leathers. D. (1986). *Nonverbal communication systems*. Boston MA: Allyn & Bacon.

Mehrabian, A. (1972). *Nonverbal communication*. Chicago IL: Aldine-Atherton.

Poyatos, F. (1988). (Ed.). *Cross-cultural perspectives in nonverbal communication*. Toronto: C. J. Hogrefe.

Samovar, L. & Porter, R. (1991). Basic principles of intercultural communication. In L. Samovar & R. Porter., (Eds.), *Intercultural Communication: A Reader*. Delmont CA: Wadsworth Publishing Company.

Contributors
(In alphabetical order)

Michael Byram

Michael Byram is Professor Emeritus in the School of Education at Durham University, England. He studied French, German and Danish at King's College Cambridge, and wrote a PhD on Danish literature. He then taught French and German at secondary school level and in adult education in an English comprehensive community school. Since being appointed to a post in teacher education at Durham in 1980, he has carried out research into the education of linguistic minorities, foreign language education and student residence abroad.

His books and articles include *Teaching and Assessing Intercultural Communicative Competence; Language Teachers, Politics and Cultures* (with Karen Risager); *Education for Intercultural Citizenship: Concepts and Comparisons* (edited with G. Alred and M. Fleming); and is the editor of *the Routledge Encyclopedia of Language Teaching and Learning*. His latest book is *From Foreign Language Education to Education for Intercultural Citizenship*. He is an Adviser to the Council of Europe Language Policy Division, and is currently interested in language education policy and the politics of language teaching.

Guo-Ming Chen

Guo-Ming Chen is Professor of Communication Studies at the University of Rhode Island. Chen is the founding president of the Association for Chinese Communication Studies. He served as Chair of the ECA Intercultural Communication Interest Group and the co-editor of International and Intercultural Communication Annual. Presently Chen is the Executive Director of the International Association for Intercultural Communication Studies and the co-editor of China Media Research. His primary research interests are in intercultural/organizational/global communication. Chen has published numerous articles, books, book chapters, and essays. Those books include Foundations of Intercultural Communication, Introduction to Human Communication, Communication and Global Society, Chinese Conflict Management and Resolution, and Theories and Principles of Chinese Communication.

Ling Chen

Ling Chen (PhD, Ohio State U. USA) is a Professor of Communication at Hong Kong Baptist University, Hong Kong SAR. Her areas of interest include Communication Competence, Intercultural Communication, Organizational Communication, Language and Social Interaction, and Chinese Communication. She has published close to 50 academic research papers and served on the editorial board of a number of international journals, including *Human Communication Research, Journal of Communication, Howard Journal of Communications, Management Communication Quarterly, Journal of Applied Communication Research, Discourse and Communication, Communication Studies*. She is currently Vice-Chair of Intercultural Communication Division of International Communication Association, and has served in other professional organizations in China and USA.

Chi Ruobing

Chi Ruobing, is the research assistant of Intercultural Institute of Shanghai International Studies University. Her M.A. degree was obtained in English language and literature at SISU in 2005. She has attended and presented papers at three national and four international conferences on intercultural communication. Her research interests include intercultural value studies, intercultural communication teaching and training, and intercultural disciplinary development. She is currently undertaking two projects for young researchers (one from SISU and one from Shanghai municipal government) and participating in another SISU key project on intercultural research. Her academic works include a co-authored (with Steve Kulich) introductory chapter to Ting-Toomey's Communicating Across Cultures (reprinted in 2007 by SFLEP) and Suggestions on Intercultural Communication Course Design and Teaching (2008, Gaoxiao Jiaoyu Yanjiu).

Dai Xiaodong

Dr. Dai Xiaodong is associate professor of Foreign Languages College of Shanghai Normal University, holding the position of executive chief of its Intercultural Research Center. He obtained his doctoral degree from Fudan University. His major research interests are cultural identity, identity negotiation and intercultural communication theory. In 2007, he won Fulbright grant and conducted research at the Department of Communication Studies of University of Rhode Island in the US. He has published numerous articles in journals such as *Chinese Journal of European Studies, American Studies Quarterly, World Economics and Politics, Contemporary International Relations, International Survey, China Media Research* and so forth. His recent book is *Canada: Cultural Security in the Context of Globalization*, published by Shanghai People's

Publication House.

Gao Yongchen

Gao Yongchen graduated from Suzhou University in 1982 and she was a visiting scholar at Anglia Poly (Cambridge Campus) during 1996-1997. Her research interests are linguistics and intercultural communication. She has been in charge of as well as participated in 7 projects with provincial and state funds. So far she has authored or co-authored over 30 journal articles and academic book chapters in both fields. In 2006, she had her own book published by Southeast University Press. She has been awarded several prizes for research and teaching. She is now professor of English in School of Foreign Languages, Suzhou University, member of the School Academic Committee, deputy dean, and supervisor of MA students.

William B. Gudykunst

William B. Gudykunst (1947-2005) was Professor of Speech Communication at the College of Communications, California State University, Fullerton. He is extremely well known in the discipline and is one of its most prolific writers/scholars in the areas of intercultural communication and human communication theory. Dr. Gudykunst was recognized as one of the leading scholars in the world in intercultural communication. The 2000 Communication Research Reports noted that he was the fourth most productive active communication scholar when weighted books and articles in communication journals were combined. He authored or co-authored 13 books or monographs and edited or co-edited 18 books or monographs; he has authored or co-authored more than 75 journal articles and published more than 60 book chapters. Professor Gudykunst presented more than 90 competitively selected and invited papers at national and international conventions. He also served on 13 editorial boards and was editor, special issue editor, and co-editor of seven journals and yearbooks. Dr. Gudykunst received many awards and honors for his scholarly work. He died on Jan. 20, 2005 at the age of 57.

Gu Jiazu

Jiazu Gu, male, born in 1941, professor, School of Foreign languages and Cultures, Nanjing Normal University and editor-in-Chief of *Chinese Semiotic Studies*. He is Vice President of China Association for Intercultural Communication and Vice President of China Association for Sino-U.S. Comparative Cultural Studies. His research orientations: intercultural communication, ethnic linguistics, semiotics and memtics.

L. Brooks Hill

L. Brooks Hill is chairman and Professor of Speech Communication at Trinity University in San Antonio, Texas, USA. His areas of specialization are public and intercultural/international communication. He has served government and industry as a consultant, trainer, and researcher. He has published extensively in the US and abroad and has over seventy presentations in Asia and the US. He was the first president of the International Association for Intercultural Communication Studies (IAICS) and for two years editor of its journal, Intercultural Communication Studies. Most recently he has been writing about new perspectives for the future study of intercultural communication.

Bates L. Hoffer

Bates Hoffer received his Ph.D. from the University of Texas at Austin. He was Assistant Professor of Japanese at the University of Hawaii, Visiting Associate Professor of Linguistics at Cornell University, and Professor of English and Linguistics at Trinity University in San Antonio, Texas, USA. He has taught with professors from 17 departments and programs, including art history, communication, computers, English, foreign languages, history, religion and sociology. He has been a keynote speaker at several international conferences in Asia, North America, and Europe. He has been an author or editor on well over 100 books and journal issues and an author on more than 200 articles, book chapters, and book reviews published in 12 different countries. He edited "Language and Literature" for 29 years. He was a founding Board member of the International Association for Intercultural Communication Studies, the General Editor of its "Intercultural Communication Studies" for 14 years, and its President from 2005-2007.

Nobuyuki Honna

Before his retirement in March 2009, Professor Nobuyuki Honna taught sociolinguistics, language policy, and international communication at the School of International Politics, Economics, and Communication, Aoyama Gakuin University. Now a professor emeritus and a research fellow at the University, he still works with international colleagues on a wide range of sociolinguistic research projects, while serving as President (2007-2009) in the U.S.-based International Association for Intercultural Communication Studies and as an editorial adviser for international journals that include *English Today*, *World Englishes*, *RELC Journal*, and *Journal of Multilingual and Multicultural Development*. With his current interest in English as an Asian language, Professor Honna also is chief editor of *Asian Englishes*, a twelve-year old international journal of the sociolinguistics of English in Asia/Pacific, published by ALC Press, Inc., Tokyo. His recent publications include *English as an Multicultural Language in Asian Contexts: Issues and Ideas* (Kuroshio Shuppan, 2008) and "East Asia" in *The Handbook of World Englishes* (Blackwell, 2006). From 2004 to 2009, Professor Honna served on the Foreign Language Committee within the Central Council of Education, the advisory organ of Japan's Ministry of Education, Culture, Sports, Science and Technology.

Jia Yuxin

Jia Yuxin is a professor of Sociolinguistics and Intercultural Communication at Harbin Institute of Technology in Harbin, China. He has taught Intercultural Communication in several universities in China and the USA and given lectures on this subject as visiting professor in quite some universities in China and abroad. He has authored and co-authored several books and served as director of the publication of the series of books of intercultural communication. He has published in Japan, Germany, the USA. Russia, France, Britain, and some other countries and many of his articles have been translated into different languages. He has given presentations, many of which are plenary or key-note presentations, in many countries around the world. He has been the director of Cross-Cultural Communication Research Center at Harbin Institute of Technology which was set up under his leadership. He is president for China Association for Intercultural Communication (CAFIC) and a member of the Board of Directors for China Association for English Education. He was president for the International Association for Intercultural Communication Studies (IAICS) in the USA and is a member of its Board Directors. He has organized many international conferences, including two yearly IAICS. He is now serving as chief editor of the journal of *Intercultural Communication Research* published by China Higher Education Press. He has also edited some issues of *Intercultural Communication Studies* (ICS) and other journals.

Young Yun Kim

Young Yun Kim is professor of communication at the University of Oklahoma, USA. She holds a BA from Seoul National University and a Ph.D. from Northwestern University. She publishes extensively in intercultural and interethnic communication. Prof. Kim was named a Fellow of the International Communication Association in 2002. In 2006, she received the Top Scholar Award for Lifetime Achievement from the Intercultural and Development Communication Division of the International Communication Association. She had given frequent keynote lectures at academic conferences and has served on the editorial board of eleven of academic journals, including the *Journal of Intercultural Communication Research*.

Steve J. Kulich

Steve J. Kulich is Executive Director of the SISU Intercultural Institute of Shanghai International Studies University (SISU) and Chief Co-editor of the "Intercultural Research" book series (Vol. 1: *Intercultural Perspectives on Chinese Communication,*" 2007, Vol. 2, 3: *Intercultural Values Studies,* forthcoming, Vol. 5, 6: *Intercultural Identity*). An intercultural communication professional with 30 years of Asia experience, he has been teaching post-graduates intercultural communication since 1999 and in 2002 became the founding Professor of the Intercultural Communication Program in the SISU Graduate School. At present, he is supervising a faculty teaching a 10-course intercultural academic program with 120 MA graduates so far (in both English and Communication Colleges). In addition to 60 publications and 30 conference presentations, he is also on the Editorial Board of the 10 volume *Intercultural Communications Series,* published by Shanghai Foreign Language Education Press (SFLEP). Recent publications include: "Values Studies: History and Concepts", and "Values Theory: Social-Cultural Dimensions and Frameworks" in Stephen W. Littlejohn & Karen A. Foss (Eds.) *The Sage Encyclopedia of Communication Theory*; and (with Zhang Rui) "The Multiple Frames of 'Chinese' Values: From Tradition to Modernity and Beyond" in Michael H. Bond's (Ed.) *The Oxford Handbook of Chinese Psychology,* 2nd ed.

Tsukasa Nishida

Tsukasa Nishida is Professor of Intercultural Relations at Nihon University in Mishima, Japan. She holds a PhD degree in sociology from University of Minnesota and Nihon University respectively. Her research fields are Educational and Social Psychology and she has published extensively on issues of Uncertainty Reduction, Management and Avoidance as well as methodological issues in intercultural communication studies. Nishida has been granted the Speech Communication Association Intercultural Communication Award for Outstanding Article. She is on the board or a member of several academic organizations, including International Academy for Intercultural Research, International Communication Association, National Communication Association.

Pan Xiaohui

PAN Xiaohui is an Associate Professor, English Department, Shenzhen University, People's Republic of China. She received her PhD from City University of Hong Kong. Her research interests are in the field of communication ranging from mass communication to intercultural communication.

Zoya G. Proshina

Doctor of Philology, Professor, Moscow State University (Russia). She has been teaching EFL, cross-cultural communication, translation and interpretation theory and practice. She has lectured on World Englishes at various Russian universities. Her books on translation, English grammar, English and Asian cultures are used at schools and universities in the Russian Far East. The author of the *English-Russian Dictionary of Asian Cultures*. She has been an editor for Russian and international journals (*World Englishes, Asian Englishes, the Journal of Asia TEFL, Humanities and Social Studies in the Far East, Culture and Language Contacts*). She served as the first and ex-president of FEELTA. She now serves as vice-president of the International Association of World Englishes.

Song Li

SONG Li is Professor of English at the School of Foreign Languages Harbin Institute of Technology. She holds an MA degree in applied linguistics from Heilongjiang University in 1990 and a PhD in English linguistics from Shanghai International Studies University in 2008. Her major research interests are the intercultural dimensions of ELT, L1 as related to L2 teaching and learning, cultural values and identity, and other issues related to intercultural communication studies as well as sociolinguistics, discourse analysis, applied linguistics and English as an international language and its variations. She has published a number of articles and book reviews in Chinese, American, and Australian academic journals. She has also written and edited a few books on intercultural communication. She has been working as deputy director of Cross-Cultural Communication Research Center at Harbin Institute of Technology. She is now Secretariat of China Association for Intercultural Communication. She is on the Advisory Board of the International Association of Intercultural Communication. She is also a member of the Editorial Board of *Intercultural Communication Studies* and works as a consulting editor for the journal.

Robert N. St. Clair

Dr. Robert N. St. Clair is a professor of communication at the University of Louisville where he teaches courses on culture theory, intercultural communication, and visual culture theory. He received the President's award for scholarship, research, and creative activity. Internationally, he served as the Executive Director of the International Association for Intercultural Communication Studies (IAICS) for over a decade. He is a founding member of Los estudos culturales de las Americas and serves on its board of directors. At the University level, he is the director of the Institute for Intercultural Communication. He is also the Senior Editor of *The Intercultural Forum*. St. Clair serves as a Faculty Affiliate and Research Affiliate in the Center for Asian Democracy. St. Clair has published over 65 refereed books and over 300 refereed academic articles.

Sun Youzhong

Professor Sun Youzhong is the dean of the School of English and International Studies at Beijing Foreign Studies University. He currently serves as Vice President of the China Association for Intercultural Communication and the Chinese Association of Global Communication respectively. He received his Ph.D. in World Civilizations from Fudan University in 1998. He has been a visiting scholar in the Department of Philosophy at Pennsylvania State University and a post-doctoral researcher in the School of Journalism at Fudan University. His research interests span intercultural communication, American media studies, American intellectual history, and Western Civilization. He is the author of *John Dewey's Social Thought* and *Decoding China's Image: A Comparative Analysis of The New York Times and The Times 1993-2002*, and co-author of *Modern American Popular Culture, Approaching America, and American Cultural Industry* respectively. He is the editor of *English Education and Liberal Arts Education and Classics of Western Thought*, and co-translator of *Individualism Old and New: Selected Works of John Dewey*. He has published numerous essays and reviews in a number of journals at home and abroad. He serves as Editor-in-Chief of *Beiwai Journal of English Studies* and Associate Editor-in-Chief of *China Communication Research*.

Svetlana Ter-Minasova

Professor Svetlana Ter-Minasova, Dean and founder of the Faculty of Foreign Languages and Area Studies at Lomonosov Moscow State University since 1988, founding President of National Association of Applied Linguistics since 1990, President of National Association of Teachers of English in Russia since its foundation in 1996, holds a doctorate in Philology. In 2002 – an honorary degree of Doctor of Letters from the University of Birmingham (UK). In 2007 – The degree of Doctor of Humane Letters, State University of New York. She has published more than 150 books and papers both in Russian and English on Foreign Language Teaching, Linguistics and Cultural Studies. She has lectured across the USSR, Russia and many other countries.

Richard L. Wiseman

Richard Wiseman was Professor of Human Communication Studies at California State University in Fullerton. He earned the Outstanding Professor Award for that university and the Wang Award for Faculty Excellence in CSU system along with many other teaching and scholarship honors. He received over 25 research grants. He authored nine books and 58 articles and book chapters in intercultural, interpersonal, and nonverbal communication and other fields. He co-authored many articles with students and gave them their first publication experience. He served as editor of *International and international Communication Annual* and guest edited an issue of *Intercultural Communication Studies*.

Xu Lisheng

Xu Li-sheng is Professor of English, Director of the Institute of Intercultural Communication, and Head of English Postgraduate Programs at School of International Studies, Zhejiang University. He is currently vise president of China Association for Intercultural Communication.

For the past twenty years and more, he has been teaching many different courses for both undergraduates and postgraduates at quite a few universities in China and abroad. His chief research interests include Intercultural Communication Studies, Linguistics, and Stylistics. Among his recent publications are some articles on language and communication and a few books such as *Studying Language and Its Use: An Intercultural Approach* (2006), *The Modern Perspective on Style* (2006), *Intercultural Communication in English* (2004; 2009), *Introducing Intercultural Communication* (2004), and *Intercultural Communication* (2008). His address is: Institute of Intercultural Communication, School of International Studies, Zhejiang University, Hangzhou 310058, China.

Zhang Hongling

Zhang Hongling (Female, born in December, 1966): Ph.D. and associate professor,

Deputy Dean of the College of Journalism and Communication, Deputy Director of the Intercultural Research Institute, Shanghai International Studies University (SISU). She graduated from SISU, obtained her MA degree in 1988 and PhD in 1999. From August, 2001 to June, 2002, she did research on intercultural communication and TESL in University of Minnesota as a Fulbright scholar. Her research interest mainly covers intercultural foreign language education and computer-assisted language teaching. She authored one book, edited and coauthored 5 books and published more than 10 articles. Her representative academic achievement An Intercultural Approach to Foreign Language Teaching is the first of its kind that systematically explores the theory and practice of the intercultural approach to foreign language teaching.

作者简介
(按姓氏英文字母顺序排列)

Michael Byram

(英国) 杜伦大学教育学院的名誉教授。他在剑桥大学King's College学习法语、德语和丹麦语,博士论文是有关丹麦文学方面的。之后,他在中学教法语和德语s,在一所社区大学进行成人教育。自从1980年在杜伦大学担任师资教育工作之后,他开始研究小语种语言者的教育、外语教学和居住海外留学生教育。他的著作和文章包括*Teaching and Assessing Intercultural Communicative Competence*、*Language Teachers, Politics and Cultures* (与Karen Risager合著)、*Education for Intercultural Citizenship: Concepts and Comparisons* (由 G. Alred and M. Fleming编辑) 和*The Routledge Encyclopedia of Language Teaching and Learning*。他最新出版的著作是*From Foreign Language Education to Education for Intercultural Citizenship*。Micheal BYRAM是欧洲文化协会语言政策部的顾问,目前感兴趣的研究领域是语言教育的政策与语言教学的政治。

陈国明 (Guo-Ming Chen)

1987年获美国肯特州立大学 (Kent State University) 传播学博士学位,目前为罗得岛大学 (University of Rhode Island) 传播学系教授。1987年美国国家传播学会 (National Communication Association) 国际与文化间传播组杰出博士论文奖得主。曾任中华传播研究学会 (Association for Chinese Communication Studies) 创会会长,美国国家传播学会立法委员,美国东部传播学会文化间传播组主席,和其他专业学会不同之职位。主要研究领域是文化间/组织间/全球传播学。目前担任国际跨文化传播研究学会执行长 (International Association for Intercultural Communication Studies),一个专业期刊编辑,以及多本期刊编辑委员。除了获得学术研究各种奖励之外,至今已发表了一百余篇论文,编著了二十本中英文专著。

陈凌 (Ling Chen)

香港特别行政区香港浸会大学传播学院教授,她的研究领域包括交际能力、跨文化交际、组织间的交际、语言与社会交往和中文交际等。发表了近50篇研究论文,担任多个国际性学术期刊的编委,包括*Human Communication Research, Journal of Communication, Howard Journal of Communications, Management*

Communication Quarterly, *Journal of Applied Communication Research*, *Discourse and Communication*和*Communication Studies*等刊物。现担任国际交际学会跨文化交际分会副主席,并在中国和美国的其他一些学术组织中任职。

迟若冰

上海外国语大学英语语言文学专业硕士学位,现为上海外国语大学跨文化研究中心助理。曾多次参加国内外跨文化方面的会议并宣读论文,目前承担上海外国语大学青年项目和上海高校选拔培养优秀青年教师两个科研项目(均为2009年底结项)。学术成果有《〈文化间的交流〉导读》(与顾力行合写,上海外语教育出版社2007年影印出版),《关于跨文化交际学课程设计及教学的几点建议》(2008,高校教育研究,69)。

戴晓东

戴晓东博士是上海师范大学外国语学院副教授,学院跨文化交际研究中心执行主任。2004年6月从复旦大学美国研究中心获得博士学位;2007年2月获得富布赖特研究学者提名,主要从事民族认同、文化认同以及跨文化交际理论研究。

高永晨

苏州大学外国语学院教授,苏州大学中国英语语言文学硕士生导师。1982年毕业于苏州大学外语系。曾作为高级访问学者赴英国剑桥Anglia大学深造。现为苏州大学外国语学院学术委员会成员,系副主任。主持并完成了国家级研究项目《大学英语教学中的跨文化交际能力培养》;省部级项目《跨文化交际与大学英语教学》、《大学生跨文化交际能力培养研究》、《全球本土化:跨文化交际研究的新视角》、《文化全球化语境下的跨文化交际研究》等。曾参加国家社会科学基金项目《汉英修辞语用比较研究》。在核心刊物以及省级以上刊物发表跨文化交际学研究系列论文30余篇。专著《文化全球化态势下的跨文化交际研究》由东南大学出版社2006年出版。先后获得江苏省教学成果奖、苏州市哲学社会科学优秀成果奖、苏州大学陆氏优秀教学奖、苏鑫奖教金、苏州大学教学成果一等奖、"21世纪·爱立信杯"、"CCTV杯"全国英语演讲比赛指导教师等奖项。

顾嘉祖

南京师范大学外国语学院教授、英文版《中国符号学研究》主编,兼任中国跨文化交际学会副会长、中国中美比较文化研究会副会长等职。研究方向:跨文化交际学、文化语言学、符号学、谜米学等。

William B. Gudykunst

美国加利福尼亚州立大学富勒顿分校交际学院言语交际已故教授,在跨文化交际研究领域享有盛名,是跨文化交际和人类交际理论研究方面最多产的作家和学者之一。他被认为是全世界跨文化交际学科的领军人。2000年的Communication Research Report这样评价：如果把出版的书籍和发表在杂志上的文章都算上的话，Gudykunst是第四名成果最丰富的交际学学者。他撰写或合著了13本书或专著，编辑或合编了18本书或专著； 在学术期刊上独立或合作发表文章75篇以上，同时他还是60多部著作部分章节的作者。他应邀曾在国内和国际会议中宣讲论文90多次。他曾是13个编辑委员成员，并担任7本期刊和年鉴的主编，因其学术著作获得很多的奖励和荣誉。W.B. Gudykunst于2005年1月20日去世，享年57岁。

L. Brooks Hill

美国得克萨斯州圣.安东尼奥三一大学言语交际学院的教授兼院长。他精通公共交际学和跨文化交际学，曾在政府部门和企业界出任咨政顾问、培训官和研究员。他的著作在美国境内外广泛发行，并在美国和亚洲做过70多次演讲。他是国际跨文化交际学会的首任会长，并担任该学会会刊*Intercultural Communication Studies*主编两年。近来，他正在撰写一部从新的视角展望跨文化交际研究未来发展的著作。

Bates L. Hoffer

美国奥斯丁的德克萨斯大学获得博士学位。曾任夏威夷大学日语副教授，康奈尔大学的语言学客座副教授，美国德克萨斯圣安东尼奥的三一大学英语和语言学教授，他和来自包括艺术史、交际、计算机、英语、外语、历史、宗教和社会学等17个院系的教授共事，在亚洲，北美和欧洲的很多国际会议上他都是主旨发言人。他撰写和编辑出版了100多本著作和期刊， 并著有200篇文章、书籍章节、书评，在12个不同的国家出版发行。他任"*Language and Literature*"的编辑达29年。他是国际跨文化交际研究会的理事和创始人之一，任其"Intercultural Communication Studies"杂志的主编14年之久，2005至2007期间担任该学会主席。

Nobuyuki Honna

曾执教于日本青山学院大学国际政治、经济和交际学院，讲授社会语言学，语言政策和国际交际，于2009年3月退休，现任该大学的荣誉教授和研究员，在很多社会语言学研究项目中与来自不同国家的学者合作，2007至2009期间担任国际跨文化交际研究会和主席，并担任包括*English Today, World Englishes, RELC Journal, and Journal of Multilingual* 和*Multicultural Development*多个国际期刊的编辑顾问。因为目前对亚洲英语达的兴趣，他还担任*Asican Englishes* 的主编。*Asian Englishes*是由东京ALC出版社出版的有关亚太地区英语社会语言学并已有12年的历史国际性期刊。他最近出版的著作包括：*Englsih as an Multicultural Language in Asian Contexts: Issues and Ideas* (Kuroshio Shuppan, 2008) 和 "East Asia" in *The Handbook of World Englishes* (Blackwell, 2006)。2004至2009年期间，他在中央教育委员会的外语委员会任职，中央教育委员会是日本教育、文化、体育和科学技术部的咨询机构。

贾玉新

哈尔滨工业大学教授，博士生导师。讲授社会语言学和跨文化交际学。曾在中国和美国多所大学讲授跨文化交际学，并在国内外多所高校担任此门学科的客座教授。曾独自撰写或与人合著图书数本，并担任跨文化交际系列图书出版的负责人。他曾在多个国家发表演讲，并且大多是主旨演讲。在国内外出版论文多篇。现任哈尔滨工业大学跨文化交际研究中心主任、中国跨文化交际学会会长，也是中国英语教育协会常务理事。曾任国际跨文化交际学会（美国）会长，现任其主任委员。多次组织承办国际会议，包括两次中国暨国际跨文化交际学会的年会。他担任由中国高等教育出版社出版的《跨文化交际研究》的主编，也曾参与编辑国际学刊 *Intercultural Communication Studies* 等一些期刊。

Young Yun Kim

美国俄克拉荷马大学交际学教授。于首尔国立大学获得学士学位，西北大学获得博士学位。她曾在跨文化交际和跨民族交际领域发表过多篇文章。2002年 Kim 教授被任命为国际交际学会研究员；2006年她获得国际交际学会跨文化与发展交际学分会授予的杰出学者终身成就奖。她经常在学术会议上做主旨发言，并担任包括 *Journal of Intercultural Communication Research* 在内的11家学术期刊编委会委员。

顾力行 (Steve Kulich)

上海外国语大学跨文化研究中心执行主任，跨文化研究系列丛书总编之一（2007年出版第一辑《跨文化视角下的中国人：交际与传播》，第二、三辑"跨文化价值观"编辑中，第四、五辑"跨文化认同"审稿中）。他有三十多年在亚洲进行跨文化交际专业教学的经验，于1999年进入上海外国语大学，2002年开始在上海外国语大学研究生部开设跨文化方向课程。迄今，该方向在顾力行教授的带领下，已拥有多名指导教师，开设了10门专业课，120名硕士研究生毕业（包括英语专业和新闻传播专业）。除此而外，他还有60多份出版物，30多个会议发表论文，同时也是上海外语教育出版社出版的10本跨文化系列丛书的编委会成员之一。他最近的学术成果有：《价值观研究：历史与概念》、《价值观理论：社会—文化维度和框架》（收入 S. W. Littlejohn 和 K. A. Foss 主编的《Sage 传播学理论百科全书》），与张睿合著的《中国价值观的多种结构：从传统到现代到未来》（收入 M. H. Bond 主编的《牛津中国人心理学手册（第二版）》）。

Tsukasa Nishida

日本三岛的日本大学跨文化关系教授，获得明尼苏达大学和日本大学的两个社会学博士学位。她的研究领域是教育和社会心理学，在不确定性的降低、管理和规避，以及跨文化交际研方法论方面都出版了很多著作。被授予言语交际协会跨文化交际优秀论文奖。她还是很多学术期刊编委会委员，这些期刊包括：*International Academy for Intercultural Research, International Communication Association , National Communication Association*。

Pan Xiaohui

中国深圳大学英语学院副教授。获香港城市大学博士学位。她感兴趣的研究领域包括大众传播和跨文化交际。

Zoya G. Proshina

俄罗斯莫斯科国立大学教授，语言学博士，讲授英语、跨文化交际、口笔译理论与实务等课程，并在多所俄罗斯大学讲授世界英语课程。俄国远东地区的很多大学和学校都使用由她编写的翻译、英语语法、英国和亚洲文化等方面的著作和教材。她还是*English-Russian Dictionary of Asian Cultures*辞典的编纂者。她还担任多个俄罗斯和国际期刊的编辑 (*World Englishes, Asian Englishes, the Journal of Asia TEFL, Humanities and Social Studies in the Far East, Culture and Language Contacts*)。她曾任远东英语教师协会的前任和第一任主席，现任世界英语协会副主席等职。

宋莉

哈尔滨工业大学外国语学院英语教授。于1990年获得黑龙江大学应用语言学硕士学位。2008年获得上海外国语大学英语语言学博士学位。其主要研究领域和成果包括跨文化交际英语教学、文化价值观与文化身份、母语语言文化与外语教学的关系、社会语言学、语篇分析、应用语言学、英语国际通用语及其变体的教学与研究等。在中国、美国和澳大利亚等学术期刊发表论文和书评多篇，并编著跨文化交际相关书刊若干。宋莉是哈尔滨工业大学跨文化交际研究中心副主任，目前担任中国跨文化交际学会秘书长、国际跨文化交际学会顾问委员、《跨文化交际研究》顾问编辑和编委等职。

Robert N. St. Clair

(美国) 路易威尔大学教授，讲授文化理论、跨文化交际学和视觉文化理论等课程。他曾因其在学业、科学研究和创造性活动等方面的成就获得总统奖。在国际上，他曾担任国际跨文化交际学会理事会执行理事达十余年之久，同时他也是*Los estudos culturales de las Americas*的创始人及理事之一。在大学里，他是跨文化交际研究所所长，同时也是Intercultural Forum的资深编辑。St.Claire是亚洲民主中心 (the Center for Asian Democracy) 的教师和研究员。St.Claire教授已出版了65本专著，并发表过300余篇学术文章。

孙有中

教授，博士生导师，北京外国语大学校长助理、英语学院院长，中国跨文化交际学会副会长，中国外国新闻传播史学会副会长。在复旦大学获世界文化史方向博士学位，在复旦大学新闻学院完成博士后研究，曾赴美国宾夕法尼亚州立大学哲学系访学。从事跨文化传播研究和美国思想文化史研究。出版专著：《美国精神的象征：杜威社会思想研究》、《解码中国形象：〈纽约时报〉和〈泰晤士报〉中国报道比较1993-2002》；合著《现代美国大众文化》、《细说美利坚》、《美国文化产业》和译著《新旧个人主义——杜威文选》；编著《西方思想经典导读》；主编《人文教育与英语教育》。在美国哲学季刊 Transactions of the Charles C. Peirce Society、《美国研究》、《外语教学与研究》、《新闻大学》、《国际新闻界》、《史学理论研究》等国内外多种核心期刊上发表了50多篇学术论文。承担有国家社科基金项目、欧盟Asia Link合作研究项目和北京市精品教材各1项。担任《中国跨文化交际研究》副主编。

Svetlana Ter-Minasova

Svetlana Ter-Minasova于1988年创建了莫斯科国立大学的外国语研究学院，并担任院长至今。1990年创建了俄罗斯国家应用语言学协会，并一直担任该学会主席一职。自1996年俄罗斯英语教师协会建立起担任主席至今。2002年于英国伯明翰大学获得文学荣誉博士学位；2007年，于美国纽约国立大学获得人类文学博士学位。她发表的关于外语教学、语言学和文化研究等方面的俄语和英语著作及论文多达150以上，并在前苏联、俄罗斯和多个国家进行讲学。

Richard L. Wiseman

美国加利福尼亚州立大学富勒顿分校人类交际学教授。他获得了该校的杰出教授奖，CSU系统的Wang Award for Faculty Excellence奖，和多项其他教学和科研奖，以及25项以上的研究奖。他撰写了有关跨文化、人际和非言语交际的9部专著和58篇文章及章节。他与学生合著了很多文章，使这些学生获得了首次发表文章的经历。他是 International and international Communication Annual 主编，也受邀主编过 Intercultural Communication Studies。他还曾是NCA和ICA的跨文化分部的领导人。

许力生

教授，博士生导师，浙江大学外语学院跨文化交际研究所所长、英语专业研究生教学中心主任，中国跨文化交际学会副会长、中国文体学研究会常务理事。主要研究方向为跨文化交际学、语言学和文体学，发表论文30余篇，出版了数部专著和译著：《语言研究的跨文化视野》（上海外语教育出版社，2006）、《文体风格的现代透视》（浙江大学出版社，2006）。主编和编写了国家"十五"和"十一五"规划教材《跨文化交际英语教程》（上海外语教育出版社，2004；新版

2009)以及《跨文化交流入门》(浙江大学出版社,2004)和研究生公共英语教材《跨文化交际》(上海外语教育出版社,2008)。

张红玲

　　博士,副教授。上海外国语大学新闻传播学院副院长,上海外国语大学跨文化研究中心副主任。1988年上海外国语大学研究生毕业,获硕士学位,1999年获应用语言学博士学位。2001年8月至2002年6月作为美国福布赖特研修学者在美国明尼苏达大学从事跨文化交际学和外语教学方向的学习和研究。长期致力于跨文化外语教学和计算机辅助外语教学研究,出版专著1本,主编或参编学术著作5部,发表论文10余篇。其代表性成果《跨文化外语教学》是国内首部系统阐述跨文化外语教学思想的论著。

《跨文化交际研究》第一辑中文摘要
(按文章出现顺序排列)

1. 文化全球化与跨文化对话——全球化视野下的跨文化交际研究

贾玉新 哈尔滨工业大学

　　本文提出以"和而不同"理念下的平等对话为平台，发展全球化时代的跨文化交际研究。跨文化交际是时代的产物，其研究与时俱进。当我们进入全球化的21世纪， 全球化为跨文化交际研究提供一个新视野，为跨文化交际研究提供一个新语境。全球化预设着文化全球化，而"全球—本土"化是当前文化全球化所可能选择的变化趋势。"和而不同"的全球社会是历史发展的必然。"和而不同"是中国文化的传统，它预设着平等和差异。"和而不同"倡导多样性文化间的平等对话，平等的文化对话 (下称"对话") 是解决全球问题和建构全球和平的出发点，"对话"为跨文化交际研究提供了理想的平台。

　　本文在对儒家"和而不同"理念理解和对西方"对话修辞"批判的基础上，提出了"和而不同"视野下的始于"倾听"的"对话修辞"概念。并以此为指导，对与"和而不同"密切相关的文化价值与言语层面上的对话，进行了阐述和分析。本文还指出，全球化视野下跨文化交际研究应采用"辩证"法，因为"辩证"法不仅能对所流行的研究理论和研究方法兼容并蓄，而且与构建全球和平的"和而不同"理念相得益彰。与西方一切二分的"二元论"截然不同，辩证法把多样性化价值、把文化全球化过程中两种不同或相对立的发展趋势 (本土化与全球化) 看作既对立又统一的有机体，在差异和对立之间寻找切入点和交汇之处，扩大共识，扩大跨文化认同。辩证法符合"和而不同"全球社会的发展趋势。但是，文章也指出，文化之融合、文化之认同必须扎根于自己传统文化土壤之中，"现代"文化镶嵌在"传统"文化之中，正是文化间传统之差异造成当今全球的文化多元性。

2. 跨文化公民概念

Michael Byram (英国) 杜伦大学

　　尽管"公民教育"是一个全新的概念，但在国家认同教育上，它与传统的学校功能是相关的。"公民教育"中的新元素是让学生走出学校活跃在社区中，并将其列为教学和学习的目标。然而，他们进入的最大社区是自己的国家，在一个需要跨越国家边界的全球化世界中，这显然是不够的。

　　本文认为外语教育在扩展公民概念及在拓展跨国公民社会和跨国社区或大或小、或长久或短暂的活动方面发挥特殊作用。以跨文化交际能力为目标的外语教育与公民教育的目标有共同之处，在拓展共同目标的同时，外语教育与公民教育将赋予学生跨国交际的能力。其共同的目标意味着公民教育和外语教育都把"践行跨国交际"作为其目标之一。公民教育使学生能够投入到社区中，而外语教育则促进学生投入到国际社区中去，践行跨国家的跨文化交际。

3. 文化空间的叠层：关于空间时间的探究
Robert N. St. Clair (美国) 路易威尔大学

文化是变化的，而理解文化变化的最佳途径就是探究在时空流转中积淀下来知识、社会实践和物质创造。因此，时空与文化之关系不是线性的而是跨越古今的空间层叠和跨越时间的文化沉淀之累积。考古学的文化研究因其能够从文化历史学家的视角更好地理解文化变化而显得尤为重要。这一文化空间模式框架将过去与现在转换生成一个新的空间："共存"。在这一新空间里，过去被现在的重构而取代。而过去在这一过程中不曾消逝；它或者是被重新界定、改进、修正，或者被重新创造。本文提出的新模式框架的重要性在于强调现时蕴涵于过去。人们只有了解过去才能通晓现在。同样，人们对未来的认识也只能求助于对现时的了解。时间就这样蕴涵于文化空间之中。

4. 中国跨文化交际学科发展现状综述
顾力行 上海外国语大学
迟若冰 上海外国语大学

本文基于顾力行在《外国语言与文化》（吴友富、冯庆华，2002-2008）发表的系列文章的主要观点，提出需对国内跨文化课程、科研和出版情况进行全面回顾、分析和评价，总结该领域在国内二十多年的发展状况。

全文以上海外国语大学硕士研究生跨文化教育为例，详细论述了如何通过课程、教学、培训、文献积累、教师培养、科研项目，以及国内外合作，为跨文化交际/传播学的学科建设服务，希望以此推动国内学者对该学科的认知和学科身份的正式确立。

5. 全球本土化：跨文化交际学科发展应关注的新视域
高永晨 苏州大学

"全球本—土化"作为全球文化与国家、民族以及区域本土文化矛盾运动的现象和结果，已成为当今文化全球化时代最为引人注目的重要特征，为跨文化交际研究以及跨文化交际学科发展洞开了一个更加崭新的视域。

全球本土化推动着各种以"跨文化"命名的学科不断涌现和日趋增多，促进着广泛而深入的跨国间的合作研究，驱使着一系列新事物和新问题成为跨文化交际研究的新课题，从而从深度和广度两个方面引领着跨文化交际学科发展。

6. 跨文化交际学的未来：二十年从事跨文化交际经验感悟
Brooks Hill (美国) 三一学院

在四十年的职业生涯中，特别是在IAICS工作的近二十年来，在做出自己的贡献的同时，我发现跨文化交际学科的某些领域里亟待更多细致的研究。在本文中我将把一生为之努力的经验所得转化为对学科未来的建议。本文将在探讨一系列密切相关问题的基础上总结出跨文化交际研究未来面临的三大挑战。本文第一部分将从理论性视角指出我们必须面对的问题，我们必须为之集中精力相互协作以在学术和实践上取得更大成就。第二部分对于我们在教学和知识应用方面不加批判地使用技术创新的成果提出了严重的警告。第三部分和最后一部分将目光转向了种族关系。在世界上的很多地方，种族关系的紧张造成了社会的分裂，我们必须更加谨慎地运用我们的知识来解决这些问题。

总之，本文将综合我个人的经历，从上述三个方面展望跨文化关系研究与实践的未来走向。文章的主题可以用这样一个问题概括：我们如何更好地挖掘潜力携手共创一个更加美好的世界？

7. 跨文化交际学的理论化:试论跨文化交际学的动态符号学、谜米学研究视角
顾嘉祖 南京师范大学

笔者完全同意Gudykunst关于加强跨文化交际理论化建设的论述，认为目前跨文化交际研究途径过于狭窄。为此，笔者提出了跨文化交际研究的新思路、新方法，其中包括谜米学和符号学的研究思路，这些思路在理论上更容易被人接受。

8. 文化与文化身份对美日个人价值观的影响
William B. Gudykunst (美国) 加州大学富乐敦分校
Tsukasa Nishida 日本大学

本文中涉及的两项研究，旨在考查文化身份的强度与文化之间的交互作用对个人层面上个人主义价值观和集体主义价值观的影响，其中被用于分析的数据取自于美国和日本。在第一项研究中，文化身份的强度与文化的交互作用影响了自由、享乐、社会认同和自我牺牲等四种价值观。在第二项研究中，文化身份的强度与文化的交互作用影响了独立、和谐和接受传统等三种价值观。这些结果表明，了解某一文化成员的价值观就必须了解其文化身份的强度。

9. 超越文化身份
Young Yun Kim (美国) 俄克拉荷马大学

本文旨在批判地审视流行于当代美国公共话语的文化身份观。作者发现，人们普遍认为文化身份是一种固定的、排他的实体，具有内在的、积极的道德规范作用。而本文则提出动态的文化身份观，强调文化身份不再墨守成规，而是持续发展的。据此本文提出了"跨文化身份"这一概念，并将其作为文化身份的延伸和对应。从一个开放的视角来看，身份的发展不再局限于单一的原文化。作者从人们在面临不同文化身份交错的种种挑战而做出的"压力—适应—成长"的心理反应来解释身份的变化发展。这种跨文化挑战被描述成推动个体在跨文化学习、认知提升和自我—他者关系取向上的进步，这既有个人意义也有普遍意义。

10. 建构跨文化认同的路径——双向拓展模型
戴晓东 上海师范大学外国语学院

　　跨文化认同超越传统的认同观,体现了交际者对他者开放、承认与欣赏差异、整合不同文化元素,以及实现自我更化与文化创新的品格。本文首先对现有论述跨文化认同建构途径的文献作回顾,然后在此基础上提出双向拓展模型,诠释其理论依据和基本内涵。文章认为,拓展文化认同,既包容个体与亚文化群体,同时又寻求跨文化协议与人类的共识,是建构跨文化认同的有效路径。建构跨文化认同并非要消除文化边界,而是要扩展它的界域,提高认同本体的开放性,使不同的文化能够有更多共享的空间和更为广阔的沟通平台。跨文化认同的建构主要涉及3个基本层面:文化间性的深化、地方意义框架的更新及其交际伦理的转变。

11. 变:"易经" 永恒的论述
陈国明 美国罗得岛大学

　　宇宙的基本原则为何?这是一个已经苦恼着中国知识分子几十个世纪的问题。两千年前出现的 "易经" 一书里,已试着从 "变" 的角度,来寻找这个问题的答案。"易经" 一书以 "变" 为核心概念,认为 "变" 为宇宙惟一不变的原则。本文从五个方面,来探讨 "易经" 对 "变" 这个概念的论述:变化的属性,变化的原则,变化的力型,变化的形态,以及变化的结果。希望借此分析,可以归纳出中国知识分子如何建构对 "变" 这个概念的各种有系统的表达形态。

12. 论中国文化中的劝说:中西传统修辞对比研究 (中西传统修辞窥探)
陈凌 香港浸会大学

　　在中国历史上,学者们将劝说视为一种理解人性、人和政治的方法,并对其进行了广泛而深入的研究。劝说与辩论是人们达到重要政治目的不可或缺的工具,也是学者们科学研究的组成部分。本文将讨论古代中国和西方的劝说策略或修辞手法的异同,以及文化对于劝说策略和研究的影响。作者指出西方古典修辞学被视为一个系统学科,而同时期的中国劝说艺术虽然相当精湛,但一般被当作达到其他目的的手段,而没有被视为一个独立的学科。

13. 跨文化英语与跨文化意识
Nobuyuki Honna (日本)青山学院大学

　　开展国际联合与协作的教育项目对于丰富英语,使其成为多元文化交际的语言,以及确保英语不同变体使用者具备跨文化交际能力是至关重要的。而将语言意识引入到学校教学中则是极为行之有效的途径。在教学中培养语言意识旨在促进学生更加明确地了解语言是如何构成的及如何使用的。因此,使学生意识到语言在多种语言和多元文化背景下的功能,对他们是很有帮助的。本文将比喻的学习作为提高跨文化素养的一种方法,而跨文化素养则是英语变体使用者之间有效交流所必需的。

14. 全球化英语对英语本族语国家的不利影响
Svetlana Ter-Minasova (俄罗斯) 罗蒙诺索夫莫斯科国立大学

全球化英语地位的确立如何使得英语民族处于危险境地？作者对此给出了七个答案。例如，语言不仅仅是隔离各民族的屏障，也是保护民族身份的盾牌；而英语全球化正在使得英语国家丢失这样一语言的保护。

15. 透过英语辞典看东亚文化
Zoya Proshina (俄罗斯) 罗蒙诺索夫莫斯科国立大学、(俄罗斯) 远东国立大学

在当今俄罗斯非常流行的认知范式使人们将辞典看作是能够通过词汇反映概念的世界观。语言强加给个人这样或者那样的世界观，并反映了一个人对于世界的理解。英语作为来自不同文化的人之间交流的中介语，也会创建一种既包含说话人源文化又具有中介语文化特点的新的世界观。本文旨在展示在英语辞典中可以反映新概念的一些东亚词汇，并借此揭示出一些在东西文化交流中极为重要的领域，这些领域可以通过第三文化的代表性词汇和概念而被认知。英语辞典中一些从东亚借来的词汇可以帮助我们认识中国、日本和韩国生活方式的差异，而另一些英语使用者创造的词汇则可以反映出他们与中国人、日本人和韩国人的关系。本研究因此也证明了语言是一种研究跨文化交际的工具。

16. 跨文化大众传播研究：一个方兴未艾的领域
孙有中 北京外国语大学

跨文化交流在不同文化的个人、组织以及全社会层面展开。跨文化交际研究通常关注的是不同文化的个体之间的交际行为。随着大众媒体在民族、国家内部和跨国范围内迅速扩张，大众传播已成为不同文化之间交流互动的日益重要的渠道。作者认为，跨文化交流研究其本意乃是对文化之间的交流现象的研究，应该把跨文化大众传播积极纳入自己的合法研究领域。作者把跨文化大众传播研究界定为对两种或多种文化之间通过大众传媒实现的文化交流现象的研究，并提出了多种有待拓展的研究课题和研究方法。作者相信跨文化大众传播研究将不仅拓展跨文化交流研究的领域，而且促进跨文化交际研究本身。

17. 跨文化教育英语教学：来自跨文化交际的挑战
宋莉 哈尔滨工业大学

全球化的进程使得跨文化交际日益成为众多世人所面临的现实。而在这一过程中，英语充当着国际通用语，并对传统的英语外语教学范式提出了挑战。单纯的英语熟练程度和对英语本族语者文化知识的了解已不足以保证英语学习者能够获得必要的跨文化交际能力，因而也不能使其并在使用英语时超越文化界限，并通过对意义、人际关系和文化身份的建构和协商，与来自不同文化背景的人有效沟通。作者认为迎接全球化时代跨文化交际现实的挑战，英语教学应该定位为跨文化教育，教

学的轴心应该转向对学习者跨文化交际能力的培养。作者首先讨论和界定了跨文化教育和跨文化交际能力，进而论证了英语在跨文化教育方面的优势，并提出英语教学应该是跨文化交际教学的理念。作者还提出了实践跨文化英语教学的基本原则。

18. 外语教师跨文化能力培训研究
张红玲 上海外国语大学

在新时代呼唤新的外语教学理念的今天，跨文化外语教学思想当仁不让地成为当今外语教学的潮流和发展趋势。然而，我国外语教师的跨文化能力还远远不能胜任这一新理念的要求。对外语教师进行跨文化培训势在必行。本文在对外语教师跨文化能力的内涵进行阐释的基础上，提出了一个外语教师跨文化能力培训框架，阐述了其目的、内容和方法，并设计了一个为期两天的培训计划以举例说明。

19. 话语内翻译与跨话语翻译：翻译与文化的新视角
许力生 浙江大学

从一个新的视角来考察和分析翻译以及翻译与文化的关系，我们很有必要区分话语内翻译与跨话语翻译，因为二者之间有着根本性的不同：跨话语翻译是跨文化的交际，而话语内翻译则不是。两类翻译各自涉及的话语系统状况不同，面对的问题也会大不相同，需要采用不同的翻译策略和技巧，对翻译本身的评判标准也应有所不同。而且，对翻译进行这样的区分有助于澄清一些长期争论不休的问题，同时可以深化我们对翻译与文化关系的认识。

20. 中国人和美国人的微笑：社会地位和情景因素对微笑行为社会得体性的影响
Richard L. Wiseman (美国) 加州大学富乐敦分校
潘晓慧 香港城市大学 深圳大学

面部表情，尤其是微笑，不仅仅用于传达个人的内心情感，同时也是展现其得体社会行为的手段。文化规约决定人的社会行为是否得体，决定人们如何在不同的时间地点，面对着不同的对象，在何等程度上表达自己的内心情感。本文将研究影响微笑之一的个人面目表情的文化因素和个人因素。

基于Hofstede (1980) 的个人主义和集体主义的文化维度观点和权势距离理论，本次调查在美国和中国设置了九个不同的情境，以此考查文化和情景对于人们微笑意图和原因的影响。共有160名美国大学生和134名中国大学生参与此次调查。在所给的"关系地位"、"熟悉程度"、"群体身分"等九个不同的情景中，参与者需指出他们是否应该笑以及为什么(比如说，情感原因，为了符合社会规范，出于谦虚，关乎他人的社会地位，为别人的面子或自尊考虑等)。分析表明文化和情景对于是否能使参与者发笑及其原因有很重要的影响， 说明了个人主义和集体主义和权势距离等文化变量与微笑的可能性及其原因有着紧密的联系。本项研究旨在提升我们对中美两国文化异同的理解，并期望以此推进中美交际。

21. 非言语跨文化交际能力面面观
Bates L. Hoffer (美国) 三一学院

跨文化交际能力包括交际者共享语言的言语能力和与之相随的非言语能力。一种语言的母语使用者会在理解他们本国其他地域人们的非言语交际时有困难，而非母语使用者通常会对别种语言的非言语交际不甚理解。对非言语系统的研究包括如下几个方面：面部表情与肢体语言、社交性非言语行为和非言语行为的文字描述。

面部表情经常被不同文化的人误解，因此交际会受到影响。肢体语言在不同文化中会被部分或错误解读，因此会导致交际的失误。社交性非言语行为是伴随言语交流过程的一些举动或者声音符号，用来表示"我正在听"，"该你说了"等等。如果交际双方使用各自的社交性非言语行为交谈，交流将变得相当困难。而作者笔下的非言语行为对语言熟练程度很高的读者而言也可能是毫无意义的。在这些情况下，读者会变得很迷惑，甚至无法捕捉到作者以微妙的方式传达的交际意图。

郑 重 声 明

高等教育出版社依法对本书享有专有出版权。任何未经许可的复制、销售行为均违反《中华人民共和国著作权法》，其行为人将承担相应的民事责任和行政责任，构成犯罪的，将被依法追究刑事责任。为了维护市场秩序，保护读者的合法权益，避免读者误用盗版书造成不良后果，我社将配合行政执法部门和司法机关对违法犯罪的单位和个人给予严厉打击。社会各界人士如发现上述侵权行为，希望及时举报，本社将奖励举报有功人员。

反盗版举报电话：(010) 58581897/58581896/58581879
反盗版举报传真：(010) 82086060
E - mail：dd@hep.com.cn
通信地址　北京市西城区德外大街4号
　　　　　　高等教育出版社打击盗版办公室
邮　　编：100120

购书请拨打电话：(010) 58581118